Designing Active Server Pages

Designing Active Server Pages

Scott Mitchell

O'REILLY®

Beijing · Cambridge · Farnham · Köln · Paris · Sebastopol · Taipei · Tokyo

Designing Active Server Pages
by Scott Mitchell

Copyright © 2000 O'Reilly & Associates, Inc. All rights reserved.
Printed in the United States of America.

Published by O'Reilly & Associates, Inc., 101 Morris Street, Sebastopol, CA 95472.

Editor: Ron Petrusha

Production Editor: Mary Sheehan

Cover Designer: Edie Freedman

Printing History:

> September 2000:   First Edition.

Library of Congress Cataloging-in-Publication Data

Mitchell, Scott
    Designing Active Server Pages/Scott Mitchell p. cm.
    ISBN 0-596-00044-8 (alk. paper)
    1. Active Server Pages. 2. Web sites --Design. 3. Web publishing I. Title.

TK5105.8885.A26 M58 2000
005.7'2--dc21   00-062331

ISBN: 0-596-00044-8
[M]

Table of Contents

Preface .... *vii*

1. *Introduction* *1*
   What Is Application Design? *1*
   What's Wrong with ASP Design? *3*
   Why Hasn't ASP Design Advanced? *4*
   What Can Be Done to Improve ASP Design? *5*
   Further Reading *18*

2. *Choosing a Server-Side Scripting Language* *19*
   The Popularity of VBScript *19*
   Specifying the Scripting Language *20*
   Creating ASP Pages with JScript *25*
   Creating ASP Pages with PerlScript *31*
   Creating ASP Pages with Python *37*
   Further Reading *37*

3. *Exception Handling* *39*
   A Bit of Terminology *40*
   Detecting When Exceptions Occur *42*
   Responding to Exceptions *65*
   Creating Custom HTTP Error Pages *73*
   Further Reading *77*

4. **Regular Expressions, Classes, and Dynamic Evaluation and Execution** *78*
     Using the RegExp Object *79*
     Using Object-Oriented Programming with VBScript *85*
     Using Dynamic Evaluation and Execution *99*
     Further Reading *103*

5. **Form Reuse** *104*
     The Importance of Code Reuse *104*
     A Primer on Form Use *106*
     Form Validation *111*
     Creating Reusable Server-Side Form Validation Routines *116*
     Developing Reusable Form Creation Routines *124*
     The Practicality of Reuse *136*
     Further Reading *137*

6. **Database Reuse** *138*
     Examining Database Usage *138*
     The Building Blocks for Creating Reusable Administration Pages ... *140*
     Creating Reusable Administration Pages *149*
     Further Reading *246*

7. **Using Components** *247*
     COM—A Quick Overview *248*
     Lesser-Known Microsoft COM Components *249*
     Enhancing Microsoft's COM Components *275*
     Building Components *276*
     Further Reading *290*

8. **Enhancing Your Web Site with Third-Party Components** *291*
     Executing DOS and Windows Applications on the Web Server
     with ASPExec *292*
     Obtaining Detailed Information About Your Users's Browsers *296*
     Grabbing Information from Other Web Servers *303*
     Encrypting Information *309*
     Uploading Files from the Browser to the Web Server *324*
     Why Reinvent the Wheel? *335*
     Further Reading *337*

Index *339*

Preface

The other day a friend called me with some problems he was having in creating an ASP script. This friend, who is relatively new to ASP but has been writing Visual Basic applications for several years, was in the midst of building a large, data-driven web site. During our conversation, he frustratedly commented that there seemed to be a lot of monotony involved in creating ASP pages.

After I asked him to elaborate, he explained there were several pages that did relatively similar things for his site: one set of ASP pages served as an administration tool for the database driving his site; another set of ASP pages allowed users to enter information into the database. Externally, these pages looked and acted differently, but their core functionality—accessing a database table and adding, editing, and removing entries—was identical. Despite these similarities, my friend was finding that he created separate ASP pages for each task, even if the tasks were related.

This friend is not alone. While the popularity and use of Active Server Pages has grown radically over the past couple of years, the quality of the code has not. As a consultant, author, and editor and founder of *4GuysFromRolla.com*—one of the largest online Active Server Pages resource sites—I've created thousands of ASP pages over the past three years. I've also worked in several teams designing large web sites using Active Server Pages and have reviewed other developers' scripts.

When developing ASP pages, I find myself (and other developers) continually reinventing the wheel. Take a moment to think about how many database administration pages you have created. About how many ASP scripts have you written to perform server-side form validation? Why is it that we put so much time into design when developing a Visual Basic or Visual C++ application but so little time when developing ASP pages?

Simply put, this book looks at why and how Active Server Page design is lacking and examines the steps that can be taken to improve this design process. It is an important topic that has received very little attention in the past.

Who This Book Is For

This book is intended for intermediate to advanced Active Server Pages developers who have solid ASP skills and are interested in learning techniques for creating reusable and robust ASP applications. Since this book focuses on writing maintainable, reusable code, if you work on large-scale ASP applications, especially with teams of ASP developers, you will find this book especially helpful.

This book is also for those who, like my friend, have found creating ASP pages to be monotonous. By spending time carefully developing Active Server Pages before writing the actual code, you will soon find yourself producing reusable, cleaner, and less error-prone code.

Finally, this book is also intended for all the ASP pros out there—those who are passionate about developing Active Server Pages, those who enjoy learning new ways to create ASP pages, and those who pride themselves on their ASP skills.

How This Book Is Organized

This book is divided into eight chapters. The first chapter serves as an introduction to the book, describing what technologies ASP offers to aid building robust, reusable applications. This chapter introduces some of the new features in ASP 3.0 and the VBScript scripting engine that are used throughout the book to assist in application design.

The next three chapters expound on the technologies briefly discussed in the introduction. Chapter 2, *Choosing a Server-Side Scripting Language*, discusses what scripting languages are available for designing ASP pages. The vast majority of books and ASP resource web sites present ASP examples in VBScript only. This chapter discusses some of the other languages that can be used and their advantages and disadvantages. When building an ASP application with a team of developers, there are times when a language other than VBScript needs to be used due to the various developers' past experiences. For example, if only one of five developers is fluent with VBScript, perhaps using JScript or PerlScript as the server-side scripting language would be a better choice.

Chapter 3, *Exception Handling*, examines exception-handling techniques as well as the new ASPError object introduced with ASP 3.0. Too often, when an error occurs in an ASP page, an unreadable, ugly message is displayed. With proper exception-handling techniques, these unreadable error messages can be avoided. In certain cases, errors that usually generate error messages can be "fixed" on the fly!

In Chapter 4, *Regular Expressions, Classes, and Dynamic Evaluation and Execution*, we look at using several of the new features available in the VBScript Scripting Engine Version 5.0. This chapter introduces VBScript classes, which are similar to classes in Visual Basic.

Chapters 5 and 6 use VBScript classes intensively to build a reusable set of classes. Chapter 5, *Form Reuse*, looks at building a server-side validation class, while Chapter 6, *Database Reuse*, focuses on building a generic database administration-generation class. At the conclusion of these two chapters you'll have created a very powerful and very reusable set of classes you can use in your own ASP applications! Furthermore, classes hide the complexity of completing a task. Therefore, if you are on a team of ASP developers that contains some beginning developers, your senior developers can work on building reusable classes while your junior-level developers can spend their time using instances of these classes within ASP pages.

Chapter 7, *Using Components*, discusses the benefits of using Microsoft-provided COM components to enhance your web site. A discussion on building custom COM components using both high-level languages and script is presented as well. Chapter 8, *Enhancing Your Web Site with Third-Party Components*, examines how to use preexisting COM components to add a variety of features to your site. There are literally hundreds of third-party COM components that can help you add various common web site features. Chapter 8 looks at some of the most widely used third-party components.

At the end of each chapter you'll find a section titled "Further Reading." This section contains a list of URLs you can visit to obtain further information on the topics discussed in the chapter.

ASP Information on the Web

One thing that fascinates me to no end is the sheer amount of free and useful Active Server Pages information on the Internet. Furthermore, there are literally thousands of ASP developers from around the world who actively participate in providing free information, answering questions, and giving feedback and encouragement. This group of people, the ASP community, is one of the nicest and most helpful groups of computer experts I've ever had the opportunity to interact with.

Some of the greatest ASP information web sites available include:

4GuysFromRolla.com
> This is the ASP web site I run. The site focuses on high-quality articles for intermediate to advanced ASP developers.

LearnASP.com
> If you are one who learns best by examining source code, seeing it run, and tinkering with it (as opposed to reading articles), then *LearnASP.com* is for

you. With thousands of code examples ready to run, *LearnASP.com* is the place to go for ASP source code.

15Seconds.com

This was one of the first ASP sites on the Internet. *15Seconds.com* serves as a gateway to ASP information, containing hundreds of links to relevant articles on a number of advanced topics.

As mentioned earlier, if you have a specific ASP question, I guarantee there are several folks who will take the time to help you find the answer. There are several web sites that focus on bringing members of the ASP community together to help answer questions and solve problems. If you have an ASP-related question that needs answering, be sure to check out these web sites:

ASPMessageboard.com

The Internet's most popular ASP-related message board, receiving hundreds of questions and answers each and every day! If you've got a question, *ASPMessageboard.com* is a great place to ask.

ASPLists.com

If you prefer ListServs over forum web sites, be sure to check out *ASPLists. com*. There are several different ListServs available from *ASPLists.com*, from the very high-volume, general lists (ASP Free For All) to the very specific, low-volume lists (Fast Code, Advanced ADSI, etc.).

Obtaining the Sample Code

All of the example Visual Basic source code from *Designing Active Server Pages* is downloadable free from the O'Reilly & Associates web site at *http://vb.oreilly.com*.

Conventions Used in This Book

Throughout this book, I have used the following typographic conventions:

`Constant width`

Indicates a language construct such as a language statement, a constant, or an expression. Interface names appear in constant width. Lines of code also appear in constant width, as do classes and function and method prototypes.

Italic

Represents intrinsic and application-defined functions, the names of system elements such as directories and files, and Internet resources such as web documents. New terms are also italicized when they are first introduced.

Constant width italic
> Indicates replaceable parameter names in prototypes or command syntax, and indicates variable and parameter names in body text.

Constant width boldface
> Indicates user input, as well as emphasized code.

How to Contact Us

The information in this book has been tested and verified, but you may find that features have changed (or even find mistakes!). You can send any errors you find, as well as suggestions for future editions, to:

> O'Reilly & Associates, Inc.
> 101 Morris Street
> Sebastopol, CA 95472
> (800) 998-9938 (in the U.S. or Canada)
> (707) 829-0515 (international/local)
> (707) 829-0104 (fax)

You can send us messages electronically. To be put on the mailing list or request a catalog, send email to:

> *info@oreilly.com*

To ask technical questions or comment on the book, send email to:

> *bookquestions@oreilly.com*

There is a web site for the book, where examples, errata, and any plans for future editions are listed. You can access this page at:

> *http://www.oreilly.com/catalog/designasp*

For more information about this book and others, see the O'Reilly web site:

> *http://www.oreilly.com*

For technical information on Visual Basic programming, to participate in VB discussion forums, or to acquaint yourself with O'Reilly's line of Visual Basic books, you can access the O'Reilly Visual Basic web site at:

> *http://vb.oreilly.com*

Acknowledgments

This book has been a dream of mine for some time. I've always considered web page design to be an extremely important topic, especially with ASP and have wanted to write a book on the subject for some time. That being said, I'd like to thank my editor, Ron Petrusha, who gave me the creative freedom and encouragement needed to write such a book. Thanks, Ron!

In January 1998, I started working with ASP with Empower Consulting, Inc., in Kansas City, Missouri. I instantly fell in love with ASP and decided to create a small web site, *4GuysFromRolla.com*, to showcase what cool things I had done with ASP. Who knew my little hobby site would grow into one of the largest ASP information sites on the Net, attracting over 15,000 ASP developers each day? A hearty thank you to all those who visit 4Guys regularly; this book is dedicated to you!

Finally, I'd like to say thanks to my great family. Our life, our decisions, our attitudes, our beliefs, and our dreams are based largely upon our upbringing. I was very fortunate to have such a loving and encouraging family; where I am today and what I am today is due, in large part, to the continual support, respect, and advice provided by my parents, brother, and relatives.

I hope you enjoy reading this book as much as I enjoyed writing it! As always, Happy Programming!

1

Introduction

As the Web has become a more integral part of everyday life and business, web sites have matured from small, static sites into rich, data-driven, complex applications. Several technologies, including dynamic scripting technologies, like Active Server Pages and Perl, have aided along the way, making the Web a more viable application medium. This book focuses on using Active Server Pages to quickly and easily build powerful and dynamic web sites.

Although the server-side tools for building web sites have experienced a nice maturation, the processes used for building these sites have not. What, specifically, is Active Server Page design? What is currently wrong with ASP design? Why hasn't the art of designing ASP pages advanced? What can be done to improve ASP design? The first three questions will be answered in this chapter. The last one, however, is a meaty one; it is addressed in this chapter, and answered over the next seven chapters.

This chapter not only addresses these questions, but also introduces functions and programming styles that will be used extensively throughout this book.

What Is Application Design?

Designing a single ASP page is trivial. The challenges involved in designing ASP pages arise when large web sites with hundreds of web pages are being crafted. These large web sites are, in their own rights, full-scale applications. Therefore, before we examine Active Server Page design, we will first take a step back and discuss application design. As we'll see shortly, application design is a long, arduous process, involving much more than simply punching out code.

Imagine that you have just been assigned the task of creating a new program that will be deployed to all of the employees in your company. This program will allow the users to query a centralized database and place the results into a number of formats that correspond to various interoffice forms your company uses. What do you do first? How do you get started?

Designing, coding, testing, and deploying an application is known as *application development*. Temporally, it can be viewed as the time span from when the program was first conceptualized to when its first stable version was available for use. (Of course, application development does not end with the first, stable release of a product. Rather, it continues as long as updates and enhancements of the given product are being made.) An entire branch of the computer science discipline is dedicated to studying various application-development methodologies. While there are a number of different methodologies, they all usually share a certain number of phases, which include:

- Design
- Coding
- Testing
- Deployment

In classical software development, developers usually follow this flow, working on the application's design before moving on to writing the actual code. For example, large software companies draft very detailed plans for their software projects before a developer writes a single line of code.

Designing for the Web

With the Web, the design stage usually focuses on the aesthetics of the web site, such as the look and feel of each web page. This makes sense, since in the Web's earlier days, the vast majority of web sites were static, their usefulness and allure directly dependent upon their HTML design. As the Web matures, though, and web sites become more dynamic, it is important that adequate time be spent on the design of the scripts that run a site.

Simply put, the design phase in web site development focuses too much on the layout and HTML issues and too little on the programmatic side. That's not to say that HTML design is unimportant: it is very important. The end users benefit directly from the HTML design. Imagine a site that had terrible HTML design, a site cumbersome to navigate and difficult to use. Chances are, after one visit to this site, you'd not come back.

Script design, on the other hand, benefits the developers directly, and the end users indirectly. For example, if your dynamic web site contains robust, easy-to-update scripts, the developers will directly benefit from reduced time spent in the coding phase when a new feature needs to be added. The end users will indirectly benefit from such well-designed scripts, since the less code a developer has to write, the less buggy her code will be. Additionally, well-designed scripts require less maintenance time, making it easier to add new functionality to existing scripts. (The benefits of code reuse and robust scripts are discussed in more detail in the next section, "What's Wrong with ASP Design?") Since both HTML design and script design are important, it is essential that adequate time be spent on both.

Since ASP pages are scripts, ASP design is the art of crafting robust, reusable code. Good design requires planning, documentation, and above all, patience. Before you begin writing code for a particular ASP page, think of what the script needs to accomplish. Is it similar to the functionality of other ASP pages on the site? Have you created a page with similar functionality in a past project? How can you build this page so that it can be easily reused in future projects?

What's Wrong with ASP Design?

In my consulting experience, I have found that many developers don't spend any time working on the design of their scripts. Rather, they just start coding once they have an understanding of what the web site needs to look like and what tasks it needs to accomplish.

Such an approach is inefficient and error-prone. If no thought is dedicated to determining the design of the ASP scripts before they are actually written, then for each similar script, the developer essentially reinvents the wheel. For example, imagine the developer has four ASP scripts that need to make modifications to a database. While these scripts may not be identical, assume they all have many functional similarities. Why should the developer spend the time to create each page separately, when one generic page would do?

There is a direct correlation between the amount of code you write and the number of bugs in your program. Typos and silly mistakes catch us all, and they occur proportionally to the amount of raw source code actually written. If we can reduce the number of total ASP scripts that need to be written by generalizing certain scripts to handle the functionality present in the previous four, we will create less buggy ASP applications.

Furthermore, intelligent ASP script design will not only save time and bugs in our current project, but also in future projects. Once a robust module is written to handle a specific task, if that task needs to be completed in a future project, we need only reuse our existing code! With hasty design techniques, code is often written without looking toward the future.

Why Hasn't ASP Design Advanced?

Despite the advantages of a lengthy ASP design stage, ASP pages are still typically designed hastily. Rigorous ASP design hasn't gained wide acceptance due to three reasons:

- Businesses are operating on Internet time. Due to the fact that businesses must operate at Internet time to stay competitive, many of the lengthier software development phases that are enjoyed in classical software development are rushed through or sidestepped completely for web applications.

- Active Server Pages are created using scripting languages. Scripting languages are meant to solve small, discrete problems. Rarely does a developer consider using a scripting language to tackle a formidable programming challenge. Therefore, when coding with a scripting language, it may seem and feel unjustifiable to spend any significant amount of time working on the design of the script.

- Active Server Pages are easy to use, and can build powerful, dynamic web sites quickly. This, of course, is an advantage of using ASP to develop a web site, but it is a bit of a double-edged sword. Due to developers' expectations concerning the ease of development and quick time frame for creating an ASP web site, a lengthy design process may seem out of place.

You may have noted a slight contradiction in the last couple of pages. In "What's Wrong with ASP Design?" I mention that ASP scripts can be used to build large, data-driven web sites, yet in the second bulleted item above, I state that rarely will a scripting language be used for a large project.

For large web projects, compiled components should be created in a high-level programming language like Visual C++, Java, or Visual Basic, and used within ASP pages. In Chapter 7, *Using Components*, we'll look at combining ASP development with compiled components.

While ASP design has been lacking, it is not because ASP makes such design difficult. In fact, quite the opposite is true; several techniques can be used to create robust, reusable ASP scripts. In the next section, "What Can Be Done to Improve ASP Design?" and throughout the rest of this book, we'll be looking at the tools and methodologies to accomplish this.

What Can Be Done to Improve ASP Design?

Even though ASP scripts are, obviously, scripts, there are several approaches that can be taken to modularize your source code and encapsulate complex tasks. These include using server-side includes, taking advantage of VBScript classes, and making calls to the *Server.Execute* and *Server.Transfer* methods.

Server-Side Includes

One of the most common approaches to creating modularized code is to use *server-side includes* (SSI). Server-side includes are used to import ASP code into an ASP page. The benefit of being able to import code from one ASP page to another is you can create individual ASP pages with common functions or classes, and have these functions and class definitions imported into the pages that require their use. Instead of having to cut and paste a particular function that is needed in several ASP web pages, you can place that function in a single file, and then use a server-side include to import the function definition into each ASP page that needs to make use of that particular function.

For example, imagine that you run an e-commerce site. Conceivably, there are a number of ASP pages in which you need to compute the sales tax. Rather than hardcode a sales tax percentage in each of these pages, you could create a single function—*ComputeTotalWithSalesTax*—that would accept the total less the sales tax as a parameter, returning the new total including sales tax. Example 1-1 contains an example of the *ComputeTotalWithSalesTax* function.

Example 1-1. Determining the Sales Tax

```
Function ComputeTotalWithSalesTax(curTotalLessSalesTax)
  Const curSalesTax = 0.0695
  ComputeTotalWithSalesTax = curTotalLessSalesTax + _
        curTotalLessSalesTax * curSalesTax
End Function
```

 The above snippet of code places business logic—determining the sales tax—within an ASP page. As we'll discuss in Chapter 7, business logic should be placed in custom components. The above code snippet only serves to show an example of using server-side includes.

If this function existed on each page that needed to calculate the sales tax, imagine what would happen if the sales tax percentage changed. You would have to poke through every ASP page, checking to see if it referenced a hardcoded sales tax value, and if it did, make the appropriate change. Of course, if you missed a page, you'd be in for a headache when certain users were being charged less tax than others.

Needless to say, such an approach is error-prone; furthermore, the developer who chooses this approach is ulcer-prone. A wiser decision would be to place a single instance of the *ComputeTotalWithSalesTax* function into a file, say */CODEREUSE/ComputeSalesTax.asp*, and then use server-side includes in each ASP page that needs to reference this function.

When using a server-side include to import the contents of one file to another, the text from the included file is just dumped straight into the file that issues the server-side include. Using a server-side include is functionally identical to copying the entire contents of the included file and pasting them into the file that initiated the server-side include. Therefore, if you have `Option Explicit` declared in the file that issues the server-side include (which you always should), you will need to have every variable you use in the included file declared in the included file. Also, the code in the file to be included should be placed within an ASP code block, using either the `<%` and `%>` delimiters or the `<SCRIPT RUNAT=SERVER LANGUAGE="VBSCRIPT">` and `</SCRIPT>` delimiters.

 ASP pages are not the only type of file that can execute server-side includes. Later in this chapter, in the section "File types that can perform server-side includes," we'll look at using server-side includes in non-ASP pages.

To revisit our sales tax example, if we created a file to hold the sales tax computing function and named that file */CODEREUSE/ComputeSalesTax.asp*, we would want to enter the following code into that file:

```
<%
Function ComputeTotalWithSalesTax(curTotalLessSalesTax)
  Const curSalesTax = 0.0695
  ComputeTotalWithSalesTax = curTotalLessSalesTax + _
        curTotalLessSalesTax * curSalesTax
End Function
%>
```

Note that the above code is nearly identical to the code in Example 1-1. The only difference is the code snippet above contains the `<%` and `%>` delimiters around the ASP code. Remember, this is needed to be properly included.

Now, for each page that needs to access this function, we need to add a single line of code. The following is an example ASP page that uses a server-side include to make the *ComputeTotalWithSalesTax* function accessible:

```
<% @LANGUAGE="VBScript" %>
<% Option Explicit %>
<!--#include virtual="/CODEREUSE/ComputeSalesTax.asp"-->
<%
  Dim curTotal
  curTotal = 46.72

  'Output the total with sales tax
  Response.Write "Cost Before Sales Tax: " & FormatCurrency(curTotal, 2)
  Response.Write "<BR>Cost After Sales Tax: " & _
          FormatCurrency(ComputeTotalWithSalesTax(curTotal), 2)
%>
```

The server-side include has two forms:

```
<!--#include file="filename"-->
```

and:

```
<!--#include virtual="filename"-->
```

If you use the **file** keyword, then *filename* is relative to the directory in which the ASP page that issues the server-side include resides. If you use the **virtual** keyword, *filename* is relative to the web server's root directory. For example, if from an ASP page in the */MyASPScripts* directory you had:

```
<!--#include file="ComputeSalesTax.asp"-->
```

then the file *ComputeSalesTax.asp* would need to exist in the */MyASPScripts* directory; if it did not, an error would result when attempting to use the server-side include.

Remember that when using the **virtual** keyword, you need to specify *filename* relative to the Web's root directory, regardless of the directory that the ASP page that issues the server-side include exists in. Therefore, if in an ASP page you used:

```
<!--#include virtual="/CODEREUSE/ComputeSalesTax.asp"-->
```

the file *ComputeSalesTax.asp* would need to exist in the */CODEREUSE* directory, regardless of what directory the ASP page that issued the server-side include existed in.

Use the virtual Keyword Religiously

When using a server-side include, there is no reason why you should use the **file** keyword. Commonly used modules should be placed in specific directories (such as */CODEREUSE*). Using the **virtual** keyword relieves any concern about being able to correctly specify the path relative to the executing ASP page.

Your include files can contain HTML formatting and/or ASP code. Also, an include file can use server-side includes itself to further modularize the code! However, if you try to perform a *cyclic include*—that is, *Page1.asp* includes *Page2.asp*, and *Page2.asp* includes *Page1.asp*—an error message will be generated. (More verbosely, the only limitation for including files in included files is included files can't include the file that included them. Be sure to check out the sidebar, "An Interesting Lingo.") Forcing a cyclic include to generate an error makes sense, because if a cyclic include did not generate an error, *Page1.asp* and *Page2.asp* would recursively include one another until the web server ran out of available memory.

An Interesting Lingo

Using include files within include files allows for confusing, yet cool-sounding, statements. Imagine what people unfamiliar with server-side includes might think if they overheard you making a comment like: "Hey, Bob, in *Report.asp*, did you want the file included by the include to include *stats.asp*, which includes another included file, or do you want *Report.asp* not to include any included files that include included files?"

Example 1-2 contains the code for *Page1.asp*, while Example 1-3 contains the code for *Page2.asp*. If you visit *Page1.asp* through a browser, the error message shown in Figure 1-1 will be generated.

Example 1-2. Page1.asp Uses a Server-Side Include to Import the Contents of Page2.asp

```
<%
    Response.Write "Preparing to include Page2.asp<P>"


    'Include the file Page2.asp
%>
<!--#include file="Page2.asp"-->
```

Example 1-3. Page2.asp Uses a Server-Side Include to Import the Contents of Page1.asp

```
<%
    Response.Write "Preparing to include Page1.asp<P>"


    'Include the file Page1.asp
%>
<!--#include file="Page1.asp"-->
```

File types that can perform server-side includes

ASP pages are not the only files that can perform server-side includes. Any file type that is mapped to *asp.dll* or *ssinc.dll* can perform server-side includes.

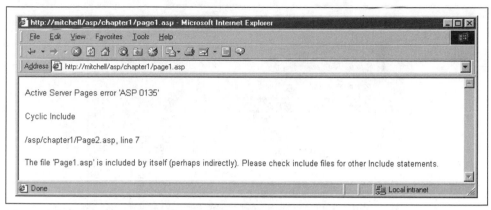

Figure 1-1. Attempting to perform a cyclic include generates an error message

When a client requests a file from an IIS web server, the web server first determines the file extension being requested by the client. Next, the web server checks to see if that extension is mapped to a particular ISAPI DLL. If there is a mapping between that file extension and an ISAPI DLL, the ISAPI DLL is invoked. This is, essentially, what happens when you request an ASP page through your web browser.

ssinc.dll is an ISAPI DLL that allows server-side directives to be executed. A server-side include is one facet of server-side directives. See the "Further Reading" section for an article that discusses server-side directives in more detail. In IIS 5.0, files with the extensions *.shtml*, *.shtm*, and *.stm* are, by default, mapped to *ssinc. dll*, and therefore can perform server-side includes. Of course, files with these extensions cannot process ASP code, unless you explicitly map these extensions to be processed by *asp.dll*.

asp.dll is capable of performing only one type of server-side directive: server-side includes. *ssinc.dll*, on the other hand, can perform all server-side directives but cannot process ASP code. For more information on all of the server-side directives, be sure to refer to the article "Using Server-Side Directives" listed at the end of this chapter in the "Further Reading" section.

You can explicitly map particular file extensions to particular ISAPI DLLs. To change a file extension mapping in Windows 2000, go to Start → Programs → Administrative Tools → Internet Services Manager (in Windows NT, open up the IIS MMC). A listing of the web sites on your computer should appear. Right-click on the web site whose file extension mapping you wish to alter, and click on Properties. A tabbed Web Site Properties dialog box will appear; select the "Home Directory" tab, and click the Configuration button. You should now be presented with the Application Configuration dialog box shown in Figure 1-2.

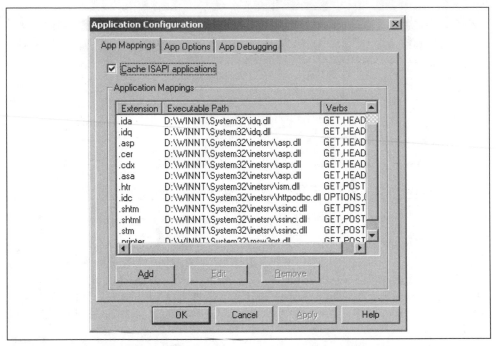

Figure 1-2. The "App Mappings" tab of the Application Configuration dialog box lists each file type's corresponding ISAPI DLL

Note that the *.asp* file extension is mapped to *asp.dll*, while the extensions *.shtml*, *.shtm*, and *.stm* are mapped to *ssinc.dll*. You can add, edit, and remove these mappings. For example, you could create a new extension mapping, having all files with the extension of *.scott* map to *ssinc.dll*. With such a mapping, files on your web site with the *.scott* extension would be functionally identical to files with extensions of *.shtml*, *.shtm*, or *.stm*; in short, *.scott* files would be able to perform server-side directives!

Be careful when adding new application mappings. There is a bug in IIS 5.0 that can arise when the *.htm* extension is mapped to *ssinc.dll* and the default document is a *.htm* file. For more information on this bug, be sure to read: *http://support.microsoft.com/support/kb/articles/ Q246/8/06.ASP*.

Dynamic server-side includes

Server-side includes are executed before any ASP code is processed. Due to this fact, you cannot specify a dynamic filename. For example, it would be nice to be able to do something like:

```
<%
  Dim strPage
  strPage = "/scripts/MyPage.asp"
%>
<!--#include virtual="<%=strPage%>"-->
```

However, since the server-side includes are performed before the ASP code is processed, the above code will cause IIS to complain that the file *<%=strPage%>* cannot be found. There are some methods available to fake dynamic server-side includes. One way is to use a `Select Case` statement, with a `Case` for each potential server-side include. For example, if you knew you would need to process the code in one of five potential include files, you could use the following code:

```
<%
Select Case strPageToExecute
   Case "IncludeFile1.asp" %>
     <!--#include virtual="/IncludeFile1.asp"-->
<% Case "IncludeFile2.asp" %>
     <!--#include virtual="/IncludeFile2.asp"-->
<% Case "IncludeFile3.asp" %>
     <!--#include virtual="/IncludeFile3.asp"-->
<% Case "IncludeFile4.asp" %>
     <!--#include virtual="/IncludeFile4.asp"-->
<% Case "IncludeFile5.asp" %>
     <!--#include virtual="/IncludeFile5.asp"-->
<% End Select %>
```

Each server-side include is issued immediately before any of the ASP code in the ASP page is run. That means all of the five server-side includes will be executed and their contents imported into the ASP page.

The downsides of this approach are that you are limited to a finite number of potential include files, and for each potential include file, you need to hardcode a case statement. As well, whenever you use an `#include` directive, the entire contents of *filename* are inserted into the ASP script before processing. If you have a large number of potential include files and these files contain large amounts of code, this could cause a performance bottleneck.

Another way to "fake" dynamic server-side includes is to use the FileSystemObject object model to read in the contents of the include file you are interested in inserting into your ASP page. The following code allows for a file to be inserted into an ASP script:

```
<% Option Explicit %>
<%
  '************************* DESCRIPTION *************************
  '* Output the entire contents of a text file, whose name can be *
  '* dynamically generated.                                        *
  '**************************************************************
  Dim strFileName, objFSO, objFile
```

```
'Create an instance of the FSO object
Set objFSO = Server.CreateObject("Scripting.FileSystemObject")

'What file do we want to import?
strFileName = "C:\InetPub\wwwroot\Adages.htm"

'Open a text file, using the OpenTextFile method
Set objFile = objFSO.OpenTextFile(strFileName)

'Output the entire contents of the text file
Response.Write objFile.ReadAll

objFile.Close       'Close the file...

'Clean up
Set objFile = Nothing
Set objFSO = Nothing
%>
```

 Note that the FileSystemObject expects full physical filenames (*C:\ InetPub\wwroot\Adages.htm*) and not virtual filenames (*/Adages.htm*).

The above code may seem like it accomplishes a dynamic server-side include, but it is a little misleading. Since the text file cannot be opened and read until the ASP script is running, if there is any ASP code within the file specified by *strFileName*, it won't be executed; rather, the ASP code will be output just like any other HTML content in the file! This method is an acceptable one if you only need a dynamic server-side include to read in an HTML header or footer. However, any ASP code in the file specified by *strFileName* will not be executed!

With ASP 2.0, truly dynamic server-side includes were impossible. However, with ASP 3.0 and the new Execute method of the Server object, true dynamic includes are possible! Server.Execute is discussed in the section "Using Server.Execute."

Naming your include files

When grouping common functions into a particular file to be included by other ASP pages, be sure to give the file an *.asp* extension. If you fail to do this, and a web surfer guesses the correct filename of an include file, the user can view the contents of the include file! Files with an *.asp* extension are safe from prying eyes because when an ASP page is requested, IIS steps in and executes the ASP page, turning the ASP code into HTML. Files *without* an *.asp* extension are not processed by IIS and are sent directly to the client. This can reveal the source code of your include files.

If for some reason, you must use include files with a non-ASP extension, be sure to place these files in a directory that has HTTP read permissions turned off. With the HTTP read permissions turned off, ASP pages can still import the contents of these include files, but if someone attempts to request these files directly through an HTTP-request (i.e., entering the full URL of the include file in their browser), they will receive an error message indicating that HTTP reads are not permitted.

Since developers often place constants, database connections, and common functions in include files, it is imperative that the contents of include files remain away from prying eyes.

It's true there is not a great chance that anyone will be able to exactly guess the name of an include file. However, that does not mean your include files are safe. Jerry Walsh has detected a potential security bug that can occur when using server-side includes. This security bug happens when you create an include file that has a programmatic error in it. For example, imagine a file named */CODEREUSE/dbConn.inc* that contained the following code:

```
<%
    Dim objConn
    Set objConn = Server.CreateObject("ADODB.Conection")

    objConn.ConnectionString = "DRIVER={Microsoft Access (*.mdb)};" & _
                "DBQ=" & Server.MapPath("/MyDatabase.mdb")
    objConn.Open
%>
```

Note that there is an error in the above code snippet: the class ID for the Connection object is misspelled, with "Conection" missing an "n." Many ASP sites use an include file to have one database connection file. However, making such a page with an error can yield disastrous results, as we'll see shortly. Now, if some page on your site uses this include file like so:

```
<% @LANGUAGE="VBScript" %>
<% Option Explicit %>
<!--#include virtual="/CODEREUSE/dbConn.inc"-->
<%
    'Do stuff with the database connection...
%>
```

an error will occur when a user visits the page, since there is an error in */CODEREUSE/dbConn.inc*. Specifically, the user will see the error message:

```
Microsoft VBScript runtime error '800a004'

Invalid Class String

/CODEREUSE/dbConn.inc, line 3
```

Notice that the full path to the include file is displayed in the error message! Since the include file does not contain an *.asp* extension, anyone who stumbles across this erroneous page can now visit your database connection script, which contains the path to your Access database (*MyDatabase.mdb*). The user can now download directly!

You might think you are safe if you do not provide some mechanism for your users to reach the ASP page that uses the erroneous include file. That is, if you provide no direct hyperlinks to this page, no user will see the error message and no user will know the include file's path. While it is true that no user will likely stumble across the ASP page, search engines may still index them!

Again, you might think that this is a minor problem and that there is an incredibly low probability that a search engine will index this odious page. However, if you go to AltaVista and enter the following search terms:

```
+"Microsoft VBScript runtime error" +".inc, "
```

you'll find that an alarming number of pages are returned that display the complete path to an include file whose contents can be read by any visitor!

The moral of this story: don't put files whose contents will be imported into ASP pages via a server-side include on your production web site until they have been thoroughly tested and do not contain any errors that will reveal their location. Or, more simply, just make sure you give your include files an *.asp* extension or place them in a directory where HTTP read permissions are turned off. Another potential solution is discussed in Chapter 3, *Exception Handling*. In that chapter, we'll look at how to have include files (and other ASP pages) handle errors more gracefully than simply spitting out an error message.

According to an article on Microsoft's web site (*http://msdn. microsoft.com/library/tools/aspdoc/iiwainc.htm*), "…it is good programming practice to give included files an *.inc* extension to distinguish them from other types of files." Be sure not to follow this suggestion unless you place these files in a directory that has read permissions disabled.

Protecting the contents of your include files from prying eyes

There are some simple steps you can take to ensure that your include files' contents won't be seen by prying eyes. The two simplest options are:

- Create a directory for all your include files, and remove the read permissions from this directory. This will prevent HTTP read requests on the specified directory. If a web visitor attempts to retrieve any file from that directory, they will receive a Permission Denied error.

- Give all include files an .asp extension. If a user tries to view a file with an *.asp* extension, IIS will attempt to process the file first with *ASP.DLL* and will send the resulting HTML instead of the actual source.

More about server-side includes

Server-side includes are extremely useful for developing and using code modules. Placing common code in modules allows for easier code reuse. Throughout this book, server-side includes are used quite frequently. Often classes will be created that are used among many ASP pages. Rather than copying the class definition into each ASP page, it makes much more sense to define the class in a single file and to use a simple server-side include in all of the pages that need to utilize the given class.

Since server-side includes are used so frequently throughout this book, it is important you have a solid understanding of how they work. If you are a little rusty on server-side includes, I highly recommend that you take the time to read the following two articles:

- "The low-down on #includes," found at *http://www.4guysfromrolla.com/webtech/080199-1.shtml.*

- "Security Alert—Using includes Improperly from non-Debugged ASP Pages can allow Visitors to View your source code," found at *http://www. 4guysfromrolla.com/webtech/020400-2.shtml.*

VBScript Classes

Since Version 5.0 of the VBScript scripting engine, developers have had the opportunity to use VB-like classes in their VBScript code. Classes provide for an object-oriented-like programming approach when developing ASP pages, which greatly enhances the reusability of a particular ASP page.

Classes are great for creating black-box modules. For other developers to use a black-box module, they do not need to know any of the specific implementation details; rather, they just use the black box through its publicly accessible methods and properties.

We will discuss classes in detail in Chapter 4, *Regular Expressions, Classes, and Dynamic Evaluation and Execution.* Classes are used extensively in Chapter 5, *Form Reuse,* and Chapter 6, *Database Reuse,* as we look at code reuse techniques. Since classes encapsulate complexity, hide implementation details, and function as a black box for the developer, classes assist greatly when creating reusable code.

In Chapters 5 and 6 we will be examining reusable scripts that make heavy use of VBScript classes.

Using Server.Execute

Server.Execute can also be used to modularize your ASP code. Server.Execute branches the control flow from one ASP page to another. When the page that was called via the Server.Execute completes processing, control is returned to the page that issued the Server.Execute command. Figure 1-3 illustrates the semantics of Server.Execute.

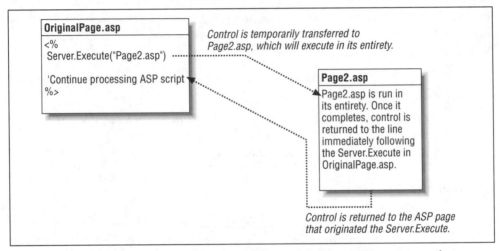

Figure 1-3. Server.Execute branches the control flow to a separate ASP page, runs the page, and returns the control flow to the original page

Server.Execute's main advantage is its ability to perform truly dynamic includes. For example, using Server.Execute, you could do the following:

```
<%
  Dim strPage
  strPage = "/scripts/MyPage.asp"
  Server.Execute(strPage)
%>
```

When an ASP page uses Server.Execute to branch control to another ASP page, all of its built-in ASP objects are passed along. For example, if *Page1.asp* issues a **Server.Execute("Page2.asp")**, *Page2.asp* will have access to *Page1.asp*'s intrinsic ASP objects. Remember that the Request object is an intrinsic ASP object and that it contains the Form and QueryString collections. Since all the intrinsic objects are shared from *Page1.asp* to *Page2.asp*, when *Page2.asp* attempts to read from either of these Request object collections, it is reading the values from *Page1.asp*'s Request object collections. Now that's a mouthful!

For example, if *Page1.asp* simply had the code:

```
Server.Execute("Page2.asp")
```

and *Page2.asp* simply had the code:

```
Response.Write Request("Age")
```

if we visited *Page1.asp* through a browser, entering the URL *http://localhost/Page1.asp?Age=21*, the Response.Write in *Page2.asp* would output 21.

To summarize: Server.Execute can be used in place of server-side includes when dynamic includes are needed. If you don't need dynamic includes, and a vanilla server-side include would suffice, I would recommend sticking with the server-side include.

Using Server.Transfer

Server.Transfer can also be used to improve ASP script design, although it cannot serve as a modularization technique like Server.Execute and server-side includes. Server.Transfer is similar to Server.Execute. If *Page1.asp* performs a:

```
Server.Transfer("Page2.asp")
```

the control flow is transferred to *Page2.asp*. When *Page2.asp* finishes executing, control is *not* returned to *Page1.asp*. Figure 1-4 illustrates the semantics of Server.Transfer.

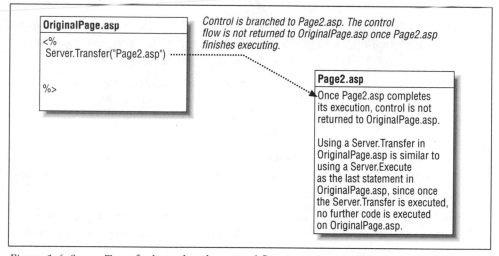

Figure 1-4. Server.Transfer branches the control flow to a separate ASP page, runs the page to completion, and stops executing

As with Server.Execute, when *Page1.asp* performs a *Server.Transfer("Page2.asp")*, *Page1.asp*'s built-in ASP objects are passed along to *Page2.asp*. Being able to access the Request.Form and Request.QueryString collections from *Page1.asp* in *Page2.asp* is an incredibly useful feature, which we'll capitalize on in Chapter 5 and in Chapter 6.

Server.Transfer improves ASP design by providing a mechanism to seamlessly move from one ASP page to another. Part of good application design is creating robust, reusable code, which usually results in the creation of several generic helper ASP pages. With Server.Transfer, we can "plug into" these helper pages, moving from one to the next. In Chapter 5 we'll look at applying Server.Transfer to gracefully hop from one ASP page to another!

Further Reading

At the end of each chapter you'll find a "Further Reading" section. These sections include links to articles that relate to the topics discussed within the chapter. These articles aren't prerequisites to understanding the topics covered in the chapter; rather, they are auxiliary readings, either describing some of the chapter topics in finer detail or providing information on related topics. In either case, I think you'll find these suggested readings worthwhile and beneficial.

- For an incredibly thorough discussion on server-side includes, be sure to check out "The low-down on #includes," available at *http://www.4guysfromrolla.com/ webtech/080199-1.shtml.*

- For a good summary of the new features added to IIS 5.0 and ASP 3.0, visit *http://www.microsoft.com/mind/0499/iis5/iis5.htm.*

- Interested in learning more about HTML design? Check out this article: *http:// webreview.com/pub/98/10/30/bookends/index.html.* Also, every developer should often visit Jakob Nielsen's usability site, *http://www.useit.com/.*

- Server-side includes form just one facet of server-side directives. To learn more about the other server-side directives (which, unfortunately, can't be used through an ASP page), be sure to check out, "Using Server-Side Directives" at *http://www.4guysfromrolla.com/webtech/082599-1.shtml.*

- For more information on using *Server.Execute* and *Server.Transfer* to alter flow control between ASP pages, be sure to read *http://msdn.microsoft.com/library/ psdk/iisref/eadg4d9v.htm.*

- Need to brush up on the FileSystemObject? If so, check out the FileSystemObject FAQ at *http://www.aspfaqs.com/webtech/faq/faqtoc.shtml#FileSystemObject.*

2

Choosing a Server-Side Scripting Language

When creating ASP pages, developers have a number of scripting languages to choose from. The most frequently used server-side scripting language is VBScript, but ASP is not limited to VBScript alone. In fact, any ActiveX scripting engine can be used as the scripting language for ASP. Microsoft provides two ActiveX scripting engines: VBScript and JScript. PerlScript and Python are two additional server-side scripting languages that can be used in an ASP page.

This chapter introduces these rarely used scripting languages, demonstrating how to accomplish some common ASP tasks. This chapter is *not* a language reference or tutorial. Extensive online resources and reference books covering the details of these scripting languages already exist.

The Popularity of VBScript

If you've read many other Active Server Pages books or are a regular at any of the large ASP resource sites on the Internet, you've no doubt noticed that the vast majority of code examples use VBScript as the server-side scripting language. In fact, this book uses VBScript for its code examples. I believe the reason that VBScript is used so frequently in code examples is that a large number of ASP developers were previous Visual Basic developers. Also, a good number of beginning ASP developers are web developers with extensive HTML skills but few programming skills. VBScript is relatively easy to learn and understand, especially for those who are new to programming.

VBScript did not achieve such popularity among ASP developers solely because it is a simple language. When ASP started to grow into a widely used tool for creating dynamic web sites, there were only two scripting engines: VBScript and

JScript. At the time, VBScript had several advantages over JScript. For one thing, VBScript allowed for error handling, while earlier versions of JScript did not.

Current versions of VBScript and JScript, though, both contain error handling, as well as a number of other enhancements. Several notable improvements were added to the Version 5.0 scripting engines; in fact, Chapter 4, *Regular Expressions, Classes, and Dynamic Evaluation and Execution*, discusses these improvements in detail.

Just because VBScript is the most popular server-side scripting language does not mean VBScript is the right scripting language for you. Each scripting language offers its own strengths and weaknesses. Also, by supporting a plethora of languages, ASP does not favor only those developers who have experience in a particular language. If your strengths lie in Perl, use PerlScript as the server-side scripting language. If you are a JavaScript guru, use JScript instead.

Specifying the Scripting Language

Since any compliant ActiveX scripting engine can be used to parse an ASP page, when a web server receives a request for an ASP page, it must first determine what ActiveX scripting engine needs to be used to parse the ASP page's code. If the ASP code consists of valid JScript syntax, but the web server attempts to have the ASP page parsed with the VBScript engine, errors will abound.

An ASP page can explicitly indicate what scripting language was used through the **Language** directive. For example, the following ASP snippet uses the **Language** directive to indicate that JScript is the scripting language used:

```
<% @LANGUAGE = "JScript" %>
<%
  var strQuote;
  strQuote = "Hello, world!";
  Response.Write(strQuote);
%>
```

The **Language** directive, like all other ASP directives, is preceded by **@**. Furthermore, directives must appear before all other ASP code. Failure to do so will result in the following error:

```
Active Server Pages error 'ASP 0140'

Page Command Out Of Order

The @ command must be the first command within the Active Server Page
```

If the Language directive is excluded (which it commonly is), the *default scripting language* is used. When first installed, both IIS and PWS set the default scripting language to VBScript. The default scripting language can be changed, though. To change the default scripting language in IIS, visit the Internet Information Services by going to Start → Programs → Administrative Tools → Internet Services Manager. The web sites on your machine should be listed. Right-click and select Properties for the web site whose default scripting language you wish to change. A tabbed dialog box should appear; select the tab titled "Home Directory." Figure 2-1 shows this dialog box with the correct tab selected.

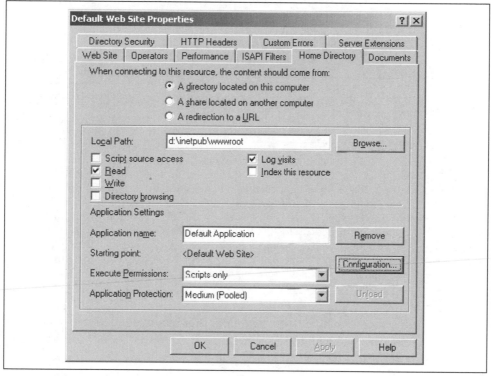

Figure 2-1. The Home Directory tab contains home directory and web application options

From the "Home Directory" tab, click the "Configuration…" button; a new tabbed dialog box will appear. Select the second tab, "App Options." One of the options will read "Default ASP language." Enter the scripting language of your choice here. Figure 2-2 displays a picture of this tab with VBScript entered as the "Default ASP language."

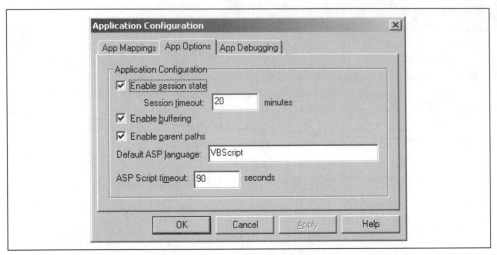

Figure 2-2. The default scripting language can be set through the "App Options" tab in the Application Configuration dialog

   If you have multiple web sites configured on your machine, you can easily set the default scripting language for all of the sites in one fell swoop. Rather than right-clicking and selecting the Properties option for a particular web site, right-click and select the Properties option for the machine name (the parent node of the various web site nodes). Next, choose to Edit the Master WWW properties. You will be presented with a dialog box identical to the one in Figure 2-1. Simply follow the same sequence of steps as you would in changing a single site's default scripting language.

While the **Language** directive is not required, it is recommended that you always explicitly use it. This will lead to less ambiguity in your ASP code. Advanced visual editors, such as Microsoft's Visual InterDev, automatically add the **Language** directive to new ASP pages.

Specifying the Server-Side Scripting Language with SCRIPT Blocks

The `<%` and `%>` delimiters are commonly used to indicate ASP code blocks. However, **SCRIPT** blocks can also be used. For example, an ASP page could consist of:

```
<SCRIPT LANGUAGE="VBSCRIPT" RUNAT="SERVER">
  Response.Write "Hello, World!"
</SCRIPT>
```

When using **SCRIPT** blocks, however, you must specify the **LANGUAGE** attribute; leaving it off will generate an error. One incentive for using **SCRIPT** blocks is they allow for multiple server-side languages in one ASP page. Example 2-1 demonstrates the use of a VBScript script block and a JScript script block, intertwined with <% and %> delimited code:

Example 2-1. Multiple Script Blocks Can Be Used in an ASP Page

```
<% @LANGUAGE="VBSCRIPT" %>
<% Option Explicit %>

<HTML>
<BODY>

<SCRIPT LANGUAGE="VBSCRIPT" RUNAT="SERVER">
  'Display a message from the VBScript script block
  Response.Write "Hello, from the VBScript block!<BR>"
</SCRIPT>

  <!--Display a message from the HTML block-->
  Hello from the HTML Block!<BR>

<%
  'Display a message from the &lt% ... %&gt block
  Response.Write "Hello from the &lt;% ... %&gt; block!<BR>"
%>

<SCRIPT LANGUAGE="JSCRIPT" RUNAT="SERVER">
  // Display a message from the JScript script block
  Response.Write("Hello, from the JScript block!<BR>");
</SCRIPT>

</BODY>
</HTML>
```

A big disadvantage of using script blocks (especially script blocks with different server-side languages) is that the order of script block execution is erratic. For example, one would expect that the output of Example 2-1 would be:

```
Hello, from the VBScript block!
Hello from the HTML Block!
Hello from the <% ... %> block!
Hello, from the JScript block!
```

However, the output from Example 2-1 is quite different, and can be seen in Figure 2-3. Note that the script block that does not contain the specified scripting language operates first. Next, the HTML and <%- and %>-delimited code operate serially; since the HTML output precedes the <%- and %>-delimited output, the HTML output is displayed first. Finally, the scripting block that contains the specified server-side scripting language is executed.

Due to this confusing fact, I find that writing ASP code using <% and %> delimiters is not only easier to read, but it is easier to follow the control flow. For this

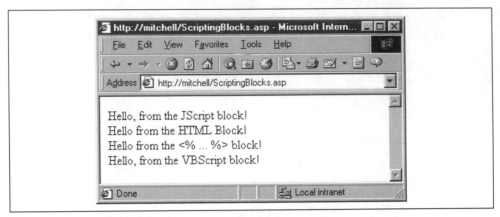

Figure 2-3. The output of script blocks is not serial

reason, the code examples presented throughout the remainder of this book use these delimiters instead of **SCRIPT** blocks.

Choosing the Right Scripting Language

Now that we've looked at how to use different scripting languages, let's look at why one might choose to use a scripting language other than VBScript. In the next three sections, "Creating ASP Pages with JScript," "Creating ASP Pages with PerlScript," and "Creating ASP Pages with Python," a discussion of the languages, benefits and drawbacks will be presented, along with code samples of each scripting language.

When deciding what scripting language to use, remember there is no *correct* scripting language. Of course, developers may feel they are being encouraged to use VBScript. After all, VBScript is the initial default scripting language for both IIS and PWS. Also, the vast majority of books on Active Server Pages use VBScript extensively in examples and sample code. However, VBScript isn't necessarily always the best choice. If it were, there wouldn't be so many other scripting languages available!

When deciding what scripting language to use, choose a language the developers working on the project are familiar with. If the developers know more than one of the available scripting languages, choose the scripting language whose features closely match the needs of the project at hand.

Finally, understand that VBScript and PerlScript are not identical to the Visual Basic and Perl languages. Rather, these scripting languages are subsets of the complete VB language and Perl. Therefore, a developer experienced in Perl should have no problem writing Active Server Pages using PerlScript.

Creating ASP Pages with JScript

Web developers who are familiar with writing client-side JavaScript code already have a good understanding of JScript's syntax and structure. JScript's syntax and control structures are also very similar to C's. For example, JScript's control structures—if ... `else`, `switch`, `while`, `do` ... `while`, and `for` statements—are syntactically identical to C's.

Statement Termination

JScript handles its statement termination a bit differently than C. In C, a semicolon is needed to end a statement; in JScript, *either* a semicolon or a newline character will suffice. Therefore, you can have a JScript statement end without a semicolon as long as the next statement begins on a new line. You can have multiple statements on one line, but then a semicolon must delimit each of these statements. For example, the following code fragment illustrates the legal and illegal use of semicolons and newline characters:

```
<% @LANGUAGE = "JScript" %>
<%
    Response.Write("Each new-line character represents")
    Response.Write("a new statement in JScript.  So does a semicolon.<P>")

    // This is legal code:
    Response.Write("Hello, "); Response.Write("World!");

    // This is not:
    Response.Write("Hello, ")  Response.Write("World!");
%>
```

I highly recommend *always* ending each statement with a semicolon, regardless of whether the next statement starts on a new line. JScript code examples in this book will adhere to this strict use of semicolons.

JScript's Variables and Datatypes

JScript does not require that you explicitly declare your variables. There is no `Option Explicit`-type command in JScript. To declare a variable, use the **var** keyword. Variable names must begin with a letter, an underscore (_), or a dollar sign ($); subsequent characters can be letters, numbers, underscores, or dollar signs.

JScript, like VBScript, is a loosely typed language. That is, every variable is of type Variant, meaning a single variable can be a string, an object, a number, or any other type. There are six datatypes available with JScript: string, number, object, Boolean, null, and undefined. The first five datatypes are fairly straightforward. The undefined datatype, however, warrants further discussion.

When a variable is first created (either implicitly or explicitly with the **var** statement), the variable is undefined. When using an undefined variable in a mathematical expression, the resulting answer will be NaN, which stands for Not a Number. If you attempt to concatenate a string variable and an undefined variable, the concatenated portion of the undefined variable will read "undefined." The following code example illustrates this point:

```
<% @LANGUAGE - "JScript" %>
<%
  var x, y;  // x and y are undefined
  y = "Hello " + x;  // y now equals "Hello undefined"
  Response.Write(y + "<P>");

  y = 4 * x;  // y now equals NaN
  Response.Write(y);
%>
```

In this example, the results would be identical if you replaced *x* in the two assignment statements with an implicitly created variable.

Case Sensitivity

JScript, like JavaScript, is case-sensitive. For this reason, it is important to know the case for the various ASP intrinsic objects and their methods and properties. Each ASP intrinsic object has the following case: Response, Request, Server, Session, Application, ObjectContext, and ASPError. Using improper case will result in an error. Try running the following code, in which the R in **Response** is not capitalized:

```
<% @LANGUAGE = "JScript" %>
<% response.Write("Case is important!!"); %>
```

Since the JScript engine does not recognize **response** as a valid object name, an error message is displayed when viewing the ASP page through a browser, as Figure 2-4 illustrates.

 If you are a VBScript developer learning JScript, you may find this case-sensitivity issue to be an annoyance. Not only do you need to know the case of the intrinsic ASP objects, but you also need to know the case of all of their methods and properties! The general rule is all of the methods and properties of the built-in objects have the first letter of each word capitalized. If the property or method contains just one word (like the Write method of the Response object), then just the first letter is capitalized. However, if the property or method contains two words (like the ExpiresAbsolute method of the Response object), then the first letter of each word is capitalized.

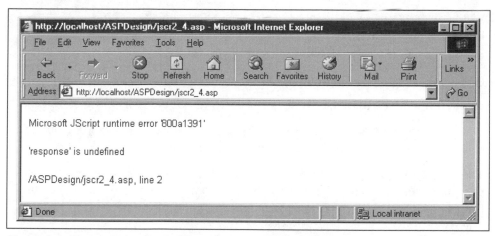

Figure 2-4. Error message caused by incorrect case of Response object

Regular Expressions

JScript contains a number of intrinsic objects, such as the Math, String, and Number objects. These objects contain useful properties and methods that make accomplishing various tasks much easier. For example, the Math object contains methods like *cos* and *sin*, which can be used to calculate the cosine and sine of a number.

The String object is especially useful, since it contains methods that allow for regular expression searching and replacing. Regular expressions are a powerful string-searching technique. If you are unfamiliar with the specifics of regular expressions, be sure to pick up a copy of O'Reilly's *Mastering Regular Expressions* by Jeffrey E. F. Friedl. This section will not attempt to teach regular expressions; rather, it will just show how to use regular expression matching and replacing in JScript.

 A short regular-expression tutorial is presented in Chapter 4.

The String object contains three methods for regular expression searching and matching: *match*, *replace*, and *search*. All three of these methods expect a Regular Expression object instance as one of their parameters. A Regular Expression object contains a valid pattern expression, and optionally, a switch. An instance of the Regular Expression object should be declared like this:

```
var RegularExpressionInstance = /pattern/[switch];
```

where *pattern* is a valid regular expression pattern and *switch* is one of the following values:

i   Ignore case.

g   Perform a global search for all occurrences of *pattern*.

gi   Perform a global search for all occurrences of *pattern*, ignoring case.

Once you have a valid Regular Expression object instance, you can use one of the regular expression methods available in the String object.

The *match* method, which expects a Regular Expression object instance as its single parameter, will return an array with the zeroth element of the array containing the last matched characters. Array elements one through *N* will contain matches to any parenthesized substrings in *pattern*.

The *search* method of the String object, like the *match* method, expects a single parameter containing a valid Regular Expression object instance. *search* returns a number, indicating the position in the string where the first match of the regular expression occurs. If no such match exists, *search* returns −1.

The *replace* method expects two parameters, a Regular Expression object instance and a string containing text to replace any matches with. The *replace* method simply searches for any matches, replacing all occurrences with the string passed in as its second parameter.

Regular expression matching can be very useful for ASP pages in server-side form validation. If we want to collect and store user information in a database, form validation can help ensure database integrity. For example, if a user submits a form with her name and telephone number, it would be nice to ensure that the telephone number is in a valid format before inserting the information into a database. Example 2-2 demonstrates several uses of JScript's regular expression capabilities. Portions of Example 2-2's code could easily be extended for use as server-side form validation. In Chapter 5, *Form Reuse*, we discuss server-side and client-side form validation in detail.

Example 2-2. Regular Expressions in JScript

```
<% @LANGUAGE = "JScript" %>
<%
    // First, examine the following statement:
    var strColdFusion;
    strColdFusion = "Using Cold Fusion is a fun, exciting way to create " +
                "dynamic Web pages!  I really like Cold Fusion.";

    // Now, let's tailor that sentence to this book!
    // We will replace all occurrences of "Cold Fusion" with "ASP"
    // Note that we have to use the global switch (g) to replace all
```

Example 2-2. Regular Expressions in JScript (continued)

```
// instances of Cold Fusion with ASP
var objRegExpr = /Cold Fusion/g;

var strASP = strColdFusion.replace(objRegExpr, "ASP");

// We have now just used the replace function to replace all instances of
// Cold Fusion with ASP.  Output the corrected sentence!
Response.Write(strASP + "<P>");



// Now, we will use the search method to make sure a particular string
// has a particular format.  If we want to make sure that the string
// strPhoneNumber has the format ###-###-####, we can do the following:
var strPhoneNumberValid = "555-555-1234";
var strPhoneNumberInvalid = "67-325533-324";

// Our regular expression object instance will search for three numbers,
// a hyphen, three numbers, a hyphen, and then four numbers.
var objRegExprPhone = /\d{3}-\d{3}-\d{4}/;

// If the phone number is valid, a match should be found starting at the
// zeroth character of the string, and the length of the string should be
// exactly 12 characters
if (strPhoneNumberValid.length == 12 &&
        strPhoneNumberValid.search(objRegExprPhone) == 0)
  // Valid phone number!
  Response.Write(strPhoneNumberValid + " is a valid phone number!");
else
  // Invalid phone number!
  Response.Write(strPhoneNumberValid + " is <B>not</b> a valid phone number!");

Response.Write("<BR>");

if (strPhoneNumberInvalid.length == 12 &&
        strPhoneNumberInvalid.search(objRegExprPhone) == 0)
  // Valid phone number!
  Response.Write(strPhoneNumberInvalid + " is a valid phone number!");
else
  // Invalid phone number!
  Response.Write(strPhoneNumberInvalid + " is <B>not</B> a valid phone number!");
%>
```

You can also perform regular expression searches using VBScript. With Version 5.0 of the scripting engines, Microsoft released a Regular Expression COM object. This object is covered in greater detail in Chapter 4.

Error Handling

The ASPError object, new to ASP 3.0, provides a mechanism to catch any errors that occur either directly from the code in an ASP page, or in an external object that is instantiated within an ASP page. This object works independently of the server-side scripting language being used.

Before ASP 3.0 and the ASPError object, though, all error handling needed to be performed by the scripting language used. VBScript has long had error-handling capabilities in the form of **On Error Resume Next**, but JScript has not had such capabilities until Version 5.0 of the scripting engine. JScript employs an error-handling syntax identical to C++'s **try ... catch** method.

With the ASPError object, however, scripting language-specific error handling has become obsolete for use in Active Server Pages development. However, these error-handling routines still matter for the developer using ASP 2.0.

Chapter 3, *Exception Handling*, is dedicated to error handling, both through the use of the ASPError object and through the VBScript and JScript scripting engines. To become acquainted with JScript's error-handling mechanism, be sure to read Chapter 3.

An ASP Example Using JScript

Now that we've examined a number of useful JScript features, it's time to present some code. This code is intended to give you a flavor of the JScript syntax and to provide a working, useful example of JScript code.

In Example 2-3, an ASP page is presented that will display detailed information for each file in a particular web directory. This ASP page shows this information only for the Web's root directory; however, only a slight modification to the code would be needed to allow the user to pass in the particular directory he is interested in viewing through the query string.

Example 2-3. A JScript Example

```
<% @LANGUAGE = "JScript" %>
<%
    // What Web directory are we interested in?
    var strDirectory = "/";

    // Translate the virtual directory into a physical directory
    var strPhysicalDirectory = Server.MapPath(strDirectory);

    // Create an instance of the FileSystemObject object
    var objFSO = Server.CreateObject("Scripting.FileSystemObject");
    var objFolder, objFile;
```

Example 2-3. A JScript Example (continued)

```
    // Use FSO's GetFolder method to obtain a copy of the
    // folder strPhysicalDirectory
    objFolder = objFSO.GetFolder(strPhysicalDirectory);

    // Now, enumerate through each file in the folder, outputting its
    // details...
    var objFiles = new Enumerator(objFolder.Files);

    Response.Write("<HTML>\n<BODY>\n");
    Response.Write("<TABLE BORDER=1 ALIGN=CENTER CELLSPACING=1>\n");
    Response.Write("<TR><TH>Name</TH><TH>Date Created</TH><TH>");
    Response.Write("Date Last Modified</TH><TH>Size (in Bytes)</TH>");
    Response.Write("<TH>Type</TH></TR>\n");

    var iFileCount = 0;

    while (!objFiles.atEnd())
    {
        objFile = objFiles.item();

        // Output the various detailed file properties
        Response.Write ("<TR>\n");
        Response.Write("\t<TD><B>" + objFile.Name + "</B></TD>\n");
        Response.Write("\t<TD>" + objFile.DateCreated + "</TD>\n");
        Response.Write("\t<TD>" + objFile.DateLastModified + "</TD>\n");
        Response.Write("\t<TD>" + objFile.Size + "</TD>\n");
        Response.Write("\t<TD>" + objFile.Type + "</TD>\n");
        Response.Write ("</TR>\n");

        objFiles.moveNext();
        ++iFileCount;
    }
    Response.Write("</TABLE>\n\n");

    Response.Write("There were " + iFileCount + " files in " + strDirectory);
    Response.Write("\n\n</BODY>\n</HTML>\n\n");
%>
```

For an extensive technical reference on the JScript syntax, along with the latest version of the JScript scripting engine, visit: *http://msdn.microsoft.com/scripting*.

Creating ASP Pages with PerlScript

If you are an experienced Perl developer, you may find PerlScript more comfortable to use than VBScript or JScript. PerlScript is syntactically similar to Perl. The PerlScript scripting engine is maintained by ActiveState, a company that describes its role as "assist[ing] with the transition of [Perl] scripts between Windows and Unix based systems" (*http://www.activestate.com/corporate/*). The PerlScript engine can be downloaded for free from ActiveState's web site, *http://www.activestate.com*.

With PerlScript, like with Perl and C/C++, each statement *must* end with a semicolon. PerlScript's control structures, which are identical to Perl's, include if ... elsif ... else, for, while, foreach, and foreach ... until. If you are new to Perl, I highly recommend that you obtain a copy of O'Reilly's *Learning Perl, Second Edition* by Randal Schwartz and Tom Christiansen.

PerlScript's Variables and Datatypes

Each PerlScript variable needs to contain a certain prefix. The prefix determines the variable's datatype. With PerlScript, as with Perl, there are three major datatypes, as illustrated by Table 2-1.

Table 2-1. PerlScript's Datatypes

Datatype	Prefix	Description
Scalar	$	Contains simple datatypes, such as strings and numbers
Array	@	Contains a variable number of scalar elements indexed by number; arrays are indexed starting at zero
Associative Array	%	Contains a variable number of scalar elements indexed by a string value; also referred to as a *hash*, and functionally identical to a Dictionary object

There are a number of ways to declare variables. The method you use determines the scope of the variable. To limit a variable's scope to the block of code in which it is declared, use the my keyword. For example, the following ASP code snippet creates and initializes a scalar variable, an array, and an associative array:

```
<% @LANGUAGE = "PerlScript" %>
<%
    my $name = "Scott";
    my @array = ("Microsoft", 74.5, -5, "4GuysFromRolla.com");
    my %grades = ("English" => 94.5, "Math" => 100.0, "Science" => 91.3);
%>
```

The second way to declare a variable is to use the local keyword. When declaring a variable as local, it is accessible within the block of code in which it was declared, as well as in subroutines called from the block of code where it was initialized. If you declare a variable with the global keyword, or do not declare the variable before using it, the variable has global scope.

Creating global-scoped variables in an ASP script can lead to some daunting problems. It is highly recommended that you declare all of your variables using the my keyword.

Take a moment to look over the previous code example. Note that the => operator is used to assign a key in the associative array to a value. Also, when you want to write or read a particular value from an array or associative array, you need to reference the array or associative array with a dollar sign (\$), since you want to deal with a particular scalar value in the array instead of the entire array. For example, imagine we wanted to assign the zeroth item from *@array* in the previous code snippet to a variable named *$BigCompany*. The following line of code would accomplish that:

```
my $BigCompany;
$BigCompany = $array[0];
```

Case Sensitivity and Object Reference

PerlScript, like VBScript, is not case-sensitive. When accessing the intrinsic ASP objects, the object name must be preceded by a dollar sign (\$). Furthermore, rather than using the period to reference a particular object's method, you must use the arrow (a dash and the greater-than sign) (->). And just to make matters more confusing, to reference an object's property, you must use the arrow *and* surround the property name with braces. The following code snippet demonstrates setting the Response object's Buffer property using PerlScript:

```
<% @LANGUAGE = "PerlScript" %>
<%
    # Turn off Buffering
    $Response->{Buffer} = 0;

    $Response->Write("Buffering has been disabled.");
%>
```

Additionally, to access an element from an object's collection, you should use the following syntax:

```
$ObjectName->CollectionName("KeyName")->Item;
```

For example, if you expected a variable named *Age* to be to be passed through the querystring, you could access the variable on your ASP page using:

```
$Request->QueryString("Age")->Item;
```

There are a lot of interesting intricacies of Perl. If you are someone who likes to have ten different ways to accomplish the same task, then you'll absolutely love Perl. An acronym used often in the Perl community is TMTOWTDI (There's More Than One Way To Do It). Entire books are dedicated to Perl's many intricacies and the plethora of ways to accomplish a given task. If you are interested in learning PerlScript, I can't stress enough the importance of owning a copy of one of these books! Again, this chapter is not going to even attempt to dive into the specifics of PerlScript. Rather, it will touch upon a few of the unique features PerlScript brings to the table and present a useful ASP application using PerlScript code.

Reading and Writing Files with PerlScript

PerlScript, unlike VBScript and JScript, has inherent support for file access. To open a file, use the *open* function. This function expects two parameters: a `filehandle` and a `filename`. The filename is simply a string, and the mode with which the file is opened is determined by an optional prefix on the filename. The following prefixes can be used to indicate what mode to open the file in:

<   Read

>   Write (erases file contents upon opening)

+>   Read and write

+<   Read and write (erases file contents upon opening)

>>   Append

If no prefix is added, the file is opened for reading. If you wanted to create an ASP page that would open the file *C:\Scott\MyFile.txt* for reading, you could use the following code:

```
open(FILEHANDLE, "<C:\\Scott\\MyFile.txt");
```

The less-than sign preceding the filename indicates to open the file for reading. Also, note the double backslashes. Perl, like JScript, uses a backslash as the escape character; therefore, to insert a literal backslash, you must use two backslashes. Be sure to close a file with the *close* function once you are finished reading or writing from the file:

```
close(FILEHANDLE);
```

PerlScript reads the contents of a file one line at a time. To loop through and display the entire contents of a file, you can use the following code:

```
<% @LANGUAGE = "PerlScript" %>
<%
    open(FILEHANDLE, "C:\\global\\WinTop.inf");

    while (<FILEHANDLE>)
    {
        $Response->Write("$_<BR>");
    }

    close(FILEHANDLE);
%>
```

The $_ symbol is a special variable in PerlScript that is beyond the scope of this book. Again, I strongly suggest you pick up a copy of a book dedicated to Perl if you decide to use PerlScript regularly in your ASP pages.

Regular Expressions

PerlScript, like JScript, offers inherent regular-expression capabilities; however, PerlScript's implementation of regular expressions differs syntactically from JScript's. To use regular expressions with PerlScript, use the =~ operator, which performs a regular expression match or replace to the scalar variable to the left of the =~ operator. To the right of the =~ operator, the following format needs to be presented:

```
operator/pattern/replacement/switch
```

The *operator* defines the action to be taken. For example, if you want to replace all matches of the *pattern* to the string variable to the left of the =~ operator, use the s operator, denoting substitution. *pattern* contains the string you are trying to match in the variable on the left side of the =~ operator. If you plan on replacing all matches found with some string, enter the string to replace the matches with in the *replacement* section. Finally, the *switch* section is identical to JScript's switches in its regular-expression implementation.

If you haven't used regular expressions in Perl before, the last paragraph is probably as clear as mud. Hopefully an example will help. In Example 2-2, JScript's regular-expression capabilities were used to perform a number of tasks. Let's perform the first task—replacing a substring (Cold Fusion) with a different substring (ASP)—using PerlScript's regular expression:

```
<% @LANGUAGE = "PerlScript" %>
<%
    # First, examine the following statement:
    my $strColdFusion;
    $strColdFusion = "Using Cold Fusion is a fun, exciting way to create ";
    $strColdFusion .= "dynamic Web pages!  I really like Cold Fusion.";

    # Now, let's tailor that sentence to this book!
    # We will replace all occurrences of "Cold Fusion" with "ASP"
    # Note that we have to use the global switch (g) to replace all
    # instances of Cold Fusion with ASP
    $strColdFusion =~ s/Cold Fusion/ASP/g;

    # Output the new value of $strColdFusion
    $Response->Write("$strColdFusion");
%>
```

A couple of quick points: the .= operator performs string concatenation, and to output a string variable, you must include it in a string delimited by double quotes (for example, "My name is $Name").

Other PerlScript Features

One of PerlScript's greatest benefits is Perl modules. Modules are prewritten code that you can easily incorporate into your PerlScript scripts. ActiveState maintains a robust library of Perl modules that you can freely use in your PerlScripts. For more information visit: *http://www.activestate.com/packages/*.

PerlScript also allows for object-oriented programming, similar to VBScript's ability to use classes (for more information, see Chapter 4). For more information, be sure to obtain a book on Perl; it's well worth the investment!

An ASP Example Using PerlScript

Now that we've worked through a number of useful PerlScript features, it's time to look at some code. As with the JScript code in Example 2-2, this code is intended to give you a flavor of the PerlScript syntax and provide a working, useful example of PerlScript code.

Many web sites today have some way to allow users to interact with one another. For example, you might have a chat application, message board, or guest book on your site. If you run a family-oriented site, it would be nice to ensure that the messages posted by your users contain no profane words. Using regular expressions, you can easily remove particular offensive words from your users' posts.

Example 2-4 provides some code that will censor a particular string. Perhaps it could be used on Microsoft's site, for it censors words like Linux, Unix, Sun, and Java! The PerlScript expects a variable named *txtMessage* to be passed through the Request.Form collection. The script then censors the string and displays it. You could easily modify the code in Example 2-3 to insert the record into a database, or perform other operations on the submitted message.

Example 2-4. Censoring with PerlScript

```
<% @LANGUAGE = "PerlScript" %>
<%
   # Read in the string from the Request.Form named txtMessage
   my $strMessage = $Request->$Form("txtMessage")->Item();

   # Now, use regular expression to remove offensive words
   $strMessage =~ s/linux/Windows/gi;
   $strMessage =~ s/UNIX/Windows/gi;
   $strMessage =~ s/Java/Visual Basic/gi;
   $strMessage =~ s/Sun/Microsoft/gi;

   # Display the new, censored Message
   $Response->Write("<HTML>\n<BODY>\n\n");
   $Response->Write("\tYour <i>new</i> message reads:<BR>$strMessage\n");
```

Example 2-4. Censoring with PerlScript (continued)

```
   $Response->Write("</BODY>\n</HTML>\n\n");
%>
```

To learn more about using PerlScript within ASP pages, visit *http://www. perlscripters.com*. To obtain the latest version of PerlScript and to access the many Perl modules freely available, visit *http://www.activestate.com*.

Creating ASP Pages with Python

Python is an object-oriented scripting language that incorporates the best features from an array of languages, such as Java, C/C++, Perl, and awk. If you're not familiar with object-oriented programming, you may find the Python syntax a bit daunting. Python is the only scripting language discussed in this chapter that *requires* you to write object-oriented code! PerlScript and VBScript have object-oriented capabilities, but do not require that you use such techniques.

To use Python in your ASP pages, you need to download the latest Python ActiveX scripting engine. You can download this for free from *http://www.python. org/download/*. Be sure to download and install both the Python interpreter and the Win32 COM extensions. Also, you have to register the Python ActiveX scripting engine on the web server before you can use it. Consult the online Python documentation for more information.

To learn more about Python, be sure to visit *http://www.python.org*. Extensive documentation exists at *http://www.python.org/doc/*. Finding good references on using Python with ASP is far from easy. There are a couple of short articles available at *Python.org*, but those articles are targeted for experienced Python developers interested in learning ASP as opposed to experienced ASP developers interested in learning Python!

Further Reading

Unfortunately, there is little in the way of documentation on these alternative server-side scripting languages. While there are a vast number of ASP-related web sites, nearly all of them focus exclusively on VBScript. The vast majority of ASP-related books focus on VBScript as well. Despite this, there are some useful articles, tutorials, and sites that deal with these alternative scripting languages.

- This tutorial is geared towards those who are more familiar with Perl than with ASP. Nevertheless, it is a very thorough tutorial on PerlScript and worth a read: *http://www.fastnetltd.ndirect.co.uk/Perl/Articles/PSIntro.html*.

- As I mentioned earlier in the chapter, the source for PerlScript and ASP information is definitely PerlScripters.com, available at *http://www.perlscripters.com*.

- If you want to ask your Jscript questions with fellow ASP developers, be sure to sign up for the JScript ListServ at *http://www.asplists.com/learn/javascript.asp.*

- Read a good tutorial discussing JScript in terms of objects at *http://www. asptoday.com/articles/19990316.htm.*

- Learn how to incorporate both VBScript and JScript code in your ASP pages. This article, available at *http://www.asptoday.com/articles/19990420.htm*, even demonstrates how to call VBScript functions from JScript code and vice versa.

- One of VBScript's advantages is its many inherent formatting functions, such as *FormatCurrency*, *FormatDateTime*, and others. Mosey on over to *http:// www.4guysfromrolla.com/webtech/vb2java.shtml* to see some JScript translations of some of the more common and useful VBScript formatting functions.

- For more information on the order in which SCRIPT blocks execute within an ASP page, refer to *http://msdn.microsoft.com/workshop/server/feature/morqa. asp#order.*

3

Exception Handling

Errors happen. Regardless of how skilled a given programmer might be, there is no way he can create truly bug-free code. Programming errors can be broken down into two broad categories: logical errors and implementation errors. Before starting to actually write code, a developer must have a solid understanding of what application she is creating, and the logic behind this application.

For example, when creating an e-commerce web application, a developer might decide that once a user decides to purchase an item, he is taken directly to a page to enter his billing and shipping information. Many users today are used to a shopping cart system, in which they can purchase multiple items online and then proceed to a "check out" page, where they can review a summary of the goods being purchased and enter the needed billing and shipping information. By not providing a shopping cart system, your users may find your site confusing and burdensome to use. Logical errors are often high-level errors, costing immense time and money to fix, since they are usually not caught until late in the product development cycle.

Implementation errors are those errors residing in the actual code. In an e-commerce site, if not all of the items selected by the user appear in the summary listing on the "check out" page, an implementation error has occurred. To summarize: flaws existing within the high-level view of the application are logical errors; errors or bugs resulting from the implementation of an idea or feature into code are implementation errors. Implementation errors are easy to detect: if the program crashes or produces incorrect output, an implementation error is at fault. Logical errors, however, are much more sinister and difficult to detect.

This chapter does *not* focus on how to reduce the number of errors you, as a developer, commit when writing code. Rather, it looks at how to gracefully handle these errors when they inevitably occur. We've all seen the patented Microsoft

Blue Screen of Death one too many times, and all know the frustration involved when a program fails to gracefully handle an error. Since bugs and errors in any decent-sized application are certain, it is vitally important to be able to respond to these errors smoothly when they occur.

A Bit of Terminology

We've already looked at the two broadest categories of errors: logical and implementation errors. Implementation errors are often described in terms of halting errors and non-halting errors. *Halting errors* cause the premature termination of a running program, whereas *nonhalting errors* produce unreliable or unpredicted output but allow the continuation of the program. Halting errors can be further divided into runtime errors and compile-time errors. *Runtime errors* are those errors that occur during the execution of a program, while *compile errors* occur during the compilation process of the program.

When an ASP script is requested, it goes through a two-phase process. First, the script is compiled into an executable version. Any syntactical errors are caught here; these are referred to as compile-time errors. For example, the following VBScript syntax, which is illegal, will generate a compile-time error:

```
<% @LANGUAGE="VBSCRIPT"%>
<%
   Dim strScott
   strScott = "Mitchell       'This will cause a compile-time error since the
                              'assignment to the string strScott is missing a
                              'closing quotation mark

%>
```

A syntactically correct script may be free of compile-time errors, but it can still contain runtime errors. Runtime errors occur when some unexpected event happens during the execution of the script. For example, dividing a number by zero is legal syntax in VBScript (therefore not generating a compile-time error), but will nevertheless generate a runtime error since the result of division by zero is undefined. The following code snippet will generate a runtime error:

```
<% @LANGUAGE="VBSCRIPT"%>
<%
   Dim iUndefined
   iUndefined = 1 / 0       'This will cause a runtime error since the division by
                            'zero is undefined

%>
```

Runtime errors are not always the fault of the programmer who developed the script that generates an error. For example, imagine that you create an ASP page to display the contents of a particular SQL Server database table. Even though your script may be flawless, containing no logic or implementation errors, if the database table being queried is renamed or the entire database is deleted, your once-perfect script will now abruptly terminate when attempting to query a non-existent database table.

A more general term for a halting error is *exception*. An exception, in the most general terms, is something unexpected. For this chapter, the definition of exception is narrowed to an unexpected event that halts script execution. Therefore, both an implementation error and an unexpected event (like a database table being renamed) qualify as exceptions. It is every programmer's goal to gracefully handle exceptions.

You may have noticed that I've been using the phrase "gracefully handle an exception" quite a bit, and as a curious reader, you may be wondering what I mean, exactly, by "gracefully." When an exception occurs, a number of things can happen. Since the developer does have a bit of control over what happens following an exception, the worst course to follow once an error occurs is to display some illegible, confusing error message to a user who may not be computer-literate.

Rather than presenting the end user with a perplexing error message, one option is to provide a more readable, friendlier message. This message would not need to alert the end user to the technical aspects of the error, but rather would let the user know a problem has occurred and the developers have been made aware of the problem. It could also suggest other web pages to visit, or could contain a link for more information (if you add the above) and the email address of the technical support team.

Error messages are usually unreadable to the end user because they usually contain information to help the developer detect the cause of the error. While an error message like:

```
General Protection Fault in module 256_1024.DRV
```

is not readable for the end user, it lets the developer know the driver in which the error occurred. In this chapter we will examine how to create readable, friendly error messages for the end user *and* how to provide detailed error information to the developer!

Displaying an understandable error message to the end user is usually the best thing that can happen when an exception occurs. However, there are rare times when an exception can be circumvented. That is, if a particular exception is detected, a sequence of steps can be undertaken to dance around the problem, continuing the execution flow, so that to the end user, it appears as though no exception had occurred. For example, imagine that every week your database's data was backed up to a secondary database. If, in your ASP page, you have trouble connecting to the primary database, rather than displaying an error message, you could show the user the backup data. Granted, this data might be out of date, and you would want to let the user know they are viewing dated information, but showing the user something useful is better than showing them an error message.

Detecting When Exceptions Occur

To be able to handle errors gracefully, it is imperative that some mechanism exists to inform us developers when an error arises. Errors occurring in an ASP page can be detected in one of two ways: through the scripting language's error-handling interface, or through ASP 3.0's new ASPError object.

The VBScript and JScript 5.0 scripting engines both contain robust runtime error-detection mechanisms. ASP pages (or other scripts) created using either of these scripting languages can use the scripting language's inherent error-handling capabilities to detect when errors occur. As we'll see in "Detecting Exceptions with Scripting Language Error-Handling Mechanisms," using either VBScript's or JScript's error-handling mechanisms often results in verbose, inelegant, and unreadable code when compared to the elegance of the ASPError object.

The ASPError object, which we'll detail in the section "Detecting Exceptions with the ASPError Object," provides detailed information about an error that just occurred in an ASP page, including a description and line number. However, the ASPError object can only be used with IIS 5.0/ASP 3.0, which, of course, requires Windows 2000 as the web server. Therefore, if you are using Windows NT as your web server's operating system, you must rely on the scripting languages' error-handling techniques to detect and gracefully respond to exceptions.

If you are using Windows 2000, though, you are in luck. To use the ASPError object, a separate error-handling web page is needed. This separate page is responsible for receiving the detailed error information and providing an understandable error message to the end user. Using this approach, an error that occurs on any line in any ASP page will result in a call to the error-handling web page. Furthermore, the ASPError object provides more detailed information on the error that occurred than either of the VBScript or JScript error-handling objects.

Using the ASPError object approach alone makes it next to impossible to detect an error, circumvent it, and continue processing. Once an error-handling web page is set up, when an error occurs, the user is sent to the error-handling web page via a `Server.Transfer`. Therefore, you can't fix the error on the error-handling web page and resume processing on the ASP page where the error originated. We'll look at the ASPError object in finer detail later in this chapter in "Detecting Exceptions with the ASPError Object."

Detecting Exceptions with Scripting Language Error-Handling Mechanisms

Both the VBScript and JScript 5.0 scripting engines provide runtime error-handling routines to assist in detecting and gracefully handling implementation errors. VBScript's error handling is very similar to Visual Basic's, using the **On Error Resume Next** notation and the Err object. JScript's error handling is similar to C++'s and Java's, using **try** ... **catch** blocks. Regardless of the scripting language used, providing adequate error handling usually results in bloating one's code severely.

If your web site is not running on IIS 5.0, then unfortunately, you do not have access to the ASPError object, and therefore must rely on the techniques discussed in this section to detect errors. If, however, you are using IIS 5.0, and all you plan on doing when an error occurs is displaying a friendly error message to the end user, then it is highly recommended that you rely on the error handling provided by the new ASP 3.0 ASPError object.

The main advantage the scripting language error-handling techniques have over the ASPError object is the ability to recover from an error. Using these techniques, a developer can detect when an error occurs and decide on some alternative course of action, keeping the script running smoothly from the perspective of the end user.

 VBScript and JScript error-handling mechanisms can only detect *runtime* errors. You cannot use these techniques to detect, recover from, or display readable error messages about compile-time errors.

Detecting errors with VBScript

If you are familiar with error handling in Visual Basic, you'll find VBScript error handling easy to pick up. By default, error handling is disabled. This means if an error occurs during the execution of a VBScript script, the script is halted and the user is presented with an error message. Usually these error messages are quite cryptic and daunting for the end user. Imagine a visitor to your web site who is presented with an error similar to:

```
Server object error 'ASP 0177 : 800401f3'

Server.CreateObject Failed

/SomePage.asp, line 14

Invalid class string
```

Would you expect this customer to return to your site in the future? This daunting error message could be modified to a more friendly error message that is less likely to scare the user away. To be able to determine when an error occurs in a script, though, error handling must be enabled.

In VBScript, error handling is enabled and disabled using the On Error statement. To enable error handling, enter the following command at the top of your ASP page:

```
On Error Resume Next
```

This informs the scripting engine that when an error occurs, it should proceed to the next line of code rather than abruptly stopping and displaying an error message. To disable error handling, use the following statement:

```
On Error Goto 0
```

Simply enabling error handling is not enough to detect when an error occurs, however. After each statement that might cause an error, an If statement needs to be used to determine whether or not an error did occur. This technique is known as

inline error handling. I find this constant inquiring whether or not an error has occurred to be rather verbose and annoying, and liken it to an inefficient manager.

Imagine that you are a manager for one employee. This employee performs a number of tasks, and as a manager, it is your job to ensure that these tasks do not cause any errors. After each task this employee performs that *might* cause an error, you take a moment out of your schedule to ask the employee whether or not an error occurred. Such a model is far from efficient and is very verbose, containing many unneeded communications between manager and employee. Ideally, the employee would know when an error occurs, and would be able to approach you, the manager, when something has gone awry. However, with VBScript and JScript error handling, we do not have this option, and must continually be bothered with having to inquire whether or not an error has occurred.

 How often should you, the manager, ask your employee if an error has occurred? Ideally, after every statement that *might* generate an error, the employee should be queried if an error occurred. Of course, what statements *might* generate an error? Deciding when to check for an error is not always easy. This topic is discussed in greater detail in the next section, "Deciding when to check if an exception occurred."

Example 3-1 contains an example of error handling. Note that at the start of the script, On Error Resume Next is issued, enabling error handling. Then, after each statement that might cause an error, a conditional statement is used to determine whether or not an error has occurred. If an error has occurred, a short error message is presented to the visitor.

Example 3-1. Using VBScript to Detect an Error

```
<%@ LANGUAGE = "VBSCRIPT" %>
<% Option Explicit %>
<%
  'Enable error handling
  On Error Resume Next

  'Create two objects
  Dim objConn, objRS
  Set objConn = Server.CreateObject("ADODB.Connection")

  'Check to see if an error occurred
  If Err.Number <> 0 then
    Response.Write "Error in creating Connection object.<BR>"
    Response.Write "Description: " & Err.Description
    Response.End
  End If

' The ProgID is invalid, so this line should generate an error
Set objRS = Server.CreateObject("Database Recordset")

  'Check to see if an error occurred
  If Err.Number <> 0 then
    Response.Write "Error in creating Recordset object.<BR>"
    Response.Write "Description: " & Err.Description
    Response.End
  End If

  'If we've reached here, no errors!
  Set objRS = Nothing
  Set objConn = Nothing
%>
```

VBScript provides an Err object to handle runtime errors. When error handling is enabled and an error occurs, the Err object's five properties are automatically populated with the error information from the latest error. These properties are presented in Table 3-1.

Table 3-1. The Err Object's Properties

Property	Description
Number	A numeric value or code uniquely identifying the error
Source	The name of the application or object that generated the error
Description	A lengthy description of the error
HelpFile	A fully qualified path to a help file
HelpContext	A context ID for a topic in a help file

To determine whether an error has just occurred, check the Number property of the Err object. If no error has occurred, this property will equal zero. If an error has occurred, the property's value will be unequal to (i.e., either greater than or less than) zero.

The Err object contains two methods: Clear and Raise. The Clear method simply resets all of the property values. If you plan on trying to recover from an error, you will need to use the Clear method once you detect an error and find some alternative path around the error. If the Clear method is not used, the next time we check `Err.Number` we will find it is not equal to zero (since it still equals the value from our first error). Therefore, if you plan on continuing execution after handling an error, be sure to issue an `Err.Clear` after recovering from each error. The following code snippet presents a case when you'd use the Clear method:

```
If Err.Number = SomeSpecificErrorNumber then
   'Some specific error occurred, circumvent the problem somehow
   Problem Circumvented Somehow...

   'Now that we took some alternative approach, we want to clear the
   'Err object
   Err.Clear           'Cleared the error... continue on with the script
End If
```

The `Raise` method generates a runtime error, and has the following definition:

```
Err.Raise Number, Source, Description, HelpFile, HelpContext
```

When developing reusable scripts, often the developer who writes a given reusable script is not the only one who uses it in practice. For example, in Chapter 5, *Form Reuse*, we will look at how to create a reusable server-side form-validation script. While I wrote the code and use it, I don't expect to be the only developer who will use it. The server-side form-validation script presented in Chapter 5 expects certain inputs from the developer using the script. If these inputs are out of acceptable ranges, an error is raised so the developer is notified immediately when trying to execute the script.

When raising errors in your own objects, Microsoft suggests that you add the VBScript constant `vbObjectError` to the custom error code. Examples in this book using the Raise method add `vbObjectError` to the error number, like so:

```
Err.Raise vbObjectError + ErrorNumber, ...
```

There is nothing magical about `vbObjectError`. It is simply a constant with a value of 80040000 hexadecimal.

Since this book focuses on building reusable, robust scripts, throughout this book we'll use the Raise method of the Err object extensively.

Deciding when to check if an exception occurred

Virtually any line of code can cause an exception. A given exception is either consistent or inconsistent. A consistent exception is one that occurs every time the script is executed. For example, the following line of code is an example of a consistent exception:

```
Dim 4GuysFromRolla        'variable names cannot begin with a number
```

This exception is consistent, since every single time an ASP page is visited with the above line of code, an error will be generated. The following lines of code demonstrate an inconsistent exception:

```
'Connect to a database
Dim objConn
Set objConn = Server.CreateObject("ADODB.Connection")
objConn.ConnectionString = "DRIVER={Microsoft Access Driver (*.mdb)};" & _
                           "DBQ=C:\InetPub\wwwroot\datastores\NWind.mdb;" & _
                           "UID=admin;PWD=;"
objConn.Open              'Open a connection to the database
```

An error would occur if the database file *NWind.mdb* did not exist in the path specified in the ConnectionString property (*C:\InetPub\wwwroot\datastores*). Such an exception is inconsistent because the above script would work flawlessly so long as the database was in the right directory. Imagine, though, that *NWind. mdb* was moved or renamed. Once that occurred, the script would start producing error messages when the Open method was reached.

Consistent exceptions are simple to detect. When testing a script that contains:

```
Dim 4GuysFromRolla
```

a developer can quickly diagnose and remedy the problem. Since inconsistent exceptions happen more unexpectedly, it is these exceptions that error detection should be employed for. After each line that may generate an inconsistent exception, be sure to place an **If** statement to check if **Err.Number** is not equal to zero. Those statements that might cause inconsistent exceptions are usually limited to methods of COM objects, such as the Open method of the ADO Connection object. Therefore, when using COM objects in your ASP scripts, be sure to check for errors immediately after calling one of the COM object methods.

In the later section "Responding to Exceptions," we look at how to gracefully handle exceptions that occur using VBScript exception handling.

Error handling in functions and subroutines

If your ASP page contains any functions or subroutines, error handling becomes somewhat trickier. If you enable error handling at the start of your ASP page and then call a function or subroutine that contains a runtime error, the function or procedure will halt and pass control back through the call stack until a procedure with enabled error handling is found. Figure 3-1 illustrates this concept graphically.

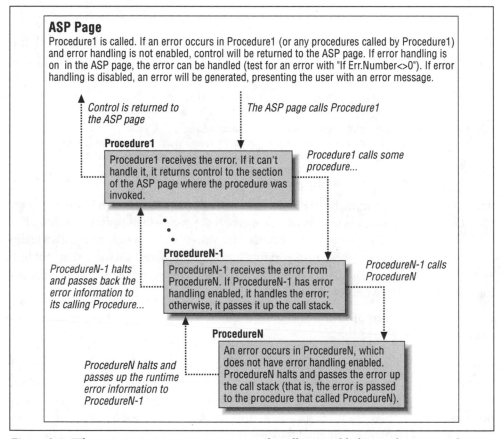

Figure 3-1. When an error occurs in a non-error handling-enabled procedure, control is passed back through the call stack until a procedure with error handling enabled is found

When a function or subroutine is called, error handling is deactivated. Therefore, if you want a function or subroutine to be able to perform error handling on its own (that is, if you don't want it to halt and pass control back to the calling procedure), you must explicitly turn on error handling in the function or subroutine with `On Error Resume Next`. Example 3-2 examines VBScript's error-handling conventions with functions and subroutines.

Example 3-2. When an Error Occurs in a Function or Subroutine, Control Is Passed Up the Call Stack Until an Error-Handling Enabled Function or Subroutine Is Found

```
<% @LANGUAGE="VBSCRIPT" %>
<% Option Explicit %>

<%
  'Enable error handling
  On Error Resume Next

  'Call Procedure1
  Procedure1

  'We can check to see if an error occurred
  If Err.Number <> 0 then
    Response.Write "An error occurred!<BR>"
    Response.Write Err.Number & " - " & Err.Description
  End If

  Sub Procedure1()
    'No error handling here
    'Call Procedure2
    Procedure2
  End Sub


  Sub Procedure2()
    'No error handling here either

    'Whoops, an error occurred!   (Using an undeclared variable)
    strScott = strMitchell

    'The above error will halt Procedure2, returning control to Procedure1. Since
    ' there is no error handling implemented there, ontrol is returned to the'line
    'immediately following the call 'to Procedure1.  Since error handling is enabled
    'there, it will handle the error. (Otherwise, the user would be shown
    'an error message.)
  End Sub
%>
```

Note that the error-handling code after the call to *Procedure1* is tripped for the error that occurred in *Procedure2*. The output of the code in Example 3-2 is as expected:

```
An error occurred!
500 - Variable is undefined
```

Streamlining VBScript error-handling code

With VBScript error handling, after each statement that might cause an exception, the developer needs to determine whether an error occurred. The following code is usually found after every potential error-causing statement:

```
If Err.Number <> 0 then
   Display an error message
End If
```

This approach can be streamlined a bit by using a subroutine to determine if an error has occurred or not. This subroutine, *CheckForError*, should have the following definition:

```
Sub CheckForError(strErrorMessage)
```

strErrorMessage is a string containing the error message that should be displayed to the user if an error occurs. After each line of code that may cause an error, the clunky:

```
If Err.Number <> 0 then
    Display an error message
End If
```

can be replaced with:

```
CheckForError strErrorMessage
```

The *CheckForError* subroutine contains fairly straightforward code, simply checking to see if **Err.Number** is nonzero. If it is, **strErrorMessage** is displayed and execution is halted with **Response.End**. Example 3-3 contains the source code for **CheckForError**.

Example 3-3. The CheckForError Subroutine Allows for More Streamlined Error-Handling Code in VBScript

```
Sub CheckForError(strErrorMessage)
  If Err.Number <> 0 then
    'An error occurred!  Display the error message
    Response.Write strErrorMessage
    Response.End
  End If
End Sub
```

Unfortunately, this subroutine needs to exist in all of your ASP pages that use scripting-language error handling. Of course, server-side includes should be used so that only one instance of this function is needed. In the later section "Responding to Exceptions," we look at how to improve this subroutine to include the ability to notify the support team of the exception's details.

A list of VBScript runtime error numbers can be found on Microsoft's scripting site at: *http://msdn.microsoft.com/scripting/default.htm?/ scripting/vbscript/doc/vsmscRunTimeErrors.htm*.

VBScript syntax error numbers are listed at: *http://msdn.microsoft.com/ scripting/default.htm?/scripting/vbscript/doc/vsmscSyntaxErrors.htm*.

Detecting errors with JScript

JScript's error handling is similar to C++'s and Java's, using `try ... catch` blocks. Error handling is fairly new to JScript; it's only available in the JScript scripting engine Version 5.0 or greater. To download the free, latest version of the JScript and VBScript scripting engines, direct your browser to *http://msdn.microsoft.com/ scripting*.

 If you have IIS 5.0 installed as your web server, the Version 5.0 scripting engines are already installed on your computer. If you are using IIS 4.0, you may have an older scripting engine version, and should upgrade your scripting engine at Microsoft's Scripting Site (*http://msdn.microsoft.com/scripting*).

In VBScript, error handling is enabled with the `On Error Resume Next` command. If an exception is raised, the Err object is populated with the error information. To detect an error, after each line of code that may be guilty of causing an error, a test is performed, checking to see if `Err.Number` is nonzero. In the earlier section "Detecting errors with VBScript," these actions were likened to an inefficient manager, continually checking on an employee to see if he had performed some erroneous task.

JScript's error handling is a bit different. In JScript, there is no single command (like VBScript's `On Error Resume Next`) that indicates that error handling should be enabled. Furthermore, JScript's error handling takes a more direct approach than VBScript's. To relate it to the manager/employee analogy used earlier, rather than asking our employee if an error occurred after he has attempted a task, we cautiously tell our employee to try a certain set of tasks. The employee then attempts to perform these tasks, and gets back to us if any of these tasks caused an error.

To let our dutiful employee know what tasks to perform, a `try` block is used, which has the following syntax:

```
try {
  possibly erroneous statements
}
```

A `try` block must be immediately followed by a `catch` block. A `catch` block contains code that is executed only if an error occurred in the commands within the preceding `try` block.

```
catch (errorObjectInstance) {
  error handling code
}
```

If an error occurs in one of the commands issued within a `try` block, the details of the error are encapsulated within an Error object. An instance of this object is assigned to the variable specified by *errorObjectInstance* immediately following the `catch` statement in the `catch` block.

The JScript Error object is similar to VBScript's Err object, but only contains two properties and no methods. The two properties of the Error object can be seen in Table 3-2.

Table 3-2. The JScript Error Object Contains Two Properties

Property	Description
description	A string containing detailed information on the exception.
Number	A 32-bit number containing both a facility code and the actual error number. The upper 16 bits are the facility code, while the lower 16 bits are the error number.

The way Microsoft chose to represent their error numbers is, in my opinion, a little confusing. The easiest way to pick apart an error number is to look at it in hexadecimal format. All error codes you'll receive through an ASP page will have the following hexadecimal format:

    800FNNNN

The *F* denotes the facility code, which indicates who raised the error. VBScript and JScript use a facility code of 10 (A, in hex). The *NNNN* represents the actual error number. Therefore, using JScript's number property, to get the *NNNN* portion of the 32-bit error number, use the following:

```
try {
  some code...
} catch (err) {
  // display the error number, less the 800F
  Response.Write("The error generated the following error code: ");
  Response.Write(err.number & 0xFFFF);
}
```

Likewise, to obtain just the facility code, use the following:

```
try {
  some code...
} catch (err) {
  // display the error number, less the 800F
  Response.Write("The error generated the following facility code: ");
  Response.Write(err.number >> 16 & 0xF);
}
```

Extracting Bits

JScript provides a number of bitwise operators that perform bit-level manipulation. The bitwise operators supported by JScript include &, |, ~, ^, >>, and <<. Respectively, these operators perform bitwise AND, bitwise OR, bitwise NOT, bitwise XOR, bitwise shift-right, and bitwise shift-left.

Bitwise operators perform operations on bits. The bitwise AND, OR, and XOR operators are binary operators, taking two bits as arguments and returning a single bit. The bitwise AND operator, which is used to extract the error number and facility code, returns a 1 if both input bits are 1; otherwise, the AND operator returns a 0. Due to this property, the bitwise AND operator is often used to extract particular bits from a numeric variable. For example, if we had an integer with the bitwise value 01100011, we could extract bits 0 through 3 by bitwise ANDing that value with 00001111. The resulting integer would be 00000011, containing the value of bits 0 through 3 of the integer.

Therefore, to extract bits 0 through 15 of the 32-bit error number, we bitwise AND the error number with 1111111111111111, or FFFF in hexadecimal. We examined how to do this in JScript:

```
err.number & 0xFFFF
```

The shift-right bitwise operator shuffles around the bits in an integer, shifting the bits to the right. For example, if we have an integer with the value 01100011 and shift-right the bits by four bits (denoted 01100011 >> 4), the result would be 00000110. Note that the four rightmost bits were truncated, and the four leftmost bits were moved over four spots. When extracting the facility code, we first need to shift-right the error number by 16 bits, since the facility code resides in bits 16 through 19. Once this has been completed, a bitwise AND is used to extract the 4 bits that make up the facility code. For example:

```
// Assume the error number is 800XYYYY, where X is the facility code and
// YYYY is the actual error number. The error number, which is a 32-bit
// number can be represented in binary with:
//    100000000000XXXXYYYYYYYYYYYYYYYY.
// The XXXX are the four bits that represent the facility code, while the
// string of Ys represents the 16-bit error number. To extract the Ys,
// a bitwise AND with the 32-bit error number and a 16-bit integer
// of 1s (FFFF)
var errorNumber = err.number & 0xFFFF;
// To grab the facility code, the XXXX must first be shifted over to
// become the rightmost bits.
var facilityNumber = err.number >> 16;
```

—Continued—

```
// Now, facilityNumber equals:
//     00000000000000000100000000000XXXX
// A bitwise AND with a 4-bit integer containing
// 4 1s is needed (F, in hexadecimal)
facilityNumber = facilityNumber & 0xF;
```

A list of JScript runtime error numbers can be found on Microsoft's scripting site at *http://msdn.microsoft.com/scripting/default.htm?/scripting/jscript/doc/jsmscRunTimeErrors.htm.*

JScript syntax error numbers are listed at *http://msdn.microsoft.com/scripting/default.htm?/scripting/jscript/doc/jsmscSyntaxErrors.htm.*

The `try` block can contain several lines of code; as soon as an error occurs, the corresponding `catch` block is visited. Therefore, a separate set of `try` ... `catch` blocks should be used for each statement that might generate an exception. As discussed in "Deciding when to check if an exception occurred," method calls to COM objects are the usual suspects for inconsistent exceptions; therefore, a `try` ... `catch` block should exist for each COM object method call.

Recall that VBScript's Err object contains a Raise method, which, as its name implies, raises an error. JScript's Error object does not contain any such method; to raise an error in JScript, use the `throw` statement. `throw` has the following syntax:

> `throw` *errorObjectInstance*;

errorObjectInstance needs to be an Error object instance with its number and description properties already set. Example 3-4 demonstrates how to use the `throw` statement.

Example 3-4. The throw Statement Raises an Error

```
<% @LANGUAGE="JSCRIPT" %>
<%
  function ThrowError()
  {
    // throw an error...
    var err;
    err = new Error();       // Create an Error object instance
    err.description = "Egad, an error!";
    err.number = 0x800A1234;

    throw err;               // throw the error (similar to Err.Raise)
  }

  // try calling the function ThrowError
  try {
    ThrowError();
```

Example 3-4. The throw Statement Raises an Error (continued)

```
  } catch (err) {
    // If we've reached here, an error occurred.  Display the error info...
    Response.Write("An error occurred!  Here are the following details:");
    Response.Write("<P><UL>Description: " + err.description);
    Response.Write("<BR>Error Number:</B> " + (err.number & 0xFFFF));
    Response.Write("<BR>Facility Code:</B> " + (err.number >> 16 & 0xF));
  }
%>
```

Nested try ... catch blocks

`try` ... `catch` blocks can be nested within one another. For example, the following is perfectly legal syntax:

```
try {  // outer try block
  try {  // inner try block
    // something
  } catch (err) {
    // this catch block is only visited if an error occurs in the
    // code within the inner try block
  }
} catch (err) {
  // this catch block is only visited if an error occurs in the
  // code within the outer try block
}
```

While explicit `try` ... `catch` block nesting isn't often used, implicit `try` ... `catch` blocks are quite common. Example 3-5 illustrates a pair of `try` ... `catch` blocks nested implicitly. The inner `try` ... `catch` block is within the function *foobar*; the outer `try` ... `catch` block contains the code that calls *foobar*.

Example 3-5. try ... catch Blocks Can Be Implicitly Nested

```
function foobar()
{
  // this is the inner try ... catch block
  try {
    // execute some code that might throw an exception...
  } catch (err) {
    // handle an error
  }
}

// this is the outer try ... catch block
try {
  foobar();
} catch (err) {
  // handle any errors thrown by foobar()
}
```

In Example 3-5, the `catch` block in the outer `try` ... `catch` block will never be visited, since if any error occurs in *foobar*, the inner `catch` block will respond. There may be times, however, when the inner `try` ... `catch` block in *foobar* might not want to respond to an error. For example, when creating reusable scripts using JScript, there may be instances when you don't want your reusable script to be responsible for handling all possible errors. In Chapter 6, *Database Reuse*, we'll examine a reusable script that creates generic database administration pages. These scripts work tightly with a database that is specified by the end developer (that is, the developer who is utilizing these reusable scripts). If the end developer specifies a database connection string that is invalid, it might be best to let the end developer handle the error rather than attempting to have the reusable script do so. The end developer might want to try a different connection string, perhaps, and if passed the error, might be able to recover from it.

To hand off the responsibility of handling an error, simply re-**throw** the error in the **catch** block. In the following code snippet, the **catch** block is only interested in working with a specific error, `0x800A1234`; all other errors are passed on:

```
try {
  some code that might throw an exception
} catch (err) {
  // only handle error 0x800A1234
  if (err.number == 0x800A1234) {
    handle the error
  } else {
    // pass off the responsibility to the outer try ... catch block
    throw err;
  }
}
```

Example 3-6 demonstrates how the responsibility of handling an error can be passed from an inner **try** ... **catch** block to an outer one.

Example 3-6. To Pass Off the Responsibility of Handling an Exception from an Inner to an Outer try ... catch Block, Re-throw the Exception

```
<% @LANGUAGE="JSCRIPT" %>
<%
  function foobar()
  {
    // foobar tries to connect to a database.  If it cannot because of an
    // an invalid data source name, the catch block re-throws the error, passing
    // off the responsibility to the outer catch block...
    try {
      // attempt to connect to the database...
      var objConn;
      objConn = Server.CreateObject("ADODB.Connection");
      objConn.ConnectionString = "DSN=NonExistentDSN";
      objConn.Open();
    } catch(err) {
      if ((err.number & 0xFFFF) == 16389)
        throw err;                          // pass off the responsibility
      else {
        // not a connection problem... handle the error
      }
```

Example 3-6. To Pass Off the Responsibility of Handling an Exception from an Inner to an Outer try ... catch Block, Re-throw the Exception (continued)

```
    }
  }

  // try calling the function ThrowError

  try {
    // Execute foobar; if there is a problem, the catch block will be visited
    foobar();
  } catch (err) {
    // at this point, we could check to see if the DSN name was bad, and, if
    // so, retry foobar or call some other function

    // Instead, for this example, we'll just output the error information
    Response.Write("An error occurred!  Here are the following details:");
    Response.Write("<P><UL><B>Description:</B> " + err.description);
    Response.Write("<BR>Error Number:</B> " + (err.number & 0xFFFF));
    Response.Write("<BR>Facility Code:</B> " + (err.number >> 16 & 0xF));
  }
%>
```

VBScript's error handling versus JScript's error handling

Now that we've examined both VBScript and JScript's error-handling mechanisms, which one is best? I find JScript's implementation of error handling to be much more elegant and readable than VBScript's. Since VBScript's error-handling approach requires the developer to inquire whether an exception occurred or not *after* the fact, the approach is more error-prone that JScript's, where the developer must set up the proper error-handling calls prior to executing the questionable statements.

I also find the JScript syntax far more elegant than VBScript's error-handling syntax. Of course, to enjoy the benefits of JScript error handling, you do have to use JScript as the server-side scripting language, something only a handful of ASP developers do.

Detecting Exceptions with the ASPError Object

As veteran web surfers, we've all stumbled across a broken link, which took us to a nonexistent web page. When clicking on a broken link, an HTTP 404 error is received. This error is generated by the web server when it cannot find a requested document.

Whenever something goes awry deep within a web server, an HTTP error is generated. These HTTP errors are three digits in length, ranging from 100–505. The first number in the three-number HTTP error code denotes the type of HTTP error. 400-level errors are client errors, such as 404 (file not found), 401 (unauthorized), and 414 (request URL too long). 500-level errors indicate intrinsic web server errors. As we'll see shortly, IIS 5.0 uses a 500-level HTTP error to signal that an error has occurred on an ASP page.

   A complete listing of HTTP error codes and their associated meanings can be seen at *http://www.webpartner.com/html/AlertsandErrors.htm.*

Prior to ASP 3.0, exception handling on an ASP page was limited to the exception-handling capabilities of the scripting language used. Due to the total lack of error handling in JScript (until Version 5.0) and the verbose nature of error handling in VBScript, ASP was long overdue for a simpler and more effective exception-handling approach. With the release of ASP 3.0 (available exclusively with IIS 5.0 and Windows 2000), a new intrinsic object, ASPError, was added to assist in exception handling. The ASPError object contains nine properties, which are detailed in Table 3-3.

Table 3-3. The Intrinsic ASPError Object Assists in Detecting and Handling Exceptions

Property	Description
ASPCode	Returns a rather detailed error code that is generated by IIS
Number	Returns the error number
Source	Returns the line of code that caused the error, if available
Category	Indicates what type of error occurred; this property will indicate if the exception was caused by the scripting language, an external COM component, or an internal ASP error
File	Returns the name of the ASP page that generated the error
Line	Returns the line number the error occurred on
Column	Returns the column the error occurred on
Description	Returns a detailed description of the error
ASPDescription	Returns a detailed description for those errors that fall under the internal Active Server Pages error Category

When an error occurs in IIS 5.0, whether it's from a COM object, the scripting language, or an internal ASP error, an HTTP 500;100 error is generated. (The 100 indicates that it is a special kind of HTTP 500 error.) Whenever an HTTP error occurs, IIS checks an error table to see what it should do in response to the error. Its choices are limited to:

- Sending a default message to the client
- Sending the client the contents of a particular file (usually an HTML file)
- Redirecting the client to an error-handling web page

Through the Internet Information Services, a developer can specify how IIS should handle particular HTTP errors. Start by opening the Internet Information Services (in Windows 2000, go to Start → Programs → Administrative Tools → Internet Services Manager). Right-click on the web site whose HTTP errors you wish to modify and choose Properties. The Web Site Properties dialog box will open; the HTTP error-handling information is under the Custom Errors tab. Figure 3-2 shows a listing of these HTTP errors for IIS on my Windows 2000 machine.

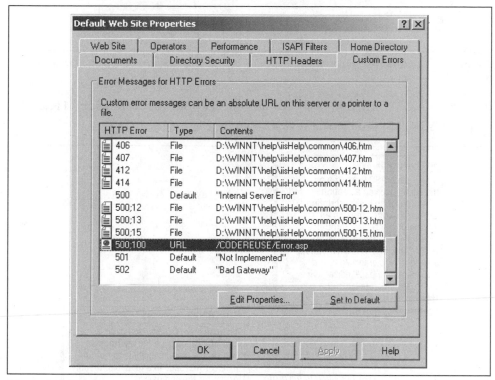

Figure 3-2. The Custom Errors tab in the Web Site Properties dialog box specifies how IIS responds to various HTTP errors

Notice that in Figure 3-2 the 500;100 HTTP error redirects the user to the URL */CODEREUSE/Error.asp*. To adjust your settings for this HTTP error, select the particular error and click the Edit Properties button. You should now be presented with the Error Mapping Properties dialog box that contains a list box and a text box. The list box contains the three various options IIS can take when an HTTP error occurs: send the default message to the client (Default), send the client a file (File), or redirect the client to a URL (URL). Figure 3-3 contains a screenshot of the Error Mapping Properties dialog box for the HTTP 500;100 error.

With the settings shown in Figure 3-3, whenever an internal web server error occurs in an ASP page, the HTTP 500;100 error will be tripped. This will send the

Error Mapping Properties
Error Code: 500 Sub Error Code: 100
Default Text: Internal Server Error - ASP error
Message Type: URL
URL: /CODEREUSE/Error.asp
OK
Cancel
Help

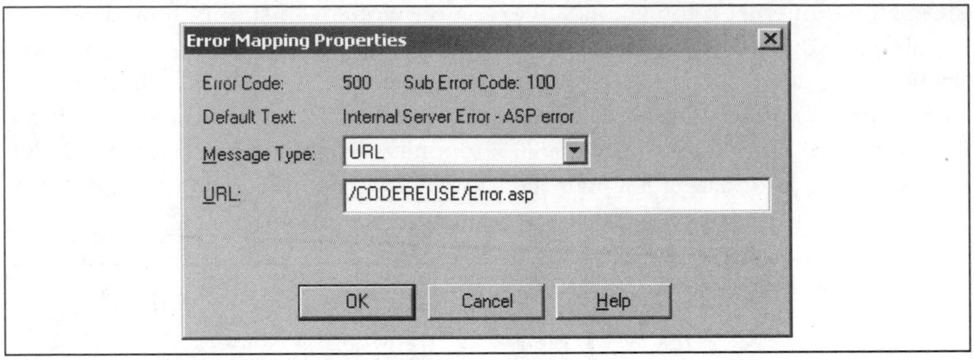

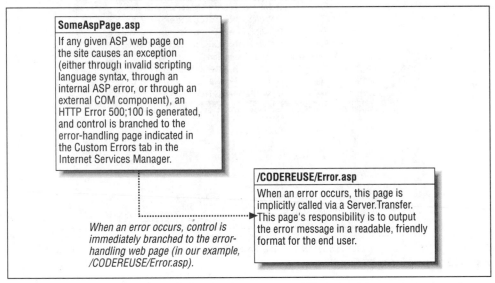

Figure 3-3. The Error Mapping Properties dialog defines how IIS handles particular server errors

user to */CODEREUSE/Error.asp* via an implicit `Server.Transfer`. Figure 3-4 graphically depicts this branch in execution.

SomeAspPage.asp
If any given ASP web page on the site causes an exception (either through invalid scripting language syntax, through an internal ASP error, or through an external COM component), an HTTP Error 500;100 is generated, and control is branched to the error-handling page indicated in the Custom Errors tab in the Internet Services Manager.
/CODEREUSE/Error.asp
When an error occurs, this page is implicitly called via a Server.Transfer. This page's responsibility is to output the error message in a readable, friendly format for the end user.
When an error occurs, control is immediately branched to the error-handling web page (in our example, /CODEREUSE/Error.asp).

Figure 3-4. When an error occurs on an ASP page, an HTTP 500;100 error is generated, branching execution to /CODEREUSE/Error.asp

When an error occurs on an ASP page, not only is a HTTP 500;100 error generated, but the details of the error are packaged into an ASPError object instance. This particular ASPError object instance can be retrieved in the error-handling web page using the GetLastError method of the Server object. Example 3-7 contains the source code for our error-handling web page, */CODEREUSE/Error.asp*.

Example 3-7. The Error-Handling Web Page Obtains Error Information Using
Server.GetLastError

```
<% @LANGUAGE = "VBSCRIPT" %>
<% Option Explicit %>
<%
  'Grab the instance of the ASPError object that contains info on
  'the error that brought us to this error-handling web page
  Dim objError
  Set objError = Server.GetLastError()
%>

<FONT SIZE=+1><B>D'oh!</B></FONT><HR NOSHADE>
An unexpected error occurred.  We apologize for this inconvenience.
<P>
<!-- Display Error Information -->
<TABLE ALIGN=CENTER BORDER=1 CELLSPACING=1>
<TR><TH COLSPAN=2>Detailed Error Information</TH></TR>
<TR>
  <TH>Property</TH>
  <TH>Value</TH>
</TR>
<TR>
  <TD>ASPCode</TD>
  <TD><%=objError.ASPCode%></TD>
</TR>
<TR>
  <TD>Number</TD>
  <TD><%=objError.Number%></TD>
</TR>
<TR>
  <TD>Source</TD>
  <TD><%=objError.Source%></TD>
</TR>
<TR>
  <TD>Category</TD>
  <TD><%=objError.Category%></TD>
</TR>
<TR>
  <TD>File</TD>
  <TD><%=objError.File%></TD>
</TR>
<TR>
  <TD>Line</TD>
  <TD><%=objError.Line%></TD>
</TR>
<TR>
  <TD>Column</TD>
  <TD><%=objError.Column%></TD>
</TR>
<TR>
  <TD>Description</TD>
  <TD><%=objError.Description%></TD>
</TR>
```

Example 3-7. The Error-Handling Web Page Obtains Error Information Using
Server.GetLastError (continued)

```
<TR>
  <TD>ASPDescription</TD>
  <TD><%=objError.ASPDescription%></TD>
</TR>
</TABLE>
<%
  Set objError = Nothing          'Clean up...
%>
```

The error-handling code in Example 3-7 uses the Server.GetLastError method to obtain information on the error that caused the HTTP 500;100 error. Next, the properties of the ASPError object are displayed in an HTML table. As we discussed earlier, the end user shouldn't be bothered with the technical details of the error, and usually we wouldn't want to display this detailed information.

As illustrated in Table 3-3, one of the ASPError object's properties is Category, which indicates which one of three categories the error falls under. The three possible error categories are:

- Scripting language error
- Internal ASP error
- External COM error

For the remainder of this section, we will examine code snippets that generate an error in a unique category. After each code snippet, we'll examine the output generated by the error-handling script in Example 3-7.

Scripting language errors

A scripting language error occurs when code that violates the scripting language's syntax is encountered. For example, in VBScript an If statement has the following syntax:

```
If condition then
  Statements
[ElseIf condition then
  ElseIf statements]
[Else
  Else statements]
End If

Or

If condition then Statements [Else Else Statements]
```

Writing an If statement that violates this expected syntax will result in a scripting language error. Example 3-8 contains the source code to *ScriptingLanguageError. asp*, which is a script with an illegal If statement. When *ScriptingLanguageError. asp* is visited through a browser, the user is automatically redirected to

/CODEREUSE/Error.asp. A screenshot of a browser visiting *ScriptingLanguageError. asp* can be seen in Figure 3-5.

Example 3-8. A C-Style If Statement Generates a Scripting Language Error When Using VBScript

```
<% @LANGUAGE="VBSCRIPT" %>
<% Option Explicit %>
<%
  if (1 = 2)
    Response.Write "What!?  1 = 2?"
%>
```

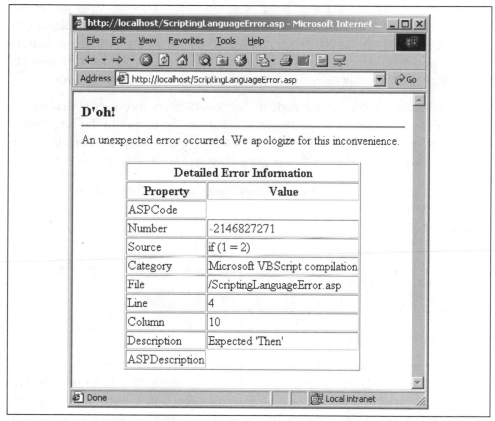

Figure 3-5. A scripting language error produces these values in the ASPError object's properties

Detecting compile-time errors with the ASPError object

Unlike the scripting language error-handling methods, the ASPError object can be used to detect compile-time errors. This is evident from the code in Example 3-8, which generates a compile-time error. Note that, according to the Category property value listed in Figure 3-5, an improperly formatted If statement results in a

"Microsoft VBScript compilation" error. This makes sense, since illegal syntax generates compile-time errors.

Internal ASP errors

When creating ASP pages, there are certain guidelines that must be followed regardless of the scripting language used. For example, server-side includes must have a certain syntax and must reference an existing file; when using the <% and %> script delimiters, these delimiters must match (that is, for every <% there must be a corresponding %>).

Internal ASP errors are a lower level of errors than scripting language errors. Scripting language errors are dependent upon the syntax of the particular scripting language used. On the other hand, internal ASP errors are scripting language-independent. When an internal ASP error occurs, the ASPDescription property of the `ASPError` object contains extra information further describing the error.

Example 3-9 contains the source code to *InternalASPError.asp*, a script that tries to include a file that does not exist. Figure 3-6 contains the output of the script when viewed through a browser. Note that the ASPDescription property contains information that was not present in the scripting language error case (Figure 3-5).

Example 3-9. Using a Server-Side Include to Import the Contents of a Nonexistent File Generates an Internal ASP Error

```
<% @LANGUAGE="VBSCRIPT" %>
<% Option Explicit %>
<%
  'An internal ASP error will be generated since we are attempting to include
  'a nonexistent ASP page...
%>
<!--#include file="NonExistentPage.asp"-->
```

External COM object errors

One of the reasons ASP is such a powerful tool for creating dynamic web pages is its ability to utilize COM components. COM components, like ADO objects, may raise errors if used improperly, or if an external exception is encountered. If such an error occurs in a COM component, the ASPError object classifies it as an external COM object error. The Category property is set to the programmatic identifier of the offending COM component.

Example 3-10 contains the source code for *COMError.asp*, a script that raises an external COM object error due to the fact that it attempts to close an ADO Connection object before it has been opened. The output of *COMError.asp*, when visited through a browser, can be seen in Figure 3-7.

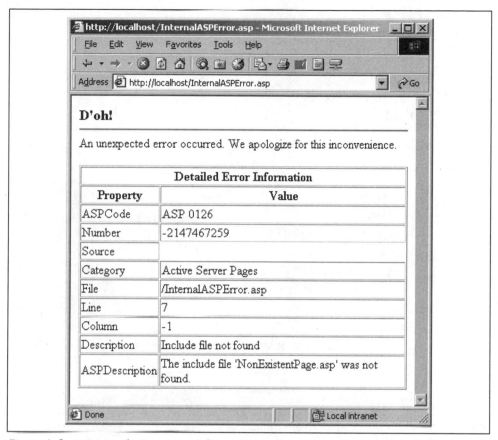

Figure 3-6. An internal ASP error produces these values in the ASPError object's properties

Example 3-10. Attempting to Close a Closed Connection Object Results in an External COM Object Error

```
<% @LANGUAGE="VBSCRIPT" %>
<% Option Explicit %>
<%
  'The following code snippet will generate a COM object error, since we
  'can't close a database connection if it's already closed!

  Dim objConn
  Set objConn = Server.CreateObject("ADODB.Connection")
  objConn.Close
%>
```

Responding to Exceptions

In the earlier section "Detecting When Exceptions Occur," we examined two methods to determine when exceptions occurred: through the server-side scripting

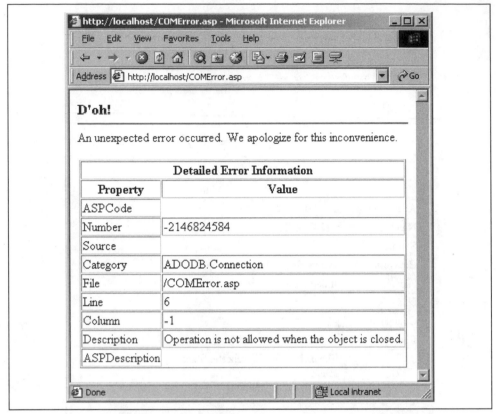

Figure 3-7. An external COM object error produces these values in the ASPError object's properties

language, and for ASP 3.0, through the ASPError object. Exception handling involves more than just detecting when an exception occurs; it also involves an appropriate response. In this section, we'll look at various ways to respond to an exception.

We'll start with a look at displaying understandable error messages. Next, a means for notifying the technical support team of the error's details is covered. Finally, we'll look at ways to recover from an error. Of course, these three approaches to responding to exceptions are not mutually exclusive. That is, when an exception occurs, you can display a readable error message, notify the support team, and attempt to recover from the error.

Displaying an Understandable Error Message

Errors are inevitable. They will happen. *Your code contains errors.* Therefore, be ready to respond to errors gracefully. Do not trivialize exception handling, expecting your code to be error-free. The worst thing that can happen when an error occurs is premature termination of the script followed by an illegible error message. As we discussed earlier, it is vitally important to provide readable, understandable error messages for your users.

Good error messages, in my opinion, contain the following four elements:

- Acknowledgement that an error occurred.
- A high-level explanation of the error.
- An apology.
- Links to other sections on a site. Links are how the Web is navigated. An error message without links to other site resources serves as a dead end, encouraging the user to leave your site altogether.

For example, a good error message for a database connection exception would be something like:

"Ah! We could not display the information you requested due to a temporary database problem. Our development team has been notified of this problem and is working diligently to resolve it as quickly as possible. We apologize for this inconvenience. In the meantime, why not check out these sections on our web site?" *Here a list of applicable links would follow.*

Personally, I find that good error messages usually contain the four elements listed above. However, I am no expert on readable error messages. For a more in-depth discussion on creating error messages, be sure to check out O'Reilly's *Developing Windows Error Messages* by Ben Ezzell.

Notifying the Support Team When an Error Occurs

Good error messages let the user know the support team has been made aware of the problems. By informing the support team when an error occurs, bugs can be quickly resolved. When an error occurs, a plethora of information is available, either through the ASPError object or the VBScript Err object. This technical information can be easily sent to the support team via email using one of the common free ASP email components.

Notifying the support team with scripting language error-handling techniques

In the earlier section "Streamlining VBScript error-handling code" we looked at a subroutine, *CheckForError*, which contained code that checked to see if `Err.Number` was nonzero. If `Err.Number` was nonzero, indicating that an error had occurred, the appropriate error message was displayed. Let's look at how this function can be expanded to include an error report email to be sent automatically to the support team.

For this example, we'll use the CDONTS email component. CDONTS is a free, lightweight email component from Microsoft that is shipped with IIS. There are plenty of good articles around the Net with information on how to use CDONTS. One such article, "Sending Emails in ASP Using CDONTS," can be found at: *http://www.4guysfromrolla.com/webtech/112298-1.shtml.*

Example 3-11 contains the new code for *CheckForError*. The error report contains the Description and Number properties from the Err object, as well as the time the error occurred, and the complete set of `ServerVariables`. This combined information should be enough to get the support team started on fixing this error.

Example 3-11. CheckForError Automatically Emails an Error Report to the Support Team in the Event of an Error

```
Sub CheckForError(strErrorMessage)
  If Err.Number <> 0 then
    'An error occurred!  Display the error message
    Response.Write strErrorMessage

    'Send error-report email to the support team
    Dim objCDO
    Set objCDO = Server.CreateObject("CDONTS.NewMail")
    objCDO.To = "support@yourdomain.com"
    objCDO.From = "support@yourdomain.com"
    objCDO.Subject = "Error Report: Error Generated at " & Now()
    objCDO.Importance = 2

    Dim strBody, strName
    strBody = "An error occured on " & Request.ServerVariables("SCRIPT_NAME") & _
              " at " & Now() & vbCrLf & vbCrLf & "Description: " & _
              Err.Description & vbCrLf & "Number: " & Err.Number & _
              vbCrLf & vbCrLf

    'Display the ServerVariables
    For Each strName in Request.ServerVariables
       strBody = strBody & strName & " - " & Request.ServerVariables(strName) & vbCrLf
    Next

    objCDO.Body = strBody
    objCDO.Send           'Send the email!
    Set objCDO = Nothing  'Clean up...

    Response.End
  End If
End Sub
```

 Since error handling is turned on, if an error occurs in sending the email message (for example, if CDONTS is not installed on the web server), the support team will never know about errors encountered by the user. For this reason, make sure CDONTS works properly on your web server *before* using it in this context.

Here is a shortened example of the error report:

```
An error occured on /CheckForError.asp at 4/5/2000 2:38:18 PM

Description: Division by zero
Number: 11

ALL_HTTP - HTTP_ACCEPT:image/gif, image/x-xbitmap, image/jpeg,
image/pjpeg, application/vnd.ms-excel, application/msword, */*
HTTP_ACCEPT_LANGUAGE:en-us
HTTP_CONNECTION:Keep-Alive
HTTP_HOST:localhost
HTTP_USER_AGENT:Mozilla/4.0 (compatible; MSIE 5.01; Windows NT 5.0)
HTTP_ACCEPT_ENCODING:gzip, deflate

ALL_RAW - Accept: image/gif, image/x-xbitmap, image/jpeg, image/pjpeg,
application/vnd.ms-excel, application/msword, */*
Accept-Language: en-us
Connection: Keep-Alive
Host: localhost
User-Agent: Mozilla/4.0 (compatible; MSIE 5.01; Windows NT 5.0)
Accept-Encoding: gzip, deflate

' ... error report shortened for brevity ...
```

A similar approach for sending error-report email can be used with JScript. Either use the CDONTS component in the **catch** block, or call a function similar to *CheckForError* in the **catch** block.

Notifying the support team with the ASPError object

Since the ASPError object contains more properties than the Err object, using the ASPError object approach will generate a more detailed error report for the support team. To send email to the support team, code similar to that in Example 3-11 will be used. Of course, the email code will exist in the error-handling web page, */CODEREUSE/Error.asp*. Example 3-12 contains a new version of */CODEREUSE/Error.asp*, one that will automatically send an error report to the support team. (The code that displayed the error information to the user has been removed for brevity. To see this code, consult Example 3-7.)

Example 3-12. /CODEREUSE/Error.asp Shoots an Error Report to the Support Team

```
<% @LANGUAGE = "VBSCRIPT" %>
<% Option Explicit %>
<%
  'Grab the instance of the ASPError object that contains info on
  'the error that brought us to this error-handling web page
  Dim objError
  Set objError = Server.GetLastError()

  'Send error-report email to the support team
  Dim objCDO
  Set objCDO = Server.CreateObject("CDONTS.NewMail")
```

Example 3-12. /CODEREUSE/Error.asp Shoots an Error Report to the Support Team (continued)

```
    objCDO.To = "support@yourdomain.com"
    objCDO.From = "support@yourdomain.com"
    objCDO.Subject = "Error Report: Error Generated at " & Now()
    objCDO.Importance = 2

    Dim strBody, strName
    strBody = "An error occured on " & Request.ServerVariables("SCRIPT_NAME") & _
              " at " & Now() & vbCrLf & vbCrLf

    'Display the ASP Error properties
    strBody = strBody & "ASPCode: " & objError.ASPCode & vbCrLf
    strBody = strBody & "Number: " & objError.Number & vbCrLf
    strBody = strBody & "Source: " & objError.Source & vbCrLf
    strBody = strBody & "Category: " & objError.Category & vbCrLf
    strBody = strBody & "File: " & objError.File & vbCrLf
    strBody = strBody & "Line: " & objError.Line & vbCrLf
    strBody = strBody & "Column: " & objError.Column & vbCrLf
    strBody = strBody & "Description: " & objError.Description & vbCrLf
    strBody = strBody & "ASPDescription: " & objError.ASPDescription & vbCrLf

    strBody = strBody & vbCrLf & vbCrLf

    'Display the ServerVariables
    For Each strName in Request.ServerVariables
        strBody = strBody & strName & " - " & Request.ServerVariables(strName) & vbCrLf
    Next

    objCDO.Body = strBody
    objCDO.Send                 'Send the email!
    Set objCDO = Nothing     'Clean up...
%>

<!-- The code to display the error message to the user has been removed for
     brevity.  It can be seen in Example 3-7.  -->

<%
    Set objError = Nothing          'Clean up...
%>
```

Recovering from an Error

Ideally, an application would be smart enough to analyze an error when it happens, take some set of actions to sidestep the error, and continue processing. Of course compile-time errors can't be recovered from (it's hard to recover from illegal syntax), but there are several runtime errors that might have viable workarounds that allow for the script to continue processing.

Recovering from an error is not possible using the ASPError method, since when an error occurs, script execution is abruptly shifted from the erroneous ASP page to the error-handling ASP page. When setting up a web site to redirect control to the error-handling page when an HTTP 500;100 error occurs, the change permeates to all web pages within the site. However, you can disable this on a page-by-page basis by turning on the scripting language's error handling.

For example, if you have successfully set up IIS to redirect to an error page upon HTTP 500;100 errors, the following ASP script, when viewed through a browser, will display any output from the error-handling page:

```
<% @LANGUAGE="VBSCRIPT" %>
<% Option Explicit %>
<%
    Dim iSomeVariable
    iSomeVariable = iSomeOtherVariable    'This will generate a runtime error since
                                          'iSomeOtherVariable was not explicitly
                                          'declared (and Option Explicit was stated)
%>
```

However, if the scripting language error handling is turned on (as it is in the code snippet below), the error-handling page won't be visited:

```
<% @LANGUAGE="VBSCRIPT" %>
<% Option Explicit %>
<%
    On Error Resume Next              'The error-handling page will not be called
                                      'since the script language error handling is
                                      'enabled.

    Dim iSomeVariable
    iSomeVariable = iSomeOtherVariable      'This will generate a runtime error
since
                                      'iSomeOtherVariable was not explicitly
                                      'declared (and Option Explicit was stated)
%>
```

To designate certain portions of your code to be handled by the scripting language error handling and other portions to be handled by the ASPError object approach, simply enable and disable the scripting language error handling at will.

To enable error handling in VBScript, use On Error Resume Next; to disable error handling, use On Error Goto 0. In JScript, there is no "enabling" error handling. Code within a try block is handled by the scripting language, while code outside of a try block is handled by the ASPError object approach.

As previously discussed, ideally a program could recover from any runtime error. However, creating such an intelligent, error-fixing program is next to impossible, and far beyond the scope of this book. It is not so far-fetched, though, to assume we can recover from a certain set of defined errors. A classic example is a backup or mirror database system. If the primary database is unreachable for some reason, rather than displaying a database connection error, an attempt can be made to connect to the backup database.

Example 3-13 contains source code to recover from such an error. The code assumes that the System DSN PrimaryDatabase specifies the primary database and that a secondary database is available through the System DSN SecondaryDatabase. The code in Example 3-13 is straightforward; it enables error handling in VBScript and attempts to connect to the PrimaryDatabase. If there is an error in the connection, it tries to connect to the SecondaryDatabase. If either database connection attempt is successful, error handling is disabled so any other errors in the script will trip the HTTP 500;100 error and redirect the user to the error-handling page.

Example 3-13. If You Have a Backup or Secondary Database, You Can Recover Nicely from Connection Errors to the Primary Database

```
<% @LANGUAGE="VBSCRIPT" %>
<% Option Explicit %>
<%
  'Enable error handling
  On Error Resume Next

  Dim objConn
  Set objConn = Server.CreateObject("ADODB.Connection")
  objConn.ConnectionString = "DSN=PrimaryDatabase"
  objConn.Open

  'Now, if there was an error, we need to try the SecondaryDatabase
  If Err.Number <> 0 then
    Err.Clear                         'clear out the error information

    objConn.ConnectionString = "DSN=SecondaryDatabase"
    objConn.Open
  End If

  'If we have an error connecting to this database as well, then that's really bad.
  If Err.Number <> 0 then
    Response.Write "Both databases are off-line."
    Response.End
  End If

  'Disable error handling, so that future errors are handled by the error-handling
  'web page
  On Error Goto 0

  '...
%>
```

When attempting to recover from an error, detailed information must be known about the recovery path. Recovering from errors is rarely an easy task. However, recovering from an error is the best course of action an application can take when an error occurs.

Creating Custom HTTP Error Pages

As discussed in the earlier section "Detecting Exceptions with the ASPError Object," when an ASP error occurs on a web page, an HTTP 500;100 error is signaled. If you correctly set up an error-handling web page through the Internet Services Manager, IIS will automatically send the user to the specified error-handling web page via a `Server.Transfer`.

Of course there are several other types of HTTP errors besides 500;100. One of the most common errors is the HTTP 404 error, which results when a client requests a page not found on the web server. There is nothing as annoying or frustrating as the default HTTP 404 error page, which is shown in Figure 3-8.

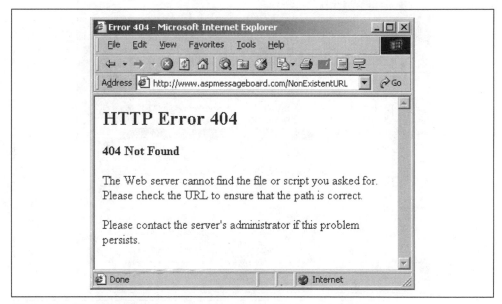

Figure 3-8. The default 404 error page serves as a dead end, frustrating users

The default 404 error page is ugly and serves as a dead end for your users. A much better approach is to provide your visitors with a custom 404 error page that apologizes for the page not being found and provides links to relevant sections on the site. Relevant sections might include a search page or a listing of popular resources on the site. The vast majority of large web sites realize the importance of custom 404 error pages. You can see some examples of real-world custom 404 error pages at the following URLs:

- *http://www.yahoo.com/NotAValidURL*
- *http://espn.go.com/NotAValidURL*
- *http://www.4guysfromrolla.com/NotAValidURL*

Custom 404 pages, unlike custom HTTP 500;100 error pages, can be implemented in both IIS 4.0 and IIS 5.0. As with creating a custom HTTP 500;100 error page, to create a custom HTTP 404 error page, start by going to the Internet Services Manager. You should see a listing of all of the web sites on your web server. Right-click on the web site for which you'd like to create a custom 404 error page and choose Properties. Choose the Custom Errors tab and locate the 404 HTTP error, as seen in the screenshot in Figure 3-9.

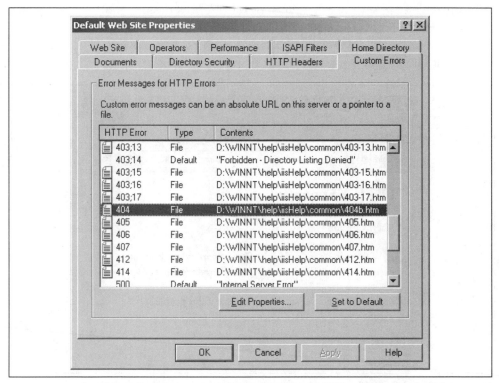

Figure 3-9. Select the 404 HTTP Error from the Custom Errors tab in the Default Web Site Properties dialog box

Next, click the Edit Properties button. You should be presented with a dialog box similar to the one shown in Figure 3-3. Select URL from the Message Type list box, and enter */CODEREUSE/404.asp* as the URL to redirect to. Now whenever a 404 error occurs on your site, your users will be automatically redirected to */CODEREUSE/404.asp*. When the custom 404 error page is called, it is passed the following information in the querystring:

```
404;URL_That_Generated_The_404
```

Through this querystring, you can determine the exact URL the user tried to enter that resulted in a 404 error. An industrious developer could create a custom 404 error page that checks the URL the user entered against valid URLs on the site.

This script could rate how close the invalid URL was to various valid URLs and automatically redirect the user to the valid URL.

Such a dynamic custom 404 error page is used at *LearnASP.com*, an ASP information resource site run by Charles Carroll. The goal of Charles's custom 404 page is to allow ASP articles and tutorials to move directories, or to change names without having users' bookmarks become invalidated.

A database table keeps track of web page filenames when they are moved or renamed. This database table's definition can be seen in Table 3-4.

Table 3-4. A Database Table Maintains the Old and New URLs for Moved or Renamed Web Pages

Column Name	Description
OldURL	The URL of the web page *before* it was moved or renamed
NewURL	The URL of the web page *after* it was moved or renamed
Frequency	A counter indicating how often a user requested the old URL and had to be redirected to the new URL

If a user enters an invalid URL, thereby causing an HTTP 404 error, the custom 404 error page is called. In the 404 error page, the invalid URL is checked against the OldURL column in the database table. If a match is found, the **Frequency** column is incremented and the user is automatically redirected to the URL specified by NewURL.

Charles is a skilled, industrious programmer, and has added many bells and whistles to this custom 404 error page. For example, the OldURL field can contain wildcard fields, such as /Tutorials/^, with a corresponding NewURL of */Learn/*.* That way, if a user enters a URL that contains the */Tutorials* directory (such as */Tutorials/ Lesson1.asp*), he or she is automatically redirected to */Learn/Lesson1.asp*.

 Charles has also added numerous other noteworthy features. To learn more about the custom 404 error page on *LearnASP.com*, be sure to visit *http://www.learnasp.com/how/notfoundintro.asp*, which includes a discussion on the motivation of the code, as well as the full source!

I, however, am not as industrious as Charles! The custom 404 page presented in Example 3-14 displays a message to the user indicating that the page could not be found. It also sends email to the webmaster, letting her know a 404 was encountered. The email contains information on the URL entered and the referring URL. That way, if the 404 came via a broken link on the site, the webmaster will be notified and able to quickly fix the broken link.

*Example 3-14. A Custom 404 Error Page Should Display an Informative Message
with Relevant Links*

```
<% @LANGUAGE = "VBSCRIPT" %>
<% Option Explicit %>
<%
  'Grab the URL of the 404.  The Querystring is in the form:
  '  404;URL
  Dim strURL
  strURL = Right(Request.QueryString, Len(Request.QueryString) - 4)

  'Send email to the webmaster
  Dim objCDO
  Set objCDO = Server.CreateObject("CDONTS.NewMail")
  objCDO.To = "webmaster@yourdomain.com"
  objCDO.From = "webmaster@yourdomain.com"
  objCDO.Subject = "404 Error Encountered on " & Now()
  objCDO.Body = "At " & Now() & " a 404 error was encountered when the user " & _
                "attempted to visit: " & strURL & ".  The referring URL was: " & _
                Request.ServerVariables("HTTP_REFERER")
  objCDO.Send
  Set objCDO = Nothing
%>

<HTML>
<HEAD>
  <TITLE>Egad!  We could not find the page you requested!</TITLE>
</HEAD>
<BODY>
  <CENTER><FONT SIZE=+2><B>
    We Could Not Find the Page You Requested
  </B></FONT></CENTER>
  <P><HR><P>
  Ah!  We could not find the page that you have requested!  Our webmaster has been
  automatically sent an email detailing this missing document.  Here are some links
  we think you will find helpful:
  <P><UL>
    <LI><A HREF="/search/">Search the Site</A><BR>
    ... <!-- More links should appear here ... -->
  </UL>
</BODY>
</HTML>
```

Here is an example email the webmaster might receive:

```
At 4/5/2000 8:09:30 PM a 404 error was encountered when the user attempted
to visit: http://localhost/NotAValidURL.  The referring URL was:
http://localhost/SomeURL.asp
```

This automatically generated email serves as a quick locator of broken links on
one's web site. Rather than requiring notification from users or expensive third-
party software to detect broken links, you can let your custom 404 error pages
indicate when a broken link is found.

Further Reading

While there are many good online articles on VBScript error handling, there are far too few JScript error-handling articles. Part of the reason, of course, is error handling wasn't available in JScript until Version 5.0. Furthermore, there are not many online articles discussing how to use the ASPError object for exception handling, also due, no doubt, to its relative newness. Keeping that in mind, here are some selected readings on the various exception-handling approaches discussed throughout this chapter.

- For a good read on using VBScript error-handling techniques to present understandable error messages to your visitors, check out "Error Handling in ASP," at *http://www.4guysfromrolla.com/webtech/060399-1.shtml*.

- A rather detailed discussion of JScript's error handling can be seen on Microsoft's site at *http://msdn.microsoft.com/workshop/languages/jscript/handling.asp*.

- On Microsoft's site, there is a rather lengthy article on new ASP 3.0 features. Unfortunately, only a short part of the article discusses using the ASPError object for exception handling. The article, "Internet Information Services 5.0," can be found at *http://www.microsoft.com/mind/0499/iis5/iis5.htm*.

- The most thorough article on the ASPError object I could find was at *http://www.asptoday.com/articles/19990308.htm*, in a piece entitled "Error Handling in IIS 5.0."

- To learn more on creating custom 404 error pages, be sure to read "Creating a Custom 404 Error Page," at *http://www.4guysfromrolla.com/webtech/061499-1.shtml*.

4

Regular Expressions, Classes, and Dynamic Evaluation and Execution

With the introduction of the VBScript 5.0 scripting engine, VBScript developers now have three very powerful techniques at their disposal which were previously unavailable with VBScript:

- The availability of a Regular Expression object, RegExp. Regular expressions provide for advanced string matching and parsing. If you are new to regular expressions, you'll soon realize their tremendous advantages and wonder how you lived without them!

- The ability to create object-oriented code! VBScript now supports classes! I am very excited about this new feature, for it allows the creation of robust and reusable ASP pages. It's also great for those working in large development teams where certain developers aren't as experienced as others with ASP. The more experienced developers can create classes that encapsulate some of the more difficult functionality, and the more novice developers can simply use these classes to accomplish the common ASP tasks!

- Dynamic evaluation and execution. Dynamic evaluation allows a code snippet contained in a string to be evaluated as though it had been entered directly by the programmer creating the script. Dynamic execution allows a code snippet contained in a string to be executed as through it had been entered directly by the programmer. By employing the use of dynamic evaluation and execution, a script can achieve flexibility not previously available. We'll discuss how to perform dynamic evaluations and executions in the section "Using Dynamic Evaluation and Execution."

If you are running ASP 3.0, you already have the VBScript 5.0 scripting engine. If you are running an older version of ASP/IIS, be sure to download the latest Microsoft scripting engines from: *http://msdn.microsoft.com/scripting/*.

Using the RegExp Object

The RegExp object provides the VBScript engine with a means to perform regular expression pattern matching. We've discussed regular expressions previously; in Chapter 2, *Choosing a Server-Side Scripting Language*, a discussion on using regular expressions in JScript and PerlScript was presented.

RegExp's Properties

Take a moment to look back at Chapter 2 to see JScript's implementation of regular expressions. Note that the regular expression syntax contains a pattern and an optional switch. The switch can have one of three values:

i   Ignore case

g   Perform a global search for all occurrences of *pattern*

gi Perform a global search for all occurrences of *pattern*, ignoring case

The RegExp object contains three properties that allow you to set the pattern and these switches for regular expression usage in VBScript. These three properties are Pattern, IgnoreCase, and Global. Pattern expects a string, and is the regular expression pattern to search for. Global is a Boolean value indicating whether the regular expression search should match all occurrences in a string or just the first one. If not specified, Global defaults to `False`. IgnoreCase is also a Boolean value, indicating whether or not a regular expression search is case-sensitive. By default, IgnoreCase is set to `False`.

Legal Regular Expression Syntax

The Pattern property contains the regular expression. A regular expression pattern is not restricted to just simple strings. The pattern can also contain special characters, which allow for much more sophisticated searches. Table 4-1 contains a listing of these special characters and their meanings.

Table 4-1. Special Characters in Regular Expression Patterns

Symbol	Description
Any alphanumeric character	Matches the alphanumeric character(s) literally.
\	Indicates that the following character is a special character or a literal. For example, a pattern containing "b" matches the character "b," while "\b" matches a word boundary.
^	Matches the beginning of a string. For example, "^A" would match only the first "A" in "ASP is Awesome."
$	Matches only the end of a string. For example "$d" would match the last "d" in "Todd is mad."

Table 4-1. Special Characters in Regular Expression Patterns (continued)

Symbol	Description
\b	Matches a word boundary. A word boundary exists between two characters, where one of the characters is a word character and the other is not. Furthermore, the beginning and end of a string are considered word boundaries. For example, if you searched for "\bscience\b" in "science has no conscience," only the first word of the string would be returned. The "science" in "conscience" would not be matched since "science" is not preceded by a word boundary.
\B	The opposite of \b. Matches any word boundary.
[abc...]	Matches any single character that exists between the braces. For example, "[aeiou]" would match the first vowel found in a string. You can also use the hyphen for a range of characters. "[a-m]" would match the first occurrence of a character belonging in the first half of the alphabet.
[^abc...]	Matches any single character not between the braces. For example, "[^aeiou]" matches the first consonant found in a string. (You can also use the hyphen to represent a range of characters.)
\w	Matches any word character. A word character is one that contains an alphanumeric character or an underscore.
\W	Matches any nonword character.
\d	Matches any digit. Functionally identical to [0–9].
\D	Matches any nondigit.
\s	Matches any space character (including a space, a newline character, a carriage return, or a tab).
\S	Matches any nonspace character.
.	Matches any character other than \n: functionally identical to [^\n].
\n	Matches a newline character.
\r	Matches a carriage return.
\t	Matches a tab.
{n}	Matches exactly *n* occurrences of a regular expression. For example, "\w{10}" matches 10 consecutive word characters.
{n,}	Matches *n* or more occurrences of a regular expression. For example, "\d{2,}" matches two or more consecutive digits.
{n,m}	Matches between *n* and *m* occurrences of a regular expression. For example, "\w{2,4}" matches either two, three, or four consecutive word characters.
?	Matches zero or one occurrences; functionally identical to {0,1}. For example, "\w\d?" matches a word character followed by zero or one digits.
*	Matches zero or more occurrences; functionally identical to {0,}.
+	Matches one or more occurrences; functionally identical to {1,}.
( )	Used to group a series of symbols. For example, "xyz?" matches "xy" and "xyz," while "x(yz)?" matches "x" and "xyz."
|	Matches either one of two groups. For example, "(Scott)|(James)" matches "Scott" or "James."

To search for a literal that is also used as a special symbol, precede the literal with a backslash. For example, to match a question mark character in a string, use the pattern "\?", since the question mark is a special symbol for regular expressions.

A regular expression can contain any number of the special symbols and literals listed in Table 4-1. Regular expressions provide a powerful tool for validating input. For example, imagine that a user will enter his social security number. The expected format is ###-##-####. This can be validated with the regular expression:

    \d{3}-\d{2}-\d{4}

which checks for three digits, followed by a dash, followed by two digits, followed by a dash, followed by four digits. A regular expression that could validate a phone number in either ###-###-#### or (###) ###-#### format could be:

    (\d{3}-\d{3}-\d{4})|(\(\d{3}\) \d{3}-\d{4})

Note that when matching a literal left or right parenthesis, the parenthesis needs to be preceded by a backslash.

RegExp's Methods

The RegExp object contains three methods: Test, Replace, and Execute. The first method, Test, accepts one parameter, which is the string to apply the regular expression to. If a match is found, Test returns **True**; otherwise, it returns **False**. For example, if you asked a user to input her name, you want to make sure only letters, apostrophes, and hyphens exist within the person's name. As Example 4-1 illustrates, you can use the Test method to quickly determine whether the name entered by the user consists of any characters other than the set of accepted characters.

Example 4-1. Using the Test Method to Validate a String

```
<% @LANGUAGE = "VBScript" %>
<% Option Explicit %>
<%
   Dim objRegExp
   Set objRegExp = New RegExp     'Create a RegExp object instance

   'Set the pattern (allow all letters, apostrophes, and hyphens)
   objRegExp.Pattern = "[^a-z' \-]"

   'Ignore case
   objRegExp.IgnoreCase = True
```

Example 4-1. Using the Test Method to Validate a String (continued)

```
    'See if the regular expression is found in strName
    Dim strName
    strName = "Scott Mitchell"
    If objRegExp.Test(strName) then
        Response.Write strName & " is not a valid name!<BR>"
    Else
        Response.Write strName & " is a valid name!<BR>"
    End If

    strName = "Roger O'Grady"
    If objRegExp.Test(strName) then
        Response.Write strName & " is not a valid name!<BR>"
    Else
        Response.Write strName & " is a valid name!<BR>"
    End If

    strName = "Tim 7sten"
    If objRegExp.Test(strName) then
        Response.Write strName & " is not a valid name!<BR>"
    Else
        Response.Write strName & " is a valid name!<BR>"
    End If
%>
```

We set the RegExp's Pattern property to search for the occurrence of a character
that is not a letter, not an apostrophe, not a space, and not a hyphen. We want to
ignore case, so we set the IgnoreCase property to **True**. Then we use the Test
method to see if any of the illegal characters exist within the string *strName*. If Test
returns **True**, then the name is invalid; if Test returns **False**, then the name is
valid. (In the above example, the first two names are valid while the last is invalid.)

The Replace method expects two string parameters. The first parameter is the
string to which to apply the regular expression; the second parameter contains the
text to be used to replace matching occurrences; a new string reflecting the appropriate substitutions is then returned by the function. For example, if we wanted to
replace all instances of the acronym "asp" with "ASP," we could use the Replace
method as shown in Example 4-2.

Example 4-2. Using the Replace Method

```
<% @LANGUAGE = "VBScript" %>
<% Option Explicit %>
<%
    Dim objRegExp
    Set objRegExp = New RegExp    'Create a RegExp object instance

    'Set the pattern (allow all letters, apostrophes, and hyphens)
    objRegExp.Pattern = "\basp\b"
```

Example 4-2. Using the Replace Method (continued)

```
    objRegExp.IgnoreCase = True   'Ignore case
    objRegExp.Global = True       'Make all possible changes

    Dim strSentence
    strSentence = "Asp is a fun language.  I aspire to learn asp!"

    Response.Write "<B>Before Replace</B><BR>" & strSentence
    Response.Write "<P><B>After Replace</B><BR> "

    'Use the replace method!
    strSentence = objRegExp.Replace(strSentence, "ASP")

    Response.Write strSentence
%>
```

Note that the regular expression used did not simply search for "asp," but rather for "\basp\b." Recall that the "\b" special symbol searches for a word boundary. If the regular expression contained just "asp," the "asp" in "aspire" would also have been capitalized.

The third and final method of the RegExp object is Execute. The Execute method takes one parameter like the Test method, a string to which to apply the regular expression. The Execute method returns a Matches collection, which contains a Match object for each successful regular expression match.

The Match object contains three read-only properties: FirstIndex, Length, and Value. FirstIndex contains the position in the string where the match occurred. Unfortunately, FirstIndex is zero-based; VBScript, as you probably know, indexes its strings starting at one. In other words, you have to add one to the value of FirstIndex to actually identify the starting position of the substring found by the Match object. As its name suggests, Length contains the total length of the matched string. The final property, Value, contains the matched text.

In Example 4-2, we used the Replace method to find all the instances of "asp" and replace them with "ASP." We can use the Execute method to grab all of the matches. The code in Example 4-3 uses the Execute method to return a Matches collection; next, the script iterates through the Matches collection, outputting the properties of each of the individual Match objects.

Example 4-3. Using the Execute Method and the Matches Collection

```
<% @LANGUAGE = "VBScript" %>
<% Option Explicit %>
<%
    Dim objRegExp
    Set objRegExp = New RegExp    'Create a RegExp object instance
```

Example 4-3. Using the Execute Method and the Matches Collection (continued)

```
    'Set the pattern (allow all letters, apostrophes, and hyphens)
    objRegExp.Pattern = "\basp\b"

    objRegExp.IgnoreCase = True  'Ignore case
    objRegExp.Global = True       'Make all possible changes

    Dim strSentence
    strSentence = "Asp is a fun language.  I aspire to learn asp!"

    'Use the execute method to obtain a matches collection
    Dim objMatches, objMatch
    Set objMatches = objRegExp.Execute(strSentence)

    Response.Write "There were " & objMatches.Count & " matches.<BR>"
    Response.Write "<P><HR><P>"

    'Loop through each Match object in the Matches collection
    Dim iCount
    iCount = 1
    For Each objMatch in objMatches
      Response.Write "<B>Match " & iCount & "</B><BR>"
      Response.Write "FirstIndex = " & objMatch.FirstIndex & "<BR>"
      Response.Write "Length = " & objMatch.Length & "<BR>"
      Response.Write "Value = " & objMatch.Value & "<BR>"
      Response.Write "<P><HR><P>"

      iCount = iCount + 1
    Next

    Set objRegExp = Nothing
%>
```

Since the Execute method returns an object, be sure to use the `Set` keyword when
assigning the Matches collection returned by Execute to a variable. Also, since the
Matches collection is, after all, a collection, you have access to the basic methods
and properties of a collection, such as the Count property. Furthermore, you can
completely iterate through the Matches collection using a `For Each ... Next` loop.

The code in Example 4-3 will generate the output shown in Figure 4-1. Note that
the first instance of "Asp" is at the beginning of the string *strSentence*, so the
Match object reports its *FirstIndex* property as zero instead of the more VBScript-
friendly one.

Personally, I find regular expressions to be neat and fun to use, partially because
no other method allows for such powerful string parsing with such convoluted
code. For example, what does the following regular expression match?

```
^\s*((\$\s?)|(£\s?))?((\d+(\.(\d\d)?)?)|(\.\d\d))\s*(UK|GBP|GB|USA|US|USD)?)\s*$
```

(This regular expression is an example from Microsoft's web site: *http://msdn.
microsoft.com/workshop/languages/clinic/scripting051099.asp*.)

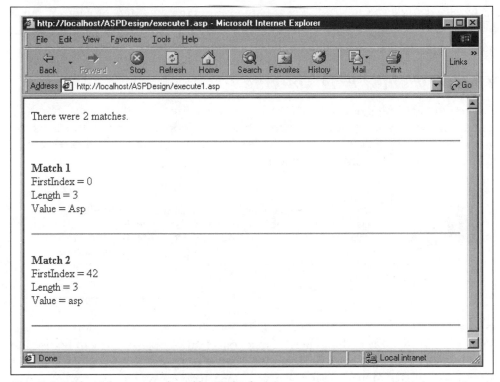

Figure 4-1. The web page produced by Example 4-3

I think you'll find regular expressions are much easier to build than to analyze after the fact. If you know what patterns you wish to search for, you will most likely be able to create a valid regular expression. However, if presented with an unwieldy regular expression, I find it a bit more difficult to work backwards and predict what type of data the regular expression was intended to validate.

That about wraps up using regular expressions in VBScript. While we looked at the code needed to perform a regular expression search in VBScript, we only touched upon how to effectively use regular expressions to achieve powerful string parsing. To truly master regular expressions, you'll almost certainly need an entire book dedicated to the subject, such as O'Reilly's *Mastering Regular Expressions*. You can also visit Microsoft's scripting site (*http://msdn.microsoft.com/ scripting/*) for more information on the RegExp object.

Using Object-Oriented Programming with VBScript

With the introduction of the VBScript 5.0 scripting engine, developers now have the ability to create classes in VBScript, much as they can in VB. The next section is intended for those new to object-oriented programming, and provides a quick introduction on the topic. The section following that discusses the VBScript syntax for creating and using classes.

Object-Oriented Programming 101

Object-oriented programming (OOP) is a programming methodology in which entities known as *bjects* are used. Objects contain properties and methods; as the names suggest, a *property* describes the features of the object, while a *method* performs some action involving the object.

> True object-oriented programming is further defined as the ability for new objects to inherit properties and methods from existing objects, and for dynamic binding of derived object methods. VBScript's implementation of OOP doesn't support these two additional requirements, and is therefore not a true object-oriented programming language.

As an ASP developer, you've already used object-oriented code written by others. For example, ADO is nothing more than a collection of objects that can be used to access a database. Having the ability to treat a complex task as a black box is indeed beneficial. When using ADO, you don't have to worry about what protocol is required to establish a connection to a database; rather, you simply use the Open method of the ADO Connection object.

An object and an instance

To fully understand object-oriented programming, it is essential to understand the difference between an object and an instance of an object.

An *object*, such as ADO's Connection object, is an abstraction. It does not physically exist. Rather, it simply serves as a template for creating instances.

An *instance* is a physical entity of an object. For example, in the following code, ADODB.Connection is an object, while *objConn* is an instance of the ADODB. Connection object:

```
'Create an instance of the ADODB.Connection object
Dim objConn
Set objConn = Server.CreateObject("ADODB.Connection")
```

You must have an instance of an object to make any method calls or to set or get any properties. A real-world example of an object/instance relationship can be seen with automobiles. A "car" is an object, a template describing the features and functionality of an automobile. A 1986 Mercury Sable GS is an instance of a car, able to have its properties modified and its methods implemented.

Encapsulating complexity

Object-oriented programming can be used to encapsulate the complexity associated with particular tasks. For example, imagine that on your web site you needed to be able to open a text file, count the number of lines in the file, and then log that information in another file. Assume you didn't have an object-oriented approach. Each time you wanted to accomplish this task, you'd need to perform the following steps:

1. Open a particular text file.
2. Count the number of lines in that text file.
3. Close the text file.
4. Open up the logging file.
5. Log the number of lines from the file in Step 2.
6. Close the log file.

Granted, these steps are not complex or too lengthy, but imagine that a novice developer is expected to perform these steps in various ASP pages. We can simplify the process by encapsulating the above steps into a single object. Let's take a look at creating such an object.

Let's call this object LogTextFileLines; it will have one property, TextFilePath, which contains the physical path to the log file. LogTextFileLines will also contain one method, UpdateLog, which is responsible for counting the number of lines in a specified text file and recording the line count in the appropriate log file. UpdateLog will have the following definition:

```
Function UpdateLog(strFileName)
```

where *strFileName* is the path to the text file whose lines need to be counted and logged. UpdateLog could return a Boolean value to indicate whether or not the operation was successful.

Once this object is created, the six-step task outlined earlier becomes much simpler:

```
'Create an instance of the LogTextFileLines object
Dim objLog
Set objLog = New LogTextFileLines

'Set the LogFile path
objLog.LogTextFileLines = "C:\Log\linecount.log"

'Count and log the number of lines in C:\TXT\Scott.txt
If objLog.UpdateLog("C:\TXT\Scott.txt") then
  Response.Write "C:\TXT\Scott.txt was logged successfully!"
Else
```

```
Response.Write "There was an error when attempting to log C:\TXT\Scott.txt"
End if
```

Being able to treat the entire process like a black box leads to less development time, and most importantly, fewer bugs.

Using Classes in VBScript

If you are not familiar with VBScript classes, but perhaps are familiar with C++'s implementation of classes, you'll no doubt find VBScript's use of classes somewhat disappointing. VBScript classes can only contain a single constructor (a *constructor* is a procedure that's executed automatically when an instance of the class is created); unfortunately, VBScript's constructor can accept no parameters. Furthermore, there is no support for inheritance in VBScript.

Inheritance is an OOP technique used to group objects into a logical hierarchy corresponding to the relationships among objects. For example, if you had a `Mammal` object, two of its children in this hierarchy might be the `Canine` and `Feline` objects. These latter two objects were *inherited* from `Mammal`. As an inherited class, `Canine` and `Feline` would have the basic methods and properties of a Mammal, as well as their own unique, specialized methods and properties.

When creating classes, keep in mind you are creating a tool to be used by other developers. In the discussion of classes throughout this book, there will be certain times when a distinction between the developer who created the class and the developer who is using the class is needed. The developer who created a class for use by other developers will be referred to as the *class developer*, while the developer using the created class will be referred to as the *end developer*.

Since VBScript classes are not compiled into binary objects like COM components, for an end developer to use a class in an ASP script, she must have the class defined within that ASP script. Rather than force the end developers to cut and paste a class definition into each ASP page they use that needs that particular class definition, it is best to create a text file that contains the class definition. Then any end developer who needs to use a class can simply use a server-side include to import the class definition into their ASP page.

As the class developer, once you have created a class, it is important that any changes to the class do not "break" any of the class's existing methods or properties. For example, if you wanted to add a new feature to an existing class, make sure that when adding it existing code utilizing that class will not break! If you need to add a new feature that changes the existing class's methods or properties to the point that errors will occur in existing code, you should create an entirely new class that utilizes the new feature. That way, old code still functions.

Creating classes

To create a class, use the **Class** statement, which has the following syntax:

```
Class ClassName
   'Define the class's properties and methods here
End Class
```

where *ClassName* is the name you choose to assign to your class; your name must follow standard VBScript variable naming conventions.

The Initialize and Terminate events

When creating classes, there are two important event handlers to be aware of: Initialize and Terminate. The Initialize event fires when a class instance is created using the **New** keyword. For example, we could create an instance of the **SomeObject** class using:

```
Dim objSomeObjectInstance
Set objSomeObjectInstance = New SomeObject
```

The Terminate event occurs when a class instance is freed. A class instance can be freed either explicitly with **Set objSomeObjectInstance = Nothing**, or implicitly, when it goes out of scope.

We can define these event handlers in our classes. The Initialize event handler can be used to initialize the class's properties or perform other needed start-up tasks. The Initialize event is often referred to as the class's *constructor*. The Terminate event can be used to perform any shutdown tasks, and is commonly referred to as the class's *destructor*. Example 4-4 contains the definition of a class with its single constructor and destructor.

Example 4-4. The Initialize and Terminate Event Handlers

```
Class SomeObject
  Private Sub Class_Initialize()
    'This event is called when an instance of the class is instantiated
    'Initialize properties here and perform other start-up tasks
  End Sub

  Private Sub Class_Terminate()
    'This event is called when a class instance is destroyed
    'either explicitly (Set objClassInstance = Nothing) or
    'implicitly (it goes out of scope)
  End Sub
End Class
```

Properties, methods, member variables, and member functions

From the end developer's standpoint, a class contains *properties* and *methods.* Properties are variables that the end developer can set that determine the state of the class. Methods are functions of the class that the end developer can call to have the class perform a given task. For example, the `ADODB.Connection` object contains properties that describe the state of the object instance, such as ConnectionString, ConnectionTimeout, and Provider, and methods that perform actions, such as Open and Close.

A class, though, can contain variables and functions that the end developer cannot directly call. These "hidden" variables and functions are referred to as *member variables* and *member functions*, respectively.

The terminology may seem a bit confusing, or at least overly verbose. To put it another way, a class contains functions and variables. If the end developer can call a class function, the function is referred to as a *method*; otherwise, it is referred to as a *member function*. Similarly, if the end developer can call a class variable, it is referred to as a *property*; otherwise, it is referred to as a *member variable.*

The public and private statements

As discussed earlier in the section "Encapsulating complexity," one of the goals of object-oriented programming is to provide a black box, hiding the implementation details from the end developer. To assist with this encapsulation of complexity, VBScript allows you to *hide* methods and properties of an object. Remember, an object should serve as a black box for the end developer; as the creator of an object, you may wish to prevent the end user from directly calling specific methods or setting certain properties.

To create member functions and member variables (methods and properties that are hidden from the end developer), precede the member variable or member function definition with the `Private` keyword. A member function can only be executed from within another one of the class's methods or member functions. A member variable can only be modified or read by code in a class method, member function, or through a `Property Get`, `Property Let`, or `Property Set` statement (which we'll discuss shortly).

 Note that the Initialize and Terminate event handlers in Example 4-1 are declared as `Private`. This prevents the end developer from explicitly triggering these events.

To create a property or method, precede the variable or function definition with the Public keyword. If you don't explicitly specify whether a function or variable should be public or private, the function or variable will be made public.

The following code creates a class with a public method and property and a private method and property:

```
Class MyClass
   'Create a public method
   Public Sub A_Public_Method()
       'Call the private method
        A_Private_Method
   End Sub

   'Create a public property
   Public A_Public_Property       ' Not a good thing to do


   'Create a private method
   Private Sub A_Private_Method()
       '...
   End Sub

   'Create a private property
   Private A_Private_Property
End Class
```

Note that when using either the Public or Private keywords with variables, you leave off the Dim statement. If you decide not to explicitly specify whether or not a variable is Public or Private, you will need to precede the property name with the Dim statement, which will make the variable Public. However, it is highly recommended that you always explicitly indicate whether or not a variable or function is either Public or Private.

Trying to access private methods or properties through an instance of *MyClass* will result in an error (see Example 4-5 and Figure 4-2). However, the method A_Public_Method can execute private methods of MyClass; for example, in the previous code snippet, A_Public_Method calls A_Private_Method.

Example 4-5. Accessing Public and Private Methods and Properties

```
'MyClass definition defined in above code snippet

'Create an instance of MyClass
Dim objMyClass
Set objMyClass = New MyClass

'Since A_Public_Method is Public, this is valid code:
objMyClass.A_Public_Method

'Since A_Public_Property is Public, this is valid code:
```

Example 4-5. Accessing Public and Private Methods and Properties (continued)

```
objMyClass.A_Public_Property = 7

'Since A_Private_Method is Private, this is code is invalid,
'and will cause an error:
objMyClass.A_Private_Method              ' Invalid

'Since A_Private_Proverty is Private, this is code is invalid,
'and will cause an error:
objMyClass.A_Private_Property = 100       ' Invalid

'Since A_Private_Proverty is Private, this is code is invalid too
Dim iValue
iValue = objMyClass.A_Private_Property       ' Invalid
```

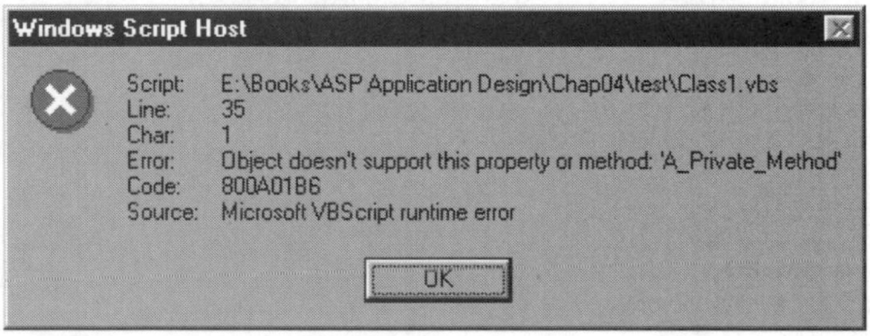

Figure 4-2. An error message generated by Example 4-5

Using Property Get

Since all variables in VBScript are Variants, if we create a public property, we have no control over what type of information the user enters. For example, imagine that we had a class with a property named PhoneNumber. Obviously this variable is intended to store a phone number. However, the developer working with our object could just as easily assign an array to this variable, or an object instance, or a currency value.

In languages like C++, the solution would be to make PhoneNumber a private property and to provide a public method, setPhoneNumber. This public method would expect one parameter: the value of the phone number the end developer wants to assign to PhoneNumber. The setPhoneNumber method would contain code to ensure that the developer couldn't insert an erroneous or improperly formatted phone number. Since PhoneNumber was made private, another public method, getPhoneNumber, would be needed to allow the developer to read the value of the PhoneNumber property.

An identical method can be implemented using VBScript; however, there is a cleaner way to do this in VB/VBScript. As with the C++ method, start by creating all of your properties as `Private`. Then if you wish to allow the end developer to *read* the value of the property, use a `Property Get` statement in your class. A `Property Get` statement has the following syntax:

```
[Public | Private] Property Get PropertyName [(arglist)]
    '... assign the value of the private property to PropertyName ...
End Property
```

Let's examine the phone number property we discussed earlier. First things first: we need to create our private property, *strPhoneNumber*:

```
Class Information
    'Create a private property to hold the phone number
    Private strPhoneNumber
End Class
```

Now, if we wanted to allow the developer using our object to be able to read the value of *strPhoneNumber*, we can add a `Property Get` like so:

```
Class Information
    'Create a private property to hold the phone number
    Private strPhoneNumber

    Public Property Get PhoneNumber()
      PhoneNumber = strPhoneNumber
    End Property
End Class
```

The developer can now read the value of *strPhoneNumber* using the following code:

```
'Assume the class Information is defined
Dim objInfo
Set objInfo = New Information

'This is a legal way to read the property
Response.Write "Phone Number = " & objInfo.PhoneNumber

'This is illegal, since strPhoneNumber is private
Response.Write "Phone Number = " & objInfo.strPhoneNumber
```

Often, developers will give their private properties a Hungarian-notation-like prefix (e.g., *strPhoneNumber*), and will give the corresponding `Property Get` statements more English-like names. For example, ADO's Connection object properties have names like ConnectionString and Timeout, not *strConnectionString* or *iTimeout*.

 Be sure to give your private properties and `Property Get` statements *different* names. If the property and `Property Get` statement share the same names, you will get a "Name redefined" error.

If the property returned by `Property Get` is an object, you must use the `Set` statement when assigning the `Property Get` name to the private property. For example, if *strPhoneNumber* was to contain a Dictionary object instead of a string, in the `Property Get` statement we'd need to use:

```
Public Property Get PhoneNumber()
   Set PhoneNumber = strPhoneNumber
End Property
```

The *arglist* component of the `Property Get` statement should be present when the property requires an argument or index to be properly used. For example, if you had an array as a private property, and wanted to allow the end developer to read a single element from the array as opposed to the entire array, you could use the following code:

```
Class Information
   'Create an array to hold the US States
   Private aStates()

   Private Sub Class_Initialize()
      'ReDim the array to hold 50 states, then populate the array
      ReDim aStates(50)
      aStates(0) = "Alabama"
      ' ... and so on ...
   End Sub

   'Create a Property Get statement to grab a certain index from
   'the aStates array
   Public Property Get States(iIndex)
      States = aStates(iIndex)
   End Property
End Class
```

Once you have an instance of the `Information` class, use the following code to read a particular value from the `aStates` array:

```
'Class Information defined above...

'Create an instance
Dim objInfo
Set objInfo = New Information

'Display the zeroth state
Response.Write objInfo.States(0)

Set objInfo = Nothing
```

Using Property Let

`Property Get` allows an end developer to *retrieve* a private property; `Property Let` enables the end developer to *assign* a value to a private property. `Property Let` statements provide assurances against property corruption. Recall our example at the start of "Using Property Get." If you created a class with a public property named strPhoneNumber, the developer utilizing your class could easily assign *anything* to strPhoneNumber. If the developer wanted strPhoneNumber to contain "Hey there, Bob," he could assign this value to the property. If the developer wanted *strPhoneNumber* to be set to an ADO Recordset object, he could easily assign this value to the property as well.

Of course, you don't want to allow end developers to enter any kind of information into your class's properties. Rather, you want to make sure they enter an accepted datatype with an accepted format. *strPhoneNumber* might require a string datatype with the format ###-###-####. The `Property Let` statement allows for datatype and format checking when an end developer attempts to assign a value to a property.

 Do not use a `Property Let` statement for properties of type Object. Rather, use the `Property Set` statement, which is discussed in detail in the next section, "Using Property Set."

Nearly syntactically identical to the `Property Get` statement, the `Property Let` statement has the following format:

```
[Public | Private] Property Let PropertyName([arglist,] value)
    '... statements: check to see if value is of the correct datatype
    '... and format.  If it is, assign value to the private property
End Property
```

To assign a value to the private property *strPhoneNumber*, we could use the following `Property Let` statement:

```
Class Information
    'Create a private property to hold the phone number
    Private strPhoneNumber

    Public Property Let PhoneNumber(strPhone)
        'Performs no format or type checking, simply assigns the
        'value passed in by the developer to strPhoneNumber
        strPhoneNumber = strPhone
    End Property
End Class
```

The above `Property Let` statement does absolutely no format or type checking on the value the end developer wants to assign to *strPhoneNumber*. The *value* parameter (*strPhone*) of the `Property Let` statement is the value entered by the end developer to the right of the equals sign. In the following code snippet,

"555-4343" would be the *value* parameter passed to the PhoneNumber `Property Let` statement:

```
'Create an instance of the object
Dim objInfo
Set objInfo = New Information

'Assign a value to the phone number
objInfo.PhoneNumber = "555-4343"
```

Of course, performing no format or type checking is silly, since if we don't care what types of data are stored in a particular property, then that property doesn't need to be defined as private. Since we do care about the format of *strPhoneNumber*, let's add some format-checking code in our `Property Let` statement.

When creating format-checking code, you have to decide which formats are acceptable and what to do if the end developer tries to assign an invalid format. For this example, we will accept a telephone format of ###-###-####, and if the end developer enters an invalid format, we'll raise an error. Example 4-6 contains the new class definition for `Information`.

Example 4-6. A More Robust Property Let Statement for PhoneNumber

```
Class Information
  'Create a private property to hold the phone number
  Private strPhoneNumber

  Public Property Let PhoneNumber(strPhone)
    'Ensures that strPhone is in the format ###-###-####
    'If it is not, raise an error
    If IsObject(strPhone) then
      Err.Raise vbObjectError + 1000, "Information Class", _
              "Invalid format for PhoneNumber.  Must be in ###-###-#### format."
      Exit property
    End If

    Dim objRegExp
    Set objRegExp = New regexp

    objRegExp.Pattern = "^\d{3}-\d{3}-\d{4}$"

    'Make sure the pattern fits
    If objRegExp.Test(strPhone) then
      strPhoneNumber = strPhone
    Else
      Err.Raise vbObjectError + 1000, "Information Class", _
              "Invalid format for PhoneNumber.  Must be in ###-###-#### format."
    End If

    Set objRegExp = Nothing
```

Example 4-6. A More Robust Property Let Statement for PhoneNumber (continued)

```
    End Property

    Public Property Get PhoneNumber()
      PhoneNumber = strPhoneNumber
    End Property
End Class
```

If the end developer attempts to execute code such as:

```
    Dim objInfo
    Set objInfo = New Information

    objInfo.PhoneNumber = "This is an invalid phone number!"
```

the error message shown in Figure 4-3 will be displayed when viewed through a browser.

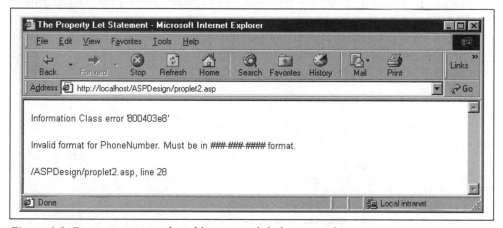

Figure 4-3. Error message produced by an invalid phone number

In the `Property Get`, `Property Let`, and `Property Set` statements, the command `Exit Property` can be used to immediately exit these three statements.

The `Property Let` statement also has an optional *arglist*. This *arglist* must be identical to the *arglist* in the property's corresponding `Property Get` statement, if it exists.

Using Property Set

Classes can have properties that are objects, but special care needs to be taken when returning an object through a `Property Get`, or when using `Property Set` to assign an object a reference. Recall from "Using Property Get" that when return-ing an object reference, it is essential to use the **Set** keyword. For example:

```
Public Property Get PropertyName()
   Set PropertyName = objPrivatePropertyObject
End Property
```

VBScript provides a **Property Set** statement to allow the end developer to assign an object instance to a property. The **Property Set** statement has the following syntax:

```
[Public | Private] Property Set PropertyName([arglist,] reference)
   '... Perform any needed checks here, then use
   'Set objPrivateProperty = PropertyName
End Property
```

The format of **Property Set** is nearly identical to that of **Property Let**. The only functional difference between the two is **Property Let** assigns non-object values to private properties, while **Property Set** assigns object instances to private prop-erties. For example, imagine we had a class that contained a private property named *objConn* that was expected to be an ADO Connection object. The class definition, with the **Property Set** and **Property Get** statements, might look something like:

```
Class MyConnectionClass
   'Create a private property to hold our connection object
   Private objConn

   Public Property Get Connection()
      Set Connection = objConn
   End Property

   Public Property Set Connection(objConnection)
      'Assign the private property objConn to objConnection
      Set objConn = objConnection
   End Property
End Class
```

The end developer would use the **Property Set** statement in the following manner:

```
'Create an instance of MyConnectionClass
Dim objMyClass, objMyRecordset
Set objMyClass = New MyConnectionClass

Set objConnection = Server.CreateObject("ADODB.Connection")

'Assign objConnection to the Connection property
Set objMyClass.Connection = objConnection
```

As with the **Property Let** statement, the **Property Set** statement has an optional *arglist*. This *arglist* must be identical to the corresponding Property Get's *arglist*.

Creating read-only or write-only properties

Using the `Property Get` and `Property Let`/`Property Set` statements enables you to make your private properties editable and readable. However, there is nothing requiring you to use both a `Property Get` and a `Property Let`/`Property Set` for a private property. In fact, you can create read-only and write-only properties by using either just `Property Get` or just `Property Let`/`Property`, respectively.

 Note that while read-only properties are fairly common, write-only properties are not. There are some objects, though, that employ write-only properties, such as the `NewMail` class of the Collaborative Data Objects for NT Server (CDONTS) object. Write-only properties can lead to headaches for developers using your classes, especially if they are unaware the property is write-only. If the property is write-only, an error will be generated if the end developer attempts to do something like the following:

```
objClass.WriteOnlyProperty = 5
Response.Write objClass.WriteOnlyProperty
```

The second line will generate an error, since the value of WriteOnlyProperty cannot be read.

Creating Useful, Reusable Code

In this chapter we discussed the fundamentals of object-oriented programming and looked at how to create classes using VBScript. In the next several chapters, we'll look at how to tie together the lessons learned in this and the previous chapter to create useful, reusable code. Having a solid understanding of object-oriented programming and the associated VBScript syntax is essential, since the next chapters will use classes extensively.

Using Dynamic Evaluation and Execution

As a programmer, you have performed *static evaluation* and *static execution* countless times. For example, the following code snippet performs both static evaluation and static execution:

```
<% @LANGUAGE="VBSCRIPT" %>
<%
  Dim iAnswer
  iAnswer = 22 / 7    'A rough approximation of pi
%>
```

The first line, `Dim iAnswer`, is an example of static execution. When a browser visits the ASP page that the above code snippet resides in, the first line of code is executed, causing a memory location to be set aside to store the value of *iAnswer*. The second line, `iAnswer = 22 / 7`, is an example of both static evaluation and static execution. Initially, the expression `22 / 7` is evaluated, returning the result `3.14285714285714`. The execution occurs when this value is stored into the variable *iAnswer*.

This type of code evaluation and execution is referred to as *static* because the statement being evaluated and the commands being executed are hardcoded into the script. The only way the expression `22 / 7` will change is if a developer edits the actual ASP file by entering a new expression.

The VBScript 5.0 scripting engine offers two functions that facilitate dynamic evaluation and execution. Let us examine each of these issues separately.

Dynamic evaluation

Imagine you wanted to present your users with a form with a single text box, into which they could enter a mathematical expression. Once the form was submitted, the result would be displayed. For example, the user might enter something like `(8 * (5 / 3.5)) - 34`. Example 4-7 contains the code to create this form, and Figure 4-4 displays the form when viewed through a browser.

Example 4-7. A Form to Solve a Mathematical Expression

```
<HTML>
<BODY>
  <FORM METHOD=POST ACTION="SolveMathProblem.asp">
    Enter a mathematical expression (like
    <CODE>5 + 4 * (9 / 4 - 10.5) + 45/2</CODE>):<BR>
    <INPUT TYPE=TEXT NAME=Expression SIZE=40>
    <P>
    <INPUT TYPE=SUBMIT VALUE="Solve this Expression!">
  </FORM>
</BODY>
</HTML>
```

When this form is submitted, *SolveMathProblem.asp* is called and is passed the user's mathematical expression in the form element **Expression**. *SolveMathProblem.asp* dynamically evaluates the user's input using the *Eval* function. The *Eval* function has the following definition:

```
[EvaluationResult = ] Eval(expression)
```

where **expression** is a string variable that contains a valid VBScript expression. *Eval* returns the result of the evaluated **expression** as though it had been hardcoded in the script. The code for *SolveMathProblem.asp*, without any error checking or validation code, is shown in Example 4-8.

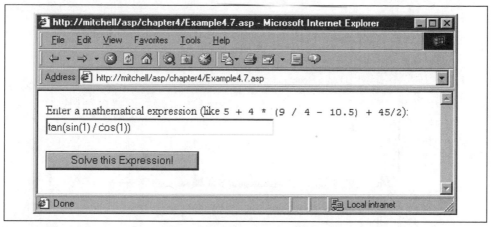

Figure 4-4. The form in Example 4-7 when viewed through a browser

Example 4-8. SolveMathProblem.asp Dynamically Evaluates the User's Input

```
<% @LANGUAGE="VBSCRIPT" %>
<% Option Explicit %>
<%
    'Read in the user's expression
    Dim strExpression
    strExpression = Request("Expression")

    'Output the result
    Response.Write "The mathematical result of:<BR><CODE>"
    Response.Write strExpression & "</CODE><P>is:<BR><CODE>"
    Response.Write Eval(strExpression) & "</CODE>"
%>
```

Eval will generate an error if the ***expression*** parameter is not a valid VBScript expression. If the user entered a non-valid VBScript expression into the text box (such as `Scott Mitchell`) in the form in Example 4-7, *SolveMathProblem.asp* would output a syntax error message, as Figure 4-5 illustrates.

 Allowing your users to directly enter the commands that will be used in dynamic evaluation or dynamic execution is a security risk, to say the least. If you permit your users to enter input that is dynamically executed, they can easily enter malicious code, such as a series of commands that will delete all of the web pages on your site using the FileSystemObject object model. Even allowing your users to directly enter commands that are dynamically evaluated poses a risk. For example, a user could output the contents of your application and session variables, which might contain connection strings or other sensitive information.

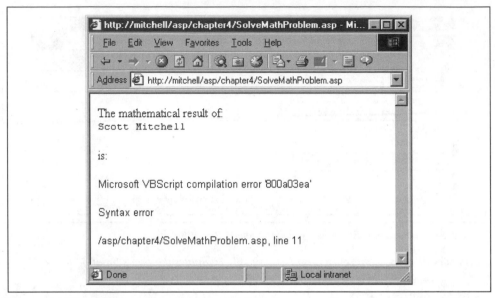

Figure 4-5. The Eval function expects a valid VBScript expression; an invalid expression results in a syntax error

Dynamic execution

The *Eval* function only allows for expression evaluation. If you need to execute a statement—such as an assignment statement, a variable declaration, or a loop—you will need to use the **Execute** statement. The **Execute** statement expects a string parameter that contains one or more statements for execution. If there are multiple statements, they must be delimited by a legal VBScript statement delimiter, namely the carriage return or the colon.

The following code snippet dynamically executes an assignment operation, assigning the value of "Hello, World!" to *strWelcomeMessage*:

```
Dim strStatement
strStatement = "strWelcomeMessage = ""Hello, World!"""
Execute strStatement
```

This next code snippet demonstrates how to execute multiple statements with one call to **Execute**. Note that each statement is delimited by a colon in the first call to **Execute**, while each statement is delimited by a carriage return in the second call to **Execute**:

```
Dim strStatement

'Delimit the statements using a colon
strStatement = "Dim iAge : iAge = 4 : Response.Write iAge"
Execute strStatement

'Delimit the statements using carriage returns
strStatement = "Dim dtBirthdate" & vbCrLf & _
```

```
                    "dtBirthDate = DateSerial(1978, 8, 1)" & vbCrLf & _
                    "Response.Write ""I was born on "" & FormatDateTime(dtBirthDate)"
        Execute strStatement
```

This final code snippet demonstrates how to create a variable-sized array *without* using `Redim`:

```
'Create an array named aPerfectSizedArray

'How many elements should the array contain?
Dim strElementsInArray
strElements = "10"

'Create the array
Dim strStatement
strStatement = "Dim aPerfectSizedArray(" & strElements & ")"

Execute strStatement
```

In VBScript, the equals operator has two functions—logical equivalence and assignment. When using the equals sign with the *Eval* statement, the equals sign serves as the logical equivalence operator. When using an equals sign within an `Execute` statement, the equals sign serves as the assignment operator.

Further Reading

To learn more about the topics covered in this chapter, be sure to read these additional resources:

- For a full list of the VBScript scripting engine version in which particular VBScript language features were implemented, check out *http://msdn. microsoft.com/scripting/default.htm?/scripting/vbscript/doc/vbsversion.htm.*

- To learn more about object-oriented programming, be sure to check out *http:// java.sun.com/docs/books/tutorial/java/concepts/.* While the site does focus on Java technology, it contains worthwhile articles on OOP design and concepts.

- For a good beginner-level discussion on regular expressions, visit *http:// hotwired.lycos.com/webmonkey/geektalk/97/33/index3a.html.*

- The best article I could find on Microsoft's site discussing regular expressions and VBScript is at *http://msdn.microsoft.com/workshop/languages/clinic/ scripting051099.asp.* This article contains a good explanation on how to use the `RegExp` object with VBScript, and supplies some basic regular expression theory.

- To obtain the latest version of the VBScript and JScript scripting engines, visit *http://msdn.microsoft.com/scripting/default.htm?/scripting/vbscript/download/ vbsdown.htm.*

5

Form Reuse

In general, the Web would be a pretty useless place if it weren't for HTML forms. Forms provide an interface for the client to submit information to the web server. The most common form interfaces include search engine interfaces, e-commerce interfaces, and data administration interfaces.

This chapter and the next focus primarily on data administration interface forms. Data administration interfaces are common in many data-driven web sites. For example, if you ran a web site that sold widgets, you'd have a pretty extensive database structure, comprised of many tables containing an assortment of relevant information. This site would also likely contain an extensive set of *administration pages*, where each administration page permitted administrators to update, insert, and delete records into the various database tables.

This chapter does not focus on creating HTML forms, or reading form variables through an ASP page—it's assumed you are familiar with those topics. (If you are a little rusty, don't worry; there's a brief discussion on each of these topics early in the chapter.) What we will be focusing on heavily throughout this chapter and the next is the art of *form reuse.*

The Importance of Code Reuse

Code reuse has many advantages, the paramount one being that developers who practice code reuse become more efficient developers, writing less buggy code. Code reuse obviously saves time in the long run, since you don't have to continuously reinvent the wheel. Code reuse also produces less buggy code. There's a positive correlation between the number of lines of code one writes and the number of bugs present. Ergo, writing fewer lines of code (through reuse) leads to fewer bugs. Furthermore, the more often a particular piece of code is reused, the more certain you can be that the reused code is bug-free. This benefits developers in the debugging phase; if there is a bug in the system, there's a much greater probability it came from a new piece of code than from a code module that has been used in several previous projects without fail.

Code reuse also benefits the end user. For example, all the Microsoft Office applications share the same code for a number of tasks, such as the toolbar functionality and the menu system. Such code reuse provides the end user with a consistent look and feel, flattening the learning curve associated with the various Office applications.

Code Reuse in ASP

ASP provides extensive opportunities for code use. Server-side includes and the Server.Execute method, which we discussed in Chapter 1, *Introduction*, allow developers to modularize their code; COM components, which we'll discuss in Chapter 7, *Using Components*, aid in business logic; as we discussed in Chapter 4, *Regular Expressions, Classes, and Dynamic Evaluation and Execution*, VBScript provides classes that enable the encapsulation of complexity and the ability to hide implementation details. Despite these features, many ASP developers fail to make a serious effort at code reuse.

I think part of the problem is that ASP pages are created using scripting languages. Generic scripts, by their nature, are often small and simple, performing a discrete task. Furthermore, scripts often each have a unique task to complete. For this reason, rarely do ideas of code reuse or modularization come into mind when developing a script.

ASP projects would benefit enormously if ASP developers paid greater attention to issues of code reuse. More often than not, a vast number of ASP scripts on your site perform nearly or even completely identical tasks. In my experience with ASP, I've identified two distinct areas in which developers usually create several common scripts: form use and database access. Creating multiple scripts to do nearly the same thing is not only cumbersome, but also error-prone and far from maintainable. These two areas would benefit the most from extensive and intelligent code reuse.

This chapter, as its name suggests, deals with form reuse. Chapter 6, *Database Reuse*, discusses techniques for code reuse in ASP scripts that utilize databases.

Examining form usage

On a data-driven web site, forms are extremely useful tools that allow visitors to query, insert, delete, or update particular bits of data from a database. Without forms, data-driven web sites are essentially useless.

When creating forms for an ASP web site, the developer will usually follow these steps:

1. Create an HTML form with the proper form fields, complete with client-side form validation.

2. Create a form-processing script and add the needed code.

3. Add server-side form validation code to the ASP page created in Step 2.

In this chapter, we'll look at ways of automating Steps 1 and 3, which are common to all forms throughout a web site. Step 2, of course, will be different depending on the form's intended purpose. However, if we are creating administration pages for use in updating, deleting, or inserting records into a database, we may be able to generalize Step 2. Chapter 6 focuses on reuse of this kind.

Before we jump into a thorough discussion of form reuse for Steps 1 and 3, it is important you have a solid understanding of forms. Specifically, it is important you understand what forms are, the HTML needed to create them, and the ASP code used to process their results. In case you are a bit rusty, the next section provides a quick review of form use.

A Primer on Form Use

Forms exist for one reason—to allow the user to send input to the web server. This input can be used in a vast variety of ways. The input may be web site feedback that is packaged into an email and sent to the webmaster; the input may be search terms for viewing a particular subset of results from a database; the input could be shipping and billing information for an item from an e-commerce web site. Therefore, to collect user input, you must use a form.

Forms play a large role in making the Web truly dynamic. A web site without forms is, most likely, a static web site. Forms have assisted web development by allowing users to visit dynamic web pages whose contents depend upon the user's input.

When using forms, often two pages are used. The first page is the form creation web page, and contains the HTML code needed to display the form and its elements (text boxes, list boxes, checkboxes, etc.). The second page is the form processing script. This is the ASP page that retrieves the form field values entered by the user and performs whatever processing needs to be done.

The next two subsections detail these two pages. The "Creating HTML Forms" section discusses how to generate a form in a web page using the proper HTML code, while the "Processing Forms Through an ASP Page" section details how to read in the form field values entered by a user and make programmatic decisions based upon these values. If you are comfortable with creating forms and reading their values through an ASP page, feel free to skip the following two sections.

Creating HTML Forms

Forms are created in HTML using the FORM tag. The FORM tag has a number of available properties or attributes, the three most important ones being NAME, ACTION, and METHOD. The NAME property gives a name to the form, which is useful when referring to a form through client-side scripting code. The ACTION property specifies the URL of the form processing script. This is the URL that is called when the user submits the form. If omitted, the ACTION property defaults to the URL of the form.

The METHOD property determines how the form data is sent to the web server when the form is submitted. The METHOD property can take one of two values: GET or POST. GET sends the form field names and values through the query string, while POST sends the values through an HTTP header. Nine times out of ten, you'll find that using POST is preferable to using GET. With POST, the form field values are not sent through the query string, which is useful under the following two circumstances:

- The user has entered sensitive information, such as a password, into the form. By displaying the form field information through the querystring, the password could be seen by an onlooker.

- Lengthy form values are expected. Some older browsers limited the total length of the querystring. When dealing with large forms, or forms that expect lengthy inputs from the user, you should use the POST method to prevent overloading of the querystring.

Using GET, though, has its advantages. One major advantage of passing the form field values through the querystring is it allows the visitor to bookmark the results of a particular set of form field values. Since a bookmark saves the entire URL, the form field values that were passed through the querystring are part of the bookmark.

The start of a form is represented with the FORM tag, and the end by a closing FORM tag (</FORM>). Here is an example of a form with no form elements:

```
<FORM NAME=frmMyForm METHOD=POST ACTION="/scripts/FormProcess.asp">
</FORM>
```

The building blocks of forms

A form without any *form elements* is pretty useless. Form elements provide for the collection of user input. Each text box, list box, checkbox, radio button, and image is considered a form element (sometimes referred to as a form field). Text boxes, checkboxes, buttons, and radio buttons are created using the INPUT tag; list boxes are created using the SELECT tag with zero to many OPTION tags; and multi-row text boxes are created using the TEXTAREA tag.

Each of these three tags has its own set of available properties. However, all have one very important property in common: the NAME property. The NAME property uniquely identifies each form field within the form. This NAME property is also what is used to retrieve the value entered for a particular form field in the form-processing script.

Since text boxes, checkboxes, and radio buttons are all created using the same HTML INPUT tag, a mechanism to specify what type of form element to create with the INPUT tag must exist. The TYPE property of the INPUT tag performs this task. The TYPE property can have one of three values: TEXT, CHECKBOX, or RADIO, which create a text box, checkbox, or radio button, respectively.

To learn more about the various properties of the form element tags, be sure to pick up a book on HTML design. Throughout the examples in this chapter, the form elements usually contain only the essential properties: NAME and TYPE.

Processing Forms Through an ASP Page

Recall that form information is sent from the client to the server via an HTTP request. It's not surprising, then, that the ASP Request object is used to obtain the form information submitted by the web visitor. The Request object contains two collections, Form and QueryString, that are useful for collecting form information.

When a user submits information through a form, the browser compacts the user's form field entries into a single string. This string contains each form element's name and value. Each form element name/value is delimited by an ampersand (&); in each name/value pair, an equals sign delimits the name and value. A raw string sent by the browser to the web server looks like:

```
FormFieldName1=FormFieldValue1&FormFieldName2=FormFieldValue2...
```

When the ASP form-processing script receives this string, it parses it into the appropriate Request object collection. If the form's METHOD parameter was set to GET, the above string is passed through the query string and the Request.QueryString collection is populated. If the form's METHOD parameter was set to POST instead, the above string is populated in the Request.Form collection. Even though ASP unpacks this string into the various collections, the string in its entirety can easily be accessed with the following code:

```
'Display the packed string that has been populated in
'the QueryString collection
Response.Write Request.QueryString
```

```
'Display the packed string that has been populated in
'the Form collection
Response.Write Request.Form
```

To access a particular element in the form field, simply specify the name of the form field like so:

```
'Return the value of the form field named FormField1
Request.QueryString("FormFieldName1")
```

If you attempt to retrieve the value of the QueryString or the Form property when the property contains no data, or if you attempt to retrieve the value of a non-existent field from either collection, an empty string will be returned; ASP does not raise an error.

Working with the QueryString and Form collections

Since Request.QueryString and Request.Form are collections, you can use the standard methods and properties of collections. For example, to return the number of elements in the Request.Form collection, use the Count property like so:

```
'Output the number of elements in the Request.Form collection
Response.Write "There are " & Request.Form.Count & " element(s) " & _
              "in the Request.Form collection"
```

To iterate through either one of these collections, use either a For Each ... Next loop or a counting loop. An example of using a For Each ... Next loop can be seen in Example 5-1. Note that when iterating through the collection using a For Each ... Next loop, each name in the name/value pairs is returned. In Example 5-1, *strName* is assigned the value of the name in the name/value pair through the For Each ... Next loop. To obtain the value in a name/value pair, use Request.QueryString(strName).

Example 5-1. Iterating with a For Each ... Next Loop

```
<%@ LANGUAGE = "VBSCRIPT" %>
<% Option Explicit %>
<HTML>
<BODY>
  <TABLE ALIGN=CENTER BORDER=1>
  <TR>
    <TH>Name</TH>
    <TH>Value</TH>
  </TR>
<%
    'Use a For Each ... Next to loop through the QueryString collection
    Dim strName
    For Each strName in Request.QueryString
      Response.Write "<TR><TD>"
      Response.Write strName
      Response.Write "</TD><TD>"
      Response.Write Request.QueryString(strName)
      Response.Write "</TD></TR>"
```

Example 5-1. Iterating with a For Each ... Next Loop (continued)

```
    Next
%>
  </TABLE>
</BODY>
</HTML>
```

The QueryString or Form collections can also be iterated by using a counting loop. Since we can obtain the number of elements in the collection using the Count property, and since the elements of a collection can be visited via an index, we can use the following code to visit each element in a collection:

```
<%@ LANGUAGE = "VBSCRIPT" %>
<% Option Explicit %>
<%
    'Use a counting loop to visit each element
    Dim iLoop, iCount
    iCount = Request.Form.Count

    For iLoop = 1 to iCount
        Response.Write "Value at " & iLoop & ": " & Request.Form(iLoop)
        Response.Write "<P><HR><P>"
    Next
%>
```

 The QueryString and Form collections are indexed starting at one.

Often you'll see code that doesn't specify whether to read from the QueryString or Form collection. For example, the code might read:

```
'Store the user's name into strName
Dim strName
strName = Request("UserName")
```

When a collection is not specified, the QueryString collection is scanned first. If the particular form field name/value pair does not exist within the QueryString collection, the Form collection is searched. If the name/value pair is not found in the Form collection either, a blank string (" ") is returned. This method's main advantage is that as a developer creating a form-processing script, you don't have to worry about the method used by the developer creating the HTML form. The disadvantage of using this method, though, is that by not explicitly specifying what collection to search for, the code becomes a bit ambiguous. As we begin to practice form reuse, you'll see that the advantage of not having to specify the correct collection greatly outweighs the disadvantage.

Form Validation

With ASP, information collected through a form interface is often used to modify a database in some way. Databases are only as good as the data within them. A database saturated with meaningless or improperly formatted data is worthless. Therefore, when creating ASP pages that will directly modify databases based upon input gathered through a form, it is vital that the user entering the form information enters valid data.

The process of ensuring that form fields contain valid input is referred as *form validation*. Form validation can occur on both the client side and server side. In the next two sections, "Client-Side Form Validation" and "Server-Side Form Validation," we'll discuss the advantages and disadvantages of each method.

Client-Side Form Validation

Client-side form validation, as the name implies, is form validation that happens on the client. A web page containing a form can optionally contain client-side JavaScript code that will execute when the user attempts to submit the form. This JavaScript code can then scan the user's form entries, making sure they have a particular format.

The main advantage of client-side form validation is the fact that the validation occurs completely on the client's computer. Therefore, if the user has entered invalid form data, they don't have to wait for a round trip to the web server before they know whether or not they've entered invalid data. Many sites employ this type of form validation. For example, an e-commerce site might provide form validation for the form fields supplied for the customer's address.

Client-side form validation is not without its disadvantages, though. If the browser being used does not support JavaScript, or the user has JavaScript disabled, then client-side form validation will not execute. Furthermore, any visitor can easily view the client-side form validation code by viewing the HTML source sent to her browser. If this user wishes to send invalid data, they could take the time to determine what types of data would "slip by" the client-side form validation. Additionally, a visitor entering the URL of the form-processing script into his or her browser and passing illegal form variable values through the querystring can circumvent client-side form validation.

Also, a malicious user can sidestep client-side form validation through the following sequence of steps:

1. Save the HTML/client-side validation source code.

2. Remove the client-side validation source code.

3. Reload the modified HTML through a browser and submit the form with invalid data.

For this reason, you should not rely on just client-side form validation; it should always be used in conjunction with server-side form validation. Client-side form validation is a nice tool, though, and can be used in addition to server-side form validation.

An example of client-side form validation can be seen in Example 5-2.

Example 5-2. Client-Side Form Validation

```
<HTML>
<HEAD>
  <SCRIPT LANGUAGE="JavaScript">
  <!--
    function ValidateData()
    {
        // Check to make sure the zip code contains either
        // ##### or #####-####
        var strZip = document.frmInfo.Zip.value, iLoop;
        if (strZip.length == 5 || strZip.length == 10)
        {
          // Ok, the zip code is the correct length, make sure
          // it contains all numeric characters if length is
          // 5, or, if length is 10, contains 5 numeric, a dash,
          // and 4 numeric
          if (strZip.length == 5)
          {
            for (iLoop=0; iLoop < strZip.length; iLoop++)
              if (strZip.charAt(iLoop) < '0' || strZip.charAt(iLoop) > '9')
              {
                  alert("You have entered an invalid zip code.");
                  return false;
              }
          } else {
            // the string is 10 characters long
            for (iLoop=0; iLoop < 5; iLoop++)
              if (strZip.charAt(iLoop) < '0' || strZip.charAt(iLoop) > '9')
              {
                  alert("You have entered an invalid zip code.");
                  return false;
              }

            if (strZip.charAt(5) != '-')
            {
                alert("You have entered an invalid zip code.");
```

Example 5-2. Client-Side Form Validation (continued)

```
                return false;
          }

          for (iLoop=6; iLoop < strZip.length; iLoop++)
            if (strZip.charAt(iLoop) < '0' || strZip.charAt(iLoop) > '9')
            {
                alert("You have entered an invalid zip code.");
                return false;
            }
        }
    } else
      {
      alert("The zip code has an invalid number of characters");
      return false;
      }

      // If we've reached this point, the data is valid, so return true
      return true;
   }
  // -->
  </SCRIPT>
</HEAD>
<BODY>
  <FORM NAME=frmInfo METHOD=POST ACTION="somePage.asp"
     ONSUBMIT="return ValidateData();">
   Enter your zip code:<BR>
   <INPUT TYPE=TEXT NAME=Zip SIZE=10>
   <P>
   <INPUT TYPE=SUBMIT>
  </FORM>
</BODY>
</HTML>
```

 Although not demonstrated in Example 5-2, regular expressions are available in JavaScript 1.2, which is available in Netscape and Internet Explorer Version 4.0 and up. Regular expressions, as demonstrated in Example 5-4, make validation much easier.

Server-Side Form Validation

Server-side form validation is form validation that occurs on the web server. Server-side form validation's major disadvantage is it requires a round trip to the web server to determine whether or not a form field contains valid data. For example, imagine you have a form that asks for the user's age. Of course, only values between 1 and 120 would be valid entries. An age of –98 is impossible; an age of "Yellow school bus" is nonsensical. If a user enters one of these invalid responses, though, he has to wait for the form field value to be sent to the web server, and have a page returned explaining the data entered was invalid.

Of course, this disadvantage is becoming less and less of an issue as Internet connection speeds become faster and faster. However, with a large number of users still connecting via a modem, this disadvantage is still a legitimate concern. This drawback of server-side validation, though, can be compensated with adequate client-side form validation. When both client-side and server-side form validation are used, the server-side form validation should duplicate the validation performed on the client side. In such a scenario, the server-side form validation serves only as a safety catch in case the user either mistakenly steps around the client-side form validation (perhaps they have JavaScript disabled), or purposely avoids client-side validation (a malicious user).

In Example 5-2, we used client-side form validation to validate a zip code. In Example 5-3, the same data is validated, but this time using server-side validation. It is recommended you use *both* client-side and server-side form validation when validating user form input.

Example 5-3. Classical Server-Side Form Validation

```
<% @LANGUAGE="VBSCRIPT" %>
<% Option Explicit %>
<%
    'Read in the form variable
    Dim strZip, iLoop
    strZip = Request("Zip")

    'Check to make sure the zip contains either ##### or #####-####
    If Len(strZip) = 5 or Len(strZip) = 10 then
        ' ok, the zip code is the correct length, make sure
        ' it contains all numeric characters if length is
        ' 5, or, if length is 10, contains 5 numeric, a dash,
        ' and 4 numeric
        If Len(strZip) = 5 then
          For iLoop = 1 to Len(strZip)
            If Asc(Mid(strZip, iLoop, 1)) < Asc("0") or _
                Asc(Mid(strZip, iLoop, 1)) > Asc("9") then
              Response.Write "You entered an invalid zip code."
              Response.End
            End If
          Next
        Else
          ' the string is 10 characters long
          For iLoop=1 to 5
            If Asc(Mid(strZip, iLoop, 1)) < Asc("0") or _
                Asc(Mid(strZip, iLoop, 1)) > Asc("9") then
              Response.Write "You entered an invalid zip code."
              Response.End
            End If
          Next

          If Asc(Mid(strZip, iLoop, 6)) <> Asc("-") then
            Response.Write "You entered an invalid zip code."
            Response.End
```

Example 5-3. Classical Server-Side Form Validation (continued)

```
        End If

        For iLoop=7 to Len(strZip)
          If Asc(Mid(strZip, iLoop, 1)) < Asc("0") or _
             Asc(Mid(strZip, iLoop, 1)) > Asc("9") then
            Response.Write "You entered an invalid zip code."
            Response.End
          End If
        Next
      End If
  Else
    Response.Write "You entered an invalid zip code."
    Response.End
  End If

  ' If we reached here, we had valid input, continue
  ' with form processing...
  Response.Write "You entered valid input, thanks!"
%>
```

In Example 5-3, classical VBScript methods were used to validate a particular input. While these methods are sufficient, they leave a lot to be desired. With the VBScript 5.0 scripting engine, a new regular expression object has been added, allowing regular expression pattern matching in VBScript!

Regular expressions offer more robust form-validation techniques than simply using the techniques in Example 5-3. Example 5-4 uses regular expression matching to perform the same form validation as in Example 5-3.

Example 5-4. Server-Side Form Validation via Regular Expressions

```
<% @LANGUAGE="VBSCRIPT" %>
<% Option Explicit %>
<%
    'Read in the form variable
    Dim strZip, iLoop
    strZip = Request("Zip")

    'Check to make sure the zip contains either ##### or #####-####
    Dim objRegExp
    Set objRegExp = New regexp

    objRegExp.Pattern = "^\d{5}(-\d{4})?$"

    If Not objRegExp.Test(strZip) then
      Response.Write "Invalid input - zip code has an invalid value!"
      Response.End
    End If

    'Otherwise, we have valid, so do stuff!
    ' ...
    Response.Write "Valid data!!!"
%>
```

For more information on form validation, be sure to check out the following on-line resources:

- "Form Validation Using JavaScript" at *http://www.4guysfromrolla.com/webtech/091998-1.shtml*

- "Server-side Form Validation" found at *http://www.4guysfromrolla.com/webtech/120199-1.shtml*

- "Advanced Form Validation" found at *http://www.asptoday.com/articles/19990708.htm*

- "Validate What? Using Regular Expressions to Validate Input" at *http://www.4guysfromrolla.com/webtech/050399-2.shtml*

Creating Reusable Server-Side Form Validation Routines

Earlier in this chapter, in the section "Code Reuse in ASP," we discussed the three common steps taken to create a form:

1. Create an HTML form with the proper form fields, complete with client-side form validation.

2. Create a form-processing script and add the needed code.

3. Add server-side form validation code to the ASP page created in Step 2.

At that time, I mentioned we would look at ways to create robust, reusable code for Steps 1 and 3. Since server-side form validation is paramount to client-side form validation, it makes sense to start by creating code for Step 1. In this section, we will look at how to create a single, reusable ASP page that uses regular expressions to validate form data. In "Developing Reusable Form Creation Routines," the discussion will switch to creating a class interface to aid in accomplishing Step 1.

Our reusable server-side form validation routine will exist on the */CODEREUSE/ValidateForm.asp* ASP page. (That means *every* form on our web site will have its ACTION property set to */CODEREUSE/ValidateForm.asp*.) This page will contain code that will iterate through the proper collection of the Request object, reading in the value of each form field and determining whether or not the value is valid.

Our validation page, */CODEREUSE/ValidateForm.asp*, needs to know what constitutes a valid entry for each and every form field. We'll supply this information in the NAME property of the form field. Since regular expressions are used to validate form field input, each form field that needs to be validated will contain the proper regular expression appended to the NAME property. For example, if we had a form field for the user to enter his telephone number, we would use the following HTML to create the text box:

```
<FORM METHOD="POST" ACTION="/CODEREUSE/ValidateForm.asp">
    <INPUT TYPE="HIDDEN" NAME="Collection" VALUE="Form">
    <INPUT TYPE="HIDDEN" NAME="Redirect" VALUE="/SomePage.asp">

    <!-- This will be validated, since the element name contains an
         exclamation point followed by the needed regular expression. -->
    Enter your phone number in the following format: ###-###-####<BR>
    <INPUT TYPE="TEXT" NAME="Phone Number!^\d{3}-\d{3}-\d{4}$">
    <P>
    <!-- This form field will NOT be subjected to any validated tests
         since it does not contain the exclamation point in its name. -->
    Enter your first name:<BR>
    <INPUT TYPE="TEXT" NAME="First Name">
    <P>
    <INPUT TYPE="SUBMIT" VALUE="Submit!">
</FORM>
```

What Format Do You Want That In?

If you are going to require that your users enter data in a particular format (such as a phone number in ###-###-#### format), make sure you let your users know what format they need to enter the information in!

A common mistake web developers make is not letting their users know what format they are expected to enter the data in. Therefore, if the user enters the data in an invalid format, she may become agitated, especially if she is continually asked to re-enter "valid" data when she doesn't know what the "valid" format is!

Note that an exclamation point separates the English-like name of the form field (*txtPhone*) and the regular expression (\d{3}-\d{3}-\d{4}). The regular expression will be used to validate the user's input in */CODEREUSE/ ValidateForm.asp*. Also note that the form's ACTION property directs the submitted form to */CODEREUSE/ValidateForm.asp*.

The above form also contains two HIDDEN form fields. The first HIDDEN form field, *Collection*, specifies what Request object collection to use. The Value for this HIDDEN form field would have been *QueryString*, had the form's METHOD been set to GET. The second HIDDEN form field, *Redirect*, specifies the ASP page that is responsible for processing the form data. This page (via a Server.Transfer) is called only if the submitted form data is valid.

Be absolutely sure to place the quotes around the form field **NAME** value! If not, any spaces in the form field **NAME** will cut off the rest of the **NAME** when passed to the server-side validation script. If you need to have double quotes in the regular expression, you must represent the double quote with some other character and have it transformed back into a double quote in the server-side validation script.

The code for */CODEREUSE/ValidateForm.asp* will perform the following steps:

1. Determine what Request collection to use. (If this isn't specified via the *Collection* **HIDDEN** variable, the Request.Form collection is used by default.)

2. Iterate through the proper collection, checking to see what form fields contain an exclamation point.

3. For those elements that do contain an exclamation point, read in the regular expression pattern and perform a regular expression match using the *Test* method of the *RegExp* object.

4. If the *Test* method returns False, then the input is invalid. Note this invalid entry in an error log.

5. Once the entire collection has been iterated, determine whether any validation errors occurred. If so, output these errors. If not, use *Server.Transfer* to forward the user onto the form-processing script specified by the **HIDDEN** variable *Redirect*.

Quite a tall order for */CODEREUSE/ValidateForm.asp*! Here is the code, with the regular expression validation emphasized:

```
<%@ LANGUAGE = "VBSCRIPT" %>
<% Option Explicit %>
<%
    Function EnglishName(str)
      'Check to see if there is an exclamation point: if so, hack off
      'all contents of the string to the right of the exclamation point
      If InStr(1,str,"!") > 0 then
        EnglishName = Left(str,InStr(1,str,"!") - 1)
      End If
    End Function


    'Determine what collection to use
    Dim strCollection
    strCollection = Request("Collection")

    'Create a reference to the property Request collection
    Dim colRequestCol
    If Ucase(strCollection) = "QUERYSTRING" then
      Set colRequestCol = Request.QueryString
    Else
```

```
       Set colRequestCol = Request.Form
     End If


     Dim strItem, strErrors, objRegExp, strErrorLog
     Set objRegExp = New regexp     ' Create a regexp instance
     objRegExp.IgnoreCase = True
     objRegExp.Global = True

     'Iterate through each of the form field elements
     For Each strItem in colRequestCol
        'See if there is an exclamation point.  If there is,
        'then we need to perform form validation
        If InStr(1,strItem,"!") > 0 then
          'Grab the regular expression pattern
          objRegExp.Pattern = Mid(strItem, InStr(1,strItem,"!") + 1, Len(strItem))
          If Not objRegExp.Test(colRequestCol(strItem)) then
            'Input invalid!  Append to the error log
            strErrorLog = strErrorLog & "<BR>Invalid Input for " & _
                        EnglishName(strItem)
          End If
        End If
     Next

     'Are there any errors?
     If Len(strErrorLog) > 0 then
        Response.Write "<B>The following validation errors occurred:</B>"
        Response.Write strErrorLog
     Else
        'No form validation errors occurred!
        'Use Server.Transfer to send the user to the proper
        'form validation script
        'If the user didn't specify a redirect, raise an error
        If Len(Request("Redirect")) = 0 then
           Raise vbObjectError + 1010, "Validation Error", "Redirect not specified"
        Else
           Server.Transfer Request("Redirect")
        End If
     End If

     Set colRequestCol = Nothing     ' Clean up
     Set objRegExp = Nothing
%>
```

Keep in mind that */CODEREUSE/ValidateForm.asp* serves only one purpose—to
perform server-side validation. If there are no validation errors, the script transfers
control to the form-processing page specified by the HIDDEN form field *Redirect*.
Due to the fact that */CODEREUSE/ValidateForm.asp* only performs server-side validation and transfers the user to the correct form-processing script, all of our HTML
pages can call this single validation page. This means once this system is implemented, when creating a form, you will not have to code its server-side validation! Figure 5-1 further illustrates the page flow that occurs when a form is
submitted.

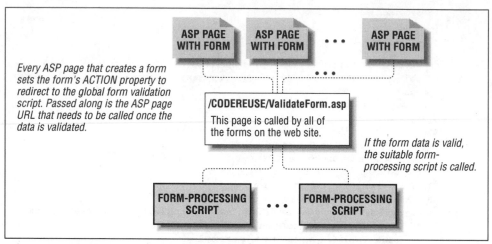

Every ASP page that creates a form sets the form's ACTION property to redirect to the global form validation script. Passed along is the ASP page URL that needs to be called once the data is validated.

Figure 5-1. /CODEREUSE/ValidateForm.asp validates all forms on the site

Beware of Malicious Users

As discussed in the previous section "Server-Side Form Validation," one of the reasons to use server-side form validation is to prevent malicious users from circumventing form validation. With the approach shown in */CODEREUSE/ ValidateForm.asp*, a malicious user could easily bypass the server-side form validation. By simply stripping the exclamation point and the regular expression that follows it from the form element NAMEs, a malicious user could send invalid data to the form-processing script that wouldn't be caught by the server-side form-validation routine.

Due to this issue, this server-side validation approach should not be used where malicious users might attempt to bypass validation. For example, on a large, publicly accessible e-commerce site, such a form-validation technique should not be applied to vital forms, such as billing information forms. This is a trade off that must be made for this application. When building a generic, reusable script, often other sacrifices must be made.

Note that this server-side form-validation approach will still work for those users who have JavaScript disabled. Since the form field validation information is stored in the form element NAMEs, and since the actual validation is performed on the server, it does not matter if the user has JavaScript enabled.

Now, let's look at how to encapsulate the logic in */CODEREUSE/ValidateForm.asp* through the use of classes!

Using Classes to Enhance Server-Side Validation

As discussed in Chapter 4, classes provide a means to encapsulate complexity. Our first implementation of */CODEREUSE/ValidateForm.asp* is rich in complexity. The developer who wishes to make any modifications to this page must know that the names of form variables may contain an exclamation point and regular expression code. It would be nice to hide such complexity.

 There is also a lot of complexity in creating the HTML forms. We'll look at ways to reduce this complexity using classes later on!

When encapsulating the server-side form-validation routines into a class, the functionality remains constant—only the implementation changes. For that reason, creating the class is mostly cut and paste work! A few enhancements have been made to the new class version, though. The major enhancement is the use of a Dictionary object to store the validation error information (*objErrorDict*). The changes made due to this enhancement are emphasized in the following code snippet:

```
<%
Class FormData
    '***************** PROPERTIES ********************
    Private colRequestCol
    Private objRegExp
    Private objErrorDict
    '************************************************

    '************* INITIALIZE/TERMINATE *************
    Private Sub Class_Initialize()
        'Determine what Request collection to use
        If Ucase(Request("Collection")) = "QUERYSTRING" then
          Set colRequestCol = Request.QueryString
        Else
          Set colRequestCol = Request.Form
        End If

        'Instantiate a regexp object
        Set objRegExp = New regexp
        objRegExp.IgnoreCase = True
        objRegExp.Global = True

        'Instantiate the error log
        Set objErrorDict = CreateObject("Scripting.Dictionary")
    End Sub

    Private Sub Class_Terminate()
        Set colRequestCol = Nothing
```

```
      Set objRegExp = Nothing
      Set objErrorDict = Nothing
End Sub
'**************************************************

'************* PROPERTY GET STATMENT **************
Public Property Get ErrorLog()
   'Return the Error Log Dictionary Object
   Set ErrorLog = objErrorDict
End Property
'**************************************************

'******************** METHODS ********************
Public Function ValidInputs()
   'Checks to see if data is valid.  If it is, returns
   'True, else returns False.  A list of errors can be
   'obtained through PrintErrors

   Dim strItem

   'Iterate through each of the form field elements
   For Each strItem in colRequestCol
      'See if there is an exclamation point.  If there is,
      'then we need to perform form validation
      If InStr(1,strItem,"!") > 0 then
         'Grab the regular expression pattern
         objRegExp.Pattern = Mid(strItem, InStr(1,strItem,"!") + 1, _
                                 Len(strItem))
         If Not objRegExp.Test(colRequestCol(strItem)) then
            'Input invalid!  Append to the error log
            objErrorDict.Add EnglishName(strItem), _
                              colRequestCol(strItem).Item
         End If
      End If
   Next

   'Did we encounter any errors?
   If objErrorDict.Count > 0 then
      ValidInputs = False
   Else
      ValidInputs = True
   End If
End Function


Private Function EnglishName(ByVal str)
   'Check to see if there is an exclamation point: if so, hack off
   'all contents of the string to the right of the exclamation point
   If InStr(1,str,"!") > 0 then
      str = Left(str,InStr(1,str,"!") - 1)
   End If
```

```
      EnglishName = Replace(str, "_", " ")
   End Function


   Public Function ErrorMessage()
     'Returns a string containing an error message
     If objErrorDict.Count = 0 then
        ErrorMessage = "There were no validation errors."
     Else
        Dim strName
        For Each strName in objErrorDict
          ErrorMessage = ErrorMessage & "Error in " & strName & _
              " - the entry " & objErrorDict(strName) & _
              " is invalid." & vbCrLf
        Next
     End If
   End Function
   '**************************************************
  End Class
%>
```

If we place the above class definition into a file, then we can use a server-side
include to import the class definition into the ASP pages that are interested in
using the class. Classes reduce complexity by hiding implementation details, and
as they say, the proof is in the pudding. Previously, */CODEREUSE/ValidateForm.
asp* consisted of 57 lines of code. Using classes and include files, the line count
has been reduced drastically to 18 lines!

```
<%@ LANGUAGE = "VBSCRIPT" %>
<% Option Explicit %>
<!--#include virtual="/CODEREUSE/FormData.Class.asp"-->
<%
    'Instantiate our class defined in FormData.Class.asp
    Dim objFormData
    Set objFormData = New FormData

    'Test to see if form inputs are valid
    If objFormData.ValidInputs() then
       'No form validation errors occurred!
       'Use Server.Transfer to send the user to the proper
       'form validation script
       'If the user didn't specify a redirect, raise an error
       If Len(Request("Redirect")) = 0 then
          Raise vbObjectError + 1010, "Validation Error", "Redirect not specified"
       Else
          Server.Transfer Request("Redirect")
       End If
    Else
       'Display an error message
       Response.Write objFormData.ErrorMessage()
    End if

    Set objFormData = Nothing
%>
```

If you are a little rusty on using include files within an ASP page, be sure to review Chapter 1 and check out the following online article "The low-down on #includes" at *http://www.4GuysFromRolla.com/ webtech/080199-1.shtml*.

Further enhancements to the server-side validation class

There are, of course, numerous improvements that could be made to the server-side validation class. One major improvement would be to have a method that not only displays the invalid form entries, but also displays the form the user just filled out, so they can quickly make the changes they need to.

One possible way to accomplish this would be to have the form supply yet another HIDDEN variable that would contain the URL to the HTML form. Then a method could be added that would perform a Server.Transfer back to the form after displaying the invalid form entries. That way, the user would see a list of the invalid form fields at the top of the HTML page, and then would be shown the form again. (This would save the user from having to click the back button when he or she has entered invalid form data.)

Developing Reusable Form Creation Routines

As promised, in this section we will examine reusable methods to create HTML forms with the proper form fields, complete with client-side form validation. These methods will hide the specific details of properly naming form fields and will not bother the developer with creating client-side form validation routines.

Form Implementation Complexity

Usually, creating a form is a trivial task; it's just a matter of HTML coding. However, due to our reusable server-side validation code, creating a form has become a much more complex issue. When using a global server-side form validation page that all forms initially submit to, all the forms need to follow a certain standard. Specifically, the NAME of each form element that requires form validation must contain an exclamation point followed by the validation regular expression. Furthermore, the form's ACTION property must direct to the validation page (*/CODEREUSE/ ValidateForm.asp*) and pass two HIDDEN variables: *Collection* and *Redirect*.

Remembering these specific details is cumbersome and serves as an easy place to make a mistake, resulting in a bug. Also, if other developers are to be working on creating the HTML forms, they will be less familiar with the conventions specified by the server-side form validation script, */CODEREUSE/ValidateForm.asp*.

As discussed earlier, client-side form validation is a nice option, although not as critical as server-side form validation. As with server-side form validation, client-side form validation lends itself to reuse.

Masking Implementation Complexity Using Classes

To reduce implementation complexity and provide a black box-like interface, we'll use classes! Two classes can be created that will provide the following benefits:

- Provide the end developer with an easy interface to create forms that contain complex implementation details.

- Provide automatic code generation for client-side form validation.

The first class defines a form field element as an object. Each form field object has a certain set of properties: **NAME**, **TYPE**, **SIZE**, and **VALUE** are four standard ones. For our custom server-side validation routines, an optional validation regular expression is yet another property. Our rather simplistic form field class, **FormElement**, contains the following definition, which is stored in the file *CODEREUSE\FormCreation.Class.asp*:

```
<%
Class FormElement
  '****************** PROPERTIES ********************
  Private strName
  Private strRegExp
  Private strType
  Private strPreHTML
  Private strPostHTML
  Private strSize
  Private strValue
  '*************************************************


  '************* PROPERTY LET STATMENTS *************
  Public Property Let Name(str)
      strName = str
  End Property

  Public Property Let RegularExpression(str)
      strRegExp = str
  End Property

  Public Property Let ElementType(str)
      'Only one of six types possible: SELECT, TEXTAREA, TEXT,
      '    RADIO, HIDDEN, or CHECKBOX (TEXT is the default)
      If Ucase(str) = "TEXT" OR Ucase(str) = "SELECT" _
            OR Ucase(str) = "TEXTAREA" OR Ucase(str) = "RADIO" _
            OR Ucase(str) = "CHECKBOX" OR Ucase(str) = "HIDDEN" then
        strType = str
```

```
   Else
     strType = "TEXT"        'TEXT is the default type
   End If
End Property

Public Property Let Size(str)
   strSize = str
End Property

Public Property Let PreHTML(str)
   strPreHTML = str
End Property

Public Property Let PostHTML(str)
   strPostHTML = str
End Property

Public Property Let Value(str)
   strValue = str
End Property
'**************************************************

'************* PROPERTY GET STATMENTS *************
Public Property Get Name()
   Name = strName
End Property

Public Property Get RegularExpression()
   RegularExpression = strRegExp
End Property

Public Property Get ElementType()
   ElementType = strType
End Property

Public Property Get Size()
   Size = strSize
End Property

Public Property Get PreHTML()
   PreHTML = strPreHTML
End Property

Public Property Get PostHTML()
   PostHTML = strPostHTML
End Property

Public Property Get Value()
   Value = strValue
End Property
'**************************************************

'******************** METHODS ********************
Public Sub Clear()
   strName = ""
```

```
            strRegExp = ""
            strType = ""
            strSize = ""
            strPreHTML = ""
            strPostHTML = ""
            strValue = ""
        End Sub
        '****************************************************
    End Class
    %>
```

A `FormElement` class instance represents a discrete form field element in a form. This implementation of `FormElement` contains only a small subset of the properties a form field element can contain. If your web site requires more elegant form fields, add the needed form field properties in the above class. The following list shows the various properties of the `FormElement` class:

Name (Read/Write)

Specifies the `NAME` property of the form element. It is essential this property is specified. Furthermore, it is recommended that you give the `NAME` property an English-like name, since if there is a validation error, this property is reported in the error message.

RegularExpression (Read/Write)

Specifies the regular expression validation code. Remember the validation routine will search to see if the user's input matches this regular expression.

ElementType (Read/Write)

Specifies the `TYPE` for the form element. This can have one of six possible values: `SELECT`, `TEXTAREA`, `TEXT`, `RADIO`, `CHECKBOX`, or `HIDDEN`, which create a list box, a multi-row text box, a single-row text box, a radio button, a checkbox, or a hidden form field, respectively.

PreHTML (Read/Write)

This property specifies any HTML that should occur before the actual `INPUT` tag.

PostHTML (Read/Write)

This property specifies any HTML that should occur after the actual `INPUT` tag.

Size (Read/Write)

This property specifies the `SIZE` property for the form element. In a multi-row text box, there are as many columns as specified by the Size property and one-fourth as many rows.

Value (Read/Write)

This property specifies the *VALUE* property of the `INPUT` tag. It is meaningless if you are creating a list box, multi-row text box, radio button, or checkbox. The Value property is very useful when creating `HIDDEN` form fields.

The `FormElement` class uses the Clear method, as described in the following definition:

Clear

The Clear method erases all of the property values. Normally such a method wouldn't be needed. The sidebar "Adding Form Elements" later in this chapter explains why I chose to supply such a method.

We'll look at how to use the `FormElement` class and its properties and methods once we examine the `GenerateForm` class.

`GenerateForm` is the class used to create the HTML that will physically construct the form on the users' browsers. Each function of `GenerateForm`'s properties is outlined here:

Collection (Read/Write)

Specifies whether to submit the form using an `ACTION` of `POST` (the default) or `GET`. To use `GET`, Collection must be set equal to QueryString. If it equals any other value, the form will submit with an `ACTION` of `POST`.

Redirect (Read/Write)

The URL of the actual form-processing script. Once the data is validated by */CODEREUSE/ValidateForm.asp*, this is the page the user is passed to.

FormName (Read/Write)

Specifies the `NAME` property of the form. If not specified, *frmForm1* is used. If you plan to use the `GenerateForm` class to create more than one form on an HTML page, it is essential that each form have its own, unique FormName for client-side form-validation purposes.

FormAction (Read/Write)

Specifies the URL of the server-side form validation script. Set to */CODEREUSE/ ValidateForm.asp* in the Initialize event, but can be modified.

SubmitTitle (Read/Write)

The title for the form's submit button. The title, if not specified, defaults to "Submit Query!"

objFormElementDict (Write (indirectly))

This property is indirectly write-only. This property is a Dictionary object that contains zero to many HTML strings that correspond to form field elements. To add a new form field element, use the AddElement method.

The following list discusses the `GenerateForm` class's methods:

AddElement(objFormElement)

Adds a form field element to objFormElementDict. *objFormElement* is expected to be an instance of the `FormElement` class. A more thorough discussion of why this technique is used to add a form element appears in a later sidebar.

GenerateForm( )

Returns the HTML that will generate a form specified by the form field elements in objFormElementDict.

GenerateValidation( )

Returns the client-side JavaScript code that will validate the form field inputs. The client-side JavaScript takes advantage of regular expressions; hence the client-side validation code will only work properly in browsers that support JavaScript 1.2 or greater: Internet Explorer or Netscape Navigator 4.0 and up.

GenerateHTMLDocument(`strTitle`)

Returns the entire HTML document in one string. Only useful if the HTML page will contain one form and one form only. The `strTitle` parameter displays a title at the beginning of the HTML page (right after the <BODY> tag). GenerateHTMLDocument(*X*) is synonymous with:

```
<HTML><HEAD>

GenerateValidation()

</HEAD><BODY>
     X

GenerateForm()

</BODY></HTML>
```

The `GenerateForm` class definition, which is listed in Example 5-5 and is also stored in the file *CODEREUSE\FormCreation.Class.asp* along with the definition of the `FormElement` class, is fairly straightforward and easy to use. To create a form, two object instances are needed: an instance of `GenerateForm` and an instance of `FormElement`. Start by creating the `GenerateForm` instance and set its properties. Next, create a single `FormElement` instance, set the needed properties in the `FormElement` instance, and call the AddElement method of the `GenerateForm` instance, passing in the `FormElement` instance. Finally, call the `FormElement` instance's Clear method and repeat the previous three steps for each element in the form.

Example 5-5. The GenerateForm Class Definition

```
<%
Class GenerateForm
   '***************** PROPERTIES ********************
   Private strRedirect
   Private strCollection
   Private strFormAction
   Private objFormElementDict
   Private strFormName
   Private strSubmitTitle
   '*************************************************
```

Example 5-5. The GenerateForm Class Definition (continued)

```
'************** INITIALIZE/TERMINATE **************
Private Sub Class_Initialize()
   'Set the default property values
   strCollection = "FORM"
   strFormAction = "/CODEREUSE/ValidateForm.asp"
   strFormName = "frmForm1"
   strRedirect = Request.ServerVariables("SCRIPT_NAME")
   strSubmitTitle = "Submit Query!"

   Set objFormElementDict = CreateObject("Scripting.Dictionary")
End Sub

Private Sub Class_Terminate()
   Set objFormElementDict = Nothing     ' Clean up
End Sub
'***************************************************


'************* PROPERTY LET STATMENTS *************
Public Property Let Collection(str)
  'Set the strCollection private property, making sure it is
  'set to either QueryString or Form (default to Form)
  If Ucase(str) = "QUERYSTRING" then
    strCollection = "QueryString"
  Else
    strCollection = "Form"
  End If
End Property

Public Property Let Redirect(str)
  'Set the strRedirect private property; if trying to assign it
  'a blank string, assign it the value of the current ASP page
  If Len(str) = 0 then
    strRedirect = Request.ServerVariables("SCRIPT_NAME")
  Else
    strRedirect = str
  End If
End Property

Public Property Let FormAction(str)
  'Set the strFormAction private property
  strFormAction = str
End Property

Public Property Let FormName(str)
  'Set the strFormName private property
  strFormName = str
End Property

Public Property Let SubmitTitle(str)
  'Set the strSubmitTitle private property
  If Len(str) = 0 then
    strSubmitTitle = "Submit Query!"
```

Example 5-5. The GenerateForm Class Definition (continued)

```
    Else
        strSubmitTitle = str
    End If
End Property
'***************************************************

'************* PROPERTY GET STATMENTS *************
Public Property Get Collection()
    Collection = strCollection
End Property

Public Property Get Redirect()
    Redirect = strRedirect
End Property

Public Property Get FormAction()
    FormAction = strFormAction
End Property

Public Property Get FormName()
    FormName = strFormName
End Property

Public Property Get SubmitTitle()
    SubmitTitle = strSubmitTitle
End Property
'***************************************************

'********************* METHODS *********************
Public Function AddElement(objFormElement)
    'Adds a form field element to the objFormElementDict object
    'Expects to be passed a valid objFormElement instance
    Dim strHTML, strTechnicalName

    'Determine if this form field needs to be validated
    If Len(objFormElement.RegularExpression) > 0 then
        strTechnicalName = objFormElement.Name & "!" & _
                        objFormElement.RegularExpression
    Else
        strTechnicalName = objFormElement.Name
    End If

    'Determine what form field type we are dealing with
    If objFormElement.ElementType = "SELECT" then
        strHTML = objFormElement.PreHTML & vbCrLf & _
                "<SELECT NAME=""" & objFormElement.Name & """"

        If Len(objFormElement.Size) > 0 then
            strHTML = strHTML & " SIZE=" & objFormElement.Size
        End If

        strHTML = strHTML & ">" & vbCrLf & _
                objFormElement.PostHTML & _
                vbCrLf & "</SELECT>" & vbCrLf & vbCrLf
```

Example 5-5. The GenerateForm Class Definition (continued)

```
    Elseif objFormElement.ElementType = "TEXTAREA" then
        strHTML = objFormElement.PreHTML & vbCrLf & _
                "<TEXTAREA NAME=""" & strTechnicalName & """"

        If Len(objFormElement.Size) > 0 then
            strHTML = strHTML & " COLS=" & objFormElement.Size & _
                " ROWS=" & objFormElement.Size / 4
        End If


        strHTML = strHTML & "></TEXTAREA>" & _
                vbCrLf & objFormElement.PostHTML & _
                vbCrLf & vbCrLf
    Else 'must be one of the other types
        strHTML = objFormElement.PreHTML & vbCrLf & _
                "<INPUT NAME=""" & strTechnicalName & """"

        If Len(objFormElement.Size) > 0 then
            strHTML = strHTML & " SIZE=" & objFormElement.Size
        End If

        If Len(objFormElement.Value) > 0 then
            strHTML = strHTML & " VALUE=""" & objFormElement.Value & """"
        End If

        strHTML = strHTML & " TYPE=" & objFormElement.ElementType & _
                ">" & vbCrLf & objFormElement.PostHTML & _
                vbCrLf & vbCrLf
    End If

    'Add the HTML to the FormElement dictionary
    objFormElementDict.Add strTechnicalName, strHTML
End Function


Public Function GenerateForm()
    'Iterates through the objFormElementDict collection and
    'generates the resulting form
    Dim strResultingForm

    strResultingForm = "<FORM NAME=""" & strFormName & _
                    """ METHOD="
    If strCollection = "QueryString" then
        strResultingForm = strResultingForm & "GET"
    Else
        strResultingForm = strResultingForm & "POST"
    End If

    strResultingForm = strResultingForm & " ACTION=""" & _
        strFormAction & """ ONSUBMIT=""return ValidateData();"">" & _
        vbCrLf

    'Add the HIDDEN form variables
    strResultingForm = strResultingForm & vbTab & "<INPUT TYPE=HIDDEN " & _
            "NAME=Collection VALUE=""" & strCollection & """>" & vbCrLf & _
```

Example 5-5. The GenerateForm Class Definition (continued)

```
            vbTab & "<INPUT TYPE=HIDDEN NAME=Redirect VALUE=""" & _
            strRedirect & """>" & vbCrLf

    'Iterate through the form element dictionary, outputting the
    'form field elements
    Dim strName
    For Each strName in objFormElementDict
      strResultingForm = strResultingForm & vbTab & objFormElementDict(strName)
    Next

    strResultingForm = strResultingForm & "<P><INPUT TYPE=SUBMIT VALUE=""" & _
          strSubmitTitle & """>" & vbCrLf & vbCrLf
    strResultingForm = strResultingForm & "</FORM>" & vbCrLf & vbCrLf

    GenerateForm = strResultingForm
  End Function



  Public Function GenerateValidation()
    'Creates the client-side validation code
    Dim strCode
    strCode = "<SCRIPT LANGUAGE=""JavaScript"">" & vbCrLf & "<!--" & vbCrLf & _
              "function ValidateData()" & vbCrLf & "{" & vbCrLf & _
              vbTab & "var iLoop;" & vbCrLf & vbCrLf

    'Now, for each form element that contains regular expression code,
    'prepare it for validation!
    Dim strName, strRegExp
    For Each strName in objFormElementDict
      If InStr(1,strName,"!") then
          'We have form validation!!  Grab the regexp
          strRegExp = Right(strName, Len(strName) - InStr(1,strName,"!"))
          strCode = strCode & vbTab & "if (document.forms['" & strFormName & _
                    "'].elements['" & Replace(strName,"\","\\") & _
                    "'].value.search(/" & strRegExp & "/) == -1) {" & vbCrLf & _
                    vbTab & vbTab & "alert('" & Left(strName, InStr(1,strName,"!") _
                    - 1) & " is not valid.');" & vbCrLf & vbTab & vbTab & _
                    "return false;" & vbCrLf & vbTab & "}" & vbCrLf
      End If
    Next

    strCode = strCode & vbCrLf & vbTab & "return true;" & vbCrLf
    strCode = strCode & "}" & vbCrLf
    strCode = strCode & vbCrLf & "// -->" & vbCrLf & "</SCRIPT>" & vbCrLf

    GenerateValidation = strCode
  End Function



  Public Function GenerateHTMLDocument(strTitleHTML)
    'This method generates the HTML/BODY tags, the form and client-side
    'form validation all in one call
    Dim strResultHTML
    strResultHTML = "<HTML><HEAD>" & vbCrLf & GenerateValidation() & _
```

Example 5-5. The GenerateForm Class Definition (continued)

```
                    "</HEAD>" & vbCrLf
    strResultHTML = strResultHTML & "<BODY>" & vbCrLf & strTitleHTML & _
            vbCrLf & GenerateForm() & vbCrLf & "</BODY></HTML>"

    GenerateHTMLDocument = strResultHTML
  End Function
  '***************************************************
End Class
%>
```

For example, the following code will create a form with four form fields (two text boxes, a text area, and a list box). The first two text boxes are validated on the client side when the form is submitted (and will also be subject to validation on the server side when submitted to */CODEREUSE/ValidateForm.asp*). For the example, the two class definitions were placed in an separate file and included in the *\05FormCreationDemo.asp* file, whose contents are as follows:

```
<%@ LANGUAGE = "VBSCRIPT" %>
<% Option Explicit %>
<!--#include virtual="/CODEREUSE/FormCreation.Class.asp"-->
<%
        'Create an instance of the GenerateForm class
        Dim objGenerateForm
        Set objGenerateForm = New GenerateForm

        'Set the objGenerateForm properties
        objGenerateForm.Collection = "Form"
        objGenerateForm.Redirect = "/scripts/Something.asp"
        objGenerateForm.SubmitTitle = "--- GO! ---"

        'Create an instance of the FormElement class
        Dim objFormElement
        Set objFormElement = New FormElement

        '*** Create the form field elements ***
        'Create an age form field element
        objFormElement.Name = "Age"
        objFormElement.Size = 4
        objFormElement.ElementType = "TEXT"
        objFormElement.RegularExpression = "\d{1,2}"
        objFormElement.PreHTML = "What is your Age?<BR>"
        objGenerateForm.AddElement objFormElement  'Add it to the form

        'Create an email form field element
        objFormElement.Clear    'clear out the form element values before reuse
        objFormElement.Name = "Email"
        objFormElement.ElementType = "TEXT"
        objFormElement.RegularExpression = "^[a-z_0-9\-\.]+@\w+\.\w+$"
        objFormElement.PreHTML = "<P>What is your email address?<BR>"
        objGenerateForm.AddElement objFormElement  'Add it to the form
```

```
            'Create a comment form field with no validation
            objFormElement.Clear     'clear out the form element values before reuse
            objFormElement.Name = "User Comments"
            objFormElement.ElementType = "TEXTAREA"
            objFormElement.PreHTML = "<P>Any comments?<BR>"
            objFormElement.Size = 40
            objGenerateForm.AddElement objFormElement  'Add it to the form

            'Create a list box
            objFormElement.Clear     'clear out the form element values before reuse
            objFormElement.Name = "Experience"
            objFormElement.ElementType = "SELECT"
            objFormElement.PreHTML = "<P>How many years have you been on the Net?<BR>"
            objFormElement.Size = 1
            objFormElement.PostHTML = "<OPTION VALUE=1>One Year</OPTION>" & vbCrLf & _
                                "<OPTION VALUE=2>Two Years</OPTION>"
            objGenerateForm.AddElement objFormElement  'Add it to the form


            'Generate the entire HTML document
            Response.Write objGenerateForm.GenerateHTMLDocument("<H1>Information</H1>")

            '(synonymous to doing:
            '  Response.Write "<HTML><HEAD>"
            '  Response.Write objGenerateForm.GenerateValidation()
            '  Response.Write "</HEAD><BODY>"
            '  Response.Write objGenerateForm.GenerateForm()
            '  Response.Write "</BODY></HTML>")


        Set objFormElement = Nothing    'Clean up!
        Set objGenerateForm = Nothing   'Clean up!
    %>
```

Note that the GenerateHTMLDocument method was used to generate the HTML output. A simple Response.Write sends the form HTML to the client. As with any generalized implementation, there are a few caveats when using the **GenerateForm** class:

- The value of the Name property of the **FormElement** class should not have a double quote. Including one will result in unexpected behavior.

- When creating a list box, it is imperative the series of HTML tags used to create the list box items be inserted in the PostHTML property. (The *Experience* form field properties provide a good example for creating a select box.)

- These classes are not designed to create complex forms. The HTML they output is not pretty, and is not intended to be so. However, refinements of the **GenerateForm** and **FormElement** classes could be made to accommodate more complex forms and more detailed form fields.

Adding Form Elements

The AddElement method expects an instance of the `FormElement` class as its single parameter. Once it receives the object instance, it refers to its various properties to create an HTML string, which is then stored in the *objFormElementDict* object.

A more sound and straightforward approach, in my opinion, would have been to have an actual instance of the `FormElement` class added to the dictionary. Then in the GenerateForm and GenerateValidation methods, the object instances in the *objFormElementDict* object would be dissected and converted into valid HTML strings.

I chose not to use this approach, though, because I didn't want to have to create an instance of the `FormElement` class for every form element. Therefore, I decided to use the current approach, so that the developer using these classes could simply reuse a single FormElement object instance. Hence, I included a Clear method in the `FormElement` class.

The Practicality of Reuse

Earlier in the chapter, the three general steps of form creation were outlined as follows:

1. Create an HTML form with the proper form fields, complete with client-side form validation.

2. Create a form-processing script and add the needed code.

3. Add server-side form-validation code to the ASP page created in Step 2.

In this chapter we examined code that took advantage of the repetitive nature of Steps 1 and 3. How practical, though, is code reuse? The answer depends on how many times we are going to repeat Steps 1 and 3. Since there is such a high initial cost in developing robust, generic, reusable code, it may not seem sensible to proceed with such code development unless you plan on reusing the code extensively.

I strongly suggest that you strive to make all of your code as reusable as possible. While this may seem time-consuming and a bit overzealous, it will be beneficial in the long run. For example, creating a reusable form class, as we did in this chapter, will save time when creating a form in *any* project! Once the reusable form-generation and validation code has been written, the timesaving benefits will be automatically included for all future projects using forms.

To summarize: although writing reusable code may seem like a great deal of initial overhead—and therefore overkill for small projects—the benefits of code reuse almost always extend far beyond the current project. For this reason, strive to apply code reuse methodologies to all of your projects.

Further Reading

To learn more about the topics covered in this chapter, be sure to read the following online articles:

- A good article on the hidden cost of code reuse. As mentioned at the end of the chapter, it may at times seem like creating reusable code has too high a cost initially. Read more at *http://www.iweek.com/708/08iuhid.htm*.

- In this chapter, we looked at using regular expressions on the client-side for form validation. For more information on this, be sure to read this article, *http://www.asptoday.com/articles/19990629.htm*, which presents a library of regular expressions for form validation.

- Another good article focusing on form validation using regular expressions can be found at *http://www.4guysfromrolla.com/webtech/050399-2.shtml*.

- When creating client-side form-validation routines, it is important you use JavaScript as the client-side scripting language, since it is the only scripting language supported by both Internet Explorer and Netscape Navigator. Detailed technical documentation on JavaScript's objects, methods, and properties can be found at: *http://developer.netscape.com/docs/manuals/index.html?content=javascript.html*.

6

Database Reuse

In Chapter 5, *Form Reuse*, we discussed how to use code reuse mechanisms to build versatile form-creation and form-validation classes. In this chapter, we will look at how to build reusable database classes. As with the previous chapter, we will begin by examining database usage from a high level and look at how to accomplish various database-related tasks using standard, procedural code. Finally, we'll convert these various procedural scripts into a robust set of classes, prime for reuse!

I think you'll find the code presented and the topics discussed in this chapter to be extremely applicable. Database access is common among ASP web sites, and any steps that can be taken to reduce the time needed to create new database interface pages are steps in the right direction. However, presenting such a large and advanced application requires a great deal of time and explanation. This chapter is, by far, the longest in this book. It will most likely take you a long while to work through this chapter. If you stick with it, though, your fortitude will pay dividends, since the application presented in this chapter is very useful in the real world.

It is assumed that you are knowledgeable in relational database design and theory. If you are unfamiliar with the SQL syntax, or have never created a relational data model, it is strongly suggested that you become more familiar with these topics before beginning on this chapter.

Examining Database Usage

As discussed in Chapter 5, there are a number of typical form interfaces. One interface used often is the administration pages interface. In this interface, a superuser is able to add, edit, and remove records from a particular database table. With this interface, there is great room for reuse, since all of the administration pages follow a particular formula:

- Provide a list of all the editable database tables. Each database table name should be a hyperlink to an administration page for that particular table.

- On each table's specific administration page, there should be three hyperlinked options: "Insert a New Record," "Edit an Existing Record," and "Delete an Existing Record."

  — In the "Insert a New Record" page, the user should be presented with a form that contains form elements for each of the columns in the table. Once the form is filled out and submitted, a new record should be added to the table with the values entered by the user.

  — In the "Edit an Existing Record" page, the user should be able to select an existing record in the table. Upon selecting an existing record, the user should be taken to a page that contains a form similar to the form in the "Insert a New Record" page. The only difference is the form fields should have the existing record's information entered into the various form fields. When the user has made changes to the record's data and has submitted the form, the specified record should be updated with the new values.

  — In the "Delete an Existing Record" page, the user should be able to select an existing record to delete.

The administration page interface lends itself well to reuse since a number of similar steps need to be repeated for each database table's administration page. The steps for creating an administration page for a specific table include:

1. Create a web page with a form that contains a form element for each of the table's columns. This is the form the user will visit when they choose "Insert a New Record."

2. Create a form-processing script for the form in Step 1 that will add the new record to the table.

3. Create a web page that lists all of the existing records for the user to choose from when they want to edit an existing record.

4. Create a web page that displays a form that contains a form element for each of the table's columns. The values of these form elements are identical to the values of the record selected by the user in Step 3.

5. Create a form-processing script for the form created in Step 4. This form-processing script is responsible for updating an existing database record (selected through the form in Step 3) with the values entered into the form in Step 4.

6. Create a web page that lists all of the existing records for the user to choose from when they want to delete an existing record.

7. Create a form-processing script for the form in Step 6 that will delete the record selected by the user.

These seven steps must be repeated for *every* table in the database that requires an administration page! Clearly, if any of these steps can be reused for each table's administration page, we will save ourselves considerable time. In this chapter, we will examine how to turn each of the above steps into reusable code. For some of the steps, a brief discussion will be presented on potential methods that could be used to make the step highly reusable. For other steps, a more in-depth analysis will occur, accompanied by code examples. These topics are discussed in detail in the next section.

 You can probably see that some of these steps can be combined, reducing the overall number of steps needed for each table's administration page. For example, the forms in Step 3 and Step 6 could share a single web page, as could the forms in Step 1 and Step 4.

The Building Blocks for Creating Reusable Administration Pages

The biggest challenge in creating truly reusable administration pages arrives when dealing with complex database tables. Imagine, for a moment, that all our tables were *simple database tables* that don't impose foreign key constraints upon other tables, and have no foreign key constraints imposed upon them (that is, a simple database table is one that has no explicit relationships with other tables). Rarely are there many simple database tables in a database. Since relational databases inherently encourage the developer to create several small, related tables, simple database tables are found only in simple data models. Therefore, we need a system that gracefully handles complex tables as well as simple tables.

In this section we'll examine the theory behind creating powerful, reusable database administration pages that can be used for complex tables. We'll begin with a discussion of what the ideal reusable administration page should contain. Since the reusable administration pages we'll later create will make heavy use of ADO schemas, an entire section is dedicated to this topic.

The Ideal Reusable Administration Page Script

Without code reuse, a developer needs to perform seven steps for each administration page. With code reuse, however, the need to repeat each of the seven steps for each administration page can be eliminated. Can code reuse help to eliminate the fact that seven steps are needed, though? The ideal situation would be to have only one step needed to create an entire set of administration pages.

Imagine that we had a page called *DatabaseAdministration.asp* that expected one parameter through the querystring, the table name. This page would then display the appropriate options for adding, deleting, and updating records, gracefully handling one-to-many and one-to-one relationships. Furthermore, the page would know what form elements would be best suited for collecting input from the user. For example, if a table had a date/time column, it might be wiser in some instances to use select boxes to represent the month, day, and year; other times, it might be wiser to use a simple text box.

This single administration page would also need to be able to determine what columns in a table had foreign key constraints and provide a mechanism to allow the user to only select applicable values from the related table. For example, imagine that we had an **Employee** table with the structure shown in Figure 6-1.

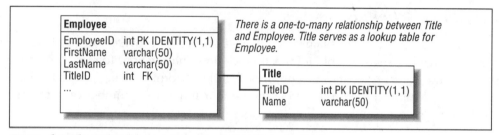

Figure 6-1. The Title table serves as a lookup table to Employee

Note that **Title** is a lookup table, and its **Name** column contains values like "President," "CEO," "Manager," "Secretary," and "Grunt." Through referential integrity, **TitleID** in **Employee** can contain only integer values that are also present in **TitleID** in **Title**.

How should our administration page handle such foreign keys when adding a new record or updating an existing record? A simple text box could be used, in which the user could enter an integer value corresponding to a value in the **Title** table. Of course, this would require the user to know that the title "CEO" had a **TitleID** of, say, 5.

This is not an acceptable solution, since the user cannot be held responsible for knowing what titles correspond to what **TitleID**s and what **TitleID**s are valid. Rather than seeing a text box, the user should be presented with a list box containing the acceptable title names. To accomplish this feat, our administration page would not only have to identify what columns are foreign keys, but would also have to decide what column from the lookup table to display in the list box!

Such a single, robust administration page is quite impossible to create, since it would require that the page be autonomous and know the *best* way to display form fields and lookup table lists. We can't expect the script to be able to make the best decisions, but what if we could give "hints" to the script to help it decide how to handle form elements and foreign keys? In this chapter, we will strive to build a collection of ASP pages that allow the end user to update, insert, and delete database records with some input from the end developer to help the administration page decide what methods to use to collect user input.

In creating this set of reusable administration pages, some mechanism for determining a particular table's columns and column properties needs to be used. Furthermore, since these pages strive to be as generic as possible, they shouldn't be dependent upon the database used; that is, these administration pages should work if we use Access, Microsoft SQL Server, or some other database system. Thankfully, ADO provides a means to collect table and column information regardless of the database provider.

Database Schemas

One of ADO's most useful features is *schemas*. Schemas provide low-level database information, such as table information, column information, foreign key constraints, and primary key information, in a high-level format. Using schemas, this system information can be collected in the same manner for a number of different database providers.

Most database systems provide their own methods for collecting such low-level information. For example, if you want to access table and column information in Microsoft SQL Server without using schemas, you would have to query system tables, like *sysobjects* or *syscolumns*. Example 6-1 illustrates how to obtain all of the tables in a SQL Server database by querying *sysobjects*.

Example 6-1. List the Tables in a SQL Server Database Using the sysobjects Table

```
<% @LANGUAGE="VBSCRIPT" %>
<% Option Explicit %>
<%
    'Open up a connection to the database
    Dim objConn
    Set objConn = Server.CreateObject("ADODB.Connection")
    objConn.ConnectionString = "DSN=MyDatabase"
    objConn.Open

    'We want to query the sysobjects table where type = 'U'
    Dim strSQL
    strSQL = "SELECT * FROM sysobjects WHERE type='U'"

    'Execute the query
    Dim objRS
```

Example 6-1. List the Tables in a SQL Server Database Using the sysobjects Table (continued)

```
Set objRS = objConn.Execute(strSQL)

'Display the table names
Do While not objRS.EOF
  Response.Write objRS("Name") & "<BR>"
  objRS.MoveNext
Loop

'Clean up...
objConn.Close
Set objConn = Nothing
%>
```

The *sysobjects* table is fairly cryptic, containing several columns with single character values that denote their purpose. Rows that have a "U" in the **Type** column are tables. I think you'll agree that the code in Example 6-1 is fairly cryptic. Furthermore, the code will only work for Microsoft SQL Server databases.

Schemas make listing database information much easier and more portable. Since the code in Example 6-1 will only work for Microsoft SQL Server databases, it is anything but portable, and portability should be a key concern when developing reusable scripts.

Importing enumerations with adovbs.inc

Before you start using schemas, it is important that you have access to the enumerations defined in ADO. There are currently two ways to do this:

- Use a server-side include to import the contents of *adovbs.inc* into each ASP page that needs to reference these database enumerations.

- Use the **METADATA** tag in *Global.asa* to import the ADO constants.

adovbs.inc is a text file that contains all of the ADO enumerations in the form of VBScript constants. To use *adovbs.inc*, copy it into the directory in which you place your include files (I recommend creating a directory named */inc* and turning off Read permissions.) *adovbs.inc* can be found in *Program Files\Common Files\System\ado*.

Once *adovbs.inc* is in a web-accessible directory, you can use a server-side include to import the contents of *adovbs.inc* into any ASP page that needs to access the ADO enumerations. Simply use the following line of code at the top of your document:

```
<% @LANGUAGE="VBSCRIPT" %>
<% Option Explicit %>
<!--#include virtual="/inc/adovbs.inc"-->
```

Take a moment to look at the contents of *adovbs.inc*. Note that it is nothing more than a lengthy list of VBScript constants assigned appropriate hexadecimal values. Below is a short excerpt from the schema section of *adovbs.inc*:

```
'---- SchemaEnum Values ----
Const adSchemaProviderSpecific = -1
Const adSchemaAsserts = 0
Const adSchemaCatalogs = 1
Const adSchemaCharacterSets = 2
Const adSchemaCollations = 3
Const adSchemaColumns = 4
```

For more information on server-side includes, be sure to read Chapter 1, *Introduction*, or check out "The low-down on #includes," available at *http://www.4guysfromrolla.com/webtech/080199-1.shtml*.

Importing enumerations with the METADATA tag

The METADATA tag imports enumerations from a type library. For example, in each ASP page that uses a server-side include to import the contents of *adovbs.inc*, we could replace:

```
<!--#include virtual="/inc/adovbs.inc"-->
```

with the following line of code:

```
<!-- METADATA
        TYPE="typelib"
        FILE="D:\Program Files\Common Files\System\ADO\msado21.tlb"
-->
```

The METADATA tag has the following syntax (the line breaks are for enhanced readability and are not required):

```
<!-- METADATA
        TYPE="typelib"
        UUID="GUID"
        FILE="FilePath"
-->
```

You only need to specify either the UUID or the FILE when importing constants from a type library. The UUID expects the type library's GUID, while the FILE expects the full, physical path to the type library. The GUID for the ActiveX Data Objects type library is: 00000201-0000-0010-8000-00AA006D2EA4. I find that specifying the *FilePath* instead of the *GUID* makes for much easier-to-read code. However, there is always the chance that the file may be renamed or moved, whereas the GUID won't change.

Now, you may be wondering why anyone would want to use the METADATA tag in place of *adovbs.inc*. Typing:

```
<!--#include virtual="/inc/adovbs.inc"-->
```

instead of:

```
<!-- METADATA
        TYPE="typelib"
        FILE="D:\Program Files\Common Files\System\ADO\msado21.tlb"
-->
```

is quicker and less prone to mistake. METADATA's advantage is that you can specify it once in *Global.asa* and have access to all of the ADO enumerations in all of your ASP pages! Also, according to Microsoft's ASP Performance Tips (*http://msdn.microsoft.com/library/psdk/bdg/bdgapp03_3rhv.htm*), using a single METADATA tag in *Global.asa* provides for better performance than using server-side includes on each page.

If you place the METADATA tag in *Global.asa*, remember that every ASP page will have access to the ADO constants. If you attempt to include *adovbs.inc* in a page, you will receive a `Name redefined: 'adOpenForwardOnly'` error. This error occurs because you are attempting to create a constant in *adovbs.inc* that already exists from the METADATA import. adOpenForwardOnly is listed because it is the first constant defined in *adovbs.inc*.

Opening schemas

To open a schema, use the OpenSchema method of the Connection object. The OpenSchema method has the following definition:

```
Set recordset = connection.OpenSchema(QueryType[, Criteria[, SchemaID]])
```

QueryType is a required parameter that specifies the type of schema to open, and must be set to a valid SchemaEnum type. There are a number of possible schema types that can return a vast array of database information. There are schemas for listing tables, columns, column privileges, foreign keys, indexes, primary keys, referential constraints, and other miscellaneous information. The valid SchemaEnums are listed in *adovbs.inc* under the heading "SchemaEnum Values." Each SchemaEnum constant defined in *adovbs.inc* is prefixed with an adSchema; some of the more commonly used SchemaEnum values (including those that will be used in code presented in this chapter) are listed in Table 6-1.

Table 6-1. Several Common SchemaEnums Are Defined in adovbs.inc

SchemaEnum	Description
adSchemaColumns	Contains detailed information about each of the columns in a database
adSchemaTables	Contains detailed information about each table in a database
adSchemaForeignKeys	Contains detailed information about all of the foreign key constraints in a database

The available `SchemaEnums` that can be specified by the *QueryType* parameter differ among the various database providers. Many database providers support a common set of `SchemaEnums` (such as `adSchemaColumns` and `adSchemaTables`), but some database providers may contain their own unique schemas that aren't represented by a value in the `SchemaEnum` list. If you need to use such a schema, set the *QueryType* to `adSchemaProviderSpecific` and specify the unique schema in the *SchemaID* parameter.

The various schemas supported depend upon the database provider. For example, the OLE DB provider for AS/400 and VSAM only supports four schemas, while the OLE DB provider for SQL Server supports several more.

Example 6-2 contains code that is functionally identical to the code presented in Example 6-1; both scripts list the tables in a database. Example 6-2, however, uses the `adSchemaTables` *QueryType* rather than `sysobjects`, which makes Example 6-2 easier to read and more portable.

Example 6-2. Listing the Tables in a Database with Schemas

```
<% @LANGUAGE="VBSCRIPT" %>
<% Option Explicit %>
<!--#include virtual="/adovbs.inc"-->
<%
    'Open a connection to the database
    Dim objConn
    Set objConn = Server.CreateObject("ADODB.Connection")
    objConn.ConnectionString = "DSN=MyDatabase"
    objConn.Open

    'Use the OpenSchema method to grab the table schema
    Dim objRS
    Set objRS = objConn.OpenSchema(adSchemaTables)

    'Loop through the contents of the schema.
    Do While Not objRS.EOF
      'Only display TABLES - not SYSTEM TABLES, not VIEWS
      If objRS("TABLE_TYPE") = "TABLE" then
        Response.Write objRS("TABLE_NAME") & "<BR>"
```

Example 6-2. Listing the Tables in a Database with Schemas (continued)

```
    End If

    objRS.MoveNext
Loop

'Clean up...
objRS.Close
Set objRS = Nothing

objConn.Close
Set objConn = Nothing
%>
```

Since a schema is returned as a Recordset object, we can use the Recordset object's properties and methods to iterate through the schema. A schema, like an ordinary database table, contains columns, which describe the properties of an abstract object, and rows, which serve as an instantiation of an object. The adSchemaTables schema we used in Example 6-2 contains several columns describing each table, including TABLE_NAME, TABLE_TYPE, DESCRIPTION, DATE_ MODIFIED, and DATE_CREATED.

The adSchemaTables schema returns the views and system tables along with the user tables. The TABLE_TYPE column specifies what type of table is being returned, and in Example 6-2 we list only user tables by assuring that TABLE_TYPE equals "TABLE" before displaying the TABLE_NAME column.

Note that we explicitly included *adovbs.inc* in Example 6-2. This explicit include would not be needed if the METADATA tag were used in *Global.asa*. It is strongly recommended that you use the METADATA approach. All the examples in this book that need to use ADO enumerations, however, will explicitly include *adovbs.inc* to assist with readability.

The Criteria parameter

The *OpenSchema* method has an optional parameter named **Criteria**. This parameter can be specified to limit the resulting schema. For example, in Example 6-2, we didn't specify a **Criteria**, and all tables were returned, including views and system tables. We could pass in a **Criteria** parameter, however, that would inform ADO to return only those tables that were user tables. Using a **Criteria** to limit the contents of a schema is similar to using a WHERE clause to limit the results of a SQL query.

Each SchemaEnum has its own predefined set of potential **Criteria** that can be used to limit the results of a schema. Some SchemaEnums have no limiting

Criteria, while others can have several columns to which *Criteria* can be applied. To accommodate the differing number of *Criteria* accepted by various SchemaEnums, the *Criteria* parameter should be passed in as an array. For example, if a particular SchemaEnum expects four *Criteria*, the array should contain four elements.

The adSchemaTables schema expects four *Criteria*: TABLE_CATALOG, TABLE_ SCHEMA, TABLE_NAME, and TABLE_TYPE. To retrieve only user tables when opening the adSchemaTables schema, we need to supply a *Criteria* parameter that was a four-element array, defined as:

```
Array(Empty, Empty, Empty, "TABLE")
```

Since we do not wish to filter on the first three *Criteria*—TABLE_CATALOG, TABLE_SCHEMA, and TABLE_NAME—we simply leave these blank by specifying the resulting array element as Empty. By using the above *Criteria*, we can alter Example 6-2 so the check for objRS("TABLE_TYPE") = "TABLE" can be avoided. Example 6-3 displays this new code using the *Criteria* parameter of the Open-Schema method.

Example 6-3. Using the Criteria Parameter to Selectively List Tables of a Database

```
<% @LANGUAGE="VBSCRIPT" %>
<% Option Explicit %>
<!--#include virtual="/adovbs.inc"-->
<%
    'Open a connection to the database
    Dim objConn
    Set objConn = Server.CreateObject("ADODB.Connection")
    objConn.ConnectionString = "DSN=MyDatabase"
    objConn.Open

    'Use the OpenSchema method to grab the table schame
    'In this example, we specify the Criteria parameter of the
    'OpenSchema method
    Dim objRS
    Set objRS = objConn.OpenSchema(adSchemaTables, _
                    Array(Empty, Empty, Empty, "TABLE"))

    'Loop through the contents of the schema.
    Do While Not objRS.EOF
      'Since the Criteria parameter returned only user table,
      'we don't need to check TABLE_TYPE here, like we did in Example 6-2
      Response.Write objRS("TABLE_NAME") & "<BR>"

      objRS.MoveNext
    Loop

    'Clean up...
    objRS.Close
    Set objRS = Nothing

    objConn.Close
```

Example 6-3. Using the Criteria Parameter to Selectively List Tables of a Database (continued)

```
    Set objConn = Nothing
%>
```

Keep in mind that Example 6-1, Example 6-2, and Example 6-3 all are functionally equivalent.

 There are several possible `SchemaEnum` values, each with their own columns and possible criteria values—far too many to list in a non-reference book like this one. You can obtain a full `SchemaEnum` listing at *http://msdn.microsoft.com/library/psdk/dasdk/mdae0wfb.htm* or through a technical reference book, like Wrox's *ADO 2.0 Programmer's Reference* (Wrox Press Inc.).

Schemas will greatly assist in the quest to create a generic database access script. Since schemas provide portable, low-level database information through an easy-to-use interface, they make an ideal solution for determining how to display particular database fields and database input mechanisms on a generic database page.

For more information on ADO schemas, be sure to read the following tutorials and articles:

- "Listing the Tables and Columns in a Database," found at *http://www.4guysfromrolla.com/webtech/101799-1.shtml*.

- Technical documentation for *OpenSchema*, found at *http://msdn.microsoft.com/library/psdk/dasdk/mdam2ppd.htm*.

- For general ADO information, check out Microsoft's ADO site at *http://www.microsoft.com/data/ado/*.

Creating Reusable Administration Pages

In our quest to build a set of truly reusable administration page generation scripts, there are three general problems we'll encounter and have to solve:

- How does one gather table and column information, and what specific table and column information is worth noting?

- How does one create easy-to-use forms for inserting, editing, and deleting records in a database table? How can the information collected about the database tables and columns be used to create easier-to-use administration page forms?

- Once the user submits an administration page form, how will the changes find their way into the database?

These questions are fairly easy to answer when one is given the liberty to create a set of administration pages for each and every database table, but when we limit ourselves to only a small set of generic administration pages, regardless of the number of database tables, these questions quickly become much more difficult to answer.

The remainder of this chapter is dedicated to answering these questions. The following sections each focus on answering a particular question:

- "Gathering Column Information" answers the question, "How does one gather column information?"

- "Gathering Foreign Key Information" answers the question, "How does one gather table information?"

- "Deciding How to Display the Table Columns in a Form" answers the question, "How can the information collected about the database tables and columns be used to create easier-to-use administration page forms?"

- "Creating the Administration Page Forms" answers the question, "How does one create easy-to-use forms for inserting, editing, and deleting records in a database table?"

- "Inserting, Updating, and Deleting Database Records" answers the question, "Once the user submits an administration page form, how will the changes find their way into the database?"

The journey to answer these questions is a long one, including multitudes of classes and over a thousand lines of source code. Each section focuses on developing a class (or set of classes) to accomplish a certain task. At the conclusion of each of these sections, we'll pause for a moment to test the class or classes we just created, and to look at how they fit into the big picture.

As classes essential to the generic administration page application are presented throughout the chapter, they will be tested against an example database. This database contains information on products and catalogs. There can be many products in a given catalog, and one product can appear in many catalogs. Each product has a specific product type, which is indicated by the `ProductType` look-up table. There are two relationships in this data model: a many-to-many relationship between `Catalog` and `Product`, and a one-to-many relationship between `ProductType` and `Product`.

The structure for this example database can be seen in Table 6-2. Some example data for the `Catalog`, `ProductType`, `Product`, and `CatalogProduct` tables can be seen in Table 6-3 through Table 6-6.

Table 6-2. The ProductInfo Database Table Structures

Table Name	Column Name	Description
Catalog	CatalogID	Primary key; int.
	Name	The name of the catalog; varchar(50).
	ReleasedDate	The date the catalog was released to the public; date/time.
	ContainsPictures	Does the catalog contain pictures? Bit.
Product	ProductID	Primary key; int.
	ProductTypeID	Foreign key; int.
	Price	The retail price; money.
	DateEntered	The date the product was entered into inventory; date/time.
	Quantity	The current, in-stock quantity; int.
ProductType	ProductTypeID	Primary key; int.
	Name	The name of the product type; varchar(50).
	Description	A description of the product type; varchar(255).
CatalogProduct	CatalogID	Primary key, foreign key; int.
	ProductID	Primary key, foreign key; int. The CatalogID and ProductID form a composite primary key.

Table 6-3. Catalog Table Example Data

CatalogID	Name	Released Date	Contains Pictures
2	Spring 2000	4/1/2000	1
3	Fall 2000	9/1/2000	0
4	2000 Year in Review	12/15/2000	0

Table 6-4. ProductType Table Example Data

ProductTypeID	Name	Description
1	Retail	For sale
2	Defective	These are defective items

Table 6-5. Product Table Example Data

ProductID	ProductTypeID	Price	Date Entered	Quantity
1	1	45	4/1/2000	555
2	1	155	4/2/2000	15
3	2	5	4/2/2000	10

Table 6-6. CatalogProduct Table Example Data

CatalogID	ProductID
3	2
3	3

Before we start presenting the classes needed for the generic administration page generation application, however, it would be prudent to take a moment and discuss some important database terms.

A Review of Database Terms

There are three terms used extensively throughout this chapter. It is imperative that I, the author, and you, the reader, speak the same lingo. So let's take a moment to make sure we are both on the same page when it comes to the following three database terms.

Primary key constraints

A primary key constraint can be placed on one or more columns in a table, and ensures that the column or columns selected contain unique values. Primary keys play an important role in relational databases, providing entity integrity. Primary keys are synonymous UNIQUE constraints that do not allow NULL values. Be sure to place primary key constraints on the column or columns that uniquely identity a particular row.

AutoNumber columns

An AutoNumber column is a numeric column that is automatically incremented each time a new record is added to the table. AutoNumber columns are created differently for each database system; in Access, an AutoNumber column is created by specifying the column's datatype as AutoNumber; in Microsoft SQL Server, the IDENTITY property is used.

An AutoNumber is not a datatype, despite the fact that in Access you set the column's datatype to AutoNumber. Rather, AutoNumber is a column property on a column that contains a numeric datatype. The AutoNumber property should only be applied to a column that is a primary key.

AutoNumbers are the easiest way to uniquely identity each row. When a new record is inserted into a table with an AutoNumber column, the developer doesn't need to specify the new AutoNumber value in the INSERT statement; the database system does this automatically, picking the next sequential AutoNumber.

A primary key column does not need to have the AutoNumber property assigned to it. For example, in a catalog of widgets, the primary key column might be the widget's serial number, which is unique among all widgets. However, the AutoNumber property should only be applied to primary key columns.

Foreign key constraints

In a relational database, tables share relationships with one another. When creating a relationship between two database tables, a *foreign key constraint* is used to ensure referential integrity.

For example, assume that you have two database tables, `Employee` and `EmployeeTitle`. The `EmployeeTitle` table represents the different titles available at your company (President, Manager, Engineer, etc.). The `Employee` table contains employee information, with a row for every employee at your company.

The `Employee` table could have many columns storing bits of information about each employee, such as social security number, birth date, name, address, and title. A relationship could be set up between the `Employee` and `EmployeeTitle` tables. The `TitleID` column in the `Employee` table would be an integer value, mapping to a specific title in the `EmployeeTitle` table. Figure 6-2 shows some values that might be found in the `Employee` and `EmployeeTitle` tables.

Employee Table

FirstName	LastName	SocialSecurityNumber	TitleID
Scott	Mitchell	123-45-6789	10
Kevin	Spacey	098-76-5432	2
Joshua	Joy	321-54-9876	7
James	Ransom	090-09-0909	10
Al	Hornets	456-12-3456	10
Skippy	Tourna	555-55-5555	2

The TitleID in the Employee table maps to a Title in the EmployeeTitle table. Therefore, to determine an employee's title, simply perform a lookup in the EmployeeTitle table.

EmployeeTitle Table

TitleID	Title
1	Engineering Systems Engineer
2	Flight Simulation Director
5	Testing Engineer
7	Secretary
9	President
10	Senior Manager

Figure 6-2. The Employee and EmployeeTitle tables are related

Note that each value in the `TitleID` in the `Employee` table maps to a value in the `TitleID` column in the `EmployeeTitle` table. Through this relationship, one can quickly determine the title of an employee. The data shown in Figure 6-2 exhibits *referential integrity*; that is, there are no logical discrepancies between the two related columns.

Imagine for a moment that the `TitleID` column for Scott Mitchell was changed to a value of 800, which is clearly not a valid value in the `EmployeeTitle` table. Or, imagine that a row in the `EmployeeTitle` table that maps to a row in the `Employee` table (such as the Secretary table, which maps to employee Joshua Joy) was deleted. Either of these events would violate referential integrity since, in either case, an `Employee` would report a nonexistent employee title.

Foreign key constraints assist by ensuring referential integrity. If a foreign key constraint was created between the `TitleID` columns of the `Employee` and `EmployeeTitle` tables, the hypothetical actions discussed in the preceding paragraph could not happen. If an attempt was made to delete an employee title that mapped to a row in the `Employee` table, a referential integrity error would be displayed and the delete command would not succeed. Similarly, if there was an attempt to alter an employee's `TitleID` to a value not present in the `EmployeeTitle` table, an error would occur and the update would not be committed.

All relational databases provide the capability to create foreign key constraints. To learn how to establish foreign key constraints for your development database, consult the database's documentation.

Since foreign key columns are usually stored as numeric data, they are a bit tricky to handle in a generic administration page. When a user creates or updates an existing record that contains foreign keys, asking the user for a numeric ID is preposterous. Instead, the user should be presented with a list box that displays a readable list of options.

Part of the challenge in creating a generic administration page generation script is determining what foreign keys exist in what tables. With the aid of schemas, however, this process is simplified. In the later section "Gathering Foreign Key Information," we'll examine how to determine the foreign key constraints in a particular database table. Another challenge is being able to map a foreign key to a set of readable options in the related table. To overcome this challenge, we'll allow the end developer to give some "hints" to the administration page generation class on how related tables should have their contents listed.

Gathering Column Information

For all aspects of the administration page interface, being able to determine the columns and column types of a given record is important. As discussed in "Database Schemas," we will use ADO schemas to ascertain column information for a given table. Example 6-2 and Example 6-3 demonstrated how to collect column information for a particular table. While this procedure is not especially difficult, it would be nice to have a class that hid the steps needed to acquire such information. An end developer using the code in Example 6-2 or Example 6-3 needs to be aware of what schemas are and how they are used. We can remove this constraint by packaging the functionality of Example 6-3 into an easy-to-use class.

Before designing the class to gather column information from a given table, it is important to know what information will need to be stored for a given database column. Since the administration pages must know a great deal of information about each column—including the name, the datatype, the default value, the column description, and whether or not the field is an AutoNumber field—it is essential that extensive information be recorded for each column in a database table.

In this section, two classes are presented: `ColumnInformation` and `Columns`. `ColumnInformation` and `Columns` are used in the generic administration page generation application to represent a generic table column and a collection of table columns, respectively. Both the `ColumnInformation` and the `Columns` classes should be placed in the same file, */CODEREUSE/Column.Class.asp*.

The ColumnInformation class

To assist with the collection of column information for a given table, a `ColumnInformation` class is presented. Each instance of this class represents a single column in a database. This class will not be used directly by the end developer, but by the `Columns` class. The `Columns` class, which we'll discuss shortly in the section "The Columns class," is used by other classes to inspect a database table's various columns. The `Columns` class contains a collection of `ColumnInformation` class instances, one for each column of a particular database table.

Since the `ColumnInformation` class is used solely for holding the needed information for a particular table column, the class contains only a number of read/write properties. Example 6-4 contains the class definition for `ColumnInformation`.

Example 6-4. The ColumnInformation Class Stores Information for a Particular Database Table Column

```
<%
Class ColumnInformation
    '************** MEMBER VARIABLES *********************
    Private strName
```

*Example 6-4. The ColumnInformation Class Stores Information for a Particular Database
Table Column (continued)*

```
Private iDataType
Private bolDefault
Private strDefault
Private bolNullable
Private strDescription
Private varValue
Private bolIdentity
Private bolPrimaryKey
'*****************************************************

'***************** GET PROPERTIES ******************
Public Property Get Identity()
  Identity = bolIdentity
End Property

Public Property Get PrimaryKey()
  PrimaryKey = bolPrimaryKey
End Property

Public Property Get Name()
  Name = strName
End Property

Public Property Get DataType()
  DataType = iDataType
End Property

Public Property Get HasDefault()
  HasDefault = bolDefault
End Property

Public Property Get DefaultValue()
  DefaultValue = strDefault
End Property

Public Property Get Nullable()
  Nullable = bolNullable
End Property

Public Property Get Description()
  Description = strDescription
End Property

Public Property Get Value()
  Value = varValue
End Property
'*****************************************************

'***************** LET PROPERTIES ******************
Public Property Let Identity(bolIdent)
  bolIdentity = bolIdent
End Property
```

Example 6-4. The ColumnInformation Class Stores Information for a Particular Database Table Column (continued)

```
    Public Property Let PrimaryKey(bolPK)
        bolPrimaryKey = bolPK
    End Property

    Public Property Let Name(str)
        strName = str
    End Property

    Public Property Let DataType(iValue)
        iDataType = iValue
    End Property

    Public Property Let HasDefault(bolHasDefault)
        bolDefault = bolHasDefault
    End Property

    Public Property Let DefaultValue(str)
        strDefault = str
    End Property

    Public Property Let Nullable(bolIsNullable)
        bolNullable = bolIsNullable
    End Property

    Public Property Let Description(str)
        strDescription = str
    End Property

    Public Property Let Value(var)
        varValue = var
    End Property
    '*****************************************************
End Class
%>
```

The class presented in Example 6-4 is very simple, containing nothing but properties. The purpose of this class is to serve as a black box for describing what, exactly, a column is.

The Columns class

Let's examine a class that collects all of the column information from a given table. Rather than having this class, `Columns`, be responsible for maintaining each discrete bit of information that pertains to a column, it simply contains a variable number of `ColumnInformation` instances. The `Columns` class takes advantage of the black box interface to a table column the `ColumnInformation` class provides.

Since the `Columns` class is quite hefty, we'll examine each part of the class separately, as opposed to listing pages of raw source code.

Columns's class properties and member variables

The `Columns` class contains a single member variable, *objColumnDict*, which is a Dictionary object, storing zero to many `ColumnInformation` instances. This collection is available to the end developer through a `Property Get` statement; furthermore, the number of elements in the *objColumnDict* Dictionary object is also available to the end developer.

Of course, the end developer won't always want to obtain the entire *objColumnDict* Dictionary object. There will be times when a developer is interested in retrieving just a specific `ColumnInformation` instance from the *objColumnDict* collection. To accommodate this, a method (GetColumnInformation) is provided to return a specific element from the *objColumnDict* Dictionary object.

Example 6-5 shows the `Columns` class definition's event handlers, member variables, and properties. The Initialize and Terminate event handlers are responsible for managing the creation and destruction of *objColumnDict*. Note the two `Property Get` statements—Count and ColumnList—that, allow for the retrieval of the number of elements in *objColumnDict* and the retrieval of *objColumnDict* itself, respectively.

Example 6-5. The Properties and Member Variable of the Columns Class

```
<%
Class Columns
    '************** MEMBER VARIABLES ********************
    Private objColumnDict              'store zero to many columns
    '***************************************************


    '****************** EVENT HANDLERS ******************
    Private Sub Class_Initialize()
      'Create an instance of the Dictionary object
      Set objColumnDict = Server.CreateObject("Scripting.Dictionary")
    End Sub

    Private Sub Class_Terminate()
      Set objColumnDict = Nothing        'Clean up...
    End Sub
    '***************************************************


    '********************** METHODS *********************
    Public Function GetColumnInformation(strColumnName)
        'Returns a specific column's information... that is, returns a
        'reference to an instance of a ColumnInformation object
        Set GetColumnInformation = objColumnDict(strColumnName)
    End Function

    ' ... Numerous methods removed here, but are presented in
    '     Example 6-6 and Example 6-7 ...
    '***************************************************
```

Example 6-5. The Properties and Member Variable of the Columns Class (continued)

```
'****************** GET PROPERTIES *******************
Public Property Get Count()
    Count = objColumnDict.Count
End Property

Public Property Get ColumnList()
    Set ColumnList = objColumnDict
End Property
'*****************************************************
End Class
%>
```

Columns's class methods

`Columns` contains a number of methods. The first method we'll look at, Populate-Columns, is responsible for reading column information from a particular database table and populating the *objColumnDict* Dictionary object with the results. The PopulateColumns method has the following definition:

```
Public Sub PopulateColumns(strTableName, objConn, strWhereClause)
```

Since `Columns` serves as a collection of database table columns, the specific database table to use must be specified by the end developer through the *strTableName* parameter. The *objConn* parameter should contain an opened connection to the database that contains the table specified by *strTableName*. PopulateColumns will use the OpenSchema method of the *objConn* Connection object passed in by the end developer. The *strWhereClause* is used only when a record is being updated and the column values for a particular row must be known. When inserting a new row, the *strWhereClause* parameter should be an empty string (`" "`).

 The end developer won't have to worry about passing the proper *strWhereClause* to PopulateColumns. Another class, `Admin-PageGenerator`, will be used to construct the various forms for updating, deleting, and inserting records. This class will also correctly call `PopulateColumns`. In fact, the end developer does not even need to know that the `ColumnInformation` and `Columns` classes exist! The `AdminPageGenerator` class is discussed in greater detail in the section "The AdminPageGenerator class."

The PopulateColumns method, which appears in Example 6-6, uses the `adSchemaColumns` schema to populate the *objColumnDict* Dictionary object. For each column in the database table specified by *strTableName*, there is a `ColumnInformation` instance created and added to *objColumnDict*. As the column information is collected, a SQL query is built up that will later be used to

determine what columns are AutoNumber columns, and if the *strWhereClause*
was specified, the values for a particular row.

*Example 6-6. The PopulateColumns Method Obtains Detailed Information About Each
Column in a Particular Database Table*

```
<%
Class Columns
    '... Member variables and Class Event Handlers not shown here;
    '    These were both shown in Example 6-5 ...

    '********************** METHODS **********************
    Public Sub PopulateColumns(strTableName, objConn, strWhereClause)
        'This sub is responsible for populating the objColumnDict
        'dictionary object with the columns from the table strTableName.
        'objConn is expected to be an opened connection to the
        'proper database

        'Make sure a proper table name was passed in
        If Len(strTableName) = 0 then
            Err.Raise vbObjectError + 1280, "Columns Class", _
                "In PopulateColumns method: TableName not supplied."
        End If

        Dim objRS        'Open up the column schema
        Set objRS = objConn.OpenSchema(adSchemaColumns, _
                            Array(Empty, Empty, strTableName, Empty))

        'Add a ColumnInformation object instance for each column that
        'exists within the table specified by strTableName.  Also,
        'build up a SQL statement
        Dim objColumn, strSQL
        strSQL = "SELECT "
        Do While Not objRS.EOF
            Set objColumn = New ColumnInformation

            objColumn.Name = objRS("COLUMN_NAME")
            objColumn.DataType = objRS("DATA_TYPE")
            objColumn.HasDefault = objRS("COLUMN_HASDEFAULT")
            objColumn.DefaultValue = objRS("COLUMN_DEFAULT")
            objColumn.Nullable = objRS("IS_NULLABLE")
            objColumn.Description = objRS("DESCRIPTION")
            objColumn.Identity = False
            objColumn.PrimaryKey = False

            objColumnDict.Add objColumn.Name, objColumn
            strSQL = strSQL & "[" & objColumn.Name & "]"

            Set objColumn = Nothing
            objRS.MoveNext

            If Not objRS.EOF then strSQL = RTrim(strSQL) & ","
        Loop

        'Now we need to grab the PrimaryKey information
```

Example 6-6. The PopulateColumns Method Obtains Detailed Information About Each Column in a Particular Database Table (continued)

```
        objRS.Close
        Set objRS = Nothing

        Set objRS = objConn.OpenSchema(adSchemaPrimaryKeys, _
                          Array(Empty, Empty, strTableName))
        Do While Not objRS.EOF
            objColumnDict(objRS("COLUMN_NAME").Value).PrimaryKey = True
            objRS.MoveNext
        Loop

        'Now we need to obtain the identity columns/column values
        strSQL = strSQL & " FROM [" & strTableName & "]"
        If Len(strWhereClause) > 0 then
            strSQL = strSQL & " WHERE " & strWhereClause
        End If

        'We need to grab a row from the database to determine if we have any
        'identity columns, and to populate our row values, if needed
        objRS.Close
        Set objRS = Nothing

        Set objRS = Server.CreateObject("ADODB.Recordset")
        objRS.MaxRecords = 1      'Get only one record
        objRS.Open strSQL, objConn

        'If there are no records in this table, we can't perform this loop
        If Not objRS.EOF then
          Dim objField
          For Each objField in objRS.Fields
            objColumnDict(objField.Name).Value = objField.Value
            If objField.Properties("ISAUTOINCREMENT") then
              objColumnDict(objField.Name).Identity = True
            End If
          Next
        End If


        'Clean up...
        objRS.Close
        Set objRS = Nothing
    End Sub

    '... Some methods and properties not shown; these methods are shown
    '    in Example 6-7; the properties were presented in Example 6-5 ...
End Class
%>
```

The tasks PopulateColumns needs to complete are pretty straightforward, but some convoluted code is needed to accomplish them. To populate the *objColumnDict* object, the adSchemaColumns schema is used with the *Criteria* set to only return columns for the database table specified by *strTableName*. As the schema contents are iterated, a ColumnInformation object instance is created at each iteration, and its properties are set according to the values for the current column in the schema. Note that the column names are also added to a SQL query as this loop progresses.

Once this loop has finished, PopulateColumns knows a great deal about each column in the database table specified by *strTableName*. However, it is still unknown what columns (if any) are AutoNumber columns and what columns (if any) are primary key columns.

To determine what columns are primary keys, we use the OpenSchema method to open the adSchemaPrimaryKeys schema, restricting the primary keys returned to the primary keys in the table *strTableName*. Next, the schema is iterated, and the columns in *objColumnDict* that match the COLUMN_NAME returned by the adSchemaPrimaryKeys have their PrimaryKey property set to True.

Determining what columns are AutoNumber columns is a tad more difficult. The AutoNumber property is not available in any schema. Part of the reason is AutoNumber is not a column datatype or column constraint; rather, it is a column property, making it a bit of an anomaly. Since AutoNumber columns are not a required standard in relational databases, ADO does not provide AutoNumber information in schemas, which is really annoying, in my opinion.

To determine whether a particular column is an AutoNumber or not, we must consult the dynamic Properties collection of the ADO Recordset. The Properties collection is available through the *Field* object, and can contain a varying number of properties. What we are looking for is a property named IS_AUTONUMBER, which, if the property exists, contains a True or False value.

At this point, PopulateColumns might also need to determine the values of the columns for a particular row (this would be the case if the user is updating an existing record, in which case the update form needs to know the current values for the column to be edited). Therefore, we'll kill two birds with one stone, gathering both the values for a particular record, if needed, and determining what columns are AutoNumbers.

To accomplish this, we need to retrieve the appropriate query from the table—this is where the dynamic SQL query that was built comes in. This SELECT statement query is used to return the particular row of interest, as specified by *strWhereClause*. If *strWhereClause* is not specified, the entire table might be returned, which is fine, but a bit of a performance drag if the table contains a large number of rows. Therefore, the MaxRecords property is set to 1, which, for database providers that support the MaxRecords property, will bring back only one row.

The Columns class contains four other methods that return information about primary key columns; these are shown in Example 6-7. When the "Edit Existing Records" administration page is run, information uniquely identifying the record being edited from all other records must be known. The GetPrimaryKeys method returns a comma-delimited list of primary key column names and values. This list of names and values will come in handy when updating a record in the database.

The QuotedValue private member function surrounds a primary key value in single quotes if the column datatype is a textual type or a date/time type. This is a requirement for SQL statements; that is, the value of a textual or date/time column must be surrounded by quotes in the WHERE clause. The Replace method is used on the column's value, replacing all instances of apostrophes with two concurrent apostrophes. This measure prevents SQL from choking on single apostrophes in textual data. To learn more about this, be sure to read "How to Deal with Apostrophes in your SQL String," available at: *http://www.4GuysFromRolla.com/webtech/ 051899-1.shtml.*

To delete a record or select a particular record to edit, the contents of a database table must be listed, and a checkbox or radio button must be present to allow the user to either select a number of records (in the case of deleting) or select a particular record (in the case of choosing which record to edit). In both of these cases, the primary key(s) and their respective value(s) must be returned for each row listed, since the primary key(s) are what uniquely identify each record in the table. To delete one or more records, it is essential that the right primary key values be known!

The GetCurrentPrimaryKeys method is nearly identical to the GetPrimaryKeys method; it differs in two ways: it expects an opened Recordset object to be passed in, and it calls the CurrentQuotedValue helper function instead of QuotedValue. The CurrentQuotedValue helper function operates just like QuotedValue, except, like GetCurrentPrimaryKeys, it expects an opened Recordset object to be passed in. Also, CurrentQuotedValue returns the value of the current row of the recordset, as opposed to the Value property of the ColumnInformation instance.

When we examine our generic administration page generation script later in the chapter, we'll see how the four methods listed in Example 6-7 aid in the administration page generation process.

Example 6-7. The Remaining Columns Class Methods

```
<%
Class Columns
    '... Member variables and Class Event Handlers not shown here;
    '    These were both shown in Example 6-5 ...

    '********************** METHODS **********************
    Public Function GetPrimaryKeys()
        Dim strColumnName, strResult
        For Each strColumnName in objColumnDict
            If objColumnDict(strColumnName).PrimaryKey then
                If Len(strResult) > 0 then strResult = strResult & " AND "
```

Example 6-7. The Remaining Columns Class Methods (continued)

```
          strResult = strResult & "[" & _
                  objColumnDict(strColumnName).Name & _
                  "] = " & QuotedValue(strColumnName)

          'Make sure we got a valid QuotedValue
          If Len(QuotedValue(strColumnName)) = 0 then
              Err.Raise vbObjectError + 1281, "Columns Class", _
                  "In method GetPrimaryKeys: Unable to Retrieve Value"
          End If
        End If
      Next

    GetPrimaryKeys = strResult
End Function

Private Function QuotedValue(strColumnName)
    'Returns the value of a column, surrounding it with
    'single tick marks if it is a text or date field
    Dim iDataType, strResult
    iDataType = objColumnDict(strColumnName).DataType

    If iDataType = adDate OR iDataType = adDBTimeStamp _
        OR iDataType = adChar OR iDataType = adVarChar _
        OR iDataType = adLongVarChar OR iDataType = adWChar _
        OR iDataType = adVarWChar OR _
        iDataType = adLongVarWChar then
            strResult = "'" & _
                Replace(objColumnDict(strColumnName).Value, "'", "''") & "'"
      Else
            strResult = objColumnDict(strColumnName).Value
      End If

    QuotedValue = strResult
End Function


Public Function GetCurrentPrimaryKeys(objRS)
    Dim strColumnName, strResult
    For Each strColumnName in objColumnDict
      If objColumnDict(strColumnName).PrimaryKey then
        If Len(strResult) > 0 then strResult = strResult & " AND "
        strResult = strResult & "[" & _
                objColumnDict(strColumnName).Name & _
                "] = " & CurrentQuotedValue(strColumnName, objRS)

          'Make sure we got a valid QuotedValue
          If Len(CurrentQuotedValue(strColumnName, objRS)) = 0 then
              Err.Raise vbObjectError + 1281, "Columns Class", _
                  "In method GetCurrentPrimaryKeys: Unable to Retrieve Value"
          End If
        End If
      Next
```

Example 6-7. The Remaining Columns Class Methods (continued)

```
    GetCurrentPrimaryKeys = strResult
End Function


Private Function CurrentQuotedValue(strColumnName, objRS)
    'Returns the value of a column, surrounding it with
    'single tick marks if it is a text or date field
    Dim iDataType, strResult
    iDataType = objColumnDict(strColumnName).DataType

    If iDataType = adDate OR iDataType = adDBTimeStamp _
        OR iDataType = adChar OR iDataType = adVarChar _
        OR iDataType = adLongVarChar OR iDataType = adWChar _
        OR iDataType = adVarWChar OR _
        iDataType = adLongVarWChar then

            strResult = "'" & _
                Replace(objRS(strColumnName).Value, "'", "''") & "'"
    Else
            strResult = objRS(strColumnName).Value
    End If

    CurrentQuotedValue = strResult
End Function
'*****************************************************

'... The PopulateColumns method and some properties are not shown;
'    the PopulateColumns method was presented in Example 6-6, and
'    the Properties were presented in Example 6-5 ...
End Class
%>
```

Testing the Columns and ColumnInformation classes

Now that we have created two classes to assist with storing database column information, let's give them a whirl!

 A "testing" section will immediately follow each major section that introduces a new class or set of classes. This testing section will show the class in use.

Since the `ColumnInformation` class contains only a set of read/write properties, a thorough example is not possible. However, Example 6-8 illustrates a simple test driver for the class.

Example 6-8. ColumnInformation Stores Information About a Table Column

```
<% @LANGUAGE="VBSCRIPT" %>
<% Option Explicit %>
<!--#include virtual="/CODEREUSE/Column.Class.asp"-->
```

Example 6-8. ColumnInformation Stores Information About a Table Column (continued)

```
<%
  'Create an instance of the ColumnInformation class
  Dim objColumnInfo
  Set objColumnInfo = New ColumnInformation

  'Set the properties of the class
  objColumnInfo.Name = "FirstName"
  objColumnInfo.DataType = adVarChar
  objColumnInfo.Nullable = False
  objColumnInfo.Identity = False
  objColumnInfo.PrimaryKey = False

  'Use the class somehow...
  Response.Write "COLUMN NAME: " & objColumnInfo.Name

  Set objColumnInfo = Nothing                'Clean up!
%>
```

To use the class, we start by importing the `ColumnInformation` class definition via a server-side include. Next, an instance of the class is created and some of its properties are assigned values. After the properties have been assigned values, feel free to do whatever testing you want. With this class you are limited to reassigning property values or reading the property values. For a simple test, Example 6-8 simply outputs the value of the Name property.

Note that the DataType property is assigned the value of an ADO constant. `adVarChar` (which has a value of 200) is a constant defined in *adovbs.inc*. The previous script does not explicitly include *adovbs.inc* since it assumes you have implemented the METADATA alternative discussed in the section "Importing enumerations with the METADATA tag." If this is not the case, however, you need to include *adovbs.inc* in each ASP page before you include any of the generic administration page generation classes.

The `Columns` class, which uses the `ColumnInformation` class internally, maintains column information for a particular database table. As discussed earlier, the PopulateColumns method, which uses the `adSchemaColumns` schema to acquire column information about a specified database table, takes three parameters, having the following definition:

```
Public Sub PopulateColumns(strTableName, objConn, strWhereClause)
```

For our test examples, we'll examine the `Products` table of our example database (see Table 6-2). Before calling the PopulateColumns method, we'll need to have successfully opened a connection to the database. The opened Connection object is the second parameter.

For our first test, we will send a blank string for the *strWhereClause* parameter. This tells PopulateColumns that we are just interested in knowing the column structure of the table. In the "Insert a New Record" administration page, where we are just interested in knowing the topology of the table, we will not supply a *strWhereClause* parameter.

If we were interested in knowing the values for a specific row in the table, we'd pass in a legal SQL WHERE clause statement as the *strWhereClause* parameter that would return exactly one row from the table. In the "Edit an Existing Record" administration page, where we'd like to know the existing values for the record being edited (so the user can see what the current values are), we'll supply a *strWhereClause* parameter.

Example 6-9 contains a test driver for the Columns class that obtains the column information for the Product table. Note that in this example the PopulateColumns method is called without specifying a *strWhereClause* parameter.

Example 6-9. The Generic Topology of the Product Table Is Obtained

```
<% @LANGUAGE="VBSCRIPT" %>
<% Option Explicit %>
<!--#include virtual="/CODEREUSE/Column.Class.asp"-->
<%
  'Open a database connection
  Dim objConn
  Set objConn = Server.createObject("ADODB.Connection")
  objConn.ConnectionString = "Provider=SQLOLEDB;Data Source=mitchell;" & _
                 "Initial Catalog=ProductInfo;User ID=sa;Password="
  objConn.Open

  'Create an instance of the Columns class
  Dim objColumns
  Set objColumns = New Columns

  'Populate the columns collection with the Product table information
  objColumns.PopulateColumns "Product", objConn, ""

  'At this point, we have access to a list of the column information in the
  'Product table.
  Dim strColumnName, objColumnInfo

  'We wish to loop through all of the columns in objColumns ColumnList
  For Each strColumnName in objColumns.ColumnList
    'Assign the specific ColumnInformation instance to a local variable
    Set objColumnInfo = objColumns.GetColumnInformation(strColumnName)

    'Output the ColumnInformation instance's properties
    Response.Write "<B>" & objColumnInfo.Name & "</B><BR>"
    Response.Write "Value: " & objColumnInfo.Value & ", "
    Response.Write "DataType: " & objColumnInfo.DataType & ", "
    Response.Write "<P><HR><P>"
```

Example 6-9. The Generic Topology of the Product Table Is Obtained (continued)

```
    Set objColumnInfo = Nothing
  Next

  Set objColumns = Nothing        'Clean up

  'Close the database
  objConn.Close
  Set objConn = Nothing
%>
```

Example 6-9 shows how easy it is to acquire detailed column information about a database table using just a few lines of code. The `Columns` class masks all the complexity in opening the proper schema and iterating through it. Since we did not specify a *strWhereClause* in our call to PopulateColumns, the Value property for each of the columns is meaningless, grabbed from a random record in the table.

Figure 6-3 contains a screenshot of Example 6-9 when viewed through a browser.

When generating the "Insert a New Record" administration page, code similar to that in Example 6-9 will be used to ascertain the topology of the administration page table. When displaying the "Edit an Existing Record" administration page, however, we will need to be able to grab information about a particular record in the database; specifically, we're interested in the record the user selected to edit.

If the *strWhereClause* parameter is specified in the call to PopulateColumns, the column values for a particular row are entered into the Value property of each `ColumnInformation` instance. Therefore, if we want to obtain column values for a particular row along with the general topology of the `Product` table, we could adjust our call to PopulateColumns to contain an *strWhereClause* parameter. For example, if we want our `objColumns` class instance in Example 6-9 to have the column values for the column where `ProductID` equals 2, we would only need to adjust our call to PopulateColumns like so:

```
    objColumns.PopulateColumns "Product", objConn, "ProductID = 2"
```

Now that we've examined how to collect column information, we'll look at how to use similar techniques to obtain foreign key constraining information.

Gathering Foreign Key Information

In "A Review of Database Terms," we discussed the importance of properly displaying foreign key columns in a database table. Remember that foreign key columns in a table will contain data that maps back to a primary key in another table. Since foreign key columns are usually stored as numeric data, foreign key columns are a bit tricky to handle in a generic administration page. When adding a

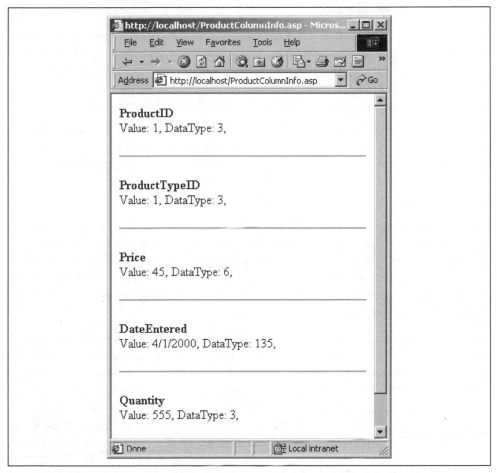

Figure 6-3. The topology of the Product table is revealed through the Columns class

new record or deleting an existing record, all foreign key constraints should be displayed as a list box of easy-to-read options.

Of course, to be able to accomplish this goal, all of the foreign key constraints in a table must be identified. The adSchemaForeignKeys schema, as its name suggests, provides a list of all of the foreign key constraints in a database.

Unfortunately, the adSchemaForeignKeys schema somewhat limits our choices of database providers. At the time of this writing, only the SQL OLE-DB and the Jet 4.0 providers support this schema. For instance, trying to access the adSchemaForeignKeys schema using an ODBC provider, will result in an error. This is a tradeoff worth making, though, since an generic administration page generation application that cannot properly handle tables with foreign key constraints is severely limited in its usefulness.

The ForeignKeyInformation class

To collect information about the columns in a database table, two classes—
ColumnInformation and Columns—were used. The ColumnInformation class
was responsible for holding the information needed to describe a particular column. The Columns class served as a container for zero to many ColumnInformation instances, representing all of the columns in a particular database table.

A very similar approach is used to gather foreign key information. A
ForeignKeyInformation class is used to store specific information on each foreign key constraint, while a ForeignKeys class serves as a container, holding zero
or more ForeignKeyInformation instances. Both of these classes should be created in a single file, */CODEREUSE/ForeignKey.Class.asp*.

As with ColumnInformation, ForeignKeyInformation simply contains read/
write properties needed to describe a foreign key constraint. Only three member
variables are needed: the column name that has the foreign key constraint placed
upon it (*strColumnName*), the name of the related table that issued the foreign
key constraint (*strPKTableName*), and the name of the primary key column in the
related table (*strPKColumn*).

With our example database (described in Table 6-2), if we wanted to identify all
foreign key constraints for the Product table, we would find that there was
exactly one foreign key constraint, which would be represented by a single
instance of the ForeignKeyInformation class. In this instance of the
ForeignKeyInformation class, the *strColumnName* member variable would be
set to the Product table's ProductTypeID column; the *strPKTableName* member variable would be set to ProductType; finally, the *strPKColumnName*
member variable would be set to ProductType's primary key, ProductTypeID.

Example 6-10 contains the ForeignKeyInformation class definition. Like the
ColumnInformation class, there are no methods or event handlers, just property
statements for the three member variables.

*Example 6-10. A ForeignKeyInformation Instance Represents a Single Foreign
Key Constraint*

```
<%
Class ForeignKeyInformation
    '************** MEMBER VARIABLES *********************
    Private strColumnName
    Private strPKTableName
    Private strPKColumnName
    '****************************************************

    '***************** GET PROPERTIES *******************
    Public Property Get ColumnName()
      ColumnName = strColumnName
    End Property
```

Example 6-10. A ForeignKeyInformation Instance Represents a Single Foreign Key Constraint (continued)

```
    Public Property Get PrimaryKeyTable()
      PrimaryKeyTable = strPKTableName
    End Property

    Public Property Get PrimaryKeyColumn()
      PrimaryKeyColumn = strPKColumnName
    End Property
    '****************************************************

    '***************** LET PROPERTIES *****************
    Public Property Let ColumnName(str)
      strColumnName = str
    End Property

    Public Property Let PrimaryKeyTable(strPKTable)
      strPKTableName = strPKTable
    End Property

    Public Property Let PrimaryKeyColumn(strPKColumn)
      strPKColumnName = strPKColumn
    End Property
    '****************************************************
End Class
%>
```

The ForeignKeys class

The `ForeignKeys` class serves as a container for zero to many `ForeignKeyInformation` instances. Like the Columns class, the `ForeignKeys` class only has a single member variable, *objFKDict*, which is a Dictionary object instance that holds information about the foreign key constraints for a particular table.

The `ForeignKeys` class contains three methods. The first method, PopulateForeignKeys, simply populates the *objFKDict* Dictionary object with the foreign key constraints from a particular table. The second method, GetForeignKeyInformation, returns a specific foreign key constraint instance from *objFKDict*. The final method, ForeignKeyExists, allows the developer to determine whether or not a particular foreign key constraint exists within the *objFKDict* Dictionary object.

The methods, properties, and event handlers for the `ForeignKeys` class are presented in Example 6-11.

Example 6-11. The ForeignKeys Class Serves as a Container for Zero to Many ForeignKeyInformation Instances

```
<%
Class ForeignKeys
  '************** MEMBER VARIABLES *****************
```

Example 6-11. The ForeignKeys Class Serves as a Container for Zero to Many
ForeignKeyInformation Instances (continued)

```
Private objFKDict
'*****************************************************

'******************** EVENT HANDLERS ******************
Private Sub Class_Initialize()
  Set objFKDict = Server.CreateObject("Scripting.Dictionary")
End Sub

Private Sub Class_Terminate()
  Set objFKDict = Nothing        'Clean up...
End Sub
'*****************************************************

'********************** METHODS **********************
Public Sub PopulateForeignKeys(strTableName, objConn)
  'This sub is responsible for populating the objFKDict
  'dictionary object with the foreign keys from the table
  'strTableName.  objConn is expected to be an opened connection
  'to the proper database.

  Dim objRS      'Open up the column schema
  Set objRS = objConn.OpenSchema(adSchemaForeignKeys, _
              Array(Empty, Empty, Empty, Empty, Empty, strTableName))

  'Add a ForeignKeyInformation object instance for each column that
  'exists within the table specified by strTableName
  Dim objFK
  Do While Not objRS.EOF
     Set objFK = New ForeignKeyInformation

     objFK.ColumnName = objRS("FK_COLUMN_NAME")
     objFK.PrimaryKeyTable = objRS("PK_TABLE_NAME")
     objFK.PrimaryKeyColumn = objRS("PK_COLUMN_NAME")

     objFKDict.Add objFK.ColumnName, objFK

     Set objFK = Nothing
     objRS.MoveNext
  Loop

  'Clean up...
  objRS.Close
  Set objRS = Nothing
End Sub

Public Function GetForeignKeyInformation(strFKName)
  'Return a specific FK's information... that is, return a
  'reference to an instance of a ForeignKeyInformation object
  If objFKDict.Exists(strFKName) then
     Set GetForeignKeyInformation = objFKDict(strFKName)
  Else
     Set GetForeignKeyInformation = Nothing
  End If
```

*Example 6-11. The ForeignKeys Class Serves as a Container for Zero to Many
ForeignKeyInformation Instances (continued)*

```
    End Function

    Public Function ForeignKeyExists(strFKName)
        ForeignKeyExists = objFKDict.Exists(strFKName)
    End Function
    '*****************************************************

    '***************** GET PROPERTIES ******************
    Public Property Get Count()
        Count = objFKDict.Count
    End Property
    '*****************************************************
End Class
%>
```

Take a moment to compare the coding styles used to create the `ForeignKeys` and
`Columns` classes. Although these two classes are nearly functionally identical, they
have differing methods. For example, the `Columns` class contains a `Property Get`
function that returns the entire *objColumnDict* Dictionary object. The
`ForeignKeys` class, however, uses a method to return the *objFKDict* collection.

The reason for these differences is to demonstrate that there is more than one way
to do things. Of course, when using several related classes to accomplish a common goal, it is usually best to have those classes share similar interfaces. That is, if
two classes are as functionally similar as `Columns` and `ForeignKeys`, it probably
only confuses an end developer who has to use different methods and properties
for each class to accomplish nearly the same thing.

A good example is the ADO objects, which share common method names. For
example, the Connection and Recordset objects both have an Open method,
which, from a high-level view, does the same thing. Since the classes presented in
this chapter are not going to be directly used in practice, I think showing multiple
ways to accomplish the same thing is useful for the reader; hence the differences
between the `Columns` class and the `ForeignKeys` class.

Additionally, `ForeignKeys` differs from the `Columns` class in that it lacks a property to return the entire collection of `ForeignKeyInformation` instances. Rather,
the `ForeignKeys` class contains only a single property that returns the number of
`ForeignKeyInformation` instances in the *objFKDict* collection, and a collection to pick out a specific element from *objFKDict* if the developer knows the
name beforehand. This makes it difficult for an end developer to iterate the
objFKDict collection, since the only way an end developer can access a
`ForeignKeyInformation` instance is if he knows the column name of the
`ForeignKeyInformation` instance.

This is not a problem, though, because in the generic administration page generation application we're creating, the end developer will have to specify how to

handle each foreign key column. Since the end developer provides this information, we know exactly what the column names of each `ForeignKeyInformation` instance will be. This may seem a bit confusing now, but it should become clearer when we discuss the `AdminPageGenerator` class in the section "Creating the Administration Page Forms."

Testing the ForeignKeys and ForeignKeyInformation classes

Like the `ColumnInformation` class, the `ForeignKeyInformation` class contains only a set of read/write properties; therefore, a detailed example is not possible. Regardless, Example 6-12 illustrates a simple test driver for the class. As with Example 6-8, in which we created a simple test driver for the `Column-Information` class, you must use a server-side include to import the class definition of `ForeignKeyInformation` in */CODEREUSE/ForeignKey.Class.asp* when using the class.

Example 6-12. The ForeignKeyInformation Class Contains Three Read/Write Properties

```
<% @LANGUAGE="VBSCRIPT" %>
<% Option Explicit %>
<!--#include virtual="/CODEREUSE/ForeignKey.Class.asp"-->
<%
  'Create an instance of the ForeignKeyInformation class
  Dim objFKInfo
  Set objFKInfo = New ForeignKeyInformation

  'Set the properties
  objFKInfo.PrimaryKeyTable = "ProductType"
  objFKInfo.PrimaryKeyColumn = "ProductTypeID"
  objFKInfo.ColumnName = "ProductTypeID"

  'Now that we have set the ForeignKeyInformation properties, do something!
  Response.Write "Primary Key Table = " & objFKInfo.PrimaryKeyTable

  Set objFKInfo = Nothing        'Clean up
%>
```

Since we cannot iterate through all the items in the *objFKDict* collection in the `ForeignKeys` class, we'll have to use a specific table that we know has a foreign key constraint for our test example of the `ForeignKeys` class. We know the `Product` table contains one foreign key constraint, from its `ProductTypeID` column to the `ProductTypeID` column of the `ProductType` table. Therefore, let's use the `ForeignKeys` class to obtain the foreign key constraint information for `Product`.

Like the `Columns` class, the `ForeignKeys` class contains a method that does all of the low-level work needed to obtain the foreign key constraint information. This method, PopulateForeignKeys, expects two parameters: a table name and an opened Connection object. The method's task is to populate the *objFKDict* Dictionary object with the foreign key constraint information for the specified database table.

Example 6-13 contains a test driver for the `ForeignKeys` class. This test driver starts by opening a connection to the database. Next, an instance of the `ForeignKeys` class is created and the PopulateForeignKeys method is called. Finally, the foreign key constraint information for the `Product` table's `Product-TypeID` column is output. The output of the code presented in Example 6-13, when viewed through a browser, can be seen in Figure 6-4.

Example 6-13. The ForeignKeys Class Canr Obtain the Foreign Key Constraints for a Particular Table

```asp
<% @LANGUAGE="VBSCRIPT" %>
<% Option Explicit %>
<!--#include virtual="/CODEREUSE/ForeignKey.Class.asp"-->
<%
  'Create a Connection object
  Dim objConn
  Set objConn = Server.CreateObject("ADODB.Connection")
  objConn.ConnectionString = "Provider=SQLOLEDB;Data Source=mitchell;" & _
                  "Initial Catalog=ProductInfo;User ID=sa;Password="
  objConn.Open


  'Create an instance of the ForeignKeyInformation class
  Dim objFKs
  Set objFKs = New ForeignKeys

  'Load the foreign key constraints for the Product table
  objFKs.PopulateForeignKeys "Product", objConn

  'Display the ForeignKeyInformation info for the ProductTypeID column
  Dim objFKInfo
  Set objFKInfo = objFKs.GetForeignKeyInformation("ProductTypeID")
  Response.Write "The Product table contains " & objFKs.Count
  Response.Write " foreign key constraints.  Specifically, the column "
  Response.Write objFKInfo.ColumnName & " of the Product table contains "
  Response.Write "a foreign key constraint to the " & objFKInfo.PrimaryKeyColumn
  Response.Write " column of the " & objFKInfo.PrimaryKeyTable & " table."

  Set objFKs = Nothing      'Clean up

  'Close the Connection to the DB
  objConn.Close
  Set objConn = Nothing
%>
```

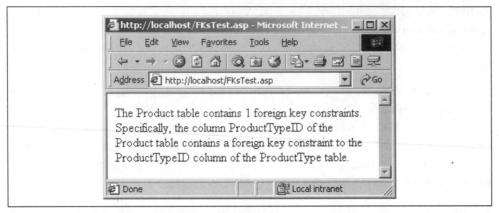

Figure 6-4. The foreign key constraint information on the Product table's ProductTypeID is displayed via the ForeignKeys class

Deciding How to Display the Table Columns in a Form

Part of the challenge of an administration page is deciding how to display the information from a database in a nice-looking HTML form. When creating an administration page for each database table by hand, once the developer decides how to display each table column in a form, all she has to do is create the needed HTML. With a generic, reusable administration page generation script, however, the situation is a bit more difficult, since the burden of deciding what form elements to use for what database table columns is placed squarely on the ASP script.

Needless to say, this makes creating nice-looking administration pages anything but easy. For example, imagine that the generic administration page generation script decided to display all numeric database types using a text box. While this will work, there are times when using a list box is easier for the end user. It's unfair to expect the generic administration page generation script to be intelligent enough to determine the *best* form field for a particular table column.

Since we can't create an all-knowing administration page generation script, we'll create the next best thing: an administration page generation script that doesn't mind receiving advice. The generic administration page generation script will have its own ideas on what the best form fields are for a given database column type, but if the end developer kindly asks the script to use a different form field for a particular database column, the script will dutifully oblige.

The DataTypeFormElementInformation class

Not surprisingly, to provide the functionality needed to determine what form element to use with what database table column, we'll employ a class. This class, `DataTypeFormElementInformation`, does exactly what its verbose name implies: it maps a particular datatype to a particular form element. A member variable, *objDataTypeDict*, is used to store a form element type for each possible datatype. When the form for updating an existing record or inserting a new record is generated, an instance of this class is consulted to aid in determining how to display the table's particular columns.

Since the *objDataTypeDict* member variable proposes to have an entry for each *possible datatype*, it is important that we define the set of possible datatypes. For our application, the set of possible datatypes are those datatypes that have constants defined in *adovbs.inc*.

Example 6-14 holds the class definition for `DataTypeFormElementInformation`, which should be stored in the file */CODEREUSE/SchemaInfo.Class.asp*. Two other member variables used in the `DataTypeFormElementInformation` class are *objFormNameDict* and *objFormDescriptionDict*; we'll look at these momentarily. For the time being, focus on the emphasized text in Example 6-14, which contains the *objDataTypeDict* member variable declaration, its initialization, and its `Property Let` and `Property Get` statements.

Example 6-14. The DataTypeFormElementInformation Class Provides Form Display Information for Specific Database Table Columns

```
<%
Class DataTypeFormElementInformation
    '************** MEMBER VARIABLES ********************
    Private objDataTypeDict
    Private objFormNameDict
    Private objFormDescriptionDict
    '******************************************************

    '****************** EVENT HANDLERS ******************
    Private Sub Class_Initialize()
        Set objDataTypeDict = Server.CreateObject("Scripting.Dictionary")
        Set objFormNameDict = Server.CreateObject("Scripting.Dictionary")
        Set objFormDescriptionDict = Server.CreateObject("Scripting.Dictionary")

        'Set the default datatype form element values
        objDataTypeDict.Add CStr(adInteger), _
            "<INPUT TYPE=TEXT SIZE=10 NAME=""col_~COLUMNNAME~""" & _
            " VALUE=""~COLUMNVALUE~"">"
        objDataTypeDict.Add CStr(adCurrency), _
            "$<INPUT TYPE=TEXT SIZE=10 NAME=""col_~COLUMNNAME~""" & _
            " VALUE=""~COLUMNVALUE~"">"
        objDataTypeDict.Add CStr(adNumeric), _
            "<INPUT TYPE=TEXT SIZE=15 NAME=""col_~COLUMNNAME~""" & _
            " VALUE=""~COLUMNVALUE~"">"
        objDataTypeDict.Add CStr(adBoolean), _
            "<SELECT NAME=""col_~COLUMNNAME~"">" & vbCrLf & _
```

*Example 6-14. The DataTypeFormElementInformation Class Provides Form Display
Information for Specific Database Table Columns (continued)*

```
                "<OPTION VALUE=""1"" ~COLUMNVALUE~>Yes</OPTION>" & vbCrLf & _
                "<OPTION VALUE=""0"" ~COLUMNVALUE~>No</OPTION>" & vbCrLf & _
                "</SELECT>"
    objDataTypeDict.Add CStr(adDate), _
                "<INPUT TYPE=TEXT SIZE=10 NAME=""col_~COLUMNNAME~""" & _
                " VALUE=""~COLUMNVALUE~"">"
    objDataTypeDict.Add CStr(adChar), _
                "<INPUT TYPE=TEXT SIZE=25 NAME=""col_~COLUMNNAME~""" & _
                " VALUE=""~COLUMNVALUE~"">"
    objDataTypeDict.Add CStr(adWChar), _
                "<INPUT TYPE=TEXT SIZE=25 NAME=""col_~COLUMNNAME~""" & _
                " VALUE=""~COLUMNVALUE~"">"
    objDataTypeDict.Add CStr(adVarChar), _
                "<INPUT TYPE=TEXT SIZE=25 NAME=""col_~COLUMNNAME~""" & _
                " VALUE=""~COLUMNVALUE~"">"
    objDataTypeDict.Add CStr(adVarWChar), _
                "<INPUT TYPE=TEXT SIZE=25 NAME=""col_~COLUMNNAME~""" & _
                " VALUE=""~COLUMNVALUE~"">"


    ' ... Several datatypes were excluded here for brevity.  Consult
    '      adovbs.inc for a full listing of possible datatypes ...
End Sub

Private Sub Class_Terminate()
  'Cleanup time!
  Set objDataTypeDict = Nothing
  Set objFormNameDict = Nothing
  Set objFormDescriptionDict = Nothing
End Sub
'*****************************************************


'***************** GET PROPERTIES *******************
Public Property Get DataTypeFormElement(iDataType)
    DataTypeFormElement = objDataTypeDict(CStr(iDataType))
End Property

Public Property Get FormElementName(strFormName)
    FormElementName = objFormNameDict(strFormName)
End Property

Public Property Get FormElementDescription(strFormName)
    FormElementDescription = objFormDescriptionDict(strFormName)
End Property
'*****************************************************


'***************** LET PROPERTIES *******************
Public Property Let DataTypeFormElement(iDataType, strFormValue)
    'Check to see if the element exists in the dictionary object.
    'If it does, update the current value, else add a new value
    If objDataTypeDict.Exists(CStr(iDataType)) then
      'Alter the current value
```

Example 6-14. The DataTypeFormElementInformation Class Provides Form Display Information for Specific Database Table Columns (continued)

```
            objDataTypeDict(CStr(iDataType)) = strFormValue
        Else
            'A new element, so add it!
            objDataTypeDict.Add CStr(iDataType), strFormValue
        End If
End Property

Public Property Let FormElementName(strFormNameValue, strFormName)
        'Check to see if the element exists in the dictionary object.
        'If it does, update the current value, else add a new value
        If objFormNameDict.Exists(CStr(iDataType)) then
            'Alter the current value
            objFormNameDict(strFormName) = strFormNameValue
        Else
            'A new element, so add it!
            objDataTypeDict.Add strFormName, strFormNameValue
        End If
End Property

Public Property Let FormElementDescription(strFormValue, strFormName)
        'Check to see if the element exists in the dictionary object.
        'If it does, update the current value, else add a new value
        If objDataTypeDict.Exists(CStr(iDataType)) then
            'Alter the current value
            objDataTypeDict(CStr(iDataType)) = strFormValue
        Else
            'A new element, so add it!
            objDataTypeDict.Add CStr(iDataType), strFormValue
        End If
End Property
'****************************************************
End Class
%>
```

In the Initialize event handler, *objDataTypeDict* is assigned to a new Dictionary object instance and is populated with the various table column datatypes and their corresponding form element values. For example, integer (`adInteger`) data is to be displayed using an HTML text box control (`<INPUT TYPE=TEXT...>`). Note that the form elements contain strings like ~COLUMNNAME~ and ~COLUMNVALUE~. These tilde-delimited strings are referred to as *placeholders*. When generating the administration page, before the HTML to display the form element is sent to the browser, these placeholders are replaced with specific values. The ~COLUMNNAME~ placeholder is replaced with the name of the database field that the form element represents. At the "Insert a New Record" administration page, the ~COLUMNVALUE~ placeholder is replaced with the column's default value, if it exists. If the column has no default value, the ~COLUMNVALUE~ placeholder is simply removed before the HTML is sent to the browser. In the "Edit an Existing Record" administration page, the ~COLUMNVALUE~ placeholder is replaced with the value of the column of the record being edited.

Note that *objDataTypeDict* is populated with a default form element string for each datatype in the Initialize event handler. For
brevity, only a subset of available datatypes is shown in the Initialize event handler. When using this class in practice, it is important
that all possible datatypes have an entry in *objDataTypeDict*. Consult *adovbs.inc* to see a complete listing of possible datatypes.

To retrieve the form element string that's used to display a particular datatype from
the *objDataTypeDict* Dictionary object, use the DataTypeFormElement property. This **Property Get** statement returns a single value from the
objDataTypeDict Dictionary object. For example, the form element string for an
Integer datatype can be obtained using the following code:

```
objDataTypeFormElementInfoInstance.DataTypeFormElement(adInteger)
```

As mentioned earlier, the end developer has an opportunity to provide the administration page generation script with some hints on how to display particular
datatypes. The DataTypeFormElement's **Property Let** statement adds a new key/
value pair to *objDataTypeDict* if the key does not already exist; otherwise, the
Property Let statement modifies the existing entry in *objDataTypeDict*, and is
used in the following manner:

```
ObjInstance.DataTypeFormElement(DataType) = strNewFormValue
```

The end developer will never call this property directly. Rather, if the
DataTypeFormElement property needs to be modified, the
AdminPageGenerator class will call it. The **AdminPageGenerator**
class, which is discussed in detail later in this chapter in "Creating
the Administration Page Forms," is responsible for creating the actual
forms needed for the various administration pages.

DataTypeFormElementInformation's other methods

The **DataTypeFormElementInformation** class has two other member variables
that have similar **Property Get** and **Property Let** statements. These two member variables, *objFormNameDict* and *objFormDescriptionDict*, are both Dictionary object instances, like *objDataTypeDict*. Like *objDataTypeDict*, these
two member variables aid in the display of a form. As the code in Example 6-14
shows, they are accessible through the read/write FormElementName and
FormElementDescription properties.

objFormNameDict can be used to give an English-like name to a form field in the
administration form, while *objFormDescriptionDict* can be used to provide a

descriptive sentence or two for each form field. Note that both of these Dictionary objects are initially empty—it is the end developer's responsibility to populate these values. If the end developer fails to do so, the literal column names are presented as the form field names, and the column's description, if it exists, is used as the form field's description.

Figure 6-5 shows the "Insert a New Record" administration page with English-like form name and description values entered by the end developer. Figure 6-6 shows the same administration page's output if the end developer did not specify these helpful names in *objFormNameDict* and *objFormDescriptionDict*.

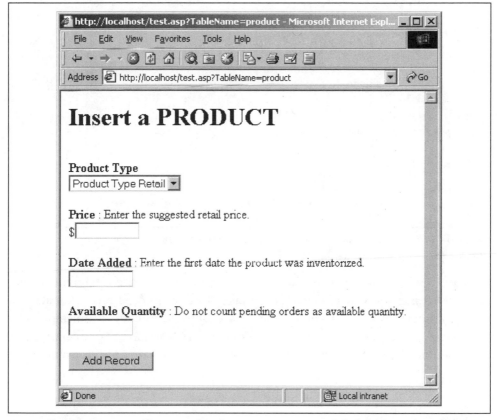

Figure 6-5. The "Insert a New Record" administration page with helpful form element names and descriptions

From the end developer's standpoint, providing labels and detailed explanations for any given number of form fields is quite simple. The end developer simply hints at what particular form fields she'd like to give a specific label or a specific description. The rest default to the column name and the column description, if it exists. An example of assigning customized names and descriptive labels to

Figure 6-6. The "Insert a New Record" administration page without the helpful form element names and descriptions

database fields is shown in Example 6-15, which contains a code fragment that might be written by an end developer to take advantage of the reusable database coding framework we're developing in this chapter. The code in Example 6-15 may seem a bit Greek, since we've yet to discuss the **AdminPageGenerator** class, but it demonstrates how simple it is to label or give a description for a number of form elements.

Example 6-15. Providing Form Element Labels and Descriptions Is an Easy Task for the End Developer

```
'Create an AdminPageGenerator instance
Dim objAdmin
Set objAdmin = new AdminPageGenerator

'Add some form element label hints for specific columns
objAdmin.FormNameHint "ProductTypeID", "Product Type"
objAdmin.FormNameHint "DateEntered", "Date Added"
objAdmin.FormNameHint "Quantity", "Available Quantity"

'Add some form element description hints for specific columns
```

*Example 6-15. Providing Form Element Labels and Descriptions Is an Easy Task for the End
Developer (continued)*

```
objAdmin.FormDescriptionHint "DateEntered", _
        "Enter the first date the product was inventoried."
objAdmin.FormDescriptionHint "Quantity", _
        "Do not count pending orders as available quantity."
objAdmin.FormDescriptionHint "Price", _
        "Enter the suggested retail price."
```

Testing the DataTypeFormElementInformation class

The `DataTypeFormElementInformation` class, like the `ColumnInformation`
and `ForeignKeyInformation` classes, is not well-suited to a detailed test case. A
simple test driver can be seen in Example 6-16. This test driver outputs the default
value of the form element HTML for the `adInteger` datatype. Next, it assigns a
new form element HTML string for `adInteger` and outputs the new value.

*Example 6-16. The DataTypeFormElementInformation Class Provides Display Information for
the Various Datatypes*

```
<% @LANGUAGE="VBSCRIPT" %>
<% Option Explicit %>
<!--#include virtual="/CODEREUSE/SchemaInfo.Class.asp"-->
<%
    'Create an instance of the DataTypeFormElementInformation class
    Dim objDTInfo
    Set objDTInfo = New DataTypeFormElementInformation

    'Use the class somehow... (display the form element for adInteger)
    Response.Write "The default form element HTML for an Integer datatype is:<BR>"
    Response.Write "<XMP>" & objDTInfo.DataTypeFormElement(adInteger) & "</XMP><BR>"
    Response.Write "<FORM>" & objDTInfo.DataTypeFormElement(adInteger) & "</FORM>"

    'Now, adjust the default form element HTML for adInteger
    objDTInfo.DataTypeFormElement(adInteger) = "<SELECT NAME=""~COLUMNNAME~"">" & _
            "<OPTION VALUE=1>1</OPTION><OPTION VALUE=2>2</OPTION></SELECT>"

    'Display the new value
    Response.Write "<P>The new form element HTML for an Integer datatype is:<BR>"
    Response.Write "<XMP>" & objDTInfo.DataTypeFormElement(adInteger) & "</XMP>"
    Response.Write "<FORM>" & objDTInfo.DataTypeFormElement(adInteger) & "</FORM>"

    Set objDTInfo = Nothing        'Clean up
%>
```

Note that Example 6-16 starts with a server-side include to import the contents of
/CODEREUSE/SchemaInfo.Class.asp, which contains the definition of the
`DataTypeFormElementInformation` class. Next, an instance of the `DataType-
FormElementInformation` class is created, and its default `DataTypeForm-
Element` value for the `adInteger` datatype is output.

Since there may be times when the end developer wishes to have a particular datatype displayed a different way, he can set a particular datatype to a particular HTML string in `DataTypeFormElement`. In Example 6-16, the `adInteger` datatype is adjusted to display a list box containing two options: 1 and 2. (This, of course, is not very practical in a real-world application, since there are far more integers than just 1 and 2!) This new form element HTML string is then output.

Figure 6-7 contains a screenshot of the code in Example 6-16 when viewed through a browser.

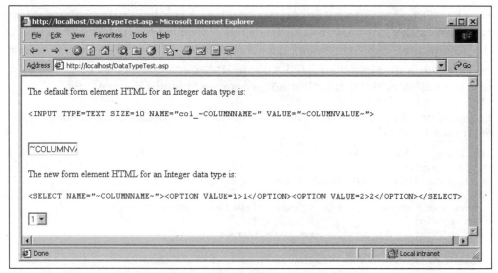

Figure 6-7. The DataTypeFormElementInformation class determines how each column in a table will be displayed in an administration page

The `XMP` tag used in Example 6-16 displays characters in a fixed-width font, ignoring HTML tags. For more information on the `XMP` tag, check out: *http://developer.netscape.com/docs/manuals/htmlguid/ tags4.htm#1424741*.

Before moving on to generating the needed HTML to create the various administration page forms, let's step back and take a look at what information we currently have at our disposal:

Column information

    The `Columns` class contains a collection of `ColumnInformation` classes, storing important information for each column in a particular database table.

Foreign key constraint information

The `ForeignKeys` class contains a collection of `ForeignKeyInformation` classes, storing important information for each foreign key constraint in a particular database table.

Form display information

`DataTypeFormElementInformation` provides detailed information about how each potential column datatype should be represented in an HTML form. This class also permits the end developer to selectively label and provide detailed information for each form field element in a form.

With this information, we can generate a form to update, insert, or delete records from a database with some ease. In the next section, "Creating the Administration Page Forms," the `AdminPageGenerator` class is dissected. This class will be responsible for creating the needed forms.

Creating the Administration Page Forms

Recall that there are three types of administration pages that need to be created:

Insert a new record

Adding a new record requires a form that presents a form field for most columns in the database table. (AutoNumber columns, for example, should not have a form field presented.) Once the user enters values into all of these form fields, a submit button should then insert a new record into the table, using the information just provided by the user.

Delete an existing record

This administration page needs to provide a listing of all of the records currently in the database table. Each record listing should have a checkbox, allowing the user to select multiple records. Once the form is submitted, those selected records should be deleted.

Edit an existing record

This administration page is a hybrid of both the "Insert a New Record" and "Delete an Existing Record" administration pages. Initially, a user needs to select a particular record to edit. This can be accomplished in a fashion similar to the "Delete an Existing Record" interface. Rather than having a checkbox beside each record, though, each record should have a radio button, so the user can only select a single record to edit.

Once the record has been selected, the user should be taken to a form similar to the one in the "Insert a New Record" interface like the ones shown earlier in Figure 6-5 and Figure 6-6. In the "Edit an Existing Record" version of this form, though, each form field should have the value of the record we're editing. The user can then make changes to the existing values and have these changes saved to the database once the form is selected.

Once we display the proper administration page form, our job is only half done; we must still alter the database to reflect this change! This section focuses just on the `AdminPageGenerator` class, which, as its name suggests, is used for creating the administration page forms. In the section "Inserting, Updating, and Deleting Database Records," we'll examine how to commit the users' changes to the database.

The AdminPageGenerator class

Creating a particular administration page form should be a simple task for the end developer using the generic administration page generator presented in this chapter. Ideally, the end developer would only have to use the following code:

```
'Create an instance of the AdminPageGenerator class
Dim objAdmin
Set objAdmin = New AdminPageGenerator

'Display the "Insert a New Record" form for the table Users
Response.Write objAdmin.DisplayInsertRecordForm("Users")

Set objAdmin = Nothing        'Clean up
```

With the `AdminPageGenerator` class, it is nearly that simple. Before we delve into the syntax for the methods that generate the various administration page forms, let's look at the member variables and properties of the `AdminPageGenerator` class.

The AdminPageGenerator member variables and properties

Since each administration page is responsible for allowing the user to insert, update, and delete records from a particular database table, the `Admin-PageGenerator` class is only concerned with the columns and foreign key constraints from a single table. This class should be placed in */CODEREUSE/ SchemaInfo.Class.asp*, which should also contain the class definition for `DataTypeFormElementInformation`. In all the examples, we'll look at showing methods, properties, or event handlers for the `AdminPageGenerator` class. Remember that these are all in one class, which should be located in */CODEREUSE/ SchemaInfo.Class.asp*.

Classes to store column and foreign key constraint information for a given database table have already been examined. As its source code in Example 6-17 shows, `AdminPageGenerator` contains two member variables—*objColumns* and *objForeignKeys*—that are instances of the `Columns` and `ForeignKeys` classes.

To generate an administration page form, we need to know not only the column and foreign key constraint information for a particular database table, but also how to display the form fields for each of the various database columns. Since we already have a class that provides information on how each potential database column datatype should be displayed as a form element, why not use an instance of this class in `AdminPageGenerator`? The *objDataTypeFormElements* member variable does exactly this, serving as an instance of the `DataTypeFormElementInformation` class.

Recall that `DataTypeFormElementInformation` contains suggestions on how to display each datatype. Although the `AdminPageGenerator` does not have any methods or properties that allow the end developer to alter these set defaults, adding such functionality is trivial. However, even with this added functionality, the `DataTypeFormElementInformation` class does not allow for total flexibility. For example, imagine the developer wanted to use two different form elements for two database columns that had the same datatype. Ugh.

To permit such flexibility, we return to a technique used previously in the chapter: hinting. If the end developer wishes to have a particular table column use a form element that is different from the default form element for the given datatype, he can give the `AdminPageGenerator` class a friendly hint. To accommodate this feature, the `AdminPageGenerator` class contains a member variable, *objFormHints*, which is a Dictionary object. For each form field hint the end developer needs to supply, a new key/value pair will be placed in this Dictionary object. The FormHint method (discussed in "The AdminPageGenerator methods" section) is available for the end developer to add hints specifying how to display a particular column as a form element.

Since the `Columns` and `ForeignKeys` classes require an opened Connection object to obtain schema information for a particular database table, the `AdminPageGenerator` class also contains private member variables that store information on how to connect to the correct database. These member variables—*strConnectionString*, *strUser*, and *strPassword*—store the connection string, user name, and password, respectively. When the end developer wishes to display a particular administration page form for a particular database table, she will need to supply the database connection information. Details on providing this information are covered in more detail in the next section, "The AdminPageGenerator methods."

Another member variable of the `AdminPageGenerator` class is *strIdentityColumn*. When adding a new record to a table in the "Insert a New Record" interface, the user should not be shown form fields for AutoNumber columns. Recall that when the `Columns` class's PopulateColumns method is called, extensive information about each column in the database table is collected. One tidbit of information collected about each column is whether it is an AutoNumber column or not. In PopulateColumns, to determine which column, if any, is an AutoNumber column, a single row is grabbed from the database table in question. Then the dynamic Properties collection of the Recordset object is examined to determine if any columns are AutoNumber columns. (The PopulateColumns method is listed in Example 6-6.)

A problem arises with this approach if there are no records in the database table to begin with, because then the Properties collection of the Recordset object isn't available for inspection. To handle this, the end developer can hint at the proper AutoNumber column. It is important that the end developer provide this information if the database table for the administration page has or always will have zero records in it.

Keep in mind that the `AdminPageGenerator` class is responsible for only one thing: creating the various administration page forms. This class is not too interested in what happens once the form is submitted, and the actual work of inserting, updating, or deleting a database record is left to another class. By default, the ASP page */CODEREUSE/AdminPageAction.asp* is called when an administration page form is submitted.

Once the administration page form is submitted and a database record has been inserted, deleted, or updated, what should happen next? The most flexible option is to have */CODEREUSE/AdminPageAction.asp* redirect the user to some other ASP page. Figure 6-8 depicts the flow between ASP pages that occurs when a user visits and submits an administration page form.

The `AdminPageGenerator` class provides the Redirect property for the end developer to specify where */CODEREUSE/AdminPageAction.asp* should send the user once the database has been modified. The Redirect property is shown in Example 6-17.

Despite the `AdminPageGenerator` class's complexity, it has only two properties, IdentityColumnHint and Redirect. (As we'll see in the next section, the meat of the `AdminPageGenerator` class is in its methods!) Example 6-17 contains the `AdminPageGenerator`'s member variables, property, and `Initialize` and `Terminate` event handlers. Note that the `Initialize` event handler instantiates the five object member variables, while the `Terminate` event handler simply cleans up.

Administration Page Form

The user is presented with a form to insert, update, or delete a record. Once the user submits the form, they are taken to the next page, /CODEREUSE/AdminPageAction.asp.

When the administration page form is submitted, AdminPageAction.asp is visited, which does the work of modifying the database.

AdminPageAction.asp

The page does the actual work of inserting, updating, or deleting a record from the database. Once the database table has been modified, the user is forwarded on to a page specified by the end developer.

After the database is modified, a Server.Transfer sends the user to a page specified by the end developer.

SomePage.asp

This can be a confirmation page of sorts. Alternatively, you could redirect the user back to the Administration Page Menu.

Figure 6-8. When a user submits an administration page form, the database is modified first, and then the user is redirected to some confirmation page

Example 6-17. The AdminPageGenerator Member Variables, Property, and Event Handlers

```
<%
    Const strAction ="/CODEREUSE/AdminPageAction.asp"
%>
<!--#include file="Column.Class.asp"-->
<!--#include file="ForeignKey.Class.asp"-->
<%
Class AdminPageGenerator
    '************** MEMBER VARIABLES ********************
    Private objColumns
    Private objForeignKeys
    Private objDataTypeFormElements
    Private objFormHints
    Private objFKHints
    Private strIdentityColumn
    Private strConnectionString
    Private strUserName
    Private strPassword
    Private strRedirect
```

Example 6-17. The AdminPageGenerator Member Variables, Property, and
Event Handlers (continued)

```
'*******************************************************

'***************** LET PROPERTIES ******************
Public Property Let IdentityColumnHint(strIdentity)
   strIdentityColumn = strIdentity
End Property

Public Property Let Redirect(str)
   strRedirect = str
End Property
'*******************************************************

'****************** EVENT HANDLERS ******************
Private Sub Class_Initialize()
  Set objColumns = New Columns
  Set objForeignKeys = New ForeignKeys
  Set objDataTypeFormElements = New DataTypeFormElementInformation
  Set objFormHints = Server.CreateObject("Scripting.Dictionary")
  Set objFKHints = Server.CreateObject("Scripting.Dictionary")
End Sub

Private Sub Class_Terminate()
  Set objFormHints = Nothing
  Set objFKHints = Nothing
  Set objColumns = Nothing
  Set objForeignKeys = Nothing
  Set objDataTypeFormElements = Nothing
End Sub
'*******************************************************

  'The AdminPageGenerator methods have been omitted.  They are discussed
  'in the next section, "The AdminPageGenerator Methods."
End Class
%>
```

The AdminPageGenerator methods

The AdminPageGenerator class is responsible for creating the "Insert a New
Record," "Edit an Existing Record," and "Delete an Existing Record" forms. The
AdminPageGenerator class contains two methods to create the "Insert a New
Record" and "Delete an Existing Record" administration page forms: CreateRecord-
Form and DeleteRecordForm, respectively. The "Edit an Existing Record" administration page requires two methods, since two forms are used. The first form,
created by the UpdateRecordList method, generates a list of potential records to
edit, from which the user can select a single record; the second form, created by
the UpdateRecordForm method, contains the form fields for the user to edit the
particular record. These four administration page form generation methods have
the following definitions:

```
Public Function CreateRecordForm(strTableName, strConnString, _
                                 strUser, strPass)
Public Function UpdateRecordList(strTableName, strConnString, _
                                 strUser, strPass)
Public Function UpdateRecordForm(strTableName, strWhereClause, _
                                 strConnString, strUser, strPass)
Public Function DeleteRecordForm(strTableName, strConnString, _
                                 strUser, strPass)
```

The parameters that need to be passed into these methods are fairly straightforward. *strTableName* specifies what database table the administration page is for. *strConnString*, *strUser*, and *strPass* contain database connection information. The *strWhereClause* in the UpdateRecordForm method specifies a valid SQL WHERE clause that will grab exactly one record from the table *strTableName*. Each of these methods returns a string that contains the HTML needed to generate the proper form.

For example, to display the "Insert a New Record" form for the ProductType database table, the following code could be used:

```
'Create an instance of AdminPageGenerator
Dim objAdmin
Set objAdmin = New AdminPageGenerator

Dim strConnString
strConnString = "Provider=SQLOLEDB;Data Source=mitchell;" & _
                "Initial Catalog=ProductInfo;User ID=sa;Password="

'Send the HTML to the client.
Response.Write objAdmin.CreateRecordForm("ProductType", strConnString, "", "")

Set objAdmin = Nothing           'Clean up!
```

Note that the connection string in the previous code snippet uses the SQLOLEDB database provider. The adSchemaForeignKeys schema is supported only by the SQLOLEDB and Jet 4.0 database providers. You can obtain the latest OLE DB providers at *http://www.microsoft. com/data/*.

These three methods will be examined in great detail over the next three sections. Before that, though, let's look at the four remaining AdminPageGenerator methods. These four methods enable the end developer to give "hints" to AdminPageGenerator. Recall that in "The DataTypeFormElementInformation class" section we discussed how DataTypeFormElementInformation provided a form field template for each possible column datatype. However, problems could arise if the developer wanted to have two columns that had the same datatype to have differing form fields.

To accommodate this, the FormHint method can be used. The FormHint method expects two parameters: the name of a particular column, and the form element code to use in place of the form element code "recommended" by `DataTypeFormElementInformation`. The form element code should be valid and complete HTML code that generates a particular form element. The placeholders ~COLUMNNAME~ and ~COLUMNVALUE~ can be used in the form element code, just as they were in the `DataTypeFormElementInformation` class. For example, if you had a column named `Price` that you wanted to create as a text box with its SIZE property set to 2, you could use the FormHint method like so:

```
objAdmin.FormHint "Price", "$<INPUT TYPE=TEXT SIZE=2 " & _
                    "NAME=""col_~COLUMNNAME~""" & _
                    " VALUE=""~COLUMNVALUE~"">"
```

The FormNameHint and FormDescriptionHint methods allow the end developer to provide English-like names and descriptions for each of the form elements. Both of these methods take two parameters: the name of the column, and the name or description to use. In "DataTypeFormElementInformation's other methods," we examined a code snippet that used these two methods.

Recall from our earlier discussions in this chapter that displaying tables that have foreign key constraints is a bit of a sticky matter. It is important that a list box be presented that contains all of the valid options. For example, imagine that we had a `Portfolio` table that had a column named `InvestmentTypeID`, which was a foreign key to an `InvestmentType` table. For this example, `InvestmentType` contains two columns, `ID` and `Name`, serving as a look-up table pairing a numeric ID to a particular type of investment (bond, stock, mutual fund, etc.). When a user is presented the "Edit an Existing Record" administration page for the `Portfolio` table, the last thing we want to do is show them a numeric field in the `InvestmentTypeID` form field. Rather, we'd like to show them a list box containing the various types of investments.

Unfortunately, `AdminPageGenerator` has absolutely no idea what columns in `InvestmentType` to display in the list box in the "Edit an Existing Record" administration page form. Therefore, it is the responsibility of the end developer to hint at what fields she'd like to see listed. The ForeignKeyHint method of the `AdminPageGenerator` class is the mechanism the end developer uses to provide foreign key constraint hints.

In our Product/Catalog example, there are a total of three foreign key constraints. The `Product` table has a single foreign key constraint with the `ProductType` table. The `CatalogProduct` table has two foreign key constraints, one to the `Catalog` table's primary key, and the other to the `Product` table's primary key.

The ForeignKeyHint method takes two parameters: the name of the column that is a foreign key, and the text to display in the list box, having the following definition:

```
Public Sub ForeignKeyHint(strColumnName, strListBoxValue)
```

In our Portfolio/InvestmentType example, the end developer might want to have the text: "*INVESTMENT NAME* Investment" appear in the list box, where *INVESTMENT NAME* is the value in the InvestmentType table's Name column. To accomplish this, the end developer could set *strListBoxValue* to: "~Name~ Investment." To insert a column value, simply enter the column name surrounded by tildes (~).

```
objAdmin.ForeignKeyHint "InvestmentTypeID", "~Name~ Investment"
```

Example 6-18 contains the code for these four methods of the Admin-PageGenerator class: ForeignKeyHint, FormHint, FormNameHint, and FormDescriptionHint.

Example 6-18. AdminPageGenerator Provides Four Methods

```
Class AdminPageGenerator
    ' ... Properties, event handlers, and other methods omitted for
    '     brevity.  The properties and event handlers are shown in
    '     Example 6-12 ...

    '********************** METHODS **********************
    Public Sub ForeignKeyHint(strColumnName, strListBoxValue)
        If objFKHints.Exists(UCase(strColumnName)) then
            objFKHints(UCase(strColumnName)) = strListBoxValue
        Else
            objFKHints.Add UCase(strColumnName), strListBoxValue
        End If
    End Sub

    Public Sub FormHint(strFormName, strFormValue)
        If objFormHints.Exists(strFormName) then
            objFormHints(UCase(strFormName)) = strFormValue
        Else
            objFormHints.Add UCase(strFormName), strFormValue
        End If
    End Sub

    Public Sub FormNameHint(strFormName, strName)
        objDataTypeFormElements.FormElementName(UCase(strFormName)) = strName
    End Sub

    Public Sub FormDescriptionHint(strFormName, strFormDesc)
        objDataTypeFormElements.FormElementDescription(UCase(strFormName)) = _
                                strFormDesc
    End Sub
    '****************************************************
End Class
```

The "Insert a New Record" administration page

Example 6-19 contains the code for *InsertRecord.asp*, which displays the "Insert a
New Record" administration page form shown in Figure 6-9. The CreateRecord-
Form method of the `AdminPageGenerator` class is responsible for generating an
administration page form that permits the user to add a new record to a table. In
Figure 6-9, you can see a screenshot of the "Insert a New Record" administration
page form for the `Product` table. Note that the `ProductTypeID` column (which is
a foreign key to the `ProductType` table) is displayed as a list box with the available product type names, rather than their corresponding product type codes.

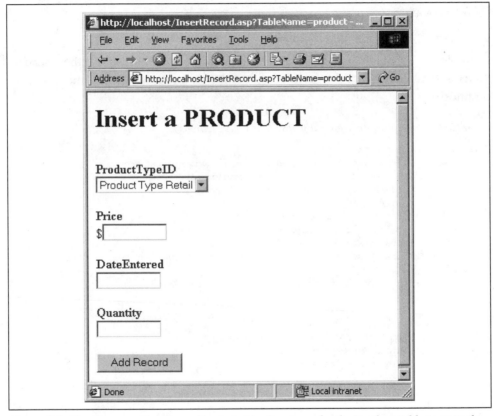

*Figure 6-9. The "Insert a New Record" administration page for the Product table permits the
user to create a new record*

*Example 6-19. The "Insert a New Record" Administration Page Can Be Created with Just a Few
Lines of Code*

```
<% @LANGUAGE="VBSCRIPT" %>
<% Option Explicit %>
<!--#include virtual="/CODEREUSE/SchemaInfo.Class.asp"-->
<%
  Dim strTableName
  strTableName = "Product"
```

Example 6-19. The "Insert a New Record" Administration Page Can Be Created with Just a Few Lines of Code (continued)

```
    Dim objAdmin
    Set objAdmin = new AdminPageGenerator

    'Set the ForeignKeyHint and the IdentityColumnHint
    objAdmin.IdentityColumnHint = "ProductID"
    objAdmin.ForeignKeyHint "ProductTypeid", "Product Type ~Name~"
%>

<HTML><BODY>
<h1>Insert a <%=UCase(strTableName)%></h1><BR>
<%
  Dim strConnString
  strConnString = "Provider=SQLOLEDB;Data Source=mitchell;" & _
                  "Initial Catalog=ProductInfo;User ID=sa;Password="

  'Display the form
  Response.Write objAdmin.CreateRecordForm(strTableName, _
                                   strConnString, "", "")

  Set objAdmin = Nothing        'Clean up...
%>
</BODY></HTML>
```

Since the administration page table name is hardcoded in Example 6-19 (`strTableName = "Product"`), *InsertRecord.asp* will only display a very specific administration page. Later in this chapter we'll look at how to make a more dynamic ASP page, able to display any administration page for any database table.

Creating an "Insert a New Record" administration page form consists of a few steps:

1. Create an instance of the `AdminPageGenerator` class.

2. Set the IdentityColumnHint property, if necessary.

3. For each foreign key constraint in the specified table, issue a call to Foreign-KeyHint.

4. Use the CreateRecordForm method, passing it the table name and database connection information, to generate the proper form.

It's that simple! In fact, later in this chapter we'll examine how to add yet another level of encapsulation to make it even *easier* to create a generic administration page form!

Now that we've looked at how an end developer uses the `AdminPageGenerator` class to create an "Insert a New Record" administration page form, it's time we examined the source code for its CreateRecordForm method, which can be seen in Example 6-20.

Example 6-20. When Creating the "Insert a New Record" Administration Page Form, CreateRecordForm Calls the Reusable CreateForm Helper Function

```
<!--#include file="Column.Class.asp"-->
<!--#include file="ForeignKey.Class.asp"-->
<%
Class AdminPageGenerator
    ' ... Properties, event handlers, and other methods omitted for
    '     brevity.  The properties and event handlers are shown in
    '     Example 6-12 ...

    '********************** METHODS **********************
    Public Function CreateRecordForm(strTableName, strConnString, _
                          strUser, strPass)
      'Assign the private member variables the values
      strConnectionString = strConnString
      strUserName = strUser
      strPassword = strPass

      'Populate the objColumns and objForeignKeys objects
      'Create a connection to the database
      Dim objConn
      Set objConn = Server.CreateObject("ADODB.Connection")
      objConn.Open strConnectionString, strUserName, strPassword

      'Populate the objColumn and objForeignKeys member variables
      objColumns.PopulateColumns strTableName, objConn, ""
      objForeignKeys.PopulateForeignKeys strTableName, objConn

      objConn.Close
      Set objConn = Nothing                           'Clean up!

      CreateRecordForm = CreateForm(True, strTableName) 'Call the helper function
    End Function
    '****************************************************
End Class
%>
```

Recall that the "Edit an Existing Record" administration page requires two forms; the first form lists the records in the database table, allowing the user to select one; the second form provides the user a chance to edit the values for that particular record. Note that the second form in the "Edit an Existing Record" administration page and the single form in the "Insert a New Record" administration page are nearly identical. The only difference is the "Edit an Existing Record" form lists the values of the record being edited in the form fields.

Due to the fact that the "Insert a New Record" and "Edit an Existing Record" administration page forms are nearly identical, it's not surprising that the source code for CreateRecordForm and UpdateRecordForm would be nearly identical as well. Rather than simply cut and paste code from these two methods, a common helper function is called from both CreateRecordForm and UpdateRecordForm. This helper function, CreateForm, which is shown in Example 6-21, expects two parameters: *bolNewRecord*, a Boolean, indicating whether or not the function is being called from CreateRecordForm or UpdateRecordForm, and *strTableName*, the name of the table that the administration page form is being created for. This helper function simplifies the code in CreateRecordForm to simply opening a connection to the database, populating the *objColumns* and *objForeignKeys* member variables of the `AdminPageGenerator` class, closing the connection, and calling CreateForm, passing it a value of `True`.

The CreateForm helper function shown in Example 6-21 returns a string containing the HTML to display the proper administration page form. Because CreateForm is a helper function only to be called by `AdminPageGenerator` methods, it is declared as `Private`. Since CreateForm is charged with the task of creating a generic insert or edit form, it's no surprise that its code is lengthy and painfully unwieldy.

Before trying to dissect the code in Example 6-21, ask yourself what the code for CreateForm needs to accomplish. Look at the problem from a high-level view. Large tasks don't seem so daunting if viewed in small, discrete chunks. The high-level tasks assigned to CreateForm include:

1. Determining if any foreign key list boxes need to be displayed. If so, a database connection must be established.

2. Looping through each of the columns in the *objColumns* member variable. For each column, display the correct form field. Displaying the correct form field consists of checking the hint collections and *objDataTypeFormElements*, the member variable instance of the `DataTypeFormElementInformation` class.

3. Creating the proper HTML tags to generate a properly functioning form, including a Submit button.

Obviously, the meat of CreateForm comes from Step 2. Note the comments in Example 6-21 that show where each of the above three steps roughly begins.

Example 6-21. CreateForm Is Responsible for Generating the Forms for the "Insert a New Record" and "Edit an Existing Record" Administration Pages

```
<%
    Const strAction ="/CODEREUSE/AdminPageAction.asp"
%>
<!--#include file="Column.Class.asp"-->
<!--#include file="ForeignKey.Class.asp"-->
<%
Class AdminPageGenerator
    ' ... Properties, event handlers, and other methods omitted for
    '     brevity.  The properties and event handlers are shown in
    '     Example 6-12 ...
```

Example 6-21. CreateForm Is Responsible for Generating the Forms for the "Insert a New Record" and "Edit an Existing Record" Administration Pages (continued)

```
'*********************** METHODS **********************
Private Function CreateForm(bolNewRecord, strTableName)
   'This function creates an HTML form to add a new record to a database
   Dim strResult, strElement, objRS, strSQL, objConn, _
       strFKHint, objField, strTemp

   '******** STEP 1: Determine if any foreign keys exist! ***************

   'If we need to access foreign keys, create/open the connection and
   'create the recordset
   If objForeignKeys.Count > 0 AND objFKHints.Count > 0 then
      Set objConn = Server.CreateObject("ADODB.Connection")
      objConn.Open strConnectionString, strUserName, strPassword

      Set objRS = Server.CreateObject("ADODB.Recordset")
   End If

   Dim strColName, objColumnInformation, strHeader, objFKInformation
   strResult = "<FORM METHOD=POST ACTION=""" & strAction & """>" & vbCrLf

   strResult = strResult & "<INPUT TYPE=HIDDEN NAME=ConnectionString " & _
                           "VALUE=""" & strConnectionString & """>" & vbCrLf

   strResult = strResult & "<INPUT TYPE=HIDDEN NAME=UserName " & _
                           "VALUE=""" & strUserName & """>" & vbCrLf

   strResult = strResult & "<INPUT TYPE=HIDDEN NAME=Password " & _
                           "VALUE=""" & strPassword & """>" & vbCrLf

   'If we are updating a record, we need to record the value of the ID
   'and record that the action is UPDATE
   If Not bolNewRecord then
      strResult = strResult & "<INPUT TYPE=HIDDEN NAME=""PrimaryKeyColumns""" & _
                  """ VALUE=""" & objColumns.GetPrimaryKeys() & """>" & vbCrLf
      strResult = strResult & "<INPUT TYPE=HIDDEN NAME=""Action"" " & _
                  "VALUE = ""UPDATE"">" & vbCrLf
   Else
      'We are inserting a new record
      strResult = strResult & "<INPUT TYPE=HIDDEN NAME=""Action"" " & _
                  "VALUE = ""INSERT"">" & vbCrLf
   End If

   'Pass along the table name
   strResult = strResult & "<INPUT TYPE=HIDDEN NAME=""TableName"" " & _
                  "VALUE = """ & strTableName & """>" & vbCrLf

   'Pass along the redirect URL (where the user is sent after the row is
   'updated/inserted)
   If Len(strRedirect) > 0 then
       strResult = strResult & "<INPUT TYPE=HIDDEN NAME=""Redirect"" " & _
           "VALUE = """ & strRedirect & "?TableName=" & strTableName & _
```

Example 6-21. CreateForm Is Responsible for Generating the Forms for the "Insert a New Record" and "Edit an Existing Record" Administration Pages (continued)

```
            """>" & vbCrLf
    End If


    '******** STEP 2: Loop through the Columns in objColumns! ************
    For Each strColName in objColumns.ColumnList
        Set objColumnInformation = objColumns.GetColumnInformation(strColName)

        'Only display the form element if the column is not an IDENTITY field
        If Not objColumnInformation.Identity And _
            Not UCase(objColumnInformation.Name) = UCase(strIdentityColumn) then
            'Determine whether this row is a foreign key or not...
            If objForeignKeys.ForeignKeyExists(objColumnInformation.Name) _
                And objFKHints.Exists(UCase(objColumnInformation.Name)) then
                Set objFKInformation = objForeignKeys.GetForeignKeyInformation( _
                                            objColumnInformation.Name)

            strFKHint = objFKHints(UCase(objColumnInformation.Name))
            If InStr(1, strFKHint, "<") then
                strElement = strFKHint
            Else
                strElement = "<SELECT NAME=""col_~COLUMNNAME~"">" & vbCrLf
                strSQL = "SELECT * FROM [" & _
                        objFKInformation.PrimaryKeyTable & "]"

            objRS.Open strSQL, objConn
            Do While Not objRS.EOF
                strElement = strElement & "<OPTION VALUE=""" & _
                                objRS(objFKInformation.PrimaryKeyColumn) & """"
                If objColumnInformation.Value = _
                        objRS(objFKInformation.PrimaryKeyColumn) then
                        strElement = strElement & " SELECTED "
                End If

                strElement = strElement & ">"

                strTemp = strFKHint
                For Each objField in objRS.Fields
                    strTemp = Replace(strTemp, "~" & objField.Name & "~", _
                                    objField.Value, 1, -1, vbTextCompare)
                Next

                strElement = strElement & strTemp & "</OPTION>" & vbCrLf

                objRS.MoveNext
            Loop

            objRS.Close            'Close the connection

            strElement = strElement & "</SELECT><P>" & vbCrLf
        End If
    Else
        'Check to see if a FormHint exists...
```

Example 6-21. CreateForm Is Responsible for Generating the Forms for the "Insert a New Record" and "Edit an Existing Record" Administration Pages (continued)

```
      If objFormHints.Exists(UCase(objColumnInformation.Name)) then
          strElement = objFormHints(UCase(objColumnInformation.Name)) & _
                      "<P>" & vbCrLf

      Else
          strElement = objDataTypeFormElements.DataTypeFormElement(_
                      objColumnInformation.DataType) & _
                      "<P>" & vbCrLf

       End If
   End If
   Set objFKInformation = Nothing            'Clean up...

   strElement = Replace(strElement, "~COLUMNNAME~", _
                      objColumnInformation.Name)
   If bolNewRecord then
     If objColumnInformation.HasDefault then
         strElement = Replace(strElement, "~COLUMNVALUE~", _
                      objColumnInformation.DefaultValue)
     Else
         strElement = Replace(strElement, "~COLUMNVALUE~", "")
     End If
   Else
     If IsNull(objColumnInformation.Value) then
         'A NULL value - this needs special care
         strElement = Replace(strElement, "~COLUMNVALUE~", "")
     Else
         strElement = Replace(strElement, "~COLUMNVALUE~", _
                      objColumnInformation.Value)
     End If
   End If

   If Len(objDataTypeFormElements.FormElementName(UCase(strColName))) > 0 _
                                                                  then
       strHeader = "<B>" & _
           objDataTypeFormElements.FormElementName(UCase(strColName)) & _
           "</B>" & vbCrLf
     Else
       strHeader = "<B>" & objColumnInformation.Name & _
                   "</B>" & vbCrLf
     End If

     If _   'long line!
   Len(objDataTypeFormElements.FormElementDescription(UCase(strColName))) _
                                                        > 0 then
         strHeader = strHeader & ": " & _
     objDataTypeFormElements.FormElementDescription(UCase(strColName)) & _
                   vbCrLf
     Elseif Len(objColumnInformation.Description) > 0 then
         strHeader = strHeader & ": " & objColumnInformation.Description & _
                   "" & vbCrLf
     End If

     strResult = strResult & strHeader & "<BR>" & strElement
   End If
```

Example 6-21. CreateForm Is Responsible for Generating the Forms for the "Insert a New Record" and "Edit an Existing Record" Administration Pages (continued)

```
            Set objColumnInformation = Nothing        'Clean up!
        Next

        '******** STEP 3: Finish up the FORM tag ************

        'Create submit button
        strResult = strResult & "<P><INPUT TYPE=SUBMIT VALUE="""

        If bolNewRecord then
            strResult = strResult & "Add Record"
        Else
            strResult = strResult & "Update Record"
        End If

        strResult = strResult & """>"
        strResult = strResult & vbCrLf & "</FORM>" & vbCrLf & vbCrLf

        CreateForm = strResult

        'Clean up if we created connection/recordset objects
        If objForeignKeys.Count > 0 AND objFKHints.Count > 0 then
            Set objRS = Nothing
            objConn.Close
            Set objConn = Nothing
        End If
    End Function
    '****************************************************
End Class
%>
```

Near the top of CreateForm, an HTML **FORM** tag is created, with its **ACTION** property set to the value in the variable *strAction*. *strAction* is a constant defined at the top of the file in which the **AdminPageGenerator** class appears (*/CODEREUSE/SchemaInfo.Class.asp*), specifying the URL of the form-processing script for the various administration page forms. For these examples, *strAction* is set as follows:

```
    Const strAction ="/CODEREUSE/AdminPageAction.asp"
```

Also, since **AdminPageGenerator** uses the **ForeignKeys** and **Columns** classes, server-side includes must be used to import both */CODEREUSE/ForeignKey.Class.asp* as well as */CODEREUSE/Column.Class.asp* into */CODEREUSE/SchemaInfo.Class.asp*.

The generic administration page generation script presented throughout this chapter is not suited to handle NULLable foreign key constraints. This feature could be added, though, and is left as an exercise to the interested reader.

The "Delete an Existing Record" administration page

As with the "Insert a New Record" administration page, the "Delete an Existing Record" administration page shares some uncanny similarities with the "Edit an Existing Record" administration page. Namely, in both the "Delete an Existing Record" administration page and the "Edit an Existing Record" administration page, a form is needed to list the records in the table. In the "Delete an Existing Record" administration page, the user can select one or more records to delete from the list of current records; in the "Edit an Existing Record" administration page, the user can select one and only one record to edit.

Before we explore this relationship further, let's step back for a moment and take a look at a screenshot of the "Delete an Existing Record" administration page, which is shown in Figure 6-10.

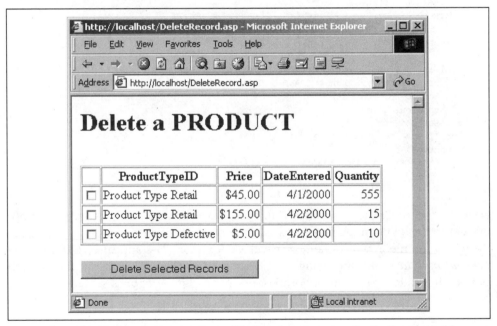

Figure 6-10. The "Delete an Existing Record" administration page for the Product table allows the user to delete one or more records

Notice that each record in the table is listed with a checkbox next to it. Also note that the `ProductTypeID` column contains the value from the `Name` column in the `ProductType` table rather than the actual numeric id in the `Product` table. In the "Insert a New Record" administration page form, the end developer could enter foreign key hints to display foreign key constraint columns as list boxes with applicable choices as opposed to a text box with a numeric id present. The same mechanism is used in the "Delete an Existing Record" to provide for translation from a numeric foreign key to a readable value.

To display the "Delete an Existing Record" administration page form, the end developer simply needs to output the returned HTML string from the DeleteRecordForm method. DeleteRecordForm, like CreateRecordForm, takes four parameters: the name of the database table whose administration page form it is to display, the connection string, the username, and the password. Also, like CreateRecordForm, DeleteRecordForm does very little in the way of actual work in displaying the "Delete an Existing Record" administration page form. Another helper function, CreateList, is responsible for actually doing the grunt work of creating the form seen in Figure 6-10.

CreateList is a generic helper function that is also called from the UpdateRecordList method. CreateList, as its name implies, creates a listing of all of the database records in a given table, and has the following definition:

```
Private Function CreateList(bolDelete, objConn, strTableName)
```

The *bolDelete* function is a Boolean value, indicating whether the user is deleting one or more records from the list of database records or is selecting a record to edit. When *bolDelete* is True, a checkbox is placed beside each listed record; when *bolDelete* is False, meaning the user is choosing a single record to edit, a radio button is used instead. CreateList expects an opened database connection to be passed in as the second parameter. The final parameter, *strTableName*, is the name of the database table for which the administration page form is being created.

DeleteRecordForm, like CreateRecordForm, populates the *objColumns* and *objForeignKeys* member variables and calls a helper function. The source code for DeleteRecordForm can be seen in Example 6-22.

Example 6-22. DeleteRecordForm Obtains Column and Foreign Key Information and Hands Display Responsibilities to CreateList

```
<!--#include file="Column.Class.asp"-->
<!--#include file="ForeignKey.Class.asp"-->
<%
Class AdminPageGenerator
    ' ... Properties, event handlers, and other methods omitted for
    '     brevity.  The properties and event handlers are shown in
    '     Example 6-12 ...


'********************** METHODS **********************
Public Function DeleteRecordForm(strTableName, strConnString, _
                            strUser, strPass)
    'Present a form that lists the database columns with a
    'checkbox next to each column.  The user can then select
    'what columns he'd like to delete.

    'Assign the private member variables the values
    strConnectionString = strConnString
    strUserName = strUser
    strPassword = strPass
```

Example 6-22. DeleteRecordForm Obtains Column and Foreign Key Information and Hands Display Responsibilities to CreateList (continued)

```
    'Create a connection to the database
    Dim objConn
    Set objConn = Server.CreateObject("ADODB.Connection")
    objConn.Open strConnectionString, strUserName, strPassword

    'Populate the objColumns and objForeignKeys objects
    objColumns.PopulateColumns strTableName, objConn, ""
    objForeignKeys.PopulateForeignKeys strTableName, objConn

    'Call the helper function CreateList
    DeleteRecordForm = CreateList(True, objConn, strTableName)

    objConn.Close                    'Close and Clean Up...
    Set objConn = Nothing
End Function
'*****************************************************

End Class
%>
```

As with the CreateForm helper function, CreateList is a colossal function, responsible for displaying a list of records for both the "Delete an Existing Record" and "Edit an Existing Record" administration page forms. Before we delve into the code of CreateList, let us step back and take a high-level view of the tasks Create-List needs to complete:

1. Determine if any foreign key constraints exist. If any do, each time a row is listed, a query will need to be run to grab the correct information to display the readable name indicated by the specific foreign key hint.

2. Set up a series of HIDDEN form fields that pass along the needed information. If CreateList is called from UpdateRecordList (that is, if *bolDelete* is False), adequate information must be passed along so that once a record is selected and the form submitted, UpdateRecordForm can be successfully called.

3. Obtain a snapshot of the database table and iterate through each record, displaying the value for each column in tabular form.

The code for CreateList is presented in Example 6-23. Note the comments in Example 6-23 that illustrate where each of the above three steps roughly begins.

Example 6-23. The Generic Helper Function CreateList Creates a List of Records, Allowing the User to Select One or More

```
<!--#include file="Column.Class.asp"-->
<!--#include file="ForeignKey.Class.asp"-->
<%
Class AdminPageGenerator
    ' ... Properties, event handlers, and other methods omitted for
    '     brevity.  The properties and event handlers are shown in
```

Example 6-23. The Generic Helper Function CreateList Creates a List of Records, Allowing the User to Select One or More (continued)

```
'        Example 6-12 ...

'********************** METHODS **********************
Private Function CreateList(bolDelete, objConn, strTableName)
  'This function creates the HTML needed to select a particular
  'record from a table

  '******** STEP 1: Determine if any foreign key constraints exist ************
  Dim objFKRS
  'If we need to access foreign keys, gather the foreign key table rows
  If objForeignKeys.Count > 0 AND objFKHints.Count > 0 then
     Set objFKRS = Server.CreateObject("ADODB.Recordset")
  End If


  Dim strResult
  strResult = "<FORM METHOD=POST ACTION=""" & strAction & """>" & vbCrLf

  '******** STEP 2: Set up the needed HIDDEN form fields ************
  strResult = strResult & "<INPUT TYPE=HIDDEN NAME=ConnectionString " & _
                          "VALUE=""" & strConnectionString & """>" & vbCrLf

  strResult = strResult & "<INPUT TYPE=HIDDEN NAME=UserName " & _
                          "VALUE=""" & strUserName & """>" & vbCrLf

  strResult = strResult & "<INPUT TYPE=HIDDEN NAME=Password " & _
                          "VALUE=""" & strPassword & """>" & vbCrLf

  If bolDelete then
    'Indicate that we are deleting a record
    strResult = strResult & "<INPUT TYPE=HIDDEN NAME=""Action"" " & _
                            "VALUE = ""DELETE"">" & vbCrLf
  Else
    'Indicate that we have selected a record to be deleted.
    strResult = strResult & "<INPUT TYPE=HIDDEN NAME=""Action"" " & _
                            "VALUE = ""UPDATESELECT"">" & vbCrLf
  End If

  strResult = strResult & "<INPUT TYPE=HIDDEN NAME=TableName " & _
                          "VALUE=""" & strTableName & """>" & vbCrLf

  'Pass along the redirect URL (where the user is sent after the row is
  'updated/inserted)
  If Len(strRedirect) > 0 then
    strResult = strResult & "<INPUT TYPE=HIDDEN NAME=""Redirect"" " & _
                            "VALUE = """ & strRedirect & "?TableName=" & _
                            strTableName & """>" & vbCrLf
  End If

  'See if we need to pass along ForeignKey hints.  If we are updating a record
  'we will need to pass along this information!
  If Not bolDelete then
    Dim objFKHintsInstance
```

Example 6-23. The Generic Helper Function CreateList Creates a List of Records, Allowing the User to Select One or More (continued)

```
    For Each objFKHintsInstance in objFKHints
        strResult = strResult & "<INPUT TYPE=HIDDEN NAME=FKName " & _
                            "VALUE=""" & objFKHintsInstance & """>" & vbCrLf
        strResult = strResult & "<INPUT TYPE=HIDDEN NAME=FKValue " & _
                            "VALUE=""" & objFKHints(UCase(objFKHintsInstance)) & _
                            """>" & vbCrLf
    Next
End If


'We need to grab the entire contents of the database
Dim objRS
Set objRS = Server.CreateObject("ADODB.Recordset")
objRS.Open "[" & strTableName & "]", objConn, , , adCmdTable

Dim objField, objColumnList
Set objColumnList = objColumns.ColumnList      'Get the list of columns

strResult = strResult & "<TABLE BORDER=1 CELLSPACING=1>"
strResult = strResult & vbCrLf & "<TR>" & vbCrLf
strResult = strResult & "<TH> </TH>"
For Each objField in objRS.Fields
    If Not objColumnList(objField.Name).Identity then
        strResult = strResult & "<TH>" & objField.Name & "</TH>" & vbCrLf
    End If
Next
strResult = strResult & "</TR>"


Dim strFKHint, objFKInformation, objColumnInformation, strElement, _
    strSQL, objFKField, strTemp

'******* STEP 3: Iterate through the Snapshot Results of the Database *******
Do While Not objRS.EOF
    strResult = strResult & "<TR>" & vbCrLf

    'Do we need to display a checkbox or a radio button?
    If bolDelete then
        strResult = strResult & "<TD><INPUT TYPE=CHECKBOX NAME=ID VALUE=""" & _
                    objColumns.GetCurrentPrimaryKeys(objRS) & """>" & vbCrLf
    Else
        strResult = strResult & "<TD><INPUT TYPE=RADIO NAME=ID VALUE=""" & _
                    objColumns.GetCurrentPrimaryKeys(objRS) & """>" & vbCrLf
    End If

    For Each objField in objRS.Fields
        If Not objColumnList(objField.Name).Identity then
            Set objColumnInformation = objColumns.GetColumnInformation(objField.Name)

            'Determine whether this row is a foreign key or not...
            If objForeignKeys.ForeignKeyExists(objColumnInformation.Name) _
                    And objFKHints.Exists(UCase(objColumnInformation.Name)) then
                Set objFKInformation = objForeignKeys.GetForeignKeyInformation(_
                                                    objColumnInformation.Name)
```

Example 6-23. The Generic Helper Function CreateList Creates a List of Records, Allowing the User to Select One or More (continued)

```
            strFKHint = objFKHints(UCase(objColumnInformation.Name))
            strSQL = "SELECT * FROM [" & objFKInformation.PrimaryKeyTable & _
                        "] WHERE [" & _
                        objFKInformation.PrimaryKeyColumn & "] = " & _
                        objRS(objFKInformation.ColumnName).Value

            objFKRS.Open strSQL, objConn
            strTemp = strFKHint
            For Each objFKField in objFKRS.Fields
                strTemp = Replace(strTemp, "~" & objFKField.Name & "~", _
                            objFKField.Value, 1, -1, vbTextCompare)
            Next
            strResult = strResult & "<TD>" & strTemp & "</TD>" & vbCrLf

            objFKRS.Close
    Else
        If IsNull(objField.Value) then
            strResult = strResult & "<TD ALIGN=RIGHT> "
        Else
            Select Case objColumnList(objField.Name).DataType
                Case adCurrency
                    strResult = strResult & "<TD ALIGN=RIGHT>" & _
                                FormatCurrency(objField.Value, 2)
                Case adDate
                    strResult = strResult & "<TD ALIGN=RIGHT>" & _
                                FormatDateTime(objField.Value, 2)
                Case adDBTimeStamp
                    strResult = strResult & "<TD ALIGN=RIGHT>" & _
                                FormatDateTime(objField.Value, 2)
                Case adVarNumeric
                    strResult = strResult & "<TD ALIGN=RIGHT>" & _
                                FormatNumber(objField.Value)
                Case adInteger
                    strResult = strResult & "<TD ALIGN=RIGHT>" & _
                                FormatNumber(objField.Value, 0)
                Case adBigInt
                    strResult = strResult & "<TD ALIGN=RIGHT>" & _
                                FormatNumber(objField.Value, 0)
                Case adTinyInt
                    strResult = strResult & "<TD ALIGN=RIGHT>" & _
                                FormatNumber(objField.Value, 0)
                Case adSmallInt
                    strResult = strResult & "<TD ALIGN=RIGHT>" & _
                                FormatNumber(objField.Value, 0)

                '... You can add special formatting for more datatypes
                '     here if you like...

                Case Else
                    strResult = strResult & "<TD>" & objField.Value
            End Select
```

Example 6-23. The Generic Helper Function CreateList Creates a List of Records, Allowing the User to Select One or More (continued)

```
                End If
                strResult = strResult & "</TD>" & vbCrLf
            End If
        End If
    Next

    strResult = strResult & "</TR>" & vbCrLf
    objRS.MoveNext
Loop
strResult = strResult & "</TABLE>" & vbCrLf

objRS.Close
Set objRS = Nothing

strResult = strResult & "<P><INPUT TYPE=SUBMIT VALUE="""
If bolDelete then
    strResult = strResult & "Delete Selected Records"">"
Else
    strResult = strResult & "Edit Selected Record"">"
End If

strResult = strResult & vbCrLf & "</FORM>" & vbCrLf & vbCrLf
CreateList = strResult
End Function
'*****************************************************

End Class
%>
```

 CreateList provides a tabular list of all of the records in a particular database table. The "Delete an Existing Record" administration page can be difficult to navigate (not to mention slow to load) if there are hundreds or thousands of records in the database table. The most obvious solution to this problem is to page the returned records. This possibility is discussed later in this chapter, in the "Limitations and Possible Enhancements" section.

The "Edit an Existing Record" administration page

The "Edit an Existing Record" administration page is a bit like a child to the "Insert a New Record" and "Delete an Existing Record" administration pages. The "Edit an Existing Record" administration page has similar functionality to the "Delete an Existing Record" administration page in that before a particular record can be edited, it must be selected from a list of all possible records. The "Edit an Existing Record" administration page is also similar to the "Insert a New Record" administration page in that once a record is selected for editing, the form used to allow the user to change the values of a particular record is identical to the form used for creating a new record.

The "Edit an Existing Record" administration page form's similarity to the "Delete an Existing Record" administration page form can be seen in a screenshot. When a user needs to edit a record, she will first be shown a listing of available records to choose from. Figure 6-11 shows this form, from which the user can select a particular record to edit from the `Catalog` table.

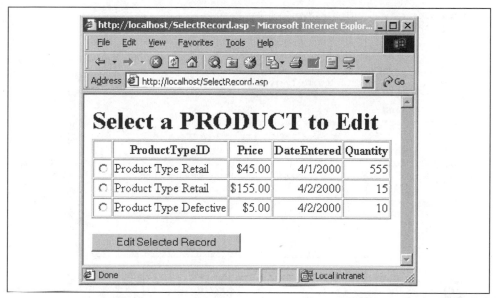

Figure 6-11. When editing an existing record, users must first choose a particular record to edit

The screenshot in Figure 6-11 looks very similar to the screenshot in Figure 6-10. The only visual difference between the user selecting a record for editing, or selecting one or more records for deleting, is that when selecting a record for editing, each record has a radio button next to it. When selecting one or more records to delete, each listed record has a checkbox next to it. These form elements were chosen due to their nature; a radio button limits the user to selecting one option out of several, whereas checkboxes permit several options to be chosen from a list.

As with both the "Insert a New Record" and "Delete an Existing Record" administration pages, from the end developer's standpoint, creating the "Edit an Existing Record" administration page requires just a few lines of code. Example 6-24 contains the code in *SelectRecord.asp* that generated the screenshot in Figure 6-11.

Example 6-24. Creating the "Edit an Existing Record" Administration Page Form Is Trivial for the End Developer

```
<% @LANGUAGE = "VBSCRIPT" %>
<% Option Explicit %>
```

*Example 6-24. Creating the "Edit an Existing Record" Administration Page Form Is Trivial for
the End Developer (continued)*

```
<!--#include virtual="/CODEREUSE/SchemaInfo.Class.asp"-->
<%
  Dim strTableName
  strTableName = "Product"

  Dim objAdmin
  Set objAdmin = new AdminPageGenerator

  objAdmin.IdentityColumnHint = "ProductID"
  objAdmin.ForeignKeyHint "ProductTypeid", "Product Type ~Name~"
%>

<HTML><BODY>
<h1>Select a <%=UCase(strTableName)%> to Edit</h1><BR>
<%
  Dim strConnString
  strConnString = "Provider=Microsoft.Jet.OLEDB.4.0;" & _
                  "Data Source=C:\InetPub\Products.mdb"

  'Display the form
  Response.Write objAdmin.UpdateRecordList(strTableName, strConnString, "", "")

  Set objAdmin = Nothing            'Clean up!
%>
</BODY></HTML>
```

 In previous code examples, the SQLOLEDB provider has been used
as the database provider for the *Connection* object. In Example 6-24,
however, the Jet 4.0 provider is used. This is just to illustrate how to
use different database providers for the administration page generation scripts.

Note that *SelectRecord.asp*, shown in Example 6-24, displays the first of two forms
for the "Edit an Existing Record" administration page. A server-side include is used
to import the contents of the file */CODEREUSE/SchemaInfo.Class.asp*, which contains the **AdminPageGenerator** class definition. The IdentityColumnHint and ForeignKeyHint methods are used to provide hints about the structure of the **Product**
table.

The code for UpdateRecordList, which is shown in Example 6-25, is strikingly similar to the code for DeleteRecordForm—both methods call the CreateList helper
function, which was shown in Example 6-23. In fact, the only difference between
UpdateRecordList and DeleteRecordForm is that UpdateRecordList calls CreateList
with the *bolDelete* parameter set to **False**.

Example 6-25. The UpdateRecordList Method Creates a Form from Which the User Can Select a Particular Record to Edit

```
<!--#include file="Column.Class.asp"-->
<!--#include file="ForeignKey.Class.asp"-->
<%
Class AdminPageGenerator
    ' ... Properties, event handlers, and other methods omitted for
    '     brevity.  The properties and event handlers are shown in
    '     Example 6-12 ...

    '********************** METHODS **********************
    Public Function UpdateRecordList(strTableName, strConnString, _
                                     strUser, strPass)
      'Present a form that lists the database columns with a
      'radio button next to each column.  The user can then select
      'what column he'd like to edit.

      'Assign the private member variables the values
      strConnectionString = strConnString
      strUserName = strUser
      strPassword = strPass

      'Populate the objColumns and objForeignKeys objects
      'Create a connection to the database
      Dim objConn
      Set objConn = Server.CreateObject("ADODB.Connection")
      objConn.Open strConnectionString, strUserName, strPassword

      objColumns.PopulateColumns strTableName, objConn, ""
      objForeignKeys.PopulateForeignKeys strTableName, objConn

      UpdateRecordList = CreateList(False, objConn, strTableName)

      objConn.Close
      Set objConn = Nothing
    End Function
    '****************************************************
End Class
%>
```

The remaining method, UpdateRecordForm, creates a form similar to that created by CreateRecordForm. Unlike CreateRecordForm, UpdateRecordForm requires a fifth parameter, *strWhereClause*. *StrWhereClause* must be a valid SQL WHERE clause (less the WHERE keyword) returning exactly one record from the database table. Figure 6-12 contains a screenshot of a particular record being edited for the Catalog table. Note the similarities between the output generated by the UpdateRecordForm method in Figure 6-8 and the CreateRecordForm method in Figure 6-5.

Example 6-26 contains the code for *EditSelectedRecord.asp*, which displays the "Edit an Existing Record" form shown in Figure 6-12. Note the second parameter

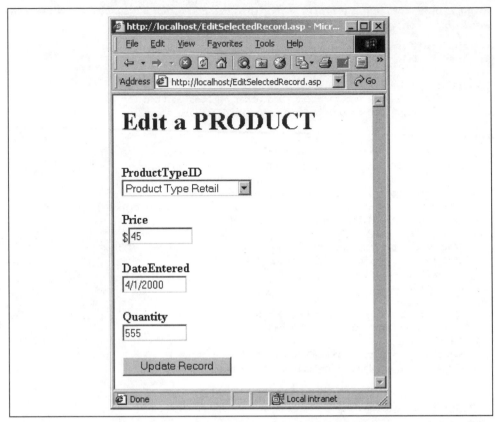

Figure 6-12. When editing an existing record, the form fields have the current column values already entered

in the UpdateRecordForm method call. This second parameter is the *str-WhereClause* parameter, which must uniquely select a single record from the table specified by *strTableName*.

Example 6-26. Creating the "Edit an Existing Record" Form Is Similar to Creating Other Administration Page Forms

```
<% @LANGUAGE = "VBSCRIPT" %>
<% Option Explicit %>
<!--#include virtual="/CODEREUSE/SchemaInfo.Class.asp"-->
<%
  Dim strTableName
  strTableName = "Product"

  Dim objAdmin
  Set objAdmin = new AdminPageGenerator
%>

<HTML><BODY>
<h1>Edit a <%=UCase(strTableName)%></h1><BR>
<%
```

Example 6-26. Creating the "Edit an Existing Record" Form Is Similar to Creating Other Administration Page Forms (continued)

```
    Dim strConnString
    strConnString = "Provider=Microsoft.Jet.OLEDB.4.0;" & _
                    "Data Source=C:\InetPub\Products.mdb"
    'Display the form
    Response.Write objAdmin.UpdateRecordForm(strTableName, "ProductID=1", _
                                             strConnString , "", "")

    Set objAdmin = Nothing          'Clean Up!
%>
</BODY></HTML>
```

In its current form, *EditSelectedRecord.asp* isn't very useful at all, since there are several hardcoded values. For one, the table name is hardcoded, displaying only a form for the **Product** table administration page. Secondly, the *strWhereClause* in the UpdateRecordForm method is also hardcoded (**ProductID = 1**). Therefore, *EditSelectedRecord.asp* will only display an update form for a particular row in a particular table. Later in this chapter, we'll examine how to make a more dynamic ASP page to generate the "Edit an Existing Record" administration page.

Not surprisingly, the code for UpdateRecordForm (which can be found in Example 6-27) is similar to CreateRecordForm. Both methods make use of the CreateForm helper function, differing in the fact that UpdateRecordForm passes in a value of **False** to *bolNewRecord* and **CreateRecordForm** passes in a value of **True**. (The code for CreateForm was presented in Example 6-21.)

Example 6-27. The UpdateRecordForm Calls the Helper Function CreateForm to Generate a Form for Editing a Particular Record

```
<!--#include file="Column.Class.asp"-->
<!--#include file="ForeignKey.Class.asp"-->
<%
Class AdminPageGenerator
    ' ... Properties, event handlers, and other methods omitted for
    '     brevity.  The properties and event handlers are shown in
    '     Example 6-12 ...

    '********************** METHODS **********************
    Public Function UpdateRecordForm(strTableName, strWhereClause, strConnString, _
                                     strUser, strPass)
      'Assign the private member variables the values
      strConnectionString = strConnString
      strUserName = strUser
      strPassword = strPass

      'Create a connection to the database
      Dim objConn
      Set objConn = Server.CreateObject("ADODB.Connection")
      objConn.Open strConnectionString, strUserName, strPassword

      'Populate the objColumns and objForeignKeys objects
```

Example 6-27. The UpdateRecordForm Calls the Helper Function CreateForm to Generate a
Form for Editing a Particular Record (continued)

```
    objColumns.PopulateColumns strTableName, objConn, strWhereClause
    objForeignKeys.PopulateForeignKeys strTableName, objConn

    objConn.Close
    Set objConn = Nothing                    'Clean up!

    UpdateRecordForm = CreateForm(False, strTableName)
  End Function
  '*******************************************************
End Class
%>
```

Inserting, Updating, and Deleting Database Records

So far, we've examined how to gather database table information and display administration page forms. We have paid little attention to how a record will be added, updated, or deleted from the database. In this section, we will examine how to gather the input from the administration page forms and apply the correct changes to the correct database table.

A single ASP page will be responsible for making all database changes specified by the various administration page forms. As discussed previously, the file */CODEREUSE/SchemaInfo.Class.asp*, which contains the class definition for `AdminPageGenerator`, also has a constant named `strAction` declared at the beginning of the file. This constant should be set to the name of the single ASP page that performs any database alterations. As mentioned previously, for these examples `strAction` is set to */CODEREUSE/AdminPageAction.asp* using the following command:

```
    Const strAction ="/CODEREUSE/AdminPageAction.asp"
```

AdminPageAction.asp utilizes—you guessed it—a class to assist in making any database changes. This class, `ModifyDatabase`, contains four methods to assist with committing the changes made by a user in one of the administration forms. These methods are InsertRecord, DeleteRecords, UpdateRecord, and UpdateSelect. Keep in mind that `ModifyDatabase` is needed only when a user submits an administration form created by `AdminPageGenerator`.

Before we look at the methods, however, let's take a moment to examine the properties and event handlers of the `ModifyDatabase` class.

 As with the other classes discussed in this chapter, the source code for the `ModifyDatabase` class should be placed in its own file. I chose to place `ModifyDatabase` in the file */CODEREUSE/ DatabaseModification.Class.asp*.

The ModifyDatabase class's properties and event handlers

The `ModifyDatabase` class has only a couple of properties. Since the class's duties focus on inserting, deleting, or updating database records, it comes as no surprise that three of the four properties provide database connection information. These three database connection properties—ConnectionString, UserName, and Password—are read/write properties and are used when connecting to the database.

The fourth property, Action, is read-only, and specifies the database action to be taken: inserting, updating, deleting, or selecting a record to update. Since there are four administration forms, and all administration forms, when submitted, lead to */CODEREUSE/AdminPageAction.asp* (which employs the `ModifyDatabase` class), there needs to be four types of possible Actions. Each of the four administration forms creates a `HIDDEN` form field named `Action`. It is through this `HIDDEN` form field that `ModifyDatabase` determines what type of action needs to be carried out.

The Initialize event handler of the `ModifyDatabase` class sets the Action property and ensures that the class is used only from */CODEREUSE/AdminPageAction.asp* (or whatever URL is specified by the `strAction` constant in */CODEREUSE/SchemaInfo.Class.asp*).

If any errors occur along the way, such as an invalid Action property being passed in from the administration page form, an error is raised. Recall that error handling was discussed in detail in Chapter 3, *Exception Handling*. The properties and event-handling code for the `ModifyDatabase` class are shown in Example 6-28.

Example 6-28. The Properties and Initialize Event Handler of the ModifyDatabase Class Determine What Database Action Will Be Performed

```
<!--#include virtual="/CODEREUSE/SchemaInfo.Class.asp"-->
<%
Class ModifyDatabase
  '************** MEMBER VARIABLES ********************
  Private strConnectionString
  Private strUserName
  Private strPassword
  Private strDBAction
  '****************************************************

  '****************** EVENT HANDLERS ******************
  Private Sub Class_Initialize()
    If UCase(Request.ServerVariables("SCRIPT_NAME")) <> _
          Ucase(strAction) then
      Err.Raise vbObjectError + 1234, "ModifyDatabase Class", _
                "ModifyDatabase can only be instantiated " & _
```

```
                              "in /CODEREUSE/AdminPageAction.asp"
    End If

    'Read in our action: UPDATE, INSERT, DELETE
    strDBAction = UCase(Request("Action"))

    If strDBAction <> "INSERT" And strDBAction <> "UPDATE" And _
            strDBAction <> "DELETE" And strDBAction <> "UPDATESELECT" then
      'Invalid Action Parameter
      Err.Raise vbObjectError + 1236, "ModifyDatabase Class", _
                  "Invalid Action - must be set to INSERT, UPDATE, or DELETE"
    End If
End Sub
'****************************************************


'***************** GET PROPERTIES ******************
Public Property Get Action()            'A read-only property
    Action = strDBAction
End Property

Public Property Get ConnectionString()
    ConnectionString = strConnectionString
End Property

Public Property Get UserName()
    UserName = strUserName
End Property

Public Property Get Password()
    Password = strPassword
End Property
'****************************************************


'***************** LET PROPERTIES ******************
Public Property Let ConnectionString(strConn)
    strConnectionString = strConn
End Property

Public Property Let UserName(strUser)
    strUserName = strUser
End Property

Public Property Let Password(strPass)
    strPassword = strPass
End Property
'****************************************************
End Class
%>
```

As shown in Example 6-28, the ModifyDatabase class must include */CODEREUSE/SchemaInfo.Class.asp*. This is due to the fact that the UpdateSelect method of ModifyDatabase uses an instance of the AdminPageGenerator class to create the second form of the "Edit an Existing Record" administration page. The file */CODEREUSE/ SchemaInfo.Class.asp* must be included since it contains the class definition for AdminPageGenerator.

ModifyDatabase's methods

The ModifyDatabase class contains four methods, one method for each of the four possible Action types. These methods have the following definitions:

```
Public Sub InsertRecord()   'Called from Insert a New Record Admin. Page Form

Public Sub UpdateRecord()   'Called when the user has finished editing a particular
                            'record in the Edit an Existing Record Admin. Page Form

Public Sub UpdateSelect()   'Called when the user selects a record to edit in
                            'the Edit an Existing Record Admin. Page Form

Public Sub DeleteRecords()  'Called from Delete an Existing Record Admin. Page
```

/CODEREUSE/AdminPageAction.asp, the form-processing script that is called when a user submits an administration page form, calls one of these four methods, depending on the Action property. If the InsertRecord, UpdateRecord, or DeleteRecords method is called, */CODEREUSE/AdminPageAction.asp* then redirects the user to the page specified by the end developer in the administration page generation script. (Recall that the AdminPageGenerator class has a Redirect property; this property determines where the user is sent after a record is inserted, updated, or deleted from the database in */CODEREUSE/ AdminPageAction.asp*.)

Since ModifyDatabase does the actual work involved in handling a submitted administration page form, the code for */CODEREUSE/AdminPageAction.asp* is fairly simple. Example 6-29 contains the complete code for *AdminPageAction.asp*.

Example 6-29. AdminPageAction.asp Is Visited When an Administration Page Form Is Submitted

```
<% @LANGUAGE="VBSCRIPT" %>
<% Option Explicit %>
<!--#include virtual="/CODEREUSE/DatabaseModification.Class.asp"-->
<%
    Dim objDB
    Set objDB = New ModifyDatabase
    objDB.ConnectionString = Request("ConnectionString")
    objDB.UserName = Request("UserName")
```

Example 6-29. AdminPageAction.asp Is Visited When an Administration Page Form Is Submitted (continued)

```
objDB.Password = Request("Password")

'Decide what ModifyDatabase method to call (based upon the Action property)
Select Case objDB.Action
  Case "INSERT":
    objDB.InsertRecord           'Insert a new database record
  Case "UPDATE":
    objDB.UpdateRecord           'Update an existing database record
  Case "DELETE":
    objDB.DeleteRecords          'Delete an existing database record
  Case "UPDATESELECT":
    objDB.UpdateSelect           'Display the UpdateRecord form
End Select

'If we actually inserted, updated, or deleted a record, redirect the user!
If objDB.Action <> "UPDATESELECT" then
  Response.Redirect Request("Redirect")
End If

Set objDB = Nothing              'Clean up...
%>
```

> Note that if a database record is inserted, updated, or deleted, the user is whisked away via a Response.Redirect rather than a Server. Transfer. I chose to use this method because I didn't want the user's browser to still show that they were at */CODEREUSE/Admin-PageAction.asp.*

Since the `ModifyDatabase` class is only used from */CODEREUSE/Admin-PageAction.asp,* which is only visited when an administration page form is submitted, the `ModifyDatabase` methods have access to the form field values passed from the administration page form. All administration page forms pass six HIDDEN form fields to */CODEREUSE/AdminPageAction.asp.* These form fields, along with a description, are listed in Table 6-7.

Table 6-7. Each Administration Page Form Passes Six HIDDEN Form Fields to AdminPageAction.asp

HIDDEN Form Field Name	Description
Action	The Action property determines what database action is to take place when the form is submitted. Each administration page form has a unique value for Action. The legal values for Action are INSERT, UPDATESELECT, UPDATE, and DELETE, and are used for the "Insert a New Record," the selecting a record to edit, the "Edit an Existing Record," and the "Delete an Existing Record" administration pages, respectively.

Table 6-7. Each Administration Page Form Passes Six HIDDEN Form Fields to AdminPageAction.asp (continued)

HIDDEN Form Field Name	Description
TableName	Specifies the name of the database table the administration page is for.
Redirect	Specifies the URL to redirect the user to once an actual insert, update, or delete is committed to the database in *AdminPageAction.asp*.
ConnectionString	Specifies the connection string for the database connection.
UserName	Specifies the username for the database connection.
Password	Specifies the password for the database connection.

These four administration page forms also have their own unique sets of form fields that are passed along to *AdminPageAction.asp* once the administration page form is submitted. Table 6-8 lists the distinctive form fields passed from each of the four administration page forms.

Table 6-8. Each Administration Page Form Also Passes Its Own, Unique Set of Form Fields to AdminPageAction.asp

Administration Page Form	Form Field Name	Description
Insert a New Record	col_*ColumnName*	Each form field that represents a column in the database table has the column as the form field name, prefixed with col_.
Edit an Existing Record—Selecting a Particular Record to Edit	FKName	For each foreign key hint supplied by the end developer, there exists a HIDDEN form field named FKName. The form field's value is set to the column name that the foreign key hint applies to.
	FKValue	Like FKName, for each foreign key hint supplied by the end developer, there exists a HIDDEN form field named FKValue. The form field's value is set to the value of the foreign key hint.
	ID	Each listed record contains a radio button named ID. The value of each radio button is a SQL WHERE clause (less the WHERE keyword itself) that uniquely identifies the row.
Edit an Existing Record— Update the Information for a Particular, Selected Record	PrimaryKeyColumns	When updating a particular record in the database, it is important to be able to select the correct record for editing. This form field contains a valid SQL WHERE clause (less the WHERE keyword itself) that uniquely identifies the row being edited.

Table 6-8. Each Administration Page Form Also Passes Its Own, Unique Set of Form Fields to AdminPageAction.asp (continued)

Administration Page Form	Form Field Name	Description
Delete an Existing Record	col_*ColumnName*	Each form field that represents a column in the database table has the column as the form field name, prefixed with col_.
	ID	Each listed record contains a radio button named ID. The value of each radio button is a SQL WHERE clause (less the WHERE keyword itself) that uniquely identifies the row.

Inserting a record into the database

A single call to the ModifyDatabase class's InsertRecord method adds a new record with the values chosen by the user into the database table specified by the TableName form field. InsertRecord, like the other three methods of ModifyDatabase, takes no parameters. InsertRecord, shown in Example 6-30, starts off by ensuring that the all-important TableName form field value was passed in correctly. If TableName was not passed in, then InsertRecord cannot possibly continue, since it has no idea which database table needs a new record added; therefore, in such a case, InsertRecord raises an error.

> All four of the ModifyDatabase methods handle errors rather ungracefully. If a needed form field is not passed in, the behavior of these methods is chaotic at best, perhaps leading to database inconsistencies. Therefore, if any of these methods becomes the slightest bit confused, it throws its arms up into the air, raising an error.

Next, a connection to the database is established using the end developer-set database connection properties. A Recordset object is explicitly created, and a snapshot of the database table specified by TableName is grabbed. The AddNew method is then used to add a new record to the table.

A For Each ... Next loop then steps through the columns in the database table. If a value was entered for a particular database column (that is, Request("col_ *ColumnName*") returns a value), then the column's value is set to the value specified by Request("col_*ColumnName*"). Once all the records have been iterated, the Update method is used to commit the changes to the database.

Example 6-30. InsertRecord Adds a New Record to the Table Specified by the TableName Form Field Value

```
<!--#include virtual="/CODEREUSE/SchemaInfo.Class.asp"-->
<%
Class ModifyDatabase
    ' ... The properties and event handlers have been omitted for brevity
```

Example 6-30. InsertRecord Adds a New Record to the Table Specified by the TableName Form Field Value (continued)

```
'       here, but are listed in Example 6-28 ...  The three other
'       methods have been left out as well.

'********************** METHODS **********************
Public Sub InsertRecord()
    'This method adds a new record to the database

    'Read in the tablename and determine what request collection we're using
    Dim strTableName
    strTableName = Request("TableName")

    'If tablename doesn't exist, that's really bad.  Throw an error
    If Len(strTableName) = 0 then
        Err.Raise vbObjectError + 1235, "ModifyDatabase Class", _
                    "TableName was not correctly passed in."
    End If

    'Open up a connection to the database
    Dim objConn
    Set objConn = Server.CreateObject("ADODB.Connection")
    objConn.Open strConnectionString, strUserName, strPassword

    'Retrieve a picture of the database table we're inserting into
    Dim objRS
    Set objRS = Server.CreateObject("ADODB.Recordset")
    objRS.MaxRecords = 1
    objRS.Open "[" & strTableName & "]", objConn, _
                adOpenForwardOnly, adLockOptimistic, adCmdTable

    objRS.AddNew    'Add a new record

    Dim objField, strFormName
    For Each objField in objRS.Fields
        'If there exists a column in the database table that matches
        'the name of a column passed in from the form with a col_ prefix,
        'set the database column's value to the form element's value
        If Len(Request("col_" & objField.Name)) > 0 then
            objField.Value = Request("col_" & objField.Name)
        End If
    Next

    objRS.Update          'commit the changes

    'Clean up...
    objRS.Close
    Set objRS = Nothing

    objConn.Close
    Set objConn = Nothing
End Sub
'****************************************************
End Class
%>
```

Selecting a particular record to edit

To edit an existing record, the user must first select which record, exactly, he'd like to edit. The UpdateRecordList method of the **AdminPageGenerator** class created the appropriate administration page form, allowing the user to pick a particular record to edit. Once the record has been chosen and the form submitted, the user is sent to *AdminPageAction.asp*, just like he is with any other administration page form.

Once the user has selected a record to edit, he needs to be presented with a form similar to the one in the "Insert a New Record" administration page. However, the "Edit an Existing Record" form the user needs to be presented with should have the selected record's column values already entered into the various form fields.

Fortunately, a class and method already exist to handle this for us! The **AdminPageGenerator**'s UpdateRecordForm method contains such functionality. Therefore, in the "Edit an Existing Record" administration page, when the user selects a record to edit, we need to display yet another administration form. For this reason, the file that contains the **AdminPageGenerator** class needs to be imported into the file that contains the **ModifyDatabase** class via a server-side include.

The UpdateSelect method of the **ModifyDatabase** class is given the responsibility for creating an appropriate administration page form. To do this, it must know what foreign key hints are needed for the database table specified by **TableName**. This information is available, of course, since we passed a number of **FKName** and **FKValue** HIDDEN form fields from the first "Edit an Existing Record" administration page form (see Example 6-24).

The UpdateSelect method generates the appropriate "Edit an Existing Record" administration page form by creating an **AdminPageGenerator** class instance. The needed foreign key hints are set, as well as the Redirect property. Finally, the administration page form is generated with a call to the UpdateRecordForm method. Example 6-31 contains the source code for UpdateSelect.

Example 6-31. UpdateSelect Is the Only ModifyDatabase Method that Doesn't Modify the Database; Rather, It Generates the Correct "Edit an Existing Record" Administration Page Form

```
<!--#include virtual="/CODEREUSE/SchemaInfo.Class.asp"-->
<%
Class ModifyDatabase
    ' ... The properties and event handlers have been omitted for brevity
    '     here, but are listed in Example 6-28 ...  The three other
    '     methods have been left out as well.

    '********************** METHODS **********************
    Public Sub UpdateSelect()
```

Example 6-31. UpdateSelect Is the Only ModifyDatabase Method that Doesn't Modify the Database; Rather, It Generates the Correct "Edit an Existing Record" Administration Page Form (continued)

```
    'This function needs to create the Update form
    Dim objAdmin
    Set objAdmin = new AdminPageGenerator       'Our instance of AdminPageGenerator

    'Read in the tablename and determine what request collection we're using
    Dim strTableName, objRequestCol, strIDs
    strTableName = Request("TableName")

    'If tablename doesn't exist, that's really bad.  Throw an error
    If Len(strTableName) = 0 then
        Err.Raise vbObjectError + 1235, "ModifyDatabase Class", _
                    "TableName was not correctly passed in."
    End If

    'Make sure the ID form field exists
    strIDs = Request("ID")
    If Len(strIDs) = 0 then
        'The user did not select a item to edit
        Response.Write "You did not select an item to edit."
        Response.End
    End If

    'We need to handle foreign key hints
    Dim aHintNames, aHintValues
    aHintNames = split(Request("FKName"), ",")
    aHintValues = split(Request("FKValue"), ",")

    Dim iLoop
    For iLoop = LBound(aHintNames) to UBound(aHintNames)
        objAdmin.ForeignKeyHint Trim(aHintNames(iLoop)), _
                            Trim(aHintValues(iLoop))
    Next

    'Set the redirect URL if needed
    If Len(Request("Redirect")) > 0 then
      objAdmin.Redirect = Left(Request("Redirect"), _
                            InStr(1, Request("Redirect"), "?") - 1)
    End If

    'Display the "Edit an Existing Record" administration page form
    Response.Write "<HTML><BODY><H1>Edit an Existing " & _
                UCase(strTableName) & "</H1><BR>" & vbCrLf
    Response.Write objAdmin.UpdateRecordForm(strTableName, strIDs, _
                                    strConnectionString, _
                                    strUserName, strPassword)
    Response.Write "</BODY></HTML>"
  End Sub
  '*****************************************************
End Class
%>
```

Specifying the Foreign Key Hints

In the UpdateSelect method, the foreign key hints used by the end developer for the particular table need to be set. The UpdateRecordList method of the `AdminPageGenerator` class, which displays the administration page form that allows the user to select a particular record to edit, provides two `HIDDEN` form fields for each foreign key hint (see Table 6-8 and Example 6-23).

When multiple form fields have the same name, say *FormName*, the Request object provides a comma-delimited list of the form field values when the form field *FormName* is requested. In UpdateSelect, the *split* function is used to convert this comma-delimited list into an array. The array is then iterated, and at each iteration, the ForeignKeyHint method of the `AdminPageGenerator` class is called.

This approach ensures that each foreign key hint specified by the end developer in the administration page form from which the user selected a record to edit is also specified for the administration page form generated by UpdateRecordForm method.

To learn more about how to use *split* to iterate through a series of form fields with the same name, be sure to read the following articles:

- "Parsing with join and split," found at *http://www.4guysfromrolla.com/webtech/050999-1.shtml*

- "Passing Arrays from One ASP Page to Another," found at *http://www.4guysfromrolla.com/webtech/101999-1.shtml*

Editing an existing database record

Editing the columns of an existing database record is handled by the UpdateRecord method of the `ModifyDatabase` class. The complete code for the UpdateRecord method can be found in Example 6-32. The code for UpdateRecord is very similar to that of the InsertRecord method shown earlier in Example 6-30. The only major difference is that UpdateRecord doesn't use the ADO Recordset object's AddNew method to create a new record in the table; rather, it uses a `SELECT` statement to grab a specific record from the table.

To obtain the correct, specific record from the database table, UpdateRecord relies on the `PrimaryKeyColumns` HIDDEN form variable passed in through the "Edit an Existing Record" administration page form. (See Table 6-8 for a description of the `PrimaryKeyColumns` form field, and refer to Example 6-21 to see the code for the CreateForm method of the `AdminPageGenerator` class, which creates the "Edit an Existing Record" administration page form.)

Note that three different situations can cause the UpdateRecord method to raise an error:

- `TableName` was not correctly passed in. If `TableName` is not supplied, UpdateRecord has no idea what database table to update.

- `PrimaryKeyColumns` was not correctly passed in. Since this form field uniquely identifies a record in the table specified by `TableName`, if this value is not supplied, UpdateRecord cannot continue, since it does not know which record to edit from `TableName`.

- The query to return a single database record returns no records at all. If this happens, a record to update does not exist, which is bad. This rare situation can happen if, between the time a record was selected for editing and the time the user submitted his changes to the record, another user deleted the record in question or altered its primary key value(s). (This possibility is discussed in more detail in "Limitations and Possible Enhancements.")

Example 6-32. UpdateRecord Applies Changes to an Already Existing Record in the Database Table

```
<!--#include virtual="/CODEREUSE/SchemaInfo.Class.asp"-->
<%
Class ModifyDatabase
    ' ... The properties and event handlers have been omitted for brevity
    '     here, but are listed in Example 6-28 ...  The three other
    '     methods have been left out as well.

    '********************* METHODS *********************
    Public Sub UpdateRecord()
        'This method updates a record in the database

        'Read in the tablename and determine what request collection we're using
        Dim strTableName
        strTableName = Request("TableName")

        'If tablename doesn't exist, that's really bad.  Throw an error
        If Len(strTableName) = 0 then
            Err.Raise vbObjectError + 1235, "ModifyDatabase Class", _
                        "TableName was not correctly passed in."
        End If

        'Read in the PrimaryKeyColumns Value
        Dim strPKColumns
        strPKColumns = Request("PrimaryKeyColumns")

        'If strPKColumns doesn't exist, that's really bad.  Throw an error
        If Len(strPKColumns) = 0 then
            Err.Raise vbObjectError + 1237, "ModifyDatabase Class", _
                        "PrimaryKeyColumns needed for an UPDATE."
        End If

        'Open up a connection to the database
```

*Example 6-32. UpdateRecord Applies Changes to an Already Existing Record
in the Database Table (continued)*

```
    Dim objConn
    Set objConn = Server.CreateObject("ADODB.Connection")
    objConn.Open strConnectionString, strUserName, strPassword

    'Retrieve a picture of the database table we're inserting into
    Dim objRS, strSQL
    strSQL = "SELECT * FROM [" & strTableName & "] WHERE " & _
                                                strPKColumns

    Set objRS = Server.CreateObject("ADODB.Recordset")
    objRS.MaxRecords = 1
    objRS.Open strSQL, objConn, adOpenForwardOnly, adLockOptimistic

    'Make sure we are on a record
    If objRS.EOF then
        'this is bad...
        Err.Raise vbObjectError + 1380, "ModifyDatabase Class", _
                "Record to update not found: Failed on - " & strSQL
    End If

    Dim objField, strFormName
    For Each objField in objRS.Fields
        'If there exists a column in the database table that matches
        'the name of a column passed in from the form with a col_ prefix,
        'set the database column's value to the form element's value
        If Len(Request("col_" & objField.Name)) > 0 then
            objField.Value = Request("col_" & objField.Name)
        End If
    Next

    objRS.Update          'commit the changes

    'Clean up...
    objRS.Close
    Set objRS = Nothing

    objConn.Close
    Set objConn = Nothing
  End Sub
  '*****************************************************
End Class
%>
```

Deleting an existing database record

The DeleteRecords method of the `ModifyDatabase` class can be used to delete
one or more records from a database table. Recall that the "Delete an Existing
Record" administration page form listed each record in a particular database table,
providing a checkbox next to each record. By using checkboxes, as opposed to
radio buttons, the user can check more than one record, thereby deleting several
records in one fell swoop.

As described in Table 6-8, each checkbox in the "Delete an Existing Record" administration page form is given the same name, ID, which contains a statement to uniquely identify the row. As with the foreign key hints in the UpdateSelect method, the value of the ID form fields will be available as a comma-delimited list. Example 6-33, which contains the code for DeleteRecords, demonstrates how this comma-delimited list can be used to delete one or more records with a single SQL statement.

Example 6-33. The DeleteRecords Method Can Delete One or More Records from a Database Table with a Single SQL Statement

```
<!--#include virtual="/CODEREUSE/SchemaInfo.Class.asp"-->
<%
Class ModifyDatabase
    ' ... The properties and event handlers have been omitted for brevity
    '     here, but are listed in Example 6-28 ...  The three other
    '     methods have been left out as well.

'********************** METHODS **********************
Public Sub DeleteRecords()
    'This method deletes one or more records from the database

    'Read in the tablename and determine what request collection we're using
    Dim strTableName, objRequestCol, strIDs
    strTableName = Request("TableName")

    'If tablename doesn't exist, that's really bad.  Throw an error
    If Len(strTableName) = 0 then
        Err.Raise vbObjectError + 1235, "ModifyDatabase Class", _
                            "TableName was not correctly passed in."
    End If

    'Make sure the ID form field exists
    strIDs = Request("ID")
    If Len(strIDs) = 0 then
        'The user did not select a item to delete
        Response.Write "You did not select an item to delete."
        Response.End
    End If

    'Open up a connection to the database
    Dim objConn
    Set objConn = Server.CreateObject("ADODB.Connection")
    objConn.Open strConnectionString, strUserName, strPassword

    Dim strSQL
    strSQL = "DELETE FROM [" & strTableName & "] WHERE "
    strSQL = strSQL & Replace(strIDs, ",", " OR ")

    objConn.Execute strSQL            'Execute the SQL statement

    'Clean up...
    objConn.Close
```

Example 6-33. The DeleteRecords Method Can Delete One or More Records from a Database
Table with a Single SQL Statement (continued)

```
    Set objConn = Nothing
End Sub
'********************************************************
%>
```

Deleting Multiple Records

The DeleteRecords method needs to be able to delete more than one record
from a database table. While a single SQL statement for each record deletion
could be used, such an approach would result in poor performance when multiple records should be deleted.

There is more than one way to delete multiple records in one SQL statement.
Example 6-33 illustrates one such way, by simply creating a lengthy SQL statement in the form of:

```
DELETE FROM TableName
WHERE ID = Value1 OR
      ID = Value2 OR . . .
      ID = ValueN
```

Another way to accomplish this same feat using a more compact and more elegant SQL statement is to use SQL's set notation. *N* records can be deleted from
a table with a SQL statement such as:

```
DELETE FROM TableName
WHERE ID IN (Value1, Value2, . . . ValueN)
```

SQL set notation is very powerful and very useful, but most importantly, it's
very cool. To learn more about SQL set notation, check out the following article, "Using SQL Set Notation to do Batch Deletes," at *http://www.*
4guysfromrolla.com/webtech/092899-1.shtml.

Tying the Administration Pages Together

Now that we have all of the classes needed to gather table and column information, display administration page forms, and store changes to the database, we're
nearly done with the generic administration page creation application. Despite all
of the hard work put into the various administration page classes thus far, and
despite all of the energy put toward making these classes as reusable as possible,
the generic administration page generation application still is not nearly as reusable as it could be.

For example, in our database example with the `Product`, `Catalog`, `ProductType`,
and `CatalogProduct` tables, to create the needed administration pages, the end
developer would be required to create a total of 12 ASP pages. These pages would

consist of an Insert, Edit, and Delete page for each database table. Each of these pages would use the `AdminPageGenerator` class to create the correct administration page form.

It would be nice to have a single, generic ASP page that served as an administration page menu, listing each database table with options for inserting, editing, or deleting records. Furthermore, it would be nice if, as new database tables were added to the database, the end developer could visit this single page to add the Insert, Edit, and Delete administration pages for the new tables.

When the user selects an administration page for a particular database table, the generic menu page should redirect the user to a single, generic ASP page responsible for displaying the correct administration page form. By having a single, generic menu page send the user to a generic administration page, our administration page application will have become truly reusable. Since each administration page form, when submitted, sends the user to a single ASP page responsible for updating the database with the requested changes, the entire generic administration page generation application has been boiled down to three ASP pages! Figure 6-13 illustrates the movement experienced throughout the three ASP pages as the user visits various administration page forms.

Before we examine the code for the generic menu page, you can see a screenshot of the menu in Figure 6-14.

To assist in creating this administration page menu, we'll need a couple of new classes. The first class, `MenuItem`, stores the information needed to create a particular table's administration pages. Information such as the table name and the various "hints" are included in this class. The second class, `AdminPageMenu`, is used to generate the actual administration page menu, and contains information pertinent to all the various tables' administration pages, such as connection information to the database.

MenuItem's methods, properties, and event handlers

Each database table has information unique to itself. Since the `AdminPageGenerator` class cannot determine these table-specific intricacies on its own, it relies on "hints" from the end developer. The `MenuItem` class serves as a container to store various hints and other table-specific information. The properties for the `MenuItem` include: TableName, Redirect, IdentityColumnHint, FormHints, FKHints, FormNameHints, and FormDescriptionHints. The last four "hint" properties are Dictionary object instances, storing zero to many end developer-supplied hints.

The TableName property simply contains the name of the database table. IdentityColumnHint contains an end developer-supplied hint as to which database column is an AutoNumber column. Recall that if a database table contains no records,

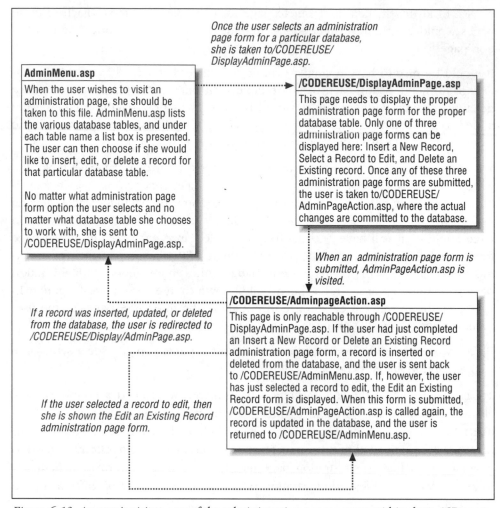

Figure 6-13. An user's visit to any of the administration pages occurs within three ASP pages

it cannot determine which column, if any, is an AutoNumber column. Therefore, the end developer should supply an IdentityColumnHint if the table contains an AutoNumber column. The Redirect property determines where the user is sent after */CODEREUSE/AdminPageAction.asp* inserts, updates, or deletes a record from the database. The diagram in Figure 6-13 assumes that the Redirect property is set to *AdminMenu.asp*. However, if the end developer would rather have a database table's administration page redirect to some sort of confirmation page, all he needs to do is set the Redirect property to the URL of the confirmation page.

The `MenuItem` class also contains four methods (AddFormHint, AddFKHint, AddFormNameHint, and AddFormDescriptionHint), which are responsible for adding hints to the four various Dictionary objects. These four methods are

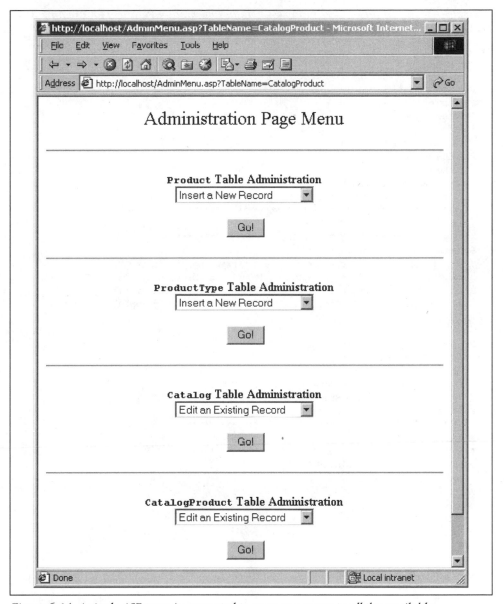

Figure 6-14. A single ASP page is generated to serve as a menu to all the available administration pages

functionally identical to the hint-adding methods in the `AdminPageGenerator` class (listed in Example 6-18).

Example 6-34 lists the `MenuItem` class, along with all of its methods, properties, and event handlers. The `MenuItem` class should be placed in a file named */CODEREUSE/ AdminPageMenu.asp*.

Example 6-34. A MenuItem Class Instance Contains Information Pertinent for Creating a Particular Database Table's Administration Page Forms

```
<%
Class MenuItem
    '************** MEMBER VARIABLES ********************
    Private strTableName
    Private strRedirect
    Private strIdentityColumn

    'Hint Dictionary objects
    Private objFormHints
    Private objFKHints
    Private objFormNameHints
    Private objFormDescriptionHints
    '*****************************************************

    '****************** EVENT HANDLERS ******************
    Private Sub Class_Initialize()
      Set objFormHints = Server.CreateObject("Scripting.Dictionary")
      Set objFKHints = Server.CreateObject("Scripting.Dictionary")
      Set objFormNameHints = Server.CreateObject("Scripting.Dictionary")
      Set objFormDescriptionHints = Server.CreateObject("Scripting.Dictionary")
    End Sub

    Private Sub Class_Terminate()
      Set objFormHints = Nothing
      Set objFKHints = Nothing
      Set objFormNameHints = Nothing
      Set objFormDescriptionHints = Nothing
    End Sub
    '*****************************************************

    '****************** LET PROPERTIES ******************
    Public Property Let TableName(str)
       strTableName = str
    End Property

    Public Property Let IdentityColumnHint(strIdentity)
       strIdentityColumn = strIdentity
    End Property

    Public Property Let Redirect(str)
       strRedirect = str
    End Property
    '*****************************************************

    '****************** GET PROPERTIES ******************
    Public Property Get TableName()
       TableName = strTableName
    End Property

    Public Property Get IdentityColumnHint()
       IdentityColumnHint = strIdentityColumn
    End Property
```

Example 6-34. A MenuItem Class Instance Contains Information Pertinent for Creating a Particular Database Table's Administration Page Forms (continued)

```
Public Property Get Redirect()
    Redirect = strRedirect
End Property

Public Property Get FormHints()
    Set FormHints = objFormHints
End Property

Public Property Get FKHints()
    Set FKHints = objFKHints
End Property

Public Property Get FormNameHints()
    Set FormNameHints = objFormNameHints
End Property

Public Property Get FormDescriptionHints()
    Set FormDescriptionHints = objFormDescriptionHints
End Property
'*****************************************************

'********************** METHODS **********************
Public Sub AddFormHint(strName, strValue)
    If objFormHints.Exists(strName) then
        objFormHints(strName) = strValue
    Else
        objFormHints.Add strName, strValue
    End If
End Sub

Public Sub AddFKHint(strName, strValue)
    If objFKHints.Exists(strName) then
        objFKHints(strName) = strValue
    Else
        objFKHints.Add strName, strValue
    End If
End Sub

Public Sub AddFormNameHint(strName, strValue)
    If objFormNameHints.Exists(strName) then
        objFormNameHints(strName) = strValue
    Else
        objFormNameHints.Add strName, strValue
    End If
End Sub

Public Sub AddFormDescriptionHint(strName, strValue)
    If objFormDescriptionHints.Exists(strName) then
        objFormDescriptionHints(strName) = strValue
    Else
        objFormDescriptionHints.Add strName, strValue
    End If
End Sub
```

*Example 6-34. A MenuItem Class Instance Contains Information Pertinent for Creating a
Particular Database Table's Administration Page Forms (continued)*

```
'*****************************************************
End Class
%>
```

Testing the MenuItem class

The MenuItem class is used to add a new administration page to the menu (see
Figure 6-14 for a screenshot). To accommodate such functionality, the MenuItem
class has a number of read/write properties. Example 6-35 contains a simple test
driver for the MenuItem class. In the example, a couple of the properties are set,
creating a MenuItem instance for the Product table.

*Example 6-35. The MenuItem Class Describes a Menu Item for the Administration
Page Menu*

```
<%@ LANGUAGE = "VBSCRIPT" %>
<% Option Explicit %>
<!--#include virtual="/CODEREUSE/AdminPageMenu.asp"-->
<%
   'Specify the redirect property (where the user should be taken to after
   '/CODEREUSE/AdminPageAction.asp updates the database)
   Const strRedirect = "/AdminMenu.asp"

   'Create an instance of the MenuItem class
   Dim objMenuItem
   Set objMenuItem = New MenuItem

   'Set some of the MenuItem proeprties
   objMenuItem.TableName = "Product"
   objMenuItem.Redirect = strRedirect
   objMenuItem.IdentityColumnHint = "ProductID"
   objMenuItem.AddFKHint "ProductTypeid", "Product Type ~Name~"

   'Output some of these values
   Response.Write "Creating a menu item for <B>" & objMenuItem.TableName
   Response.Write "</B><BR>"

   Set objMenuItem = Nothing        'Clean up
%>
```

> The output of the test driver in Example 6-35, when viewed through
> a browser, is simply "Creating a menu item for Product."

AdminPageMenu's properties and event handlers

The AdminPageMenu class is responsible for generating the menu interface shown
in Figure 6-14. Since every single administration page form is shown through a sin-

gle ASP page (*/CODEREUSE/DisplayAdminPage.asp*), the information needed to display a particular administration page form must be passed from the menu page (*AdminMenu.asp*) to a page that can correctly display the proper administration page form. As shown in Figure 6-13, the page that is responsible for displaying the administration page form has been named */CODEREUSE/DisplayAdminPage.asp*. However, you can specify that the users be sent to a different page once they choose an administration page from the menu. A constant, `strAction`, defines what ASP page the user should be sent to from the administration page menu (*AdminMenu.asp*).

Recall that database table-specific information already exists in each `MenuItem` instance. However, we have not yet accounted for certain pieces of information needed by every database table's administration page, namely the database connection information. The `AdminPageMenu` class contains the information required by all administration pages.

`AdminPageMenu` contains three properties used for maintaining database connection information: ConnectionString, UserName, and Password. The `AdminPageMenu` class also contains a private member variable, *objMenuDict*, which is a Dictionary object instance containing `MenuItem` instances. For each database table that needs to be listed on the administration page menu, a `MenuItem` instance representing this database table's information must exist in the *objMenuDict* Dictionary object. In the next section, "AdminPageMenu's methods," we'll look at how `MenuItem` instances are inserted into the *objMenuDict* member variable.

The `AdminPageMenu` class source code should be placed in the same file as the `MenuItem` class, */CODEREUSE/AdminPageMenu.asp*. Example 6-36 contains the properties and event handlers for the `AdminPageMenu` class.

Example 6-36. The AdminPageMenu Class Contains Database Connection Information

```
<%
'strAction specifies where the Adminitration Menu should take the user once
'they select a particular administration menu option.
Const strAction = "/CODEREUSE/DisplayAdminPage.asp"

Class AdminPageMenu
    '************* MEMBER VARIABLES *********************
    Private objMenuDict
    Private strConnString
    Private strUserName
    Private strPassword
    '***************************************************

    '****************** EVENT HANDLERS *****************
    Private Sub Class_Initialize()
        'Initialize objMenuDict
```

Example 6-36. The AdminPageMenu Class Contains Database
Connection Information (continued)

```
       Set objMenuDict = Server.CreateObject("Scripting.Dictionary")
   End Sub

   Private Sub Class_Terminate()
       Set objMenuDict = Nothing          'Clean up...
   End Sub
   '*****************************************************

   '***************** GET PROPERTIES ******************
   Public Property Get Count()
      Count = objMenuDict.Count
   End Property
   '*****************************************************

   '***************** LET PROPERTIES ******************
   Public Property Let ConnectionString(str)
      strConnString = str
   End Property

   Public Property Let UserName(str)
      strUserName = str
   End Property

   Public Property Let Password(str)
      strPassword = str
   End Property
   '*****************************************************

   ' ... The methods of AdminPageMenu are presented in Example 6-37 ...
End Class
%>
```

The `strAction` constant appearing at the beginning of Example 6-36 indicates where the user should be sent once he or she selects a particular administration page to visit from the administration page menu.

AdminPageMenu's methods

Since the `AdminPageMenu` class is responsible for generating the actual administration page menu, a method is needed to accomplish this. This method, GenerateMenu, iterates through the objMenuDict collection. For each `MenuItem` instance, GenerateMenu creates a form containing a list box with three options: Insert a New Record, Edit an Existing Record, and Delete an Existing Record. The form also contains a number of `HIDDEN` form variables that */CODEREUSE/ DisplayAdminPage.asp* needs to present the user with the correct administration page form.

AdminPageMenu also contains a method for adding a MenuItem instance to the objMenuDict member variable. The method, AddMenuItem, expects a MenuItem instance as a single parameter, and adds this instance to *objMenuDict*.

The two methods of AdminPageMenu can be seen in Example 6-37. Note that when the FORM tag is created, the ACTION property is set to a constant named strAction. strAction specifies the URL the user is sent to once he selects the administration page form he'd like to visit. strAction, a constant that needs to be defined before the AdminPageMenu class definition, should be set to */CODEREUSE/ DisplayAdminPage.asp*.

Example 6-37. The GenerateMenu Method of the AdminPageMenu Class Creates the HTML to Display the Administration Page Menu

```
<%
'strAction specifies where the Administration Menu should take the user once
'they select a particular administration menu option.
Const strAction = "/CODEREUSE/DisplayAdminPage.asp"

Class AdminPageMenu
        ' ... The properties and event handlers for AdminPageMenu are
        '       presented in Example 6-36 ...

    '********************** METHODS *********************
    Public Sub AddMenuItem(objMenuItem)
        'Add a new MenuItem instance to the objMenuDict Dictionary object
        objMenuDict.Add objMenuItem.TableName, objMenuItem
    End Sub


    Public Function GenerateMenu()
        'This function returns an HTML string containing the Admin. Page Menu
        Dim strResult, strName, objMenuItem, strTmp, objFormHints, _
            objFKHints, objFormNameHints, objFormDescriptionHints

        strResult = "<CENTER>" & vbCrLf
        For Each strName in objMenuDict
            Set objMenuItem = objMenuDict(strName)
            strResult = strResult & "<FORM METHOD=POST ACTION=""" & _
                                        strAction & """>" & vbCrLf

            '********* Create HIDDEN variables **********
            strResult = strResult & "<INPUT TYPE=HIDDEN NAME=ConnectionString " & _
                            "VALUE=""" & strConnString & """>" & vbCrLf

            strResult = strResult & "<INPUT TYPE=HIDDEN NAME=UserName " & _
                            "VALUE=""" & strUserName & """>" & vbCrLf

            strResult = strResult & "<INPUT TYPE=HIDDEN NAME=Password " & _
                            "VALUE=""" & strPassword & """>" & vbCrLf

            strResult = strResult & "<INPUT TYPE=HIDDEN NAME=TableName " & _
                            "VALUE=""" & objMenuItem.TableName & """>" & vbCrLf
```

Example 6-37. The GenerateMenu Method of the AdminPageMenu Class Creates the HTML to Display the Administration Page Menu (continued)

```
strResult = strResult & "<INPUT TYPE=HIDDEN NAME=Redirect " & _
                        "VALUE=""" & objMenuItem.Redirect & """>" & vbCrLf

strResult = strResult & "<INPUT TYPE=HIDDEN NAME=IdentityColumnHint " & _
                "VALUE=""" & objMenuItem.IdentityColumnHint & """>" & vbCrLf


Set objFormHints = objMenuItem.FormHints
Set objFKHints = objMenuItem.FKHints
Set objFormNameHints = objMenuItem.FormNameHints
Set objFormDescriptionHints = objMenuItem.FormDescriptionHints

For Each strTmp in objFormHints
    strResult = strResult & "<INPUT TYPE=HIDDEN NAME=FormHintsName " & _
                "VALUE=""" & strTmp & """>" & vbCrLf
    strResult = strResult & "<INPUT TYPE=HIDDEN NAME=FormHintsValue " & _
                "VALUE=""" & objFormHints(strTmp) & """>" & vbCrLf
Next
For Each strTmp in objFKHints
    strResult = strResult & "<INPUT TYPE=HIDDEN NAME=FKHintsName " & _
                "VALUE=""" & strTmp & """>" & vbCrLf
    strResult = strResult & "<INPUT TYPE=HIDDEN NAME=FKHintsValue " & _
                "VALUE=""" & objFKHints(strTmp) & """>" & vbCrLf
Next
For Each strTmp in objFormNameHints
    strResult = strResult & "<INPUT TYPE=HIDDEN NAME=FormNameHintsName" & _
                " VALUE=""" & strTmp & """>" & vbCrLf
    strResult = strResult & "<INPUT TYPE=HIDDEN NAME=" & _
                "FormNameHintsValue VALUE=""" & _
                objFormNameHints(strTmp) & """>" & vbCrLf
Next
For Each strTmp in objFormDescriptionHints
    strResult = strResult & "<INPUT TYPE=HIDDEN NAME=" & _
                "FormDescriptionHintsName " & _
                "VALUE=""" & strTmp & """>" & vbCrLf
    strResult = strResult & "<INPUT TYPE=HIDDEN NAME=" & _
                "FormDescriptionHintsValue VALUE=""" & _
                objFormDescriptionHints(strTmp) & """>" & vbCrLf
Next

Set objFormHints = Nothing
Set objFKHints = Nothing
Set objFormNameHints = Nothing
Set objFormDescriptionHints = Nothing
'********** End Create HIDDEN variables **********

strResult = strResult & "<B><CODE>" & objMenuItem.TableName & _
                "</CODE>" & " Table Administration</B><BR>" & vbCrLf
strResult = strResult & "<SELECT SIZE=1 NAME=Action>" & vbCrLf & _
        "<OPTION VALUE=INSERT>Insert a New Record</OPTION>" & vbCrLf & _
        "<OPTION VALUE=UPDATE>Edit an Existing Record</OPTION>" & vbCrLf & _
        "<OPTION VALUE=DELETE>Delete an Existing Record</OPTION>" & vbCrLf & _
        "</SELECT>" & vbCrLf
```

Example 6-37. The GenerateMenu Method of the AdminPageMenu Class Creates the HTML to Display the Administration Page Menu (continued)

```
            strResult = strResult & "<P><INPUT TYPE=SUBMIT VALUE=""  Go!  "">" & _
                            vbCrLf

            strResult = strResult & "</FORM><P><HR><P>" & vbCrLf & vbCrLf

        Set objMenuItem = Nothing
      Next
      strResult = strResult & "</CENTER>" & vbCrLf

      GenerateMenu = strResult
   End Function
   '****************************************************
End Class
%>
```

Generating a menu with the AdminPageMenu and MenuItem classes

Now that we've looked at the properties and methods of the `MenuItem` and `AdminPageMenu` classes, its time we examine how to apply these classes to generate the administration page menu. In this example, we've used *AdminMenu.asp* as the ASP page that generates the administration page menu.

The source code for *AdminMenu.asp* can be seen in Example 6-38. Note that a server-side include is used to import the contents of */CODEREUSE/ AdminPageMenu.asp*, which contains the class definition for `AdminPageMenu` and `MenuItem`. Also notice that the Redirect property for each `MenuItem` instance is set to */AdminMenu.asp*.

Example 6-38. A Single Instance of the AdminPageMenu Class Is All It Takes to Generate the Administration Page Menu

```
<%@ LANGUAGE = "VBSCRIPT" %>
<% Option Explicit %>
<!--#include virtual="/CODEREUSE/AdminPageMenu.asp"-->
<HTML>
<BODY>
  <CENTER>
    <FONT SIZE=+2>
      Administration Page Menu
    </FONT>
  </CENTER>
  <P><HR><P>
<%
  Const strRedirect = "/AdminMenu.asp"

  Dim objAdminMenu, objMenuItem
  Set objAdminMenu = New AdminPageMenu

  objAdminMenu.ConnectionString = "Provider=SQLOLEDB;Data Source=mitchell;" & _
                        "Initial Catalog=ProductInfo;User ID=sa;Password="
```

Example 6-38. A Single Instance of the AdminPageMenu Class Is All It Takes to Generate the
Administration Page Menu (continued)

```
'Add a MenuItem instance to objAdminMenu for each database table
Set objMenuItem = New MenuItem
objMenuItem.TableName = "Product"
objMenuItem.Redirect = strRedirect
objMenuItem.IdentityColumnHint = "ProductID"
objMenuItem.AddFKHint "ProductTypeid", "Product Type ~Name~"
objAdminMenu.AddMenuItem objMenuItem
Set objMenuItem = Nothing


Set objMenuItem = New MenuItem
objMenuItem.TableName = "Catalog"
objMenuItem.Redirect = strRedirect
objMenuItem.IdentityColumnHint = "CatalogID"
objAdminMenu.AddMenuItem objMenuItem
Set objMenuItem = Nothing


Set objMenuItem = New MenuItem
objMenuItem.TableName = "CatalogProduct"
objMenuItem.Redirect = strRedirect
objMenuItem.AddFKHint "ProductID", "Product ~Quantity~ at $~Price~"
objMenuItem.AddFKHint "CatalogID", "Catalog ~Name~"
objAdminMenu.AddMenuItem objMenuItem
Set objMenuItem = Nothing

'Display the administration page menu
Response.Write objAdminMenu.GenerateMenu()

Set objAdminMenu = Nothing              'Clean up
%>
</BODY></HTML>
```

In Example 6-38, a `MenuItem` instance is created for each database table that
needs a set of administration pages. There may be times when you don't want to
allow users to alter particular database tables. To prevent them from doing so, simply do not add a `MenuItem` instance for that database table. (Note that there is no
MenuItem instance being added for the **ProductType** table in Example 6-38.) Furthermore, if your data model expands to encompass new tables in the future, creating administration pages for those tables is as simple as adding a `MenuItem`
instance in *AdminMenu.asp*.

A screenshot of the code presented in Example 6-38 can be seen in Figure 6-15.

Note that the administration page menu in Figure 6-15 is nearly identical to that in
Figure 6-14. The only difference is the administration page menu in Figure 6-15 is
lacking an administration page option for the **ProductType** table. There may be

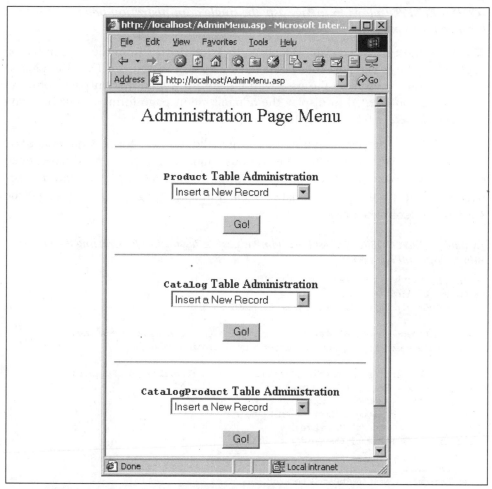

Figure 6-15. A generic Administration Page Menu allows the user to select from three administration pages for each database table

situations in which you wish to present administration pages only to a subset of database tables. Since the end developer can limit what administration page options appear in the administration page menu, such control is possible.

It would also be nice to be able to limit what type of administration pages each database table could have. For example, the end developer may not want anyone deleting records from the Catalog table. Adding such functionality would be relatively simple and would serve as a great exercise for the interested reader.

/CODEREUSE/DisplayAdminPage.asp: the single administration page form generation script

Whenever the user selects an administration page to visit from the administration page menu, he is taken to */CODEREUSE/DisplayAdminPage.asp*. This ASP page is responsible for presenting the user with the correct administration page form. All the information needed to display the administration page form is available, having been passed in from *AdminMenu.asp*.

To display the proper administration page, the proper `AdminPageGenerator` method must be called after the various "hints" and properties have been entered. Example 6-39 shows the code for */CODEREUSE/DisplayAdminPage.asp*, which creates the appropriate administration page form using the `AdminPageGenerator` class.

Example 6-39. /CODEREUSE/DisplayAdminPage.asp Is Responsible for Creating the Proper Administration Page Form

```
<% @LANGUAGE="VBSCRIPT" %>
<% Option Explicit %>
<!--#include virtual="/CODEREUSE/SchemaInfo.Class.asp"-->
<%
   'This ASP page is called when the user submits the form in AdminMenu.asp.
   'This page needs to display the proper administration page...

   Dim strTableName, strFormAction, strConnString, strUserName, strPassword
   strTableName = Request("TableName")
   strFormAction = Request("Action")
   strConnString = Request("ConnectionString")
   strUserName = Request("UserName")
   strPassword = Request("Password")

   Dim objAdmin
   Set objAdmin = New AdminPageGenerator

   '******** BEGIN: ADD ALL HINTS ENTERED BY END DEVELOPER ***************
   If Len(Request("IdentityColumnHint")) > 0 then
      objAdmin.IdentityColumnHint = Request("IdentityColumnHint")
   End If

   If Len(Request("Redirect")) > 0 then
      objAdmin.Redirect = Request("Redirect")
   End If

   Dim aTmpNames, aTmpValues, strTmpName, strTmpValue, iLoop

   'Add Form Hints
   strTmpName = Request("FormHintsName")
   strTmpValue = Request("FormHintsValue")

   aTmpNames = split(strTmpName, ",")
   aTmpValues = split(strTmpValue, ",")
```

Example 6-39. /CODEREUSE/DisplayAdminPage.asp Is Responsible for Creating the Proper
Administration Page Form (continued)

```
For iLoop = LBound(aTmpNames) to UBound(aTmpNames)
   objAdmin.FormHint Trim(aTmpNames(iLoop)), Trim(aTmpValues(iLoop))
Next

'Add FK Hints
strTmpName = Request("FKHintsName")
strTmpValue = Request("FKHintsValue")

aTmpNames = split(strTmpName, ",")
aTmpValues = split(strTmpValue, ",")

For iLoop = LBound(aTmpNames) to UBound(aTmpNames)
   objAdmin.ForeignKeyHint Trim(aTmpNames(iLoop)), Trim(aTmpValues(iLoop))
Next

'Add Form Name Hints
strTmpName = Request("FormNameHintsName")
strTmpValue = Request("FormNameHintsValue")

aTmpNames = split(strTmpName, ",")
aTmpValues = split(strTmpValue, ",")

For iLoop = LBound(aTmpNames) to UBound(aTmpNames)
   objAdmin.FormNameHint Trim(aTmpNames(iLoop)), Trim(aTmpValues(iLoop))
Next

'Add Form Description Hints
strTmpName = Request("FormDescriptionHintsName")
strTmpValue = Request("FormDescriptionHintsValue")

aTmpNames = split(strTmpName, ",")
aTmpValues = split(strTmpValue, ",")

For iLoop = LBound(aTmpNames) to UBound(aTmpNames)
   objAdmin.FormDescriptionHint Trim(aTmpNames(iLoop)), Trim(aTmpValues(iLoop))
Next
'********** END: ADD ALL HINTS ENTERED BY END DEVELOPER ***************

'Output the FORM
Response.Write "<HTML><BODY><h1>" & vbCrLf

'Decide what administration page form to display
Select Case strFormAction
  Case "INSERT":
    Response.Write "Insert a New " & UCase(strTableName) & "</H1>" & vbCrLf
    Response.Write objAdmin.CreateRecordForm(strTableName, strConnString, _
                                    strUserName, strPassword)
  Case "UPDATE":
    Response.Write "Select an Existing " & UCase(strTableName) & _
                " to Edit</H1>" & vbCrLf
    Response.Write objAdmin.UpdateRecordList(strTableName, strConnString, _
                                    strUserName, strPassword)
  Case "DELETE":
```

*Example 6-39. /CODEREUSE/DisplayAdminPage.asp Is Responsible for Creating the Proper
Administration Page Form (continued)*

```
        Response.Write "Delete an Existing " & UCase(strTableName) & "</H1>" & vbCrLf
        Response.Write objAdmin.DeleteRecordForm(strTableName, strConnString, _
                                        strUserName, strPassword)
    Case Else:
        'Uh-oh, shouldn't get here...
        Response.Write "Invalid Action parameter specified..."
        Response.End
    End Select
    Response.Write "</BODY></HTML>"

    Set objAdmin = Nothing                  'Clean up...
%>
```

With *AdminMenu.asp* displaying the administration page menu, */CODEREUSE/
DisplayAdminPage.asp* serving as the sole administration page form generation
script, and */CODEREUSE/AdminPageAction.asp* making all requested database
modifications, the generic administration page generation application now has the
flow illustrated in Figure 6-13.

Limitations and Possible Enhancements

Every application has its shortcomings and room for improvements; when using an
application, it is important that you are aware of its limitations. The generic administration page generation application is not without its fair share of handicaps.

For starters, when creating robust, reusable code, it is important to ensure that the
code will work under a variety of different circumstances. Unfortunately, the
administration page generation is limited to working with only two database providers: the SQLOLEDB provider, and the Jet 4.0 (or greater) provider. The application is limited to these two providers due to its use of the `adSchemaForeignKeys`
schema, which currently is only supported by the SQLOLEDB and Jet 4.0 database
providers. Since the majority of ASP sites use either Microsoft SQL Server or
Microsoft Access, this isn't too great of a problem, but it would have been nice to
have the administration page generation application work for all database
providers.

Another limitation of the system is the difficulty presented in obtaining information on AutoNumber columns. While AutoNumber information can be found from
a SQL Server database through examination of the `syscolumns` system table, the
only generic way to obtain the AutoNumber column for a particular database table
is to use the dynamic Properties collection of the Recordset object. This presents a
problem when attempting to determine the AutoNumber column in a table with
no records. To compensate for this, the IdentityColumnHint property is available
in the `AdminPageGenerator` class, but this solution is far from graceful.

Another limitation of the administration page reveals itself when a database table has a foreign key column that is nullable. A simple enhancement could be made to check whether a foreign key column allowed NULLs, and if so, the list box of available foreign key values could also contain an N/A entry.

Yet another shortcoming of the application arises when there are multiple users making concurrent or near-concurrent changes to the same database tables through the administration pages. For example, imagine that the following situation occurred:

- User A chooses to Edit an Existing Record from the `Catalog` table. Our user chooses to edit the "Fall, 2000" catalog record, and is whisked away to the administration page form where he can alter various column values.

- While User A is making some changes to the "Fall, 2000" catalog record, User B decides to delete the "Fall, 2000" catalog record from the `Catalog` table. Uh-oh!

- User A finishes making his changes and submits the form. An error is returned (since the UpdateRecord method of the `ModifyDatabase` class couldn't grab the record being edited from the `Catalog` table), confusing and irritating User A.

This shortcoming is common among Internet applications, or any distributed application for that matter, and is a difficult one to overcome. Unfortunately, this is a limitation the users of the administration page generation application will have to live with. Since it is unfeasible and impractical to implement some sort of locking system on these database tables, concurrent users working with the same database table may inadvertently cause errors to occur for one another.

A note on performance

The administration page generation application was written to be as robust and reusable as possible. Furthermore, an important goal of the application was ease of use. Often there is a tradeoff between reusability and performance. Likewise, a tradeoff also exists between code readability and performance. Classes enhance readability and maintainability, but are often not as efficient as their procedural counterparts.

How important is performance, though? For a web application that will be used by many concurrent users, performance is key. Computers have trained us to be impatient, and there's nothing worse than having to wait for your computer! With the administration page generation application, however, performance is not paramount, since just a few "superusers" will use it occasionally. Therefore, it's not terribly important to have a blazingly fast administration page. With an application focusing so heavily on reusability, readability and maintainability are far more important qualities than performance.

Note that we now have a very powerful, generic administration page generation application. To add a new set of administration pages for a new database table, a new `MenuItem` instance needs to be added to */CODEREUSE/DisplayAdminPage.asp*. *That's all that needs to be done!* In the beginning of this chapter, I groaned at how much work was involved in creating administration pages the classical way. With this application, administration pages to insert, update, and delete records from a database table require only five lines of code!

Hopefully this chapter has illustrated the benefits of code reuse. While building reusable applications takes a tremendous amount of upfront effort (I spent over two weeks creating the various classes presented in this chapter), the rewards are immeasurable. The end results were definitely worth the initial hard work!

Further Reading

It is an understatement to say that this chapter discussed numerous topics. As such, certain topics were skimmed over a bit. This futher reading should provide more detailed information about a number of topics covered in this chapter.

- The technical documentation for database schemas is available on Microsoft's site at *http://msdn.microsoft.com/library/psdk/dasdk/mdam2ppd.htm.*

- To learn how to use the `METADATA` tag to import DDL constants, be sure to read "Using METADATA to Import DDL Constants," available at *http://www. 4guysfromrolla.com/webtech/110199-1.shtml.*

- If you are looking for some more detailed information on how to use various data providers with ADO, be sure to check out "Using Providers with ADO" at *http://msdn.microsoft.com/library/psdk/dasdk/mdap99m7.htm.*

- To learn how to create a generic database insertion script similar to the one used in the InsertRecord method of the `ModifyDatabase` class, be sure to read "A Very Generic Database Insertion ASP Page," at *http://www. 4guysfromrolla.com/webtech/122299-1.shtml.*

- In this chapter we discussed a number of advanced database techniques. For database-related questions and answers, be sure to check out the Database ListServs over at *http://www.asplists.com/asplists/database.asp.*

7

Using Components

One of the most powerful features of ASP is its tight integration with COM. Due to this relationship, Active Server Pages can easily use COM objects, thereby extending the feature set of ASP. Microsoft provides several ready-to-use COM objects with IIS, which will be the focus of this chapter; however, there is an entire market of third-party COM objects created by companies independent from Microsoft, which will be discussed in length in the next chapter. Furthermore, you, the developer, can create your own custom COM objects for use in your ASP projects, which we'll touch upon briefly in this chapter.

Being able to use COM objects in ASP pages—be it Microsoft-created, third-party-created, or custom-built—is what gives Active Server Pages their great flexibility. Without the ability to use COM objects, ASP would be painfully limited in its scope. After all, ASP only provides a handful of intrinsic objects for the developer to use. These built-in ASP objects don't grant the developer much more than the ability to read from the HTTP request stream, write to the HTTP response stream, and gather information about the web server. To extend ASP, components must be used.

To fully understand the importance of being able to use COM components in an ASP page, imagine for a moment that suddenly, ASP's ability to use COM objects is taken away. Since ADO is nothing more than a collection of Microsoft-provided COM components that aid in database interactions, if an ASP page could not instantiate and utilize a COM component, developers would not be able to create data-driven web sites using Active Server Pages.

Using a high-level programming language like Java, Visual C++, or Visual Basic, developers can create custom COM components for use in ASP pages. Using custom COM components is a virtual necessity for large web sites with complex business rules. In this chapter we'll examine what benefits custom COM components bring to the table and when they should be used. We'll also discuss Windows Script Components, which are scriptable COM objects, and compare them to classical, binary COM components.

In this chapter we'll also look at some of the lesser-known Microsoft COM components. Almost every developer is familiar with ADO, but not as many have had working experience with Ad Rotator, Browser Capabilities, and Content Linker.

COM—A Quick Overview

This book has focused on code reuse and design for ASP applications. Throughout the past seven chapters, we've created various scripts and classes that could easily be reused in other ASP scripts and web projects with minimal effort. While following rigorous ASP application design techniques makes future ASP projects a breeze, it does not lend itself well to future projects using other development tools.

For example, if you wanted to create a banner rotation system on your web site, you could write a class that would randomly pick one advertising banner from a set of potential banners based upon some developer-defined weighting of the various banners. Creating such a system wouldn't be too difficult, and could be done in a highly reusable way using classes. Now, imagine that you were interested in creating a random image-viewing program using Visual C++. You ought to be able to reuse the random banner rotation script to display a random image, since both programs are incredibly alike. However, since the banner rotation system was written as a VBScript class, you cannot directly use it in your Visual C++ random image viewing program.

 A COM component to assist in banner rotation already exists. This component, named Ad Rotator, is discussed in detail in this chapter.

It has long been the dream of developers to be able to write and compile a program just once, and have it able to be used by any program on any platform on any computer with maximum ease. COM, which stands for Component Object Model, is a Microsoft-backed standard for creating "use anywhere, anytime, anyhow" components. With COM, a developer only needs to write the code and compile the object once. With this compiled object in hand, any programming language or tool that can utilize COM can then create an instance of the COM object.

This chapter does not contain a thorough explanation of COM. If you are interested in learning the nitty-gritty details of COM, I highly suggest you read *Inside COM*, by Dale Rogerson, published by Microsoft Press.

COM components can be created in a wide array of programming languages, including Java, Visual C++, and Visual Basic. A fully functional COM component can be instantiated and used from a wide array of programming tools and languages. If you are proficient in any of these languages, you can create custom COM objects for use in your ASP pages. Later in this chapter, we'll discuss the benefits of custom COM objects and when they should be used. This chapter does not, however, delve into a detailed discussion on how to build custom COM components. For a great resource on building custom COM components for use in ASP pages, be sure to read Shelly Powers's *Developing ASP Components* (O'Reilly & Associates).

In summary, COM components allow for the development of components in a plethora of languages that can be compiled once and used virtually anywhere.

COM components can also be developed using any ActiveX Scripting Engine, such as VBScript, JScript, PerlScript, or Python. We will discuss these COM components, referred to as Windows Script Components, in the section "Building COM Components with Script" later in this chapter.

Lesser-Known Microsoft COM Components

Microsoft has created a wide range of COM components for developers to freely use in their applications. Many of these COM components are intended for use in a number of application settings. For example, ActiveX Data Objects (ADO), which were used extensively in Chapter 6, *Database Reuse*, are nothing more than a collection of COM objects to aid with database access. Due to the nature of COM, ADO is not limited to use in Active Server Pages alone. In fact, ADO is commonly used in stand-alone Visual Basic and Visual C++ applications that need to access a database.

Microsoft provides a bevy of useful COM components for Active Server Pages other than ADO. In this section, we will quickly examine the basic functionality of these lesser-known COM components, and then look at how to improve their functionality with the same design techniques we've used throughout the first seven chapters. Table 7-1 shows a listing of the COM components included with IIS for ASP. This chapter will examine the first two, Ad Rotator and Content Linker, in detail.

Table 7-1. Installable ASP Components

Component Name	Description
Ad Rotator	Provides a random banner rotation system.
Content Linker	Useful for creating a table of contents page for a collection of related URLs. Also provides navigational functionality to step through related URLs sequentially.
Content Rotator	Randomly displays text or HTML on a web page.
Browser Capabilities	Useful for determining your visitor's browser's capabilities. For example, this component can be used to determine if your visitor can support client-side VBScript, ActiveX controls, and other information.
Counters	Provides for web page hit counting, letting your visitors see how many people have visited a given page.
Permission Checker	Can be used to determine if a user has access to a certain file or directory. Especially useful when Basic or NT Challenge/ Response password authentication has been enabled.
MyInfo	Keeps track of web server information in one object. The MyInfo component tracks information like the name, address, and phone number of the webmaster, company, or organization running the web site.
Tools	A nifty little collection of helpful tools for accomplishing basic server-side tasks.

For a list of the various methods and properties for these Installable Active Server Pages Components, check out *http://msdn.microsoft. com/library/psdk/iisref/comp275c.htm*.

Creating a Random Banner Rotation System with Ad Rotator

Nearly every web site these days supports itself financially through the sale of advertising banners. For example, the web site I run, *4GuysFromRolla.com*, offers free ASP information to tens of thousands of developers each day. To help pay for the web hosting for *4GuysFromRolla.com*, I sell advertising space to companies that specialize in ASP web hosting or companies that build custom COM components.

 In Chapter 8, *Enhancing Your Web Site with Third-Party Components*, we'll examine some of these custom COM components.

Multiple advertisers mean, of course, that multiple banners are available for display on the user's browser. To display them, a *banner rotation system* is essential. A banner rotation system is one that randomly displays a single advertising banner from a list of advertising banners.

Microsoft provides a free custom COM component to assist in creating a banner rotation system. This component, named Ad Rotator, is installed by default with Personal Web Server, IIS 4.0, and IIS 5.0.

Creating a rotator schedule file

The Ad Rotator generates the HTML to display an advertising banner randomly selected from a *rotator schedule file*. The rotator schedule file contains information on each of the banners in the banner rotation system. When clicked, an advertising banner should redirect the user to the appropriate URL. For example, if you were running a banner for *4GuysFromRolla.com* on your site, when the user clicked the banner, they would be automatically transferred to *http://www.4GuysFromRolla.com*.

The Ad Rotator does this in an indirect way. Rather than just displaying a banner that is hyperlinked to the appropriate URL, like so:

```
<A HREF="http://www.4GuysFromRolla.com">
  <IMG SRC="/images/4GuysBanner.gif">
</A>
```

the Ad Rotator uses a *redirection file*, which is an optional ASP page that can be used to record how many times a specific banner was clicked. Figure 7-1 illustrates the control flow when using the redirection file.

All this information—the redirection file URL, the banner information, and other tidbits of information—is stored in the rotator schedule file. The rotator schedule file is a simple text file that has the form shown in Example 7-1.

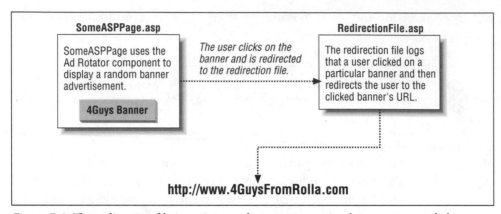

Figure 7-1. The redirection file is an intermediate step occurring between a user clicking a banner and that user being redirected to the banner's corresponding URL

Example 7-1. The Rotator Schedule File Contains Information on Each Banner in the Rotation

```
REDIRECT RedirectionFileURL
WIDTH BannerWidthInPixels
HEIGHT BannerHeightInPixels
BORDER BorderValueForImages
*
Path to banner image 1
Banner redirection URL 1
ALT tag text 1
Weight 1
Path to banner image 2
Banner redirection URL 2
ALT tag text 2
Weight 2
Path to banner image N
Banner redirection URL N
ALT tag text N
Weight N
```

The first four lines in the rotator schedule file apply to all the banners in the rotation. The REDIRECT line specifies the URL of the redirection file. Recall that the redirection file script is responsible for sending the user to a URL when a specific banner is clicked. Later in this chapter, in the section "The redirection file," we'll examine the details of a redirection file.

The URL of the redirection file should not be relative to the directory of the ASP page using the Ad Rotator. Non-relative URLs can be specified in one of two ways: either through a full URL listing (*http://www.yourserver.com/scripts/somescript.asp*) or by specifying a fully qualified virtual path (*/scripts/somescript.asp*). A relative URL, like *somescript.asp*, limits the directories in which pages utilizing the Ad Rotator component can be found.

The `REDIRECT` line in the rotator schedule file is optional; however, it is strongly recommended that you supply it. If you do not supply a `REDIRECT` line, when the user clicks a banner, the ASP page on which the banner appeared will be reloaded with a new query string indicating the redirect URL specified for the particular banner (which we'll discuss shortly).

The following three lines—`WIDTH`, `HEIGHT`, and `BORDER`—are all optional. The `WIDTH` line specifies the width, in pixels, of all the banners in the rotator schedule file. If `WIDTH` is omitted, a value of 440 is used. The `HEIGHT` line indicates the height, in pixels, of all the banners in the rotator schedule file. If `HEIGHT` is omitted, a value of 60 is used. The `BORDER` line specifies the `BORDER` value in the `IMG` tag, which indicates whether a border should be placed around an image. If the `BORDER` property is not specified, it defaults to a value of 1.

The asterisk following the first four lines separates the global properties from the banner-specific properties and is *not* optional. Therefore, as an absolute minimum, the first two lines of the rotator schedule file should be:

```
REDIRECT BannerRedirectURL
*
```

After the asterisk, four lines are needed for each banner in the rotation. The four lines provide the following information for each specific banner:

- The path to the image. As with the global `REDIRECT` line, this should be a non-relative URL (*http://www.yourserver.com/images/someBanner.gif* or */images/someBanner.gif*). If you specify the image as a relative URL (*someBanner.gif*), you will experience broken images when using the same rotator schedule file in ASP pages in a different directory.

- The URL the user should be redirected to when they click the banner. The URL is oftentimes a fully qualified web address, like *http://www.someserver.com*. When a banner is clicked, this URL will be passed to the redirection file through a query string variable.

- The `ALT` tag text. An image's `ALT` tag is displayed while the graphic is loading or if the visitor has images disabled or is surfing from a text-only browser (such as lynx). Also, in both Internet Explorer and Netscape for Windows, if the user moves her mouse over the image, the `ALT` tag appears as a tool tip.

- The weight of the banner. This weight specifies how often the banner is displayed, relative to the other banners in the rotation system. If the banner rotation system contained two banners, one with a weight of 2 and the other with a weight of 1, the first banner would be displayed, on average, twice as often as the second. Commonly, developers will ensure that the various weights add up to 100 so that by looking at a specific banner's weight, one can quickly determine the percentage of times the banner will be displayed.

Example 7-2 contains a working rotator schedule file with three banners.

Example 7-2. AdRot.asp, a Rotator Schedule File Containing Three Banners

```
REDIRECT /CODEREUSE/AdRedirect.asp
WIDTH 468
HEIGHT 60
BORDER 1
*
/images/4GuysFromRolla.gif
http://www.4GuysFromRolla.com
When you think ASP, think 4GuysFromRolla.com!
40
/images/ASPMessageboard.gif
http://www.ASPMessageboard.com
Got ASP Questions?  Find Answers!
40
/images/OReilly.gif
http://www.oreilly.com
Books by O'Reilly
20
```

Our rotator schedule file starts by specifying our redirection file, */CODEREUSE/ AdRedirect.asp*. When any of the banners displayed by Ad Rotator are clicked, the user will be taken to this script. The next three lines contain global information on each of our banners for this rotator schedule file. These first four parameters that specify global properties for all advertisement banners are separated from the banner-specific information by a line containing just an asterisk. This line is vitally important, and if omitted, will generate errors when the Ad Rotator attempts to display a banner. Following the asterisk, each of the groups of four lines describes a banner in the rotation.

The rotator schedule file shown in Example 7-2 is used shortly in a couple of examples. For these examples, assume the rotator schedule file has been saved as */CODEREUSE/AdRot.asp*.

Often developers will create rotator schedule files with a *.txt* extension. This can be dangerous if you wish to keep the rotator schedule file from prying eyes. If the rotator schedule file is saved with a *. txt* extension and placed in a web-accessible directory, anyone who knows or guesses the filename can easily view the source of the rotator schedule file. Therefore, it is recommended that you give the rotator schedule file an *.asp* extension or place it in a directory that has HTTP read access disabled.

Displaying a banner

To display a banner, use the GetAdvertisement method of the Ad Rotator. The GetAdvertisement method has the following definition:

GetAdvertisement(*RotatorScheduleFile*)

The GetAdvertisement method returns HTML that displays a hyperlinked image. Therefore, to display an advertisement, simply use the following code:

```
<%
  Dim objAdRot
  Set objAdRot = Server.CreateObject("MSWC.AdRotator")
  Response.Write objAdRot.GetAdvertisement(RotatorScheduleFile)
%>
```

It's that simple. Example 7-3 contains an ASP page that displays a random banner from the rotator schedule file shown in Example 7-2. The output of the script in Example 7-3, when viewed through a browser, can be seen in Figure 7-2.

Example 7-3. Use the GetAdvertisement Method Where You Wish to Have an Ad Inserted

```
<%@ LANGUAGE = "VBSCRIPT" %>
<% Option Explicit %>
<%
  Dim objAdRot
  Set objAdRot = Server.CreateObject("MSWC.AdRotator")
%>

<HTML>
<BODY>
  <!--Display a banner ad-->
  <CENTER>
    <%=objAdRot.GetAdvertisement("/CODEREUSE/AdRot.asp")%>
  </CENTER>

  <H1>Welcome to our Website!</H1>
  Blah blah blah blah
  <P>

  <!--Display a banner ad-->
  <CENTER>
    <%=objAdRot.GetAdvertisement("/CODEREUSE/AdRot.asp")%>
  </CENTER>
</BODY>
</HTML>

<%
  Set objAdRot = Nothing     'Clean up!
%>
```

The GetAdvertisement method simply returns the HTML to display a particular banner with a hyperlink to the ASP page specified by the REDIRECT line in the

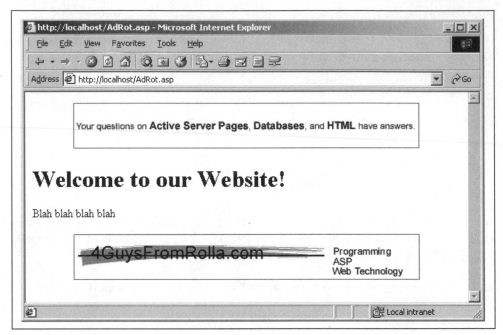

Figure 7-2. The rotator schedule file is consulted to display a random banner at the top and bottom of the document

rotator schedule file. The HTML generated by GetAdvertisement for the top banner in Figure 7-2 (with line breaks added for readability) is:

```
<A HREF="/CODEREUSE/AdRedirect.asp?
    url=http://www.ASPMessageboard.com&
    image=/images/ASPMessageboard.gif" >
        <IMG SRC="/images/ASPMessageboard.gif"
            ALT="Got ASP Questions?  Find Answers!"
            WIDTH=468 HEIGHT=60 BORDER=1>
</A>
```

When clicked, the banner directs the user to the redirection file, passing the banner's particular image path and redirection URL through the query string.

The redirection file

The redirection file, which is specified by the **REDIRECT** line in the rotator schedule file, is visited whenever a user clicks on a banner advertisement generated by the Ad Rotator component. This file should contain a redirection script that is responsible for handling any click-through statistical logging and for forwarding the user to the correct URL.

Note that your code in the redirection script is responsible for forwarding the user to the banner ad's URL; the Ad Rotator component doesn't handle that process automatically. The minimal code needed for the redirection file is simply:

```
<% Response.Redirect Request.QueryString("URL") %>
```

which will send the user to the banner's specific URL.

The redirection file's only requirement is to send the user to the clicked banner's URL. Before sending the user off the site, though, the redirection script can take a moment to record the fact that the particular banner was clicked.

Tracking banner statistics

Often advertisers (who pay their hard-earned money to purchase banner advertisements) are interested in viewing various statistics for their banners. The three major statistics advertisers are interested in are *impressions*, *click-throughs*, and *click-through percentage*. A banner impression occurs when a banner is displayed to the user, whereas a click-through only occurs when a user clicks on the displayed banner. The click-through percentage is the number of click-throughs divided by the number of impressions. These three statistics give the advertiser a pretty good view of their banner advertising's effectiveness.

To keep track of these statistics, we'll need to use a database table. This database table, `AdInfo`, contains the needed rows for advertising statistics tracking, and is described in Table 7-2.

Table 7-2. The AdInfo Table Is Designed to Track Advertising Banner Statistics

Column	Description
URL	Specifies the URL to which the banner points (i.e., *http://www. someserver.com/*). Forms a composite primary key with the `ImageURL` column.
ImageURL	Specifies the URL for the banner graphic (i.e., *images/banners/ someBanner.gif*). Forms a composite primary key with the URL column.
Impressions	An integer field with a default of zero. Keeps track of the total number of impressions for a particular banner.
ClickThroughs	An integer field with a default of zero. Keeps track of the total number of click-throughs for a particular banner.
Description	Provides a textual description of the banner to be used in a report screen. This report screen should show the description, impressions, click-throughs, and click-through percentages for each banner.

There is no need to have a `ClickThroughPercentage` column in the `AdInfo` table, since the click-through percentages can be determined by dividing the value of `ClickThroughs` by the value of `Impressions`.

With the Ad Rotator, calculating the total number of click-throughs is rather simple. Each time a banner is clicked, the redirection file is visited. Since the URL of the banner image and the URL to redirect to are passed to the redirection file, a simple **UPDATE** statement could be issued to increment the number of `ClickThroughs`.

Example 7-4 presents a redirection file that increments the number of click-throughs for the clicked banner. Note that the script assumes a row has already been entered into the `AdInfo` table that contains the URL and image URL. Therefore, for this approach to accurately track the click-through stats, before adding a new banner to the rotator schedule file, be sure to add a corresponding row to the `AdInfo` database table.

Example 7-4. The Redirection Script Can Track Click-Through Statistics

```
<% @LANGUAGE="VBSCRIPT" %>
<% Option Explicit %>
<%
  'Read in the URL/Image
  Dim strURL, strImageURL
  strURL = Request.QueryString("url")
  strImageURL = Request.QueryString("image")

  'Now, open a connection to the database.  We need to
  'increment the click-through count by 1 for this banner
  Dim objConn
  Set objConn = Server.CreateObject("ADODB.Connection")
  objConn.Open "DSN=AdvertisingInfo"

  Dim strSQL
  strSQL = "UPDATE AdInfo SET ClickThroughs = ClickThroughs + 1 " & _
           "WHERE URL = '" & strURL & "' AND ImageURL = '" & strImageURL & "'"

  objConn.Execute strSQL        'Execute the SQL statement

  objConn.Close                 'Clean up...
  Set objConn = Nothing

  'Redirect the user
  Response.Redirect strURL
%>
```

The banner rotation script makes tracking click-through statistics simple. However, tracking impression statistics with Ad Rotator is far from easy; it can be done, but requires some clever (and messy) hacks. You may wonder how important impression tracking is. One may think that advertisers are only interested in how many people actually clicked on their banner, but in my experience, I've found that many advertisers regard impressions as just as important. Furthermore, since advertisers usually prefer to buy blocks of impressions (that is, an advertiser may be willing to pay x dollars for y banner impressions), being able to track the number of impressions is important as well.

Since the GetAdvertisement method of the Ad Rotator component simply spits out HTML, there are no straightforward hooks or event handlers to use to increment the number of impressions when a particular banner is shown. Therefore, if tracking banner impressions is critical, many developers will give up on Ad Rotator and look for other solutions.

There are a number of articles sprinkled throughout the Web on how to create a custom banner rotation system using ASP. Here are a few of these articles:

- "Creating a Banner Rotation System" at *http://www. 4guysfromrolla.com/webtech/061399-4.shtml.*
- "Dynamic Banner Administration" at *http://www.15seconds.com/ issue/pv980220.htm.*
- "Rotating Banner Ads Using a Database" at *http://www. 4guysfromrolla.com/webtech/091299-1.shtml.*

However, using a bit of a hack, we can implement banner impression tracking with the Ad Rotator. For this hack to work properly, it is essential that for each banner you wish to add to the rotator schedule file, you *first* add a record to the `AdInfo` table.

OK, now comes the hack! Rather than simply calling the GetAdvertisement method and sending it directly to the HTML output stream, we can instead store it to a variable. Having intercepted it, we can quickly scan it, looking for the `URL` (wedged between `url=` and the following ampersand (`&`)) and the `ImageURL` (wedged between the `image=` and the closing quotes). Since these two pieces of information uniquely identify each record in the `AdInfo` table, once we have the values for `URL` and `ImageURL`, we can increment the correct row's `Impressions` column! A huge, ugly, disgraceful hack, I know, but with the Ad Rotator, there is no cleaner way to track impressions.

To accomplish this, we'll create a function named *ShowAd*, which returns the HTML to generate the clickable advertising banner. *ShowAd* has the following definition:

```
Function ShowAd(AdRotatorInstance, strScheduleFile)
```

The *AdRotatorInstance* must be a valid Ad Rotator object instance. The *strScheduleFile* parameter (the same parameter required by the GetAdvertisement method, incidentally) expects a virtual path to the rotator schedule file. *ShowAd* will call the GetAdvertisement method of the *AdRotatorInstance* component, saving the HTML for analysis. The URL and ImageURL values are then picked out of the saved HTML, and a database call is executed to increment the number of impressions for the specific banner.

The full source code for *ShowAd* can be seen in Example 7-5.

Example 7-5. Impression Tracking Is Possible with the Ad Rotator Component

```
Function ShowAd(objAdRotator, strScheduleFile)
  'Save the HTML
  Dim strHTML
  strHTML = objAdRotator.GetAdvertisement(strScheduleFile)

  'Now, get the URL (between url= and &) and ImageURL (between image and ")
  Dim strURL, strImageURL, iImageStart
  strURL = Mid(strHTML, InStr(1, strHTML, "url=") + 4, _
               InStr(1, strHTML, "&") - InStr(1, strHTML, "url=") - 4)

  iImageStart = InStr(1, strHTML, "image=") + 6
  strImageURL = Mid(strHTML, iImageStart, InStr(iImageStart, strHTML, """") _
               - iImageStart)

  'Update the database info
  Dim objConn
  Set objConn = Server.CreateObject("ADODB.Connection")
  objConn.Open "DSN=AdvertisingInfo", "sa"

  Dim strSQL
  strSQL = "UPDATE AdInfo SET Impressions = Impressions + 1 " & _
           "WHERE ImageURL = '" & strImageURL & "' AND URL = '" & _
           strURL & "'"

  objConn.Execute strSQL

  objConn.Close
  Set objConn = Nothing

  ShowAd = strHTML
End Function
```

In Example 7-3, we used the GetAdvertisement method to display a banner. This method, of course, lacks impression tracking. To display a banner and increment its **Impressions**, use the *ShowAd* function where you previously used the GetAdvertisement method, like so:

```
<%
  'Create an instance of the Ad Rotator
  Dim objAdRot
  Set objAdRot = Server.CreateObject("MSWC.AdRotator")
%>

<!--Display a banner ad-->
<CENTER>
  <%=ShowAd(objAdRot, "/CODEREUSE/AdRot.asp")%>
</CENTER>
```

 Note that the ShowAd method expects an instance of the Ad Rotator as its first parameter. Be sure to have created such an instance of the Ad Rotator object *before* calling the ShowAd method.

Providing impression and click-through tracking via a class

Clearly, implementing impression tracking adds considerable complexity in using the Ad Rotator component. As we've seen countless times before in this book, when faced with a task with complicated implementation details, it is often wise to encapsulate the task in a class. Therefore, let us create a class to ease impression and click-through tracking with the Ad Rotator component.

This class, **AdRotation**, will have an Ad Rotator instance as a member variable, which will be used to generate the HTML for the advertisements. Along with a single private member variable, the **AdRotation** class contains the following properties:

ScheduleFile
Specifies the rotator schedule file the Ad Rotator component should consult when displaying a banner.

ConnectionString
Specifies the connection string to the database that contains the **AdInfo** table.

UserName
Specifies the username to use when connecting to the database, if one is needed.

Password
Specifies the password to use when connecting to the database, if one is needed.

Example 7-6 contains the properties and event handlers for the **AdRotation** class. This class definition should be placed in the file */CODEREUSE/AdRotation.Class.asp*.

*Example 7-6. The AdRotation Class Contains Three Database Connection Properties and a
Property for the Rotator Schedule File*

```
<%
Class AdRotation
  '************** MEMBER VARIABLES ********************
  Private objAdRotator
  Private strScheduleFile

  'Database connection info
  Dim strConnectionString
  Dim strUserName
  Dim strPassword
  '***************************************************

  '****************** EVENT HANDLERS *****************
  Private Sub Class_Initialize()
    'Create an instance of the Ad Rotator component
    Set objAdRotator = Server.CreateObject("MSWC.AdRotator")
  End Sub

  Private Sub Class_Terminate()
    Set objAdRotator = Nothing        'clean up!
  End Sub
  '***************************************************

  '***************** GET PROPERTIES ******************
  Public Property Get ScheduleFile()
    ScheduleFile = strScheduleFile
  End Property

  Public Property Get ConnectionString()
    ConnectionString = strConnectionString
  End Property

  Public Property Get UserName()
    UserName = strUserName
  End Property

  Public Property Get Password()
    Password = strPassword
  End Property
  '***************************************************

  '***************** LET PROPERTIES ******************
  Public Property Let ScheduleFile(str)
    strScheduleFile = str
  End Property

  Public Property Let ConnectionString(str)
    strConnectionString = str
  End Property

  Public Property Let UserName(str)
    strUserName = str
  End Property
```

Example 7-6. The AdRotation Class Contains Three Database Connection Properties and a Property for the Rotator Schedule File (continued)

```
Public Property Let Password(str)
    strPassword = str
End Property
'******************************************************

'... The two methods for the AdRotation class have been omitted for
brevity; they are both presented in Example 7-7 ...
End Class
%>
```

The `AdRotation` class has only two methods: ShowAd and SendOffSite. The ShowAd method randomly picks a banner based upon the rotator schedule file and updates the number of `Impressions` in the `AdInfo` table, returning the HTML to generate the banner. This method should be called each time you wish to display an advertising banner. SendOffSite, on the other hand, is only called once from the banner rotation script. SendOffSite increments the `ClickThroughs` column value and uses a Response.Redirect to send the user on to the URL the clicked banner points to.

Example 7-7 contains the source code for the two AdRotation methods. Note that the ShowAd method is nearly identical to the *ShowAd* function presented in Example 7-5, and the SendOffSite method is nearly identical to the redirection file shown in Example 7-3.

Example 7-7. The Two AdRotation Methods Assist with Impression and Click-Through Statistic Tracking

```
<%
Class AdRotation
    '... The properties and event handlers for the AdRotation class
    were presented in Example 7-6 ...

    '********************** METHODS **********************
    Public Function ShowAd()
      'Save the HTML
      Dim strHTML
      strHTML = objAdRotator.GetAdvertisement(strScheduleFile)

      'Now, get the URL (between url= and &) and ImageURL (between image and ")
      Dim strURL, strImageURL, iImageStart
      strURL = Mid(strHTML, InStr(1, strHTML, "url=") + 4, _
                   InStr(1, strHTML, "&") - InStr(1, strHTML, "url=") - 4)

      iImageStart = InStr(1, strHTML, "image=") + 6
      strImageURL = Mid(strHTML, iImageStart, InStr(iImageStart, strHTML, """") _
                        - iImageStart)

      'Update the database info
      Dim objConn
```

Example 7-7. The Two AdRotation Methods Assist with Impression and Click-Through
Statistic Tracking (continued)

```
    Set objConn = Server.CreateObject("ADODB.Connection")
    objConn.Open strConnectionString, strUserName, strPassword

    Dim strSQL
    strSQL = "UPDATE AdInfo SET Impressions = Impressions + 1 " & _
             "WHERE ImageURL = '" & strImageURL & "' AND URL = '" & _
             strURL & "'"

    objConn.Execute strSQL      'Update the impressions

    objConn.Close
    Set objConn = Nothing       'close/clean up

    ShowAd = strHTML
  End Function


  Public Sub SendOffSite()
    'Read in the URL/Image
    Dim strURL, strImageURL
    strURL = Request.QueryString("url")
    strImageURL = Request.QueryString("image")

    'Now, open a connection to the database.  We need to
    'increment the click-through count by 1 for this banner
    Dim objConn
    Set objConn = Server.CreateObject("ADODB.Connection")
    objConn.Open strConnectionString, strUserName, strPassword

    Dim strSQL
    strSQL = "UPDATE AdInfo SET ClickThroughs = ClickThroughs + 1 " & _
             "WHERE URL = '" & strURL & "' AND ImageURL = '" & strImageURL & "'"

    objConn.Execute strSQL          'Execute the SQL statement

    objConn.Close                   'Clean up...
    Set objConn = Nothing

    Response.Redirect strURL        'Redirect the user
  End Sub
  '*****************************************************
End Class
%>
```

Before you use the AdRotation class in a production environment, be sure to add exception-handling code in both ShowAd and Send-OffSite. Both methods assume the information needed to extract URL and ImageURL is present and in the correct format.

Using the AdRotation class

As we've examined throughout this book, classes hide implementation details and mask complexity through encapsulation. As we'll see in a moment, by wrapping the impression and click-through tracking features into a class, the Ad Rotator is now even easier to use than before! In Example 7-3, we looked at how to display an advertisement using the Ad Rotator. Example 7-8 shows how to use the `AdRotation` class not only to display an add, but also to increment the ad's impression count.

 In Example 7-8, the `AdRotation` class has been placed inside a file named */CODEREUSE/AdRotation.Class.asp*, and is imported into the code using a server-side include.

Example 7-8. Use the ShowAd Method to Display a Banner Advertisement with the AdRotation Class

```
<%@ LANGUAGE = "VBSCRIPT" %>
<% Option Explicit %>
<!--#include virtual="/CODEREUSE/AdRotation.Class.asp"-->
<%
    'Create an instance of the AdRotation class
    Dim objAdRot
    Set objAdRot = New AdRotation

    'Set the database connection properties and the schedule file
    objAdRot.ConnectionString = "DSN=AdvertisingInfo"
    objAdRot.ScheduleFile = "/CODEREUSE/AdRot.asp"

    'Wherever an ad is to be displayed, simply call the ShowAd() method and
    'send its output to the client!
%>

<HTML>
<BODY>
    <!--Display a banner ad-->
    <CENTER>
        <%=objAdRot.ShowAd()%>
    </CENTER>

    <H1>Welcome to our Website!</H1>
    Blah blah blah blah
    <P>

    <!--Display a banner ad-->
    <CENTER>
        <%=objAdRot.ShowAd()%>
    </CENTER>
</BODY>
</HTML>
```

*Example 7-8. Use the ShowAd Method to Display a Banner Advertisement with the
AdRotation Class (continued)*

```
<%
  Set objAdRot = Nothing       'Clean up!
%>
```

When a banner is clicked, the user will be taken to the redirection file, which
should have been specified in the first line of the rotator schedule file (which contains the REDIRECT keyword). From the redirection file, we will need to send the
user to the URL the clicked banner points to, but first we need to update the banner's ClickThroughs value. Both of these tasks are accomplished through the
SendOffSite method.

Using the AdRotation class, all we need to do in the redirection file is:

• Create an instance of the AdRotation class.

• Set its properties.

• Call the SendOffSite method.

That's all! The SendOffSite method will correctly increment the ClickThroughs
value and redirect the user to the proper URL! Example 7-9 shows the source code
for the redirection file.

*Example 7-9. With the AdRotation Class, the Redirection File Needs Only to Call the
SendOffSite Method*

```
<% @LANGUAGE="VBSCRIPT" %>
<% Option Explicit %>
<!--#include virtual="/CODEREUSE/AdRotation.Class.asp"-->
<%
  'Create an instance of the AdRotation class
  Dim objAdRot
  Set objAdRot = New AdRotation

  'Set the properties...
  objAdRot.ScheduleFile = "/CODEREUSE/AdRot.asp"
  objAdRot.ConnectionString = "DSN=AdvertisingInfo"

  objAdRot.SendOffSite       'Increment ClickThroughs and redirect the user!

  Set objAdRot = Nothing     'Clean up...
%>
```

When using the AdRotation class, you must have the AdInfo table properly set
up and have an entry in the table for every banner in the rotator schedule file.
(The database table AdInfo was presented in Table 7-2.) With the current implementation, this results in having to enter the same information twice: once in the
AdInfo table and once in the rotator schedule file. An industrious developer
would create a script that would accomplish both tasks in one fell swoop.

Possible enhancements to the AdRotation class

One obvious enhancement to the `AdRotation` class would be to add a reporting method. This method, when called, would return either an HTML string or a Recordset object that contained the various banner information in the `AdInfo` table. The pertinent information would be each banner's description, impressions, click-throughs, and click-through percentages.

Another needed enhancement is some sort of administration tool. Currently, banner information must be stored in two places: the rotator schedule file and the database. It is essential that the banner's image URL and redirect URL in the rotator schedule file match the `AdInfo` table's `ImageURL` and `URL` columns, respectively. Rather than having to make these two identical entries by hand, an administration page that made the needed changes in both the rotator schedule file and the database would be ideal, saving time and errors resulting from typos.

Did we really accomplish anything?

At the start of this chapter, I listed some of the benefits of COM objects over VBScript classes. Namely, COM objects are highly portable, able to be accessed by multiple development tools and programming languages. VBScript classes, on the other hand, are only really useful in programming tools that can utilize VBScript, such as ASP, client-side browser code, and the Windows Script Host.

However, as soon as I introduced a useful COM component (the Ad Rotator), I almost immediately provided a more functional version using a class. Isn't this chapter about components and not classes? While this VBScript `AdRotation` class is not portable, it is still worth the time to develop the class. When developing components, I find it intelligent to keep the components fairly simple, allowing a particular component to have only a small subset of core features.

Once this focused component has been created, developers working with various development tools and programming languages can extend the core functionality of the portable component using non-portable methods. That is exactly what we have done with the `AdRotation` class.

Managing Web Site Content with the Content Linker

One of the greatest challenges of running a web site is adding new content. As a site grows, adding a new web page to the site often involves adding links to several other pages. Microsoft provides a free component with IIS 4.0 and IIS 5.0 called the Content Linker, which makes managing content-rich, frequently updated web sites much easier.

Specifically, the Content Linker provides dynamic hyperlinks between a series of ordered web pages. To use the Content Linker, a *Content Linker list file* is needed, which provides an ordered list of related URLs and descriptions. When the Content

Linker is used in one of the pages listed in the Content Linker list file, hyperlinks can be generated to point to the next and previous URLs in the list. To add a new URL to the list of related URLs, simply add a reference to the new web page in the Content Linker list file. We'll look at the specifics of the Content Linker list file shortly.

Content Linker is especially useful in web sites that contain several related web pages, especially if those web pages can be related sequentially. If you think of a web site's layout in terms of a tree structure (see Figure 7-3), after using the Content Linker, it quickly becomes apparent that it was designed for sites with a flat organization of web pages. In sites with a deep organizational structure, the Content Linker can still be used, but will not be as useful or helpful. Figure 7-3 shows both flat and deep tree structures representing two web site layouts.

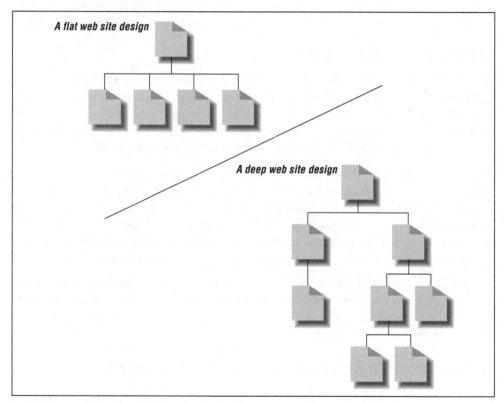

Figure 7-3. A flat web site design lends itself to use of the Content Linker

A great example of the Content Linker in use is *LearnASP.com*, a site dedicated to providing various ASP tutorials. *LearnASP.com* breaks down each tutorial into several related lessons, giving the site a flat web page structure. The Content Linker component is used to generate dynamic hyperlinks between each lesson and tutorial. Take a moment to check out the *LearnASP.com* tutorial layout (*http://www.LearnASP.com/learn*).

The Content Linker list file

To use the Content Linker, a Content Linker list file is needed. The Content Linker list file contains a list of ordered URLs, each appearing on a separate line. Each URL can contain three tab-delimited values:

    URL   Description   Comment

The URL field is the web page URL. Unfortunately, URL must be a relative URL. URLs in the form of *http://someAddress* are invalid and will be ignored by the Content Linker component. Furthermore, non-relative URLs in the form */Address* are also invalid. I find this to be extremely annoying and a painful shortcoming of the Content Linker component.

The Description parameter provides a description for the specific URL. For example, if you ran a web site with several related products for sale, the Content Linker would be a wise choice to use to provide a simple means of navigation among the products. Since the URL might be cryptic (something like *Product. asp?PID=5623932*, perhaps), a textual description of the page would be in order. This description should appear in the Description parameter in the Content Linker list file.

The final parameter, Comment, is not used at all by the Content Linker component. Rather, it serves as a place to add comments for the developer creating the Content Linker list file.

In the Content Linker list file, only the URL parameter is required. Description and Comment are optional.

Example 7-10 contains a valid Content Linker list file for a web site that provides a step-by-step tutorial for learning JScript's control structures. For this entire example, all our files will be placed in the */JscriptTutorial* directory. The Content Linker list file shown in Example 7-10 should be named *JScriptContLink.asp*.

Example 7-10. The Content Linker List File Provides a List of Related Web Pages

```
default.asp   Tutorial Menu    Menu page for the tutorial
if.asp    if ... else Statement Tutorial
for.asp   for Statement Tutorial
while.asp   while Loops Tutorial
switch.asp   switch Statement Tutorial
```

As with the Ad Rotator's rotator schedule file, the Content Linker list file is often given a *.txt* extension. Such an extension, however, enables users to download your Content Linker list file over the Web. By giving the file an *.asp* extension, IIS will attempt to process the file as an ASP page before sending the output to the client. Since the Content Linker list file does not contain valid ASP code, an error will be generated, and the user will not see the file's source code. Of course, if this is not a concern to you, feel free to give the Content Linker list file a *.txt* extension.

In our example, *default.asp* will serve as a menu, containing a link to each of the tutorials. All of the other files in the Content Linker list file contain a tutorial on a particular JScript control structure.

Providing a next and previous hyperlink in each tutorial

In each tutorial it would be nice to provide a next and previous hyperlink, so that the user can quickly and easily traverse through the various JScript control structure tutorials. Of course, this is what the Content Linker is intended for, and now that we have our Content Linker list file, adding such dynamic hyperlinks is a breeze.

To use the Content Linker in an ASP page, we must first create an instance of it. To do this, we can use the following code:

```
Dim objContentLinkerInstance
Set objContentLinkerInstance = Server.CreateObject("MSWC.NextLink")
```

The Content Linker component contains eight methods that can be used to generate dynamic hyperlinks among web pages in the Content Linker list file. These methods are:

GetListCount(`ContLinkList`*)*

Returns the number of web pages represented by the Content Linker list file `ContLinkList` (essentially returns the number of lines in the text file `ContLinkList`).

GetListIndex(`ContLinkList`*)*

Returns the *index number* of the current page within the Content Linker list file. The various lines in the Content Linker list file are given index numbers sequentially, with the first line having an index of 1. If a page whose URL is not found in `ContLinkList` executes GetListIndex, a value of 0 will be returned.

GetNextURL(ContLinkList)

Returns the next URL in the Content Linker list file. If the page that executes the GetNextURL method is the last file listed in the Content Linker list file, the GetNextURL method returns the URL of the first item in the Content Linker list file.

GetNextDescription(ContLinkList)

Returns the description of the next page in the Content Linker list file. If a description was not specified in the Content Linker list file for the next URL, a blank string is returned.

GetPreviousURL(ContLinkList)

Returns the previous URL in the Content Linker list file.

GetPreviousDescription(ContLinkList)

Returns the description of the previous page in the Content Linker list file.

GetNthURL(ContLinkList, Index)

Returns the URL of the page with the specified *Index* value.

GetNthDescription(ContLinkList, Index)

Returns the description of the page with the specified *Index* value.

To display the next and previous links in our JScript control structure tutorial pages, we'll use the GetPreviousURL, GetPreviousDescription, GetNextURL, and GetNextDescription methods. Example 7-11 contains the source code for *if.asp*, which contains a (very) short tutorial on using the if ... else JScript control structure.

Example 7-11. The if ... else Tutorial Contains a Dynamic Hyperlink to the Next and Previous Tutorials

```
<% @LANGUAGE="VBSCRIPT" %>
<% Option Explicit %>
<%
  'Create an instance of the Content Linker
  Dim objContLink
  Set objContLink = Server.CreateObject("MSWC.NextLink")
%>
<HTML>
<BODY>
  <CENTER><H1>if ... else Control Structure Tutorial</H1></CENTER>
  <HR NOSHADE>

  <PRE>
  if (<i>condition</i>)
    <i>statement</i>
  [else <i>statement</i>]
  </PRE>

  <P>
  <!-- Display previous / next links -->
  <TABLE WIDTH=100% BORDER=0>
```

Example 7-11. The if ... else Tutorial Contains a Dynamic Hyperlink to the Next and Previous Tutorials (continued)

```
<TR><TD WIDTH=50% ALIGN=LEFT>
  <A HREF="<%=objContLink.GetPreviousURL("JScriptContLink.asp")%>">
    &lt;&lt; <%=objContLink.GetPreviousDescription("JScriptContLink.asp")%>
  </A>
</TD><TD WIDTH=50% ALIGN=RIGHT>
  <A HREF="<%=objContLink.GetNextURL("JScriptContLink.asp")%>">
    <%=objContLink.GetNextDescription("JScriptContLink.asp")%> &gt;&gt;
  </A>
</TD></TR>
  </TABLE>
</BODY>
</HTML>

<%
  Set objContLink = Nothing              'Clean up!
%>
```

A screenshot of *if.asp*, when viewed through a browser, can be seen in Figure 7-4. Note the two hyperlinks at the bottom of the page, providing easy access to the next and previous URLs in the Content Linker list file. As you can see, the Description field from the Content Linker list file is used as the hypertext, and if we were to examine the page's HTML source, we would find that the URL field is used as the value of the HREF attribute for forward and backward navigation.

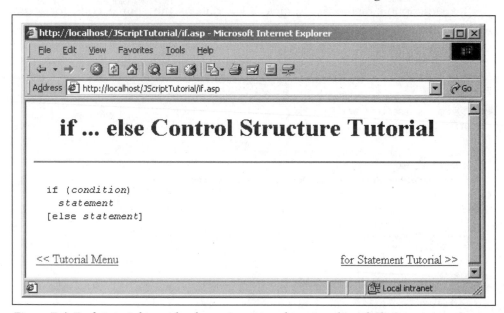

Figure 7-4. Each tutorial provides dynamic next and previous hyperlinks

To provide a previous and next hyperlink on every JScript Control Structure tutorial, simply cut and paste the HTML TABLE near the bottom of Example 7-11. (Of course, rather than cutting and pasting the code into each tutorial page, it is recommended that you place the table in a separate file and use a server-side include in all tutorial pages.)

In the next section, we will look at displaying a dynamically created table of contents as the tutorial's start page (*/JscriptTutorial/ default.asp*)!

With the Content Linker list file in place, to create a new JScript Control Structure tutorial, simply perform the following three tasks:

1. Create the new tutorial, saving it in the */JscriptTutorial* directory.

2. Add the code that generated the dynamic next and previous links in our new tutorial.

3. Add the new tutorial's URL and description to *JScriptContLink.asp*, the Content Linker list file for the JScript Control Structure tutorials.

It's that simple! There's no need to go poking through existing tutorials and updating links to include the new tutorial. Rearranging the order of the tutorials is also a breeze with the Content Linker. If we were not using the Content Linker and wished to completely reorder the tutorials, we'd have to edit the hardcoded next/previous links in all the tutorials. With only four tutorials, this isn't much of a headache, but imagine if we had hundreds!

However, since we are using the Content Linker, we can reorder the tutorials by simply rearranging the order of the tutorials in the Content Linker list file. Since the next and previous links are generated upon demand, after saving the changes to the Content Linker list file, the next and previous links on the various tutorials will automatically reflect the changes!

Creating an index listing of the JScript Control Structure tutorials

When users first visit our JScript Control Structure tutorial section, it might be nice to show them a quick overview of the available tutorials, rather than immediately starting on the first tutorial. Such a listing of available tutorials would be a pain to manage without Content Linker, especially if new tutorials were added frequently.

With the Content Linker component, however, maintaining a listing of available tutorials is quite simple. For our example, *default.asp* will contain a listing of available tutorials. Figure 7-5 presents a screenshot of what we want *default.asp* to look like when viewed through a browser.

To generate such an index listing, we'll loop from the first tutorial's index value to the maximum index value of the various pages in the Content Linker list file. Recall that the GetListCount method returns the total number of pages in the

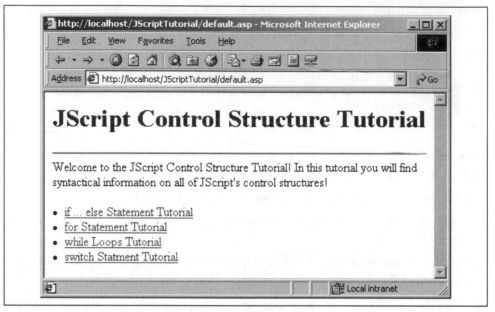

Figure 7-5. The first page in the JScript Control Structure tutorial series should present a listing of the available tutorials

Content Linker list file. Also, recall that two methods exist that allow us to pick out a specific URL and description: GetNthURL and GetNthDescription.

To create a listing of available tutorials, we'll loop through the available indexes, displaying a hyperlink for each index using the GetNthURL and GetNthDescription methods. Example 7-12 contains the source code of *default.asp*, displaying a listing of the available tutorials.

Example 7-12. Listing the Available Tutorials Is a Simple Task with the Content Linker

```
<% @LANGUAGE="VBSCRIPT" %>
<% Option Explicit %>
<%
  'Instantiate the Content Linker component
  Dim objContLink
  Set objContLink = Server.CreateObject("MSWC.NextLink")
%>
<HTML>
<BODY>
  <CENTER><H1>JScript Control Structure Tutorial</H1></CENTER>
  <HR NOSHADE>

  Welcome to the JScript Control Structure Tutorial!  In this
  tutorial you will find syntactical information on all of JScript's
  control structures!

  <P>
  <%
```

Example 7-12. Listing the Available Tutorials Is a Simple Task with the Content Linker

```
    'Since default.asp is listed as the first entry in the Content Linker file,
    'start the For loop at 2, so as not to include default.asp in the listing of
    'available tutorials
    Dim iLoop
    For iLoop = 2 to objContLink.GetListCount("JScriptContLink.asp")
%>
    <LI><A HREF="<%=objContLink.GetNthURL("JScriptContLink.asp", iLoop)%>">
        <%=objContLink.GetNthDescription("JScriptContLink.asp", iLoop)%>
    </A><BR>
<%
    Next

    Set objContLink = Nothing          'Clean up...
%>
</BODY>
</HTML>
```

Enhancing Microsoft's COM Components

As we saw in the Ad Rotator example, VBScript classes can be used to enhance existing COM components. Rarely will you find an existing COM component that meets every single one of your requirements for a given project. Rather than scrapping the notion of using the existing COM component, though, why not use it as a foundation and use VBScript classes to include the needed extra functionality?

This is exactly what was done in this chapter with the Ad Rotator. A random banner rotation application with impression and click-through tracking was needed. Ad Rotator met some of those requirements, but not all. Rather than dismissing Ad Rotator altogether, we embraced the random banner display and click-through tracking capabilities of Ad Rotator and wrote our own VBScript wrapper class to add the impression tracking. Existing COM components are great building blocks, and in my opinion, should be used as often as possible.

Using existing COM components is a lot like buying an existing house and applying your own add-ons, as opposed to building your own made-to-order home. For example, if you wanted a home with a deck and the only homes on the market were those without decks, you would have two options:

- Buy an existing home and add on a deck.

- Build a new home from scratch with, of course, a deck.

Buying an existing home and adding a new deck requires less time, effort, and money than building a new home from scratch does. Similarly, using existing COM components and adding the extra needed functionality is a lot less time-consuming, and less prone to error, than building your own COM component from scratch.

Building Components

Since COM components can be created in a number of high-level programming languages, such as Visual C++, Java, and Visual Basic, if you are proficient in any of these languages, you can create your own custom COM components (or COM objects, as they are sometimes called). For an object to be considered a COM object (and therefore to be able to be instantiated from the wide range of development tools and programming languages), it must follow certain guidelines. These low-level guidelines are far past the scope of this book, and will not be discussed in detail.

Thankfully, high-level programming languages ensure that most of these low-level implementation details are taken care of for you. For example, when creating a COM component in Visual Basic, these low-level details can be completely ignored, and the developer can focus on creating classes that will be translated into full-fledged COM components by Visual Basic.

This book also refrains from stepping through the process of creating a COM object with any programming language. There are already several great books on the topic. If you are looking for an entire book dedicated to building COM objects in various languages, let me recommend Shelly Powers's *Developing ASP Components* (O'Reilly), which shows how to create components in Java, Visual C++, and Visual Basic in great detail.

What this book does focus on is a particular type of custom COM component, one used to ensure business logic integrity.

Wrapping Business Logic Within a COM Object

Custom COM components usually fall into one of two categories:

- Components that provide some type of added functionality to the web site
- Components that define the business logic a site must abide by

The two Microsoft COM components we examined earlier in this chapter were both examples of COM components that provided added functionality. The Ad Rotator component provided a generic advertising banner rotation system, while the Content Linker provided a simpler means for adding and updating content to a large web site. In Chapter 8, we'll look at a number of commercially available COM components that also fall within this category.

The second category of custom COM components is not nearly as glamorous as the first, but in large web sites, is incredibly important. Pause for a moment and think of any large e-commerce web site. When purchasing an item from that site, a number of complicated transactions must occur: taxes must be computed; credit card balances must be checked; orders must be sent to the warehouse via some mechanism. Now, imagine that all of these complicated transactions were handled by logic in each ASP page from which a user could purchase an item.

While ASP may be able to handle such complex business rules, it would not be wise to place complicated business rules within an ASP page, for a number of reasons. Imagine, for a moment, that all the business rules were hardcoded into the applicable ASP pages. What would happen if a tax law changed, requiring the taxes to be calculated differently? Since the tax calculations were hardcoded into a number of ASP pages, a developer must hunt through the site, making the needed changes. The more changes the developer is required to make, the more likely he is to miss a needed change or commit a typo, resulting in a tax-calculation error.

As we've seen throughout this book, complex tasks become incredibly simpler when the task is wrapped inside of a class. With a class, the end developer can treat the class like a black box and not worry about how the black box performs its tasks. With classes, the responsibility for a particular task is removed from the developer and placed squarely on the shoulders of the class. Custom COM components that handle business logic provide a similar black box interface.

In an e-commerce web site, business logic might include tax information, credit card handling, shipping procedures, and mechanisms to notify complementary computer systems (such as sending an order to the warehouse, which might use a different computer system). If changes occur in the business logic, only the custom COM component's code needs to be modified. All the ASP pages using the COM component are unaware of the business logic changes that occurred.

Custom COM components responsible for business logic also provide a level of abstraction between an ASP page and the database. In a large, data-driven web site that does not use COM objects for business logic, when some piece of information needs to be committed or retrieved from the database, the ASP page is responsible for executing the SQL statement. In this book, we've looked at several examples of using the ADO objects to insert, update, and delete database records.

However, in a large site with several developers and a complex data model, having the ASP pages handle database transactions is asking for trouble. Since similar database actions are taken on various ASP pages, there are bound to be typos or mistakes, resulting in database or ASP errors. Granted, stored procedures could be used to help alleviate this problem, but what happens if the data model is changed? Those ASP pages that reference tables that no longer exist or have been altered need to be fixed to reflect the changes in the data model.

On a large web site, where there may be hundreds of ASP pages, such a data model change can be a logistical nightmare. When custom COM components are involved, the ASP pages make calls to the COM component; it is then the responsibility of the component to make the appropriate database access calls. That way, if there is a data model change, only the custom COM object needs to be modified; the ASP pages that reference the COM component can go unchanged!

Custom COM components can therefore encapsulate the database and business logic, providing a black box for ASP pages to use. Custom COM components make up the middle layer of a *three-tiered web site*. A three-tiered web site is one that consists of three parts, each distinct from one another and responsible for a unique set of tasks. The three tiers, which are illustrated in Figure 7-6, include:

- *A Data Services tier*, which includes data storage tools, such as databases.

- *A Business Services tier*, which includes components that contain business logic information.

- *A User Services tier*, which contains the front end of the application that is presented to the user.

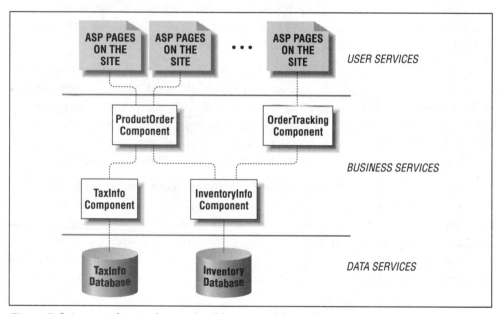

Figure 7-6. Large, robust web sites should consist of three distinct tiers

 For a more detailed explanation of the motivation behind and the advantages of a three-tiered client-server application, be sure to read "Building Three-Tiered Client-Server Business Solutions," a Microsoft white paper available at *http://www.microsoft.com/TechNet/Analpln/ 3tierwp.asp*.

Imagine the steps that occur when a user visits an order-tracking page in a three-tiered e-commerce web site. When a user enters his or her ordering specifics, the

ASP page creates an instance of the `OrderTracking` component (see Figure 7-6). This component may interact with other custom COM components (such as the `InventoryInfo` component). The order-tracking ASP page, though, is not concerned with how the `OrderTracking` component provides the order information details.

As illustrated in Figure 7-6, the `OrderTracking` component performs some calculations and then requests information from the `InventoryInfo` component. This component grabs the requested information from the Inventory database, which is in the Data Services tier.

Using custom COM components also makes for easier-to-read, simplified ASP code. Imagine the several lines of cryptic ASP code that would be needed to handle a sale from an e-commerce web site. Using custom COM components that assume responsibility for the business logic, the ASP code would be greatly simplified to something like:

```
'Instantiate the object
Dim objBuySomething
Set objBuySomething = Server.CreateObject("Product.Purchase")

'Set the properties
objBuySomething.ProductID = 458734582
objBuySomething.Quantity = 1
objBuySomething.CreditCardNumber = 1234432112344321
objBuySomething.AddressLine1 = ...
'...

'Now that all the properties have been set, make the purchase
objBuySomething.Purchase
```

Using COM Objects in a Multienvironment Scenario

One of the major advantages of COM components is they can be used by a vast array of high-level languages and programming tools. This enables developers to create a single COM component that can be used in a wide array of situations. This fact is especially useful when creating custom COM objects to encapsulate business logic.

In the previous section, "Wrapping Business Logic Within a COM Object," we looked at how to wrap the business logic involved in an e-commerce web site into a set of COM objects. These COM objects housed business logic like sales tax information, and were used as a layer of abstraction between the ASP pages and the data store.

Might there be other applications besides an ASP web site that need access to these business rules? For example, imagine that besides having an e-commerce site, the company also takes orders over the phone. Employees using a simple Visual Basic program would likely fill these phone orders. This Visual Basic program would need to adhere to the same business logic rules that customers shopping on the web site follow. Therefore, the custom COM components developed for the e-commerce site could also be used in the phone-ordering program.

Building COM Components with Script

Despite the performance and reusability advantages of custom COM components written in a high-level programming language in your ASP pages, such COM components suffer a couple of shortcomings that make them difficult and annoying to use.

For starters, ASP pages are not written in the existing programming languages that can create compiled COM objects. While this may seem irrelevant, imagine that you already have a complex routine written in VBScript in an ASP page that performs the business logic your site needs to adhere to. To put this in, say, a Visual Basic COM object, you must translate the VBScript to Visual Basic syntax. While such a translation may be light work, what if you wrote your ASP code in JScript or PerlScript, or if you needed to create your COM component using Java or Visual C++? Such a translation would be exceedingly difficult.

Another shortcoming of COM components occurs when you need to make a change to an existing component that's currently in use. Making a change requires, at minimum, recompilation and reregistration of the component, and at worst, a restart of the web services. Anyone who's developed COM components with a high-level language is far too familiar with this annoyance.

To address these shortcomings, Microsoft offers Windows Script Components (WSC), which, as the name implies, are COM components created with script as opposed to a high-level programming language. Since Windows Script Components can be created using any ActiveX scripting engine, you can simply cut and paste your ASP code and create a COM component, regardless of what scripting language you used to create your ASP page! Also, since these are scripts, no lengthy recompilation process is needed when changes need to be made to an existing component.

Once you create a COM object and make it publicly available, any future changes made to the object must not break existing code. If you need to make changes to a COM object that will cause existing code to break, it is essential that you create a new component rather than alter the existing one.

To be able to create COM components with script, you must download and install the Windows Script Component from Microsoft's Script site, *http://www.microsoft. com/msdownload/vbscript/scripting.asp*. Windows Script Components are simple text files and must be created using a predefined XML format. Rather than forcing developers to fully learn the rather terse XML format, Microsoft provides a freely available Windows Script Component Wizard. In this section we'll look at how to create Windows Script Components using this wizard.

For starters, you'll need to get yourself a copy of the Windows Script Component Wizard from the Microsoft Scripting Site, *http://msdn.microsoft.com/scripting.* At the time of this writing, the wizard was directly available at *http://msdn.microsoft. com/scripting/scriptlets/wz10en.exe.*

For this example, let's create a COM component that would be similar to a compiled custom COM component. Assume we have a database table named `Employee` that has the following columns:

`FirstName`
> The employee's first name

`LastName`
> The employee's last name

`Salary`
> The employee's salary

`BirthDate`
> The employee's date of birth

Our COM component will contain a property for each column in the `Employee` table and a single method, AddEmployee, that will add a new row to the `Employee` table. The COM component will apply some business logic, ensuring that the employee is over 18 years of age and that the `Salary` is greater than or equal to $25,000. By placing this database insertion into a component, we are encapsulating the database complexity from the ASP developer. The developer does not need to concern himself with the structure of the `Employee` table or worry about adhering to any business rules.

Now let's create our Windows Script Component! Once the Windows Script Component Wizard has been downloaded and installed, start the wizard by going to Start → Programs → Microsoft Windows Script → Windows Script Component Wizard. The first step of this six-step wizard prompts for the name and ProgID of your component, as well as the version and filename for the script file.

The ProgID is what you will use in an ASP page to instantiate the Windows Script Component:

```
Dim objInstance
Set objInstance = _
        Server.CreateObject("ProgID")
```

Let's name our component Employee and give it a ProgID of `Employee.Insert`. A screenshot of the first page of the Windows Script Component Wizard can be seen in Figure 7-7.

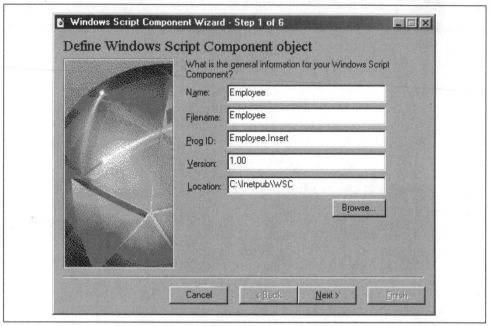

Figure 7-7. Enter the component's registration and file information in Step 1 of the wizard

In Step 2 of the wizard, we are asked to specify the scripting language to use, as well as what special implementations to support. To have access to the built-in ASP objects, be sure to select the "Support Active Server Pages" option. Note that the Error checking and Debugging options have been disabled. These should be enabled only when in the development stages of the component, and not when the component is ready to be publicly used. If selected, the Error checking option will display error messages interactively; if the debugging option is selected, the Microsoft Script Debugger can be launched when an error occurs.

Figure 7-8 shows what Step 2 of the wizard should look like.

Step 3 prompts for the properties of the component and allows us to define whether the property is read/write, read-only, or write-only, as well as to set the property's default value. For this example, we need a read/write property for each database column in the `Employee` table. Figure 7-9 provides a screenshot of Step 3 of the Windows Script Component Wizard.

Step 4 prompts for the component's methods. Since we will only have one method, AddEmployee, there is only one entry here. Furthermore, this method expects no parameters, since there is a property for each database column;

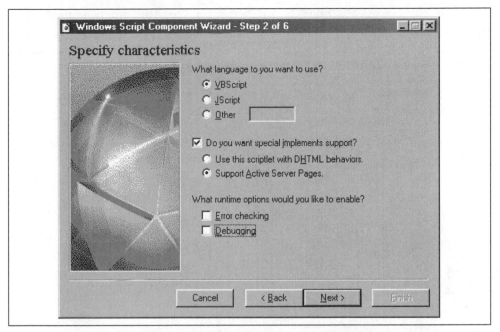

Figure 7-8. In Step 2 of the wizard, specify the scripting language that you wish to use and whether to implement ASP support

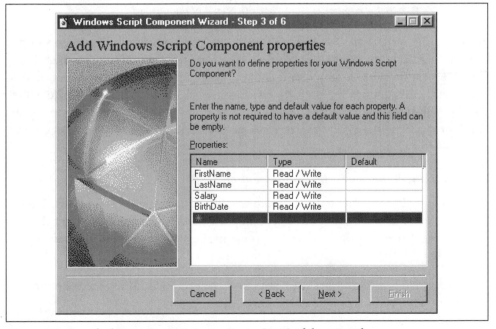

Figure 7-9. Specify the component's properties in Step 3 of the wizard

therefore, the parameters entry is left blank for the AddEmployee method. A screenshot of Step 4 of the wizard can be seen in Figure 7-10.

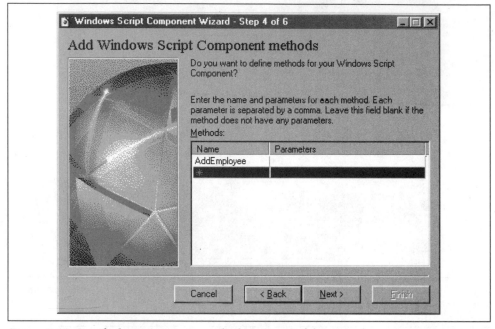

Figure 7-10. Specify the component's methods in Step 4 of the wizard

Step 5 of the wizard prompts for any events for the component. For this example, we will not add any events, so proceed on to the next step. Step 6, which is the final step in the wizard, provides summary information. Once you've checked to make sure everything is in order, go ahead and click Finish. This will create a shell for the Windows Script Component. It is now up to us to fill in the code for the AddEmployee method. The wizard has already written the rest of the component's code for us!

Dissecting the Windows Script Component file

The generated Windows Script Component file contains several sections. Take a moment to look at the component's source. At the start of the document there is the XML tag, since Windows Script Components are XML-formatted documents:

```
<?xml version="1.0"?>
```

The remainder of the file's contents are placed within a `<component>` ... `</component>` block.

The first tag in the `<component>` tag is the `<?component?>` tag. This tag indicates whether or not the component supports error checking and debugging. The `<?component?>` tag has the following form:

```
<?component error="boolean" debug="boolean" ?>
```

If error checking and debugging were not selected in Step 2 of the wizard, as was the case in our example, then this tag will not exist. For completeness, feel free to add it in:

```
<?component error="false" debug="false" ?>
```

Next, a `<registration>` tag defines the description of the class, its ProgID, ClassID, and version number. Note that except for the ClassID, these values were entered into Step 1 of the wizard:

```
<registration
   description="Employee"
   progid="Employee.Insert"
   version="1.00"
   classid="{b31aab60-1fb8-11d4-8013-0000216d54d6}"
>
</registration>
```

The next block of code defines what properties and methods are public. Public properties and methods in a Windows Script Component are synonymous to public properties and methods in a VBScript class. Also note that each of the properties is marked as both read and write with the `<get/>` and `<put/>` tags:

```
<public>
   <property name="FirstName">
      <get/>
      <put/>
   </property>
   <property name="LastName">
      <get/>
      <put/>
   </property>
   <property name="Salary">
      <get/>
      <put/>
   </property>
   <property name="BirthDate">
      <get/>
      <put/>
   </property>
   <method name="AddEmployee">
   </method>
</public>
```

Next, the `<implements>` tag is used to indicate that this component has access to the built-in ASP objects:

```
<implements type="ASP" id="ASP"/>
```

The remainder of the file is a `<script>` block that contains the actual code for the component (in this case, VBScript code). Note that the `<script>` block is immediately followed by a funky-looking `<![CDATA[` tag, and right before the closing script tag, its ending `]]>` tag. This is a special XML reference indicating that the text between the `<![CDATA[` and `]]>` tags is source code and not to be interpreted by the XML parser. If the `<![CDATA[` tag were left out, the parser would raise an error if any reserved XML names or characters were found in the component's source code.

 The CDATA tag is similar to the opening and closing HTML comment tags (`<!--` and `//-->`) that should be used when writing client-side JavaScript. Both indicate to the parser that the content between these tags is not to be interpreted by the parser.

At this time, the AddEmployee method is just a skeleton function:

```
function AddEmployee()
    AddEmployee = "Temporary Value"
end function
```

It is up to us to add the necessary code. We do need to make one other slight modification to the WSC file before writing our code. Since the AddEmployee method will add a record to a database, we will need an instance of the ADO Connection object. This should be declared using the `<object>` tag after the `<implements>` tag and before the `<script>` tag:

```
<object id="objConn" progid="ADODB.Connection" />
```

The ID parameter in the `<object>` tag defines how the object will be referred to in our component's code.

Now that everything is ready to go, let's write the code for the AddEmployee method. This method needs to insert a record into the **Employee** table based upon the four properties. If one of these properties is not supplied, or if the supplied value of the property violates one of the business logic rules, an error will be raised. Otherwise, if the data is valid, a record will be inserted into the database.

Example 7-13 contains the source code for the AddEmployee method.

Example 7-13. The AddEmployee Method, upon Validating the Inputs, Inserts a Row into the Employee Table

```
function AddEmployee()
  'Ensure that all of the properties have been entered
  If Len(CStr(FirstName)) = 0 or Len(CStr(LastName)) = 0 _
     or Len(CStr(Salary)) = 0 or Len(CStr(BirthDate)) = 0 then
   'Raise an error
   Err.Raise vbObjectError + 1000, "Employee.Insert", "Property not supplied."
  End If


  'Ensure that the business logic rules have not been violated
  'Is employee 18 or over as of today?
  If DateDiff("yyyy", BirthDate, Date()) < 18 then
    'Raise an error
    Err.Raise vbObjectError + 1001, "Employee.Insert", "Employee under 18!"
  End If


  'Is the salary under 25k?
  If Salary < 25000 then
    'Raise an error
    Err.Raise vbObjectError + 1002, "Employee.Insert", _
              "Employee Salary cannot be less than $25,000!"
  End If



  'OK, there is no problem with the insertion data, so insert a
  'record into the Employee table!
  Dim strSQL
  strSQL = "INSERT INTO Employee (FirstName, LastName, Salary, BirthDate) " & _
           "VALUES('" & Replace(FirstName, "'", "''") & "','" & _
           Replace(LastName, "'", "''") & "'," & Salary & ",'" & _
           BirthDate & "')"

  'Open the connection to the database
  Const strConnection = "DSN=EmployeeDatabase"
  objConn.ConnectionString = strConnection
  objConn.Open

  objConn.Execute strSQL          'Add the record

  objConn.Close                   'Close the database connection
end function
```

Note that the AddEmployee method begins by checking to ensure that all data is passed in, that the Employee being added is at least 18 years of age, and that the salary is at least $25,000. If any of these checks fail, an error is raised using the Raise method of the Err object. Since the error-checking option was not selected in Step 2 of the wizard, when an error is raised it will be passed to the calling application (the ASP script using this component). Assuming these checks all pass, a row is added to the Employee table.

The validation in the AddEmployee method is far from complete. Measures should be taken not only to ensure that values were entered for each of the parameters, but that they match their expected datatypes. For example, an error should be raised if the Salary property is assigned a value of "More, please."

Before using this component in an ASP page, we must register it. To register a Windows Script Component, right-click on the Windows Script Component file and select the Register option. Figure 7-11 shows how to register the component.

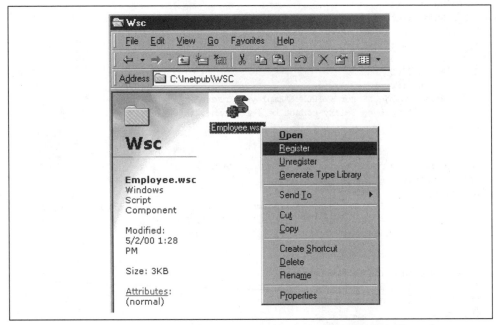

Figure 7-11. To register a Windows Script Component, right-click the .wsc file and choose Register

Once the component is registered, you can create an instance of the object in an Active Server Page (or in a Visual Basic, Visual C++, or Java program). Also, if you ever need to alter the component, all you need to do is simply edit the appropriate *.wsc* file! There is no complicated unregistering/reregistering as there can be with compiled COM objects, and you don't need to stop and restart the web services when making changes to an existing Windows Script Component.

Example 7-14 provides a quick example of how to use the Windows Script Component we just created within an ASP page. Note that instantiating and using a Windows Script Component is identical to instantiating and using a compiled COM component. The ASP developer does not need to concern herself with whether the COM component was created as a binary or is in script form. Note that an instance of the Windows Script Component we just created is instantiated using the ProgID that we specified in Step 1 of the wizard (`Employee.Insert`).

Example 7-14. Using a Windows Script Component Is Identical to Using a Classical, Binary COM Component

```
<% @LANGUAGE="VBSCRIPT" %>
<% Option Explicit %>
<%
  'Create an instance of the Employee.Insert Windows Script Component
  Dim objEmployeeInsert
  Set objEmployeeInsert = Server.CreateObject("Employee.Insert")

  'Set the Employee.Insert properties
  objEmployeeInsert.FirstName = "Scott"
  objEmployeeInsert.LastName = "Mitchell"
  objEmployeeInsert.Salary = 78000
  objEmployeeInsert.BirthDate = "8/1/78"

  objEmployeeInsert.AddEmployee          'Add the employee to the database

  Set objEmployeeInsert = Nothing        'Clean up!
%>
```

Windows Script Components versus classical, binary COM components

Since Windows Script Components are interpreted scripts as opposed to compiled binary files, they will obviously suffer from poor performance when compared to binary files. Therefore, if you expect your site to have many concurrent users, it is best to stick with binary COM objects.

Also, since classical COM components are created using high-level languages, chances are you will be developing them using a mature development environment. With Windows Script Components, however, you will likely be using a development tool like Notepad to edit the component! While this is not a huge issue when dealing with a single, small component, imagine that you needed to develop a slew of large, robust, interactive components. Managing these large, interrelated files using Notepad would be difficult, at best, especially if a team of developers were working on the project.

 A side benefit of compiled COM components is the source is hidden from prying eyes. Developers creating COM components for sale would want to make sure that the final COM component product is in binary form so that those purchasing the components cannot share the component's source code with other potential customers.

The advantages Windows Script Components have over compiled COM components include the ease in making changes to existing components and the ability to dump ASP code into a component with little or no translation. Windows Script Components should be used as a stepping-stone to compiled COM objects. For example, in the development stages, use Windows Script Components. During development, you'll enjoy being able to quickly make changes to existing, in-use components. As the project grows larger and moves toward shipping, be sure to move the components to a compiled, binary form, where they'll benefit from improved performance.

Personally, I find Windows Script Components to be very neat and cool. In smaller projects, I have a hard time convincing myself that the advantages of using COM objects outweigh the burdens involved in needing to make changes to the COM object as the project progresses. Since altering an existing COM object requires recompilation and reregistration, it's much easier to not use components. With Windows Script Components, however, that is no longer true! Also, I find it really cool that you can grab a snippet of useful ASP code and quickly stick it into a Windows Script Component, creating a COM component from working ASP code with little or no translation.

Further Reading

If you are in charge of a large ASP/IIS web site, or are working on one, chances are you are familiar with building and using custom COM components. If you do not have much experience with custom COM objects, these articles should help!

- I know I mentioned it earlier, but if you need information on Microsoft's Browser Capabilities component, you should definitely check out ASPTracker: *http://www.asptracker.com.*

- For some real-world code examples of using the Content Linker, check out the "Content Link Tutorial" at *http://www.learnasp.com/learn/cl.asp.*

- For a plethora of articles on building components for ASP applications, check out the Component Building section on *15Seconds.com, http://www. 15seconds.com/focus/Component%20Building.htm.*

- For a good article on the pros of placing business logic in custom COM components, be sure to read "Using Business Objects in your Web Application", *http://www.4guysfromrolla.com/webtech/110198-1.shtml.*

- For a ListServer discussion on component building, check out *http://www. asplists.com/asplists/components.asp.*

- For a good example of how to create a Windows Script Component be sure to check out "A Simple Windows Scripting Component" at *http://www.asptoday. com/articles/19990729.htm.*

Enhancing Your Web Site with Third-Party Components

One of ASP's greatest features is its tight integration with COM. As we examined in Chapter 7, *Using Components*, Active Server Pages can instantiate complex COM objects written in high-level languages like Visual C++, Visual Basic, or Java. Microsoft provides several such components for use in Active Server Pages, such as the ActiveX Data Objects (ADO), the Ad Rotator, and the Content Linker.

As the popularity of Active Server Pages has grown, many developers have started their own companies that focus solely on developing COM components for use in Active Server Pages. These components can be used to greatly enhance the functionality provided by your web site. In this chapter, we'll look at several of these components, focusing on what they do, when they should be used, and how to use them.

ASP was designed to intrinsically support only a small core of functionality, with the premise that if a developer needed further functionality, he could create his own COM component. Some people find this to be a shortcoming of ASP. For example, to open, read, and write to files with ASP, you must use the FileSystemObject; other server-side web scripting languages, like Perl, have file-handling capabilities already built in. While needing to instantiate a component to simply read a text file may seem like a superfluous performance hit, by omitting file-handling capabilities, ASP is more streamlined.

Personally, I find ASP's implementation to be ideal. ASP is very streamlined, consisting of only a few needed built-in objects. All other functionality should be (and can be) imported from a COM component. Tools to develop COM components are widely accessible (Visual Basic, for instance, is the most popular programming language in the world, with an installed base in the millions), and both ASP and COM have spawned a lively third-party market that focuses on add-on tools for Active

Server Pages. The components presented in this chapter help to greatly extend the capabilities of ASP pages.

Executing DOS and Windows Applications on the Web Server with ASPExec

There may be times when you'd like an ASP page to be able to execute an application on the web server. For example, you may wish to provide the webmaster with the ability to execute certain maintenance programs residing on the web server through a web page. In "Executing Applications on a Server Through an ASP Web Page" (available at *http://www.4guysfromrolla.com/webtech/072199-2. shtml*), author Neema Moraveji discusses how he needed to be able to remotely start a setup program on the web server from a web page. In "Creating a Component Using Visual C++ to Manipulate Virtual Directories" (available at *http://www. 15seconds.com/issue/990107.htm*), author Shai Vaingast needed to be able to execute a command-line program through an ASP page.

Rarely will you want to let your users execute an application on the web server. Imagine the performance ramifications of hundreds of users running an application simultaneously on your web server!

In both of these articles, the authors turned to the ASPExec component, which allows developers to execute DOS and Windows applications on the web server through an ASP page. ASPExec is a free component available from Stephen Genusa's company, ServerObjects (download it now from *http://www.serverobjects. com/products.htm#free*). Once you download the component, you must use *regsvr32* to install it before you can use it in your ASP pages. To do so, copy *ASPExec.DLL* to the Windows system directory (*Windows\System* or *Winnt\ system32*). Next, run *regsvr32* to register the DLL as follows:

```
regsvr32 aspexec.dll
```

Instructions on installing the ASPExec component are included with the download at *http://www.serverobjects.com/products.htm#free*.

ASPExec's Properties and Methods

The ASPExec object contains four properties and three methods. The ASPExec properties can be seen in Table 8-1 and the methods in Table 8-2.

Table 8-1. ASPExec Contains Four Properties

Property	Description
Application	Specifies the path (optional) and the executable's filename.
Parameters	Specifies the command-line parameters. The property's value is a single string containing all command-line parameters separated by spaces.
TimeOut	Specifies the amount of time to wait in milliseconds if either the ExecuteDOSApp or ExccuteWinAppAndWait method is used. Its default value is 30 milliseconds.
ShowWindow	Specifies whether or not a window is displayed on the web server for the executing application (only applicable when either the ExecuteWinAppAndWait or ExecuteWinApp method is used.)

Table 8-2. ASPExec Contains Three Methods

Method	Description
ExecuteDOSApp	Executes a DOS application specified by the Application property, returning the output of the application.
ExecuteWinAppAndWait	Executes the Windows application specified by the Application property and waits for the timeout specified by the TimeOut property.
ExecuteWinApp	Executes the Windows application specified by the Application property.

Executing a Command-Line Program with ASPExec

ASPExec can execute both command-line programs (using ExecutcDOSApp) and Windows programs (using ExecuteWinApp or ExecuteWinAppAndWait). To execute a command-line program using ASPExec, you must first create an instance of the ASPExec component. To do so, use the following code:

```
Dim objASPExecInstance
Set objASPExecInstance = Server.CreateObject("ASPExec.Execute")
```

Next, set the Application and Parameters properties to indicate the program you'd like to execute and the command-line arguments you wish to pass to the application. Once these two properties have been set, simply call the ExecuteDOSApp method to execute the DOS application.

One such DOS application you can execute through an ASP page is *ping*. *ping* sends an echo request to a server. When the server receives this request, it returns a confirmation. Oftentimes *ping* is used to ensure that a web site is up and functional. *ping* has many command-line argument options, but the only required one is the IP, hostname, or domain name of the server to contact.

Try it out! Drop to the command prompt (go to Start → Run and enter command if you are using Windows 95/98, cmd if you are using Windows NT or Windows 2000) and type in ping www. 4GuysFromRolla.com. This will send an echo request to the web server *4GuysFromRolla.com* runs on.

For a full list of *ping*'s command-line arguments, enter ping /? at the command prompt.

Example 8-1 contains an ASP page that will execute *ping* through an ASP page. The page first creates a form in which the developer can enter the name of the computer he wishes to ping. When the developer enters a domain name (or IP or hostname) to ping, the form reloads the page and the ASPExec component is instantiated. Its Application property is set to *ping* and its Parameters property is set to the hostname entered by the user in the form. The code in Example 8-1, which should be saved as */AspPing.asp*, is nearly identical to one of the example ASP pages that is included with the ASPExec download.

Example 8-1. You Can Execute ping from an ASP Page Using ASPExec

```
<% @LANGUAGE="VBSCRIPT" %>
<% Option Explicit %>

<html>
<body>
<H3>ASPExec Ping Test</H3>

<% if Request.QueryString("host") = "" then %>
  <!-- The user has no entered a hostname to search yet.  Present them
       with a form to select a hostname. -->
  <form action="AspPing.asp" method=get>
    Enter Host to Ping:
    <input type=text size=45 name=host value="localhost"><P>
    <input type="Submit">
  </form>

<% else
    Dim Executor, strResult

    'Create an instance of the ASPExec object
    Set Executor = Server.CreateObject("ASPExec.Execute")

    'Indicate that we want to run the ping program with the hostname as the
    'only parameter
    Executor.Application = "ping"
    Executor.Parameters = Request.QueryString("host")

    'Execute ping, storing the results in strResult
    strResult = Executor.ExecuteDosApp
```

Example 8-1. You Can Execute ping from an ASP Page Using ASPExec (continued)

```
    'Output the contents of strResult
    Response.Write "<pre>" & strResult & "</pre>"
  end if
%>

</body>
</html>
```

Figure 8-1 shows */AspPing.asp* when first visited. Note that a form is displayed where the user can enter the hostname of the computer he or she wishes to ping.

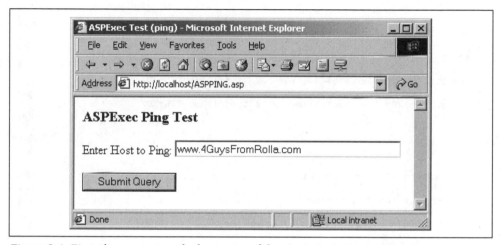

Figure 8-1. First, the user enters the hostname of the computer to ping

Once the user enters a hostname (or an IP or a domain name) and submits the form, */AspPing.asp* will be called again. This time, however, an instance of the ASPExec component will be created and *ping* will be executed with the hostname entered by the user as the only command-line argument. The output is returned by the ExecuteDOSApp method and stored in *strResult*. This output is then displayed. Figure 8-2 shows the output of */AspPing.asp* after the user has selected a hostname to ping.

The ASPExec download includes several examples of using ASPExec. One example uses ASPExec to output the contents of a DOS command (such as `dir C:\`). This idea can easily be extended into a remote DOS window on a web page, which would serve as a great administrative tool for remote webmasters. (Of course, such an application is also a scary security risk. With the proper procedures, however, you could guarantee that only a select set of users have access to such a powerful administration tool.)

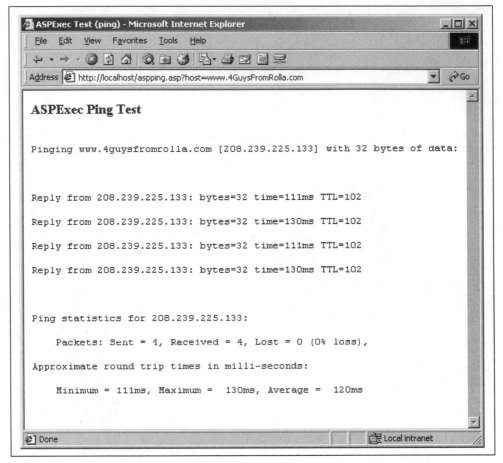

Figure 8-2. The results of ping are output

Obtaining Detailed Information About Your Users's Browsers

One of the difficulties in designing web pages for the Internet is your users may be using a number of different browsers. The fierce competition between Netscape and Microsoft has led to differing "standards." Internet Explorer, for example, supports client-side VBScript and ActiveX controls. Netscape, however, supports Java-Script as the only client-side scripting language, and ActiveX controls can only be used with a plug-in. Similarly, both Internet Explorer and Netscape have their own protocol and extensions for Dynamic HTML and cascading style sheets.

While Internet Explorer and Netscape are by far the two most popular browsers on the market, there are many other browsing options available. If users may visit your site through the WebTV browser, AOL's custom browser, lynx (a text-based

Unix browser), Opera, or any other non-mainstream browser, it is important that you ensure that your site still looks pleasant and is easy to use. For example, if you had a set of web pages that utilized DHTML and a user visited your site using a browser that didn't support DHTML (older versions of Internet Explorer and Netscape, lynx, etc.), you would want to redirect the user to a set of pages that accomplished the same tasks but refrained from using DHTML.

Using Microsoft's Browser Capabilities Component

As mentioned in Chapter 7, Microsoft provides a free COM component to accomplish this task: the Browser Capabilities component. This component has a couple of drawbacks, though. For starters, to use the Browser Capabilities component, a browser capabilities file is needed and must be updated each time a new browser comes to market or a new browser version is released. This file, named *browscap. ini*, contains information about all of the popular browser types and each browser's capabilities.

 For the latest version of *browscap.ini*, visit *http://www.asptracker.com*.

Another disadvantage of the Browser Capabilities component is it only reports on a small set of available browser properties. Furthermore, the Browser Capabilities component only indicates whether or not the user's browser *supports* a certain property. For example, Internet Explorer 5.0 supports client-side JavaScript; however, users can easily disable JavaScript support. The Browser Capabilities component, therefore, would indicate that a visitor who was using Internet Explorer 5.0 supported client-side JavaScript, even if the user had disabled JavaScript from their browser.

A More Versatile Solution: cyScape's BrowserHawk

To compensate for the disadvantages of the Browser Capabilities component, you can use BrowserHawk, a third-party component from cyScape, Inc. Like the Browser Capabilities component, BrowserHawk maintains a list of potential browser types and versions and their various capabilities. Unlike the Browser Capabilities component, however, BrowserHawk will automatically check for and download updates to this list of the various browsers' capabilities. Furthermore, BrowserHawk contains a much more thorough list of browser capabilities than the Browser Capabilities component.

Determining the User's Browser Information

How does a component like the Browser Capabilities component know what browser a visitor is using?

Each time a browser requests a web page from a web site, the browser sends along some information about itself in the request header. This information, referred to as the User-Agent string, contains the name and version of the web browser and the visitor's operating system.

To access this string in your ASP page, examine the **HTTP_USER-AGENT** variable in the Request.ServerVariables collection. Creating a simple ASP page with the following code:

```
<%=Request.ServerVariables("HTTP_USER-AGENT")%>
```

I received the following output when visiting the page with an Internet Explorer 5.0 browser:

```
Mozilla/4.0 (compatible; MSIE 5.0; Windows 98; DigExt)
```

The Browser Capabilities component takes this string and searches for an entry in the *browscap.ini* file that corresponds to the browser type and version indicated by the User-Agent HTTP header. Following this header in the *browscap.ini* file is a list of capabilities supported by the particular browser. The following is a partial list of the capabilities under the IE 5.0 header in the *browscap.ini* file:

```
[IE 5.0]
browser=IE
Version=5.0
majorver=5
minorver=0
frames=True
tables=True
cookies=True
backgroundsounds=True
vbscript=True
javascript=True
javaapplets=True
ActiveXControls=True
Win16=False
beta=False
AOL=False
MSN=False
CDF=True
DHTML=True
XML=True
```

A free 30-day evaluation copy of BrowserHawk can be downloaded from cyScape's web site at *http://www.cyscape.com/products/bhawk/start.asp*. At the time this book was published, BrowserHawk offered Standard, Professional, and Enterprise editions costing $119, $274, and $489 USD, respectively.

Once BrowserHawk is installed, you can start using it in your ASP pages to detect your visitor's browser information! BrowserHawk contains an extremely lengthy set of properties for each possible browser type and version. Table 8-3 contains a list of some of the more useful properties. A complete list can be found online at *http://www.cyscape.com/showbrow.asp*.

Table 8-3. BrowserHawk Indicates the Properties Your Users's Browsers Support

Property	Description
ActiveXControls	Boolean; indicates whether or not the user's browser supports ActiveX controls.
Cookies	Boolean; indicates whether or not the user's browser supports cookies.
CookiesEnabled	Boolean; indicates whether or not the visitor has cookies enabled. For browsers that accept cookies, this property checks to ensure the user has cookies enabled. (For a browser that supports cookies but has disabled cookies, the Cookies property would return `True`, while the CookiedEnabled property would return `False`.)
DHTML	Boolean; indicates whether or not the user's browser supports DHTML.
Frames	Boolean; indicates whether or not the visitor's browser supports frames.
Height	Returns the height of the visitor's screen resolution. For example, a visitor who was viewing your site at 800x600 would have a Height property of 600.
IPAddr	Returns the IP address of the visitor.
JavaApplets	Boolean; indicates whether or not the user's browser supports Java applets.
JavaEnabled	Boolean; similar to the CookiesEnabled property, this property indicates whether or not the visitor has Java applets enabled.
JavaScript	Boolean; indicates whether or not the user's browser supports client-side JavaScript.
JavaScriptEnabled	Boolean; similar to the CookiesEnabled property, this property indicates whether or not the visitor has client-side JavaScript enabled.

Table 8-3. BrowserHawk Indicates the Properties Your Users's Browsers Support (continued)

Property	Description
StyleSheets	Boolean; indicates whether or not the user's browser supports cascading style sheets (CSS).
VBScript	Boolean; indicates whether or not the user's browser supports client-side VBScript code.
Version	Returns the version of the browser.
Width	Returns the width of the visitor's screen resolution. For example, a visitor who was viewing your site at 800x600 would have a Width property of 800.
XML	Boolean; indicates whether or not the user's browser supports XML.

 The Enabled properties—CookiesEnabled, JavaEnabled, and JavaScriptEnabled—only work with the Professional or Enterprise editions of BrowserHawk.

Using the BrowserHawk component

Once you have run through the BrowserHawk installation process, the Browser-Hawk DLL will be registered on your machine. You are now ready to start using BrowserHawk in your ASP pages! To create an instance of the BrowserHawk component, use the following lines of code:

```
Dim objBrowserHawkInstance
Set objBrowserHawkInstance = Server.CreateObject("cyScape.browserObj")
```

Before reading the Height, Width, JavaScriptEnabled, or JavaEnabled properties, you must call the GetExtProperties method. This method sends a blank page to the client to assess which of these properties, if any, are disabled. Likewise, before reading the CookiesEnabled property, call the CookieDetector method. The BrowserHawk documentation details what properties need to have a method called before being read.

Example 8-2 demonstrates how to use the BrowserHawk component to determine what properties your visitor supports. Note that the GetExtProperties and Cookie-Detector methods are called prior to listing the capabilities of the user's browser.

Example 8-2. BrowserHawk Determines What Properties Are Supported by a Visitor's Browser

```
<% @LANGUAGE="VBSCRIPT" %>
<% Option Explicit %>
<%
  Dim objBHawk
```

Example 8-2. BrowserHawk Determines What Properties Are Supported
by a Visitor's Browser (continued)

```
  Set objBHawk = Server.CreateObject("cyScape.browserObj")

  'Get the extended properties
  objBHawk.GetExtProperties

  'Call the cookie detector
  objBHawk.CookieDetector
%>
<HTML>
<BODY>
  <H1>Fun Facts About Your Browser!</H1>
  Your resolution: <%=objBHawk.Width%>x<%=objBHawk.Height%><BR>
  Cookies Enabled: <%=objBHawk.CookiesEnabled%><BR>
  Support VBScript: <%=objBHawk.VBScript%><BR>
  Support XML: <%=objBHawk.XML%><BR>
  JavaScript Enabled: <%=objBHawk.JavaScriptEnabled%><BR>
  Java Applets Enabled: <%=objBHawk.JavaEnabled%>
</BODY>
</HTML>

<%
  Set objBHawk = Nothing      'Clean up!
%>
```

When the ASP page presented in Example 8-2 is visited through a browser, the
output will differ on depending what browser is used to visit the page! I visited
this page with Microsoft's Internet Explorer 5.0; a screenshot can be seen in
Figure 8-3.

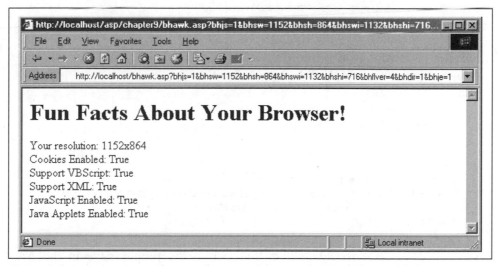

Figure 8-3. As you can see, I have cookies, JavaScript, and Java applets enabled

Redirecting users based on their browser's enabled capabilities

Web developers face a real dilemma when trying to create easy-to-use web sites. While many new technologies have arisen to help make the web experience more interactive (Macromedia Flash, for example, or Dynamic HTML), these add-ons are not standard across all browsers and all versions. Therefore, many web developers choose to create two sets of web pages. One set utilizes the advanced features—such as cascading style sheets, Java applets, and XML—supported by the more recent browsers. The second set of pages provides similar functionality but uses the older technologies—vanilla HTML and simple client-side JavaScript commands.

When a visitor first arrives at the site, he is redirected to the appropriate set of pages, depending upon his browser. For example, the following snippet of code could be used on the start page (*/default.asp*) to send the user to a certain set of web pages based upon his browser's support of DHTML:

```
<% @LANGUAGE="VBSCRIPT" %>
<% Option Explicit %>
<%
  Dim objBHawk
  Set objBHawk = Server.CreateObject("cyScape.browserObj")

  'Redirect the user based on the browser's ability to support DHTML
  If objBHawk.DHTML then
    'Supports DHTML
    Response.Redirect "/DHTMLSupport/default.asp"
  Else
    'Does not support DHTML
    Response.Redirect "/NonDHTML/default.asp"
  End If
%>
```

Then, for each ASP page in the */DHTMLSupport* directory, you'd want to use a server-side include to add the following ASP code:

```
<%
  Dim objBHawk
  Set objBHawk = Server.CreateObject("cyScape.browserObj")

  'Redirect the user to the NonDHTML section if they don't support DHTML
  If Not objBHawk.DHTML then
    'Does not support DHTML
    Response.Redirect Replace(Request.ServerVariables("SCRIPT_NAME"), _
                  "DHTMLSupport", "NonDHTML")
  End If
%>
```

This snippet of code would redirect the user to the proper page in the *Non-DHTML* directory if the browser didn't support DHTML. That way, if some user entered the URL *http://www.yoursite.com/DHTMLSupport/SomePage.asp* into their non-DHTML supporting browser, they would be automatically redirected to *http:// www.yoursite.com/NonDHTML/SomePage.asp*. Similarly, in all of the ASP pages in the */NonDHTML* directory, you'd want to add a similar block of ASP code to the one above that would check to see if DHTML was supported, and if so, would redirect the user to the appropriate page in the */DHTMLSupport* directory.

Grabbing Information from Other Web Servers

One of the most frequent questions I hear from ASP developers is "How can I grab information from another web server?" Specifically, they're interested in the HTML generated by a particular URL, be it a static web page or an ASP page.

There are many reasons a developer may be interested in using an ASP page to obtain a web page fresh from another server. One of the most popular reasons is to obtain some real-time data. For example, several of the portals maintain updated stock quotes and weather information. Many developers would like to be able to snatch this information and display it on their own web page.

Many sites that provide weather or stock information have the actual temperature or quotes in a specific column and row in an HTML table. An excellent article on *4GuysFromRolla.com*, "Grabbing Table Columns From Other Web Pages," by Thomas Winningham, presents an application to quickly and easily grab a particular column and row from an HTML table residing on a different web server. The article is available at: *http://www.4guysfromrolla.com/webtech/ 031000-1.shtml*.

To grab information from a web page, we need look no further than to Stephen Genusa's excellent set of objects. The ASPHTTP object, available for $49.95 at *http:// www.serverobjects.com/products.htm#asphttp*, allows developers to download HTML content from another web server. Furthermore, while using ASPHTTP, you can save the downloaded content to a file if you so choose!

When you download the ASPHTTP DLL from *ServerObjects.com*, you will need to move it to your Windows System directory and register it using *regsvr32*. Once it is registered, you are ready to start using the component in your ASP pages.

ASPHTTP's Properties and Methods

ASPHTTP contains a vast array of properties. A full listing of these properties can be seen at: *http://www.serverobjects.com/comp/asphttp3.htm*. Table 8-4 contains a listing of some of the more commonly used properties.

Table 8-4. The ASPHTTP Properties

Properties	Description
BinaryData	Returns the data obtained by ASPHTTP in binary format. This is useful if you are using ASPHTTP to grab binary images, such as GIFs, from other web sites.
Headers	Returns the response HTTP headers sent by the web server contacted by ASPHTTP.
Port	Indicated what port to connect to on the remote web server (defaults to 80, the standard HTTP port).
PostData	Specifies the data to send through the HTTP POST.
SaveFileTo	Used to save the resulting HTML or binary data to a file.
URL	Specifies the URL to grab the information from (must start with `http://`).

The most common ASPHTTP method is the GetURL method, which returns the response of the HTTP request to the URL specified by the URL property.

Retrieving a Web Page with ASPHTTP

Since ASPHTTP is designed to request data through the HTTP protocol from other servers, let's look at an example of doing just that. When using ASPHTTP, as with any of the other components discussed in this chapter, you must first create an instance of the object. To create an instance of ASPHTTP, simply use the following two lines of code:

```
Dim objASPHTTPInstance
Set objASPHTTPInstance = Server.CreateObject("AspHTTP.Conn")
```

To retrieve the contents of an HTML page, all you need to do is set the URL property accordingly and call the GetURL method. Example 8-3 contains ASP code that will grab the HTML content from the *LearnASP.com* homepage and display the HTML syntax.

Example 8-3. Grabbing the HTML of a Web Page on a Remote Web Server Is Easy with the ASPHTTP Component

```
<% @LANGUAGE="VBSCRIPT" %>
<% Option Explicit %>
<%
  Dim objAspHTTP, strHTML
  Set objAspHTTP = Server.CreateObject("AspHTTP.Conn")

  'Grab the HTML from http://www.LearnASP.com
  objAspHTTP.URL = "http://www.LearnAsp.com/default.asp"

  strHTML = objAspHTTP.GetURL()
%>
<HTML>
<BODY>
```

Example 8-3. Grabbing the HTML of a Web Page on a Remote Web Server Is Easy with the ASPHTTP Component (continued)

```
<H1>Here is the HTML to display LearnASP.com!</H1>
<XMP>
<%=strHTML%>
</XMP>
</BODY>
</HTML>

<%
  Set objAspHTTP = Nothing      'Clean up!
%>
```

Once the GetURL method is called, the *LearnASP.com* web site is contacted through an HTTP Get, and the response is stored in the variable *strHTML*. Understand that *strHTML* simply contains the HTML returned by */default.asp* on *LearnASP.com*. When the contents of *strHTML* are output, the HTML source is shown due to the surrounding XMP tags. A screenshot of the code in Example 8-3, when viewed through a browser, can be seen in Figure 8-4.

Retrieving Binary Data with ASPHTTP

ASPHTTP is not restricted to grabbing just textual HTML information from remote servers; binary data, such as GIFs, JPGs, and ZIPs, can also be obtained by ASPHTTP. Furthermore, with the SaveFileTo property, you can save these files to the web server.

You can also use the SaveFileTo property to save textual HTML data from remote servers.

Imagine that a News web site had a GIF that showed any major accidents on the expressways in your location. This GIF was updated as accidents occurred and were cleared, and was always stored in one location, perhaps *http://www. TrafficNews.com/Chicago/map.gif*. If you wanted to provide a picture of this GIF on your site, you could do so with a simple IMG tag, like so:

```
<IMG SRC="http://www.TrafficNews.com/Chicago/map.gif">
```

However, if your site attracts a lot of visitors during the day, the webmasters at *TrafficNews.com* might not appreciate your linking directly to their image and eating up their bandwidth. To appease these webmasters, you might decide to copy this GIF to your web server. However, if this traffic map is updated frequently, the copy on your web server would become quickly outdated.

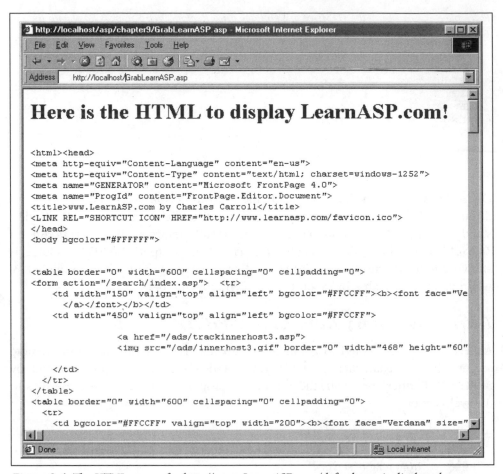

Figure 8-4. The HTML source for http://www.LearnASP.com/default.asp is displayed

The following situation would be ideal, and is quite possible using ASPHTTP:

- A user visits a web page on your server that displays the accident map. Before displaying the map, the date and time the image was saved to the web server are compared to the current time. If the accident map on the local web server is less than one hour old, the user is shown that image.

- If, however, the image is more than an hour old, the current accident map is downloaded from *TrafficNews.com*, the user is shown the more recent map, and the downloaded accident map is saved to the local web server.

To accomplish this, we will use an ASP page, */images/TrafficReport.asp*, that outputs the correct traffic report image (either the local copy or the one on the *TrafficNews.com* web site) in binary GIF form. Since */images/TrafficReport.asp* will output the GIF in binary format, you can display the GIF from any other ASP or HTML page using the IMG HTML tag, like so:

```
<IMG SRC="/images/TrafficReport.asp">
```

Using ASP Pages to Provide Non-HTML Output

By default, ASP pages send HTML to the browser, which renders the output like any other HTML page. However, ASP pages can send non-HTML output. When sending data to a client, it is important to let the client know the MIME type of the data so it can properly display it. The MIME (Multipurpose Internet Mail Extensions) type lets the browser know how to display the data. HTML has a MIME type of text/html. For example, if you send a web browser the binary contents of a GIF file, you need to send the data with a MIME type of image/gif.

To let the browser know what type of output you are sending, use the ContentType property of the Response object. Try the following quick example. Create an ASP page named */ShowImage.asp* and enter the following code:

```
<%
   Response.ContentType = "image/gif"
   Response.Redirect "/images/SomeImage.gif"
%>
```

where */images/SomeImage.gif* is a valid GIF file on your web server. Then, from any ASP page, include the following line of HTML:

```
<IMG SRC="/ShowImage.asp">
```

When you view an ASP page with the above IMG tag, you will see the contents of */images/SomeImage.gif*!

There are a vast number of MIME types available. A rather thorough list can be found at: *ftp://ftp.isi.edu/in-notes/iana/assignments/media-types/media-types*.

In the file */images/TrafficReport.asp*, we will need to perform the following tasks:

1. Check to see if a version of the traffic report GIF exists on the local web server. If there is no local copy, proceed to Step 4.

2. Since the file exists, compare its date last modified property to the current time. If the file is more than an hour old, proceed to Step 4.

3. If we've reached this point, the traffic report GIF on the local web server is less than one hour old, so show this GIF and end.

4. If we've reached this point, either a local copy of the traffic report does not exist, or it is out of date. In either case, use ASPHTTP to grab the recent version from *TrafficNews.com*, saving the GIF to the local web server.

The source code for */images/TrafficReport.asp* can be seen in Example 8-4. Note the comments in Example 8-4 illustrating the start of the four steps outlined.

Example 8-4. The Traffic Report GIF Is Only Downloaded from TrafficNews.com if the Local Version Is Outdated or Nonexistent

```
<% @LANGUAGE="VBSCRIPT" %>
<% Option Explicit %>
<%
  'We are going to be outputting a GIF, so set the ContentType
  Response.ContentType = "image/gif"

  'strVirtualName is the virtual file name of the traffic report GIF
  'on the local Web server
  Const strVirtualFileName = "/TrafficReport.gif"

  'strFileName stores the physical file name of the traffic report GIF
  Dim strFileName
  strFileName = Server.MapPath(strVirtualFileName)

  'Create an instance of the FileSystemObject component
  Dim objFSO
  Set objFSO = Server.CreateObject("Scripting.FileSystemObject")

  '******** STEP 1: Determine if the file exists ***********
  If objFSO.FileExists(strFileName) then
    'Since the file exists, we need to check when it was created
    Dim objFile
    Set objFile = objFSO.GetFile(strFileName)

    '********* STEP 2: Compare the local copy's DateLastModified property
                       with the current date/time (Now()) ******************
    Dim dtDateModified
    dtDateModified = objFile.DateLastModified
    Set objFile = Nothing

    If DateDiff("h", dtDateModified, Now()) = 0 then
      '****** STEP 3:  The local copy is up to date - show it to the user! ******
      Response.Redirect strVirtualFileName
      Response.End
    End If
  End If

  Set objFSO = Nothing

  '********** STEP 4 **************
      'If we get here, the file either doesn't exist on the web server, or it
      'is outdated. Use ASPHTTP to grab the current version and save it to disk.
  '*********************************
  Dim objAspHTTP, strHTML
  Set objAspHTTP = Server.CreateObject("AspHTTP.Conn")

  'Grab the traffic report banner and save it to disk
  objAspHTTP.URL = "http://www.TrafficNews.com/reports/TrafficReport.gif"
```

can't be encrypted (since the receiver wouldn't have a key to decrypt it), a security hole exists if this transfer occurs over an insecure communication medium. The major advantage of this algorithm is it is a fast and efficient one.

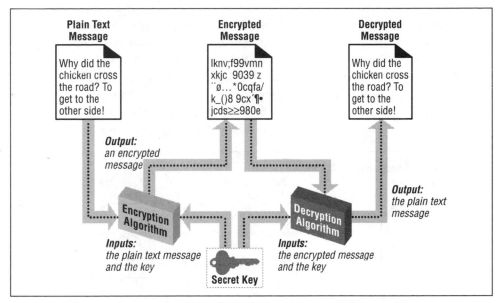

Figure 8-5. Symmetric cryptography performs both encryption and decryption with a single key

Cracking Symmetric Cryptography

As with any key-based encryption algorithm, the encryption algorithm is only as strong as its key size. DES, a symmetric cryptographic encryption algorithm that has been a standard since 1976, uses a 56-bit key. This key length was more than sufficient when the algorithm was first devised, but has since become far too short. With modern machines, such short keys can be cracked via a brute force method within hours or days.

As keys grow larger, the time required to apply a brute-force algorithm increases exponentially, making a brute-force approach for a single computer a near impossibility. However, if the brute-force algorithm can be distributed over hundreds or thousands of computers, cracking large keys might be possible.

There is currently such a project underway at *http://distributed.net*. By installing a small program on your computer, during idle periods your computer will work on a brute-force algorithm to decrypt an encrypted message.

Asymmetric cryptography

Asymmetric cryptography uses two mathematically related keys. These two keys include a *private key*, which is never revealed, and a *public key*, which is available to everyone. These two keys are related mathematically in such a way that a document encrypted by a public key can only be decrypted by the corresponding private key. So, as Figure 8-6 illustrates, if Person A wishes to send Person B an encrypted message, Person A will encrypt the message with Person B's public key. Once this is accomplished, the only key that will decrypt the message is Person B's private key, which is known *only* by Person B. This has the advantage that anyone can send Person B an encrypted message that only Person B can decrypt, since everyone knows Person B's public key and only Person B knows his private key.

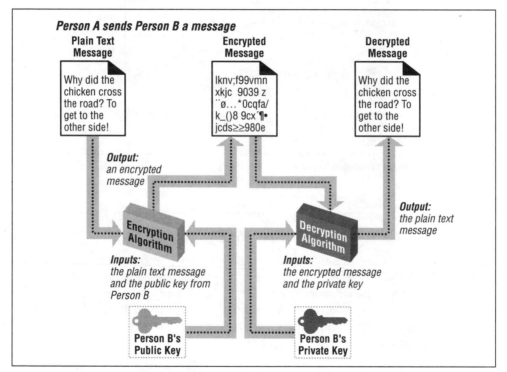

Figure 8-6. Asymmetric cryptography utilizes mathematically related public and private keys for encryption and decryption

 The most common asymmetric cryptography approach is RSA, named after its inventors: Ron Rivest, Adi Shamir, and Len Adleman. RSA keys are based on the products of large prime numbers. RSA's strength lies in the fact that computers have an extremely difficult time factoring large numbers.

Authentication

Encryption can be used to garble the information sent between two computers, but how can a user be sure that when he or she receives a piece of information such as email, it came from whomever claimed to have sent it? While authentication may not seem vitally important, it is essential to protect from the "Man in the Middle" attack.

In the "Man in the Middle" attack, a malicious hacker intercepts communications between a sender and a receiver and masquerades as the sender. For example, say that Person A was interested in obtaining some sensitive information from Person B. In a normal, asymmetric cryptography scheme, the following events would unfold:

1. Person A sends Person B his public key and asks for a sensitive document.
2. Person B knows that A has rights to see that sensitive document, so Person B encrypts the sensitive document with Person A's public key, so that only Person A's private key can decrypt the information.
3. Person A receives the encrypted message containing the sensitive document and decrypts it with his private key.

This is how it's supposed to work, but what if a hacker interjected himself into the middle of this scenario? Imagine that the following sequence of steps occurred:

1. Person A sends Person B his public key and asks for a sensitive document.
2. The hacker intercepts this request and alters the request. The hacker replaces Person A's public key in the request with his own public key.
3. Person B receives the request. Thinking the request contains Person A's public key, the information is encrypted with the hacker's public key. The encrypted message is then sent to Person A.
4. That hacker again intercepts the message en route to Person A. Since the message was encrypted with the hacker's public key, the hacker can decrypt the message with his private key and read the sensitive documents!
5. So as not to alert Person A to a potential security attack, the hacker can encrypt the plain text secure document with Person A's public key and send it to Person A. At this point, Person A can decrypt the message with his private key. No one except the hacker is aware that any breach in security has occurred!

Figure 8-7 illustrates the "Man in the Middle" attack.

The reason the "Man in the Middle" attack works is because Person A and Person B have no means to verify that the message hasn't been altered in transit. To

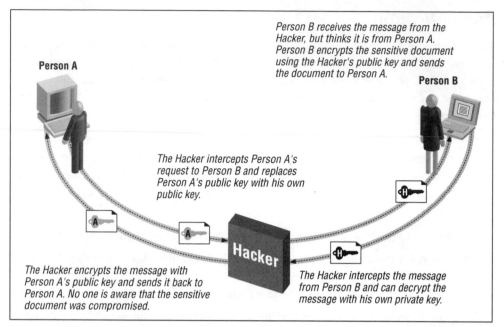

Figure 8-7. Without authentication, asymmetric cryptography is vulnerable to a "Man in the Middle" attack

account for this, *digital signatures* are used. Digital signatures reverse the public key/private key roles. If a sender encrypts his message using his own private key, anyone can decrypt it with the sender's public key. Since the sender is the only one who has access to his private key, a message received that can be successfully decrypted by the sender's public key must have been sent from the sender.

Understand that digital signatures are not used to encrypt data; rather, they are used solely for authentication. Encryption and authentication are two different things; the former garbles the message so it is only readable by the intended recipient(s), while the latter is used to guarantee the message was sent by the person claiming to have sent it. There is no reason why, though, a message can't be both digitally signed and encrypted.

Digital Certificates

Asymmetric cryptography, which is widely used, requires a public and private key pair for all parties interested in participating in secure communications. Who is responsible, though, for generating these public and private keys? Obviously, if by chance two people were using the same public or private keys, all the advantages for the public/private key system would go flying out the window.

To overcome these problems, *digital certificates* are used. Digital certificates bind an individual to a public key. Since asymmetric cryptography fails if multiple users have identical public or private keys, trusted third-party companies known as *certificate authorities* have arisen. The job of certificate authorities is to issue digital certificates, thereby assigning unique public and private keys. There are many certificate authorities available that can easily be found by searching the web for "Certificate Authorities." A popular certificate authority is VeriSign (*http://www.verisign.com*).

 For more information on digital certificates, be sure to check out *http://www.aspencrypt.com/crypto101_certs.html.*

Client and server certificates

Digital certificates come for both clients (individual users) and servers (web servers, for example). A web server that wishes to establish the Secure Socket Layer (SSL) needs to use a server certificate. Individuals who wish to receive encrypted documents using an asymmetric cryptography algorithm (such as encrypted email) must have a client digital certificate set up on their computer. In the next section, "Sending Digitally Signed, Encrypted Email with ASPEncrypt," we'll examine how to set up a client certificate.

Sending Digitally Signed, Encrypted Email with ASPEncrypt

There are many potential situations in which it would be nice to be able to send an encrypted email. An online stock-trading web site, for example, might offer its users an option to have their stock portfolio's current worth emailed to them at the close of the market each day. Sending such information in plain text email poses a potential security threat, since anyone who can intercept the email can easily view its contents. The email could be most likely be intercepted in one of two ways: by some hacker who was eavesdropping on the network communications, or by a nosy technical engineer at the user's ISP.

To keep the portfolio information secure, one option would be for the online trading company to send encrypted email. When encrypting email, it is important to ensure that the email is encrypted so only the person the email is intended for can decrypt it. Furthermore, it would be nice to encrypt the message using a standard technology so the user receiving the email can decrypt the message without needing to download or use any type of add-on component.

Such a scenario is possible using S/MIME Certificate-based encryption. S/MIME, which stands for Secure/Multipurpose Internet Mail Extensions, aims at adding security measures to email messages using the MIME format. S/MIME provides for secure email by providing two mechanisms that were discussed throughout the past few pages:

- Authentication
- Encryption

To reiterate, authentication ensures the recipient of an email message that the email was indeed sent by the person who claimed to send it. Encryption is used to secure the email message, ensuring that only the person the email is intended for can read it. To accomplish both of these tasks, S/MIME uses digital certificates.

S/MIME is currently supported by a number of popular email clients, including Netscape Communicator, Microsoft Outlook, and Microsoft Outlook Express. A full list of S/MIME-enabled email clients can be found at: *http://www.rsasecurity.com/standards/smime/products.html.* The RSA Security web site also contains a list of S/MIME-compatible third-party encryption components, which can be found at: *http:// www.rsasecurity.com/standards/smime/interop_center.html.*

For a web server to send encrypted email to a visitor, that visitor must have a digital certificate and must present the web server with his public key. For the web server to digitally sign email, thereby proving to the recipient of the email that it truly came from the source it claims to have come from, the web server must have a digital certificate. Therefore, to just encrypt email, only the client is required to have a certificate; to just sign email, only the web server must have a certificate; to both encrypt and sign email, both the web server and client must have a certificate.

In this section, we will look at how to encrypt and digitally sign email using ASPEncrypt. For information on how to perform a number of other security-related tasks with ASPEncrypt, be sure to check out the ASPEncrypt task list at *http://www. aspencrypt.com/tasks.html.*

Besides being able to authenticate and encrypt email, ASPEncrypt can also encrypt files on the web server, be used to implement secure uploads and downloads of sensitive information, and encrypt sensitive information like credit-card numbers!

Obtaining the client's certificate

To encrypt email, you need to know the public key of the intended email recipient. To obtain this information, you need to have access to the recipient's client certificate, which you can obtain in one of two ways:

Obtaining Client and Server Certificates

To obtain a client or server certificate, you will need to visit one of the Certificate Authorities, such as VeriSign. At the time of this writing, VeriSign offers a free 60-day trail for their client certificates and a free 14-day trial for their server certificates. After the trial period, client certificates run at $14.95 per year while various server certificate options can cost from $395 to $1,295.

To obtain a trial client certificate, visit *http://www.verisign.com/client/*. For a quick reference guide on how to set up your email client to be able to receive encrypted email, be sure to read VeriSign's encrypted email guide: *http://www. verisign.com/securemail/guide/*. To help install a client certificate, *ASPEncrypt. com* provides an easy-to-use web page at: *http://www.aspencrypt.com/get_cert. htm*.

To obtain a trial server certificate, visit *http://www.verisign.com/server/*. The server certificate, which is used for authentication, will also enable you to perform secure web site communications (using SSL) from your web site.

---

1. Have the client upload their certificate.

2. Obtain the client's certificate through the ClientCertificate property of the Request object.

The first method is a little cumbersome for the end user, requiring them to export their certificate to a text file and then upload that text file. The second method, using the ClientCertificate property, is preferred, but only works over an SSL connection (where the URL contains `https://`). I recommend you use the second method if possible. The first method is error-prone, since the client has to export his or her certificate. Furthermore, asking the client to take the time to export their certificate seems unprofessional to me.

Since the ClientCertificate property requires the web server to use SSL, you must first set up SSL. There are several great online articles that include examples on how to set up SSL on IIS:

- "How to Request and Install an SSL Certificate on IIS 4.0," found at *http://www. 4guysfromrolla.com/webtech/062299-1.shtml*.

- "SSL: Both Secure and Friendly: Why and How to use SSL," found at *http:// www.asptoday.com/articles/19991206.htm*.

- "Untangling Web Security: Getting the Most from IIS Security," found at *http:// msdn.microsoft.com/workshop/server/iis/Websec.asp*.

When installing SSL on your server, be sure to opt to accept client certificates. The default Client Certificate Authentication option is not to accept client certificates.

When a web visitor visits a SSL-enabled page that requests a client certificate, she will be prompted to select which client certificate she'd like to present to the web server. This certificate contains the piece of information we are after, which is the client's public key. Figure 8-8 contains a screenshot of the client certificate selection dialog box.

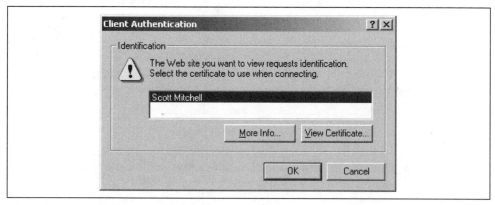

Figure 8-8. When visiting an SSL-enabled web page that accepts client certificates, the visitor must choose what certificate to present to the web site

The Request object's ClientCertificate property is a collection containing the client certificate information. Since the property is a collection, it can be iterated through using a **For Each ... Next** loop, as Example 8-5 illustrates.

Example 8-5. The Contents of the Client Certificate are Displayed While Iterating Through the ClientCertificate Collection

```
<% @LANGUAGE="VBSCRIPT" %>
<% Option Explicit %>
<%
  Dim strKey

  'Loop through each key in the ClientCertificate collection
  For Each strKey in Request.ClientCertificate
    Response.Write "<B>" & strKey & "</B> - " & _
              Request.ClientCertificate(strKey) & "<P>"
  Next
%>
```

The client certificate contains information on the issuer of the certificate, the email address of the client, the certificate's serial number, the date the certificate is valid until, and other related information. Figure 8-9 contains the output of the code in

Example 8-5 when viewed through a browser. Note that the URL in the address bar is prefixed by the SSL-required *https://* instead of the standard *http://*.

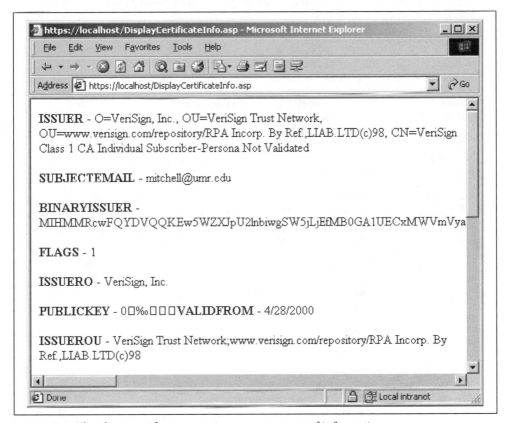

Figure 8-9. The client certificate contains an assortment of information

 One bit of information contained in the client certificate, which is used in Example 8-6 to send encrypted email, is the *Certificate*, which is a binary representation of the entire certificate.

Sending encrypted email

To send encrypted email using the client's public key, the ASPEncrypt component can be used in conjunction with the ASPEmail component. Example 8-6 contains an ASP page named */SendEncMail.asp* that sends encrypted email using the recipient's public key. This page needs to accomplish three tasks:

1. Read in the client certificate.
2. Create the email message.
3. Send the encrypted email.

These three steps are outlined with comments in the code in Example 8-6.

Example 8-6. ASPEncrypt and ASPEmail Provide for Encrypted Email Delivery

```vbscript
<% @LANGUAGE="VBSCRIPT" %>
<% Option Explicit %>
<%
  Dim objMail, objCM, objContext, objBlob
  Dim objCert, strMsg, strEmail

  Set objMail = Server.CreateObject("Persits.MailSender")
  Set objCM = Server.CreateObject("Persits.CryptoManager")
  Set objContext = objCM.OpenContext("mycontainer", True)

  ' Retrieve the client certificate from the ClientCertificate property
  Set objBlob = objCM.CreateBlob

  '****** STEP 1: Read in the certificate **********
  objBlob.Binary = Request.ClientCertificate("Certificate")

  'Ensure that the client certificate was correctly received.
  If Len(objBlob.Hex) > 0 Then
    Set objCert = objCM.ImportCertFromBlob(objBlob)

    'See if the certificate contains an email address
    strEmail = objCert.Subject("E")
    If strEmail <> "" Then
      Set strMsg = objContext.CreateMessage
      strMsg.AddRecipientCert objCert

      '******** STEP 2: Create the Email Message **********
      objMail.Host = "mail.yourserver.com"
      objMail.Subject = "This is an Encrypted Message"
      objMail.From = "Mitchell@4GuysFromRolla.com"
      objMail.FromName = "Scott Mitchell"
      objMail.AddAddress strEmail
      objMail.Body = "This message is encrypted!  Only the visitor who supplied " & _
                     "the certificate will be able to view this message."

      '******* STEP 3: Send the encrypted email ***********
      objMail.SendEncrypted strMsg

      Response.Write "Message was successfully sent to " & strEmail
    Else
      'the certificate does not contain an email address; can't send the
      'encrypted email!
      Response.Write "Certificate does not contain an Email address."
    End If
  Else
    'objBlob.Hex = 0, ergo no client certificate was presented
    Response.Write "No certificate received."
  End if
%>
```

Note that the email is sent using the SendEncrypted method. This method of the ASPEmail component encrypts the email message using the public key provided in the client certificate before sending the email message. This encrypted email message can only be viewed by the client who provided the client certificate and can be displayed only in an S/MIME-compliant email program.

> Only the body of the email is encrypted. The subject, however, is not encrypted, so be sure not to place any sensitive information in the email's subject line.

Sending digitally signed emails

To digitally sign email, the sender of the email must have a certificate. Recall that when a sender wishes to digitally sign email, he will use his private key to encrypt the message. If the receiver of the email message can successfully decrypt the message using the sender's public key, then the message must have come from the person claiming to have sent the message, since no one else has access to the sender's private key.

> The purpose of digitally signing an email is not to hide the message of the email from prying eyes, but rather to provide authentication. This will prove the email was really sent from the person who claimed to have sent it, and that it wasn't tampered with in transit.

Sending digitally signed email requires the message to be encrypted with the server certificate's private key. This sensitive key is located in the registry, and naturally, should not be able to be read by anyone but the owner of the certificate (the web server). To access this registry information, you must either set the registry permissions to allow the anonymous user to have read access or use the ASPEncrypt object's LogonUser method to log on as a user who has rights to read the registry.

To send digitally signed email, we must be able to get our hands on the server certificate, which contains the private key. Unlike reading the client's certificate, there is no simple mechanism to read the server certificate through an ASP page. To get to the server certificate, we must know the server certificate's *serial number*. The certificate authority assigns a serial number that uniquely identifies each certificate.

Sending Digitally Signed Email—A Security Risk?

Logging on as a user with permissions proves to be a security risk, in my opinion, since the username and password must be entered into the ASP page like so:

```
Set CM = Server.CreateObject("Persits.CryptoManager")
CM.LogonUser "Domain", "Administrator", "password"
```

While anonymous web users are not supposed to be able to see the source to your ASP pages, there have been a couple of security holes in IIS over the years that have revealed the source to ASP pages. For example, in ASP's early days, there was the *::$DATA* bug, in which anyone could view the source to an ASP page if they entered *::$DATA* at the end of the URL in their browser:

```
http://www.someserver.com/SomeASPPage.asp::$DATA
```

While the *::$DATA* and other similar security holes are patched quickly by Microsoft, there is still often a period during which unscrupulous individuals can view the source code to any of your ASP pages. While the probability that someone may decide to view the source to the one ASP page on your entire site that contains a superuser's username and password is extremely low, it is still something you should take into account before implementing this approach.

The server certificate's serial number can be found through the Internet Services Manager. Start by opening the Internet Services Manager (Start → Programs → Administrative Tools → Internet Services Manager). A list of web sites will be brought up; right-click on the web site that will send digitally signed email and click on Properties. Select the Directory Security tab and click on View Certificate. This will bring up a dialog box containing the server certificate's information. The second tab, Details, contains the properties. Click on the Serial Number property, and the certificate's serial number is displayed in the text box below. Figure 8-10 shows this dialog box and the server certificate's numerous properties.

Digitally signed email messages are created using the ASPEncrypt and ASPEmail component in tandem. As we saw in Example 8-6, sending encrypted email utilizes both the ASPEncrypt component and a special send method from the ASPEmail component, SendEncrypted. Creating and sending digitally signed email follows a similar pattern: the ASPEncrypt component must be used to read in the server certificate's private key and encrypt the message, and a special ASPEmail component method (SendSigned) needs to be called to send the signed email. Example 8-7 contains the source code to send digitally signed email using ASPEncrypt and ASPEmail.

Figure 8-10. The server certificate's serial number can be found through the Internet Services Manager

Example 8-7. Digitally Signed Email Is Used for Authentication of the Sender

```
<% @LANGUAGE = "VBSCRIPT" %>
<% Option Explicit %>
<%
  Dim objCM, objMail, objStore, objSignerCert, objContext, objMsg
  Set objCM = Server.CreateObject("Persits.CryptoManager")

  'Log on as a user who has the proper registry permissions
  objCM.LogonUser "domain", "Administrator", "password"

  'Grab the server certificate by serial number
  Set objStore = objCM.OpenStore( "my", True )
  Set objSignerCert = objStore.Certificates("60D3 2D8D D833 43DF 079B 83E9 3CA1 AEE3")

  'Create the digitally signed email
  Set objContext = objCM.OpenContext("my", True )
  Set objMsg = objContext.CreateMessage
  objMsg.SetSignerCert objSignerCert ' Specify signer certificate

  'Send Signed Message
  Set objMail = Server.CreateObject("Persits.MailSender")
  objMail.Host = "mail.yourcompany.com"
  objMail.Subject = "This is a Digitally Signed message"
  objMail.From = "Mitchell@4guysfromrolla.com"
  objMail.FromName = "Scott Mitchell"
  objMail.AddAddress "yourname@yourcompany.com"
```

Example 8-7. Digitally Signed Email Is Used for Authentication of the Sender (continued)

```
  objMail.Body = "This message is digitally signed, proving its authenticity!"

  objMail.SendSigned objMsg    'Send the signed message
%>
```

In Example 8-7, we used the LogonUser method to read the server certificate from the web server's registry. Also note that we used the SendSigned method of the ASPEmail component to send the digitally signed email. For more information on sending digitally signed email using ASPEncrypt and ASPEmail, check out: *http://www.aspencrypt.com/task_mail.html*.

Sending digitally signed, encrypted email

If you need to send an email message that contains sensitive material and you wish to provide authentication so the user can be assured that the email came from the person claiming to have sent it, you will need to both digitally sign and encrypt the email message. Recall that digitally signing an email message does not hide the email's contents from prying eyes—it only serves to authenticate that the email was sent by the person who claimed to have sent it. Furthermore, encryption alone does not provide any sort of authentication of the sender.

ASPEncrypt and ASPEmail can be used together to send digitally signed, encrypted emails. The ASPEmail component has a special method, SendSignedAndEncrypted, that is used for sending email messages that need to be both encrypted and signed. Details on sending signed and encrypted email are available on the ASPEncrypt web site at: *http://www.aspencrypt.com/task_mail.html*. Not surprisingly, this approach involves the union of the code to encrypt the message (shown in Example 8-6) and the code to digitally sign an email message (shown in Example 8-7).

Uploading Files from the Browser to the Web Server

One of the most frequently asked questions on the ASP Messageboard (*http://www.aspmessageboard.com*) is how to upload files from the client to the web server via an ASP page. Allowing your web visitors to upload binary documents has a number of practical applications. For example, a community site might allow its members to upload pictures of themselves; a job-hunting site might allow its applicants to upload their resumes in Word format; a software distribution site, like *Tucows.com*, might allow developers to upload their programs for download.

Uploading binary information to a web server is possible using existing HTML forms. To upload binary data, alter the HTML form tag so it contains an ENCTYPE and uses the POST METHOD:

```
<FORM ENCTYPE="MULTIPART/FORM-DATA"
      METHOD="POST"
      ACTION="URL for Form processing script">
```

 You must explicitly set METHOD="POST" in your form tag; if you fail to do this, your ASP page that attempts to save the uploaded file will report an error. Also, if your visitors are using out-of-date browsers, they may not be able to upload files to the web server, since older browsers did not support the multipart/form-data standard. Internet Explorer started supporting the standard in Version 3.02, and Netscape has supported the standard since Version 2.0.

Then, to provide a text box and browse button in the form so the user can select a file to upload, use the INPUT tag with the TYPE set to FILE:

```
<INPUT TYPE="FILE" NAME="FormElementName">
```

Clicking the Browse button will open the Choose file dialog box, from which the user can select a local file to upload.

 The multipart/form-data ENCTYPE was adopted with RFC 1867. More detailed documentation can be found at: *http://www.w3.org/1999/07/NOTE-device-upload-19990706.*

While providing the ability for the client to send a binary file up to the web server through an HTML form is easy, saving this binary data as a file through an ASP page is not practical without using a third-party component.

 ASP pages can access files on the web server using the FileSystemObject (FSO). This object, however, was built to handle text files only. Accessing binary files with FSO can be impractical, especially for large binary files, since a byte-by-byte conversion must occur each time the FileSystemObject accesses a binary file. Therefore, file uploads using just the FileSystemObject are quite impractical; your best bet is to turn to a solid third-party component. For information on accessing binary files using the FileSystemObject, be sure to check out the "Further Reading" section.

There are a number of ASP upload components available on the Net, all of which can be seen at: *http://www.aspalliance.com/components/.* For this chapter, I will be discussing how to use Software Artisans's SA-FileUp component. SA-FileUp, which can be downloaded from *http://www.softartisans.com/softartisans/saf.html,* costs $129 per server or $1,999 for a site license.

In this section, we will look at how to upload a file from the client to the web server and how to upload a file from the client into a database BLOB column. If you don't already own a copy of SA-FileUp, you will need to download and install the evaluation copy before proceeding with the examples.

Creating a Simple "Upload a File" ASP Page

SA-FileUp is a very robust component, offering more than the simple ability to upload a file from the client to the server. We will look at these more advanced functionalities in a bit, but first I'd like to just go through an example of creating a simple "Upload a File" ASP page. For this example, we will create two files: *UploadFile.htm*, an HTML page using the multipart/form-data method to allow a user to upload a local file, and *SaveUploadedFile.asp*, an ASP page that will save the uploaded file to the web server.

Example 8-8 contains the HTML for *UploadFile.htm*. Note the use of the attributes `ENCTYPE="form/multi-part"`, `TYPE="FILE"`, and `METHOD="POST"`; all of these are needed to allow for the client to upload a file.

Example 8-8. UploadFile.htm Creates a Form from Which the User Can Select a Local File to Upload

```
<HTML>
<BODY>
  <FORM ENCTYPE="multipart/form-data" METHOD="POST" ACTION="SaveUploadedFile.asp">
    Enter the file to upload:<BR>
    <INPUT TYPE="FILE" NAME="UploadFile">

    <P><INPUT TYPE="SUBMIT" VALUE="Upload File!"
  </FORM>
</BODY>
</HTML>
```

Figure 8-11 shows a screenshot of *UploadFile*. Note that clicking the Browse button will open the Choose file dialog box, from which the user can select a local file to upload.

To save the file, we will use the SA-FileUp component in *SaveUploadedFile.asp*. To instantiate the component, use the following code:

```
Dim objSAFileUpInstance
Set objSAFileUpInstance = Server.CreateObject("SoftArtisans.FileUp")
```

Before we look at the source code for *SaveUploadedFile.asp*, let's take a moment to examine SA-FileUp's properties and methods. The pertinent properties are listed first in Table 8-5, while the pertinent methods are outlined in Table 8-6.

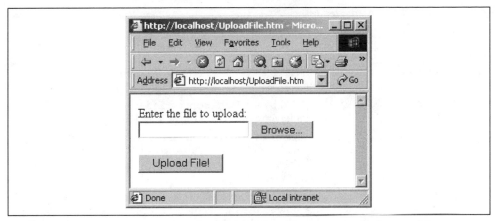

Figure 8-11. Using an INPUT tag with its TYPE Set to FILE creates a text box and Browse button to aid the user in selecting a local file to upload

Table 8-5. SA-FileUp Contains Many Properties. The Following Is a Listing of the More Commonly Used Properties.

Property	Description
ContentDisposition	Contains the MIME content disposition of the data submitted by the client. This should be **multipart/form-data** when uploading a file.
IsEmpty	A Boolean value specifying whether or not the user selected a file to upload.
MaxBytes	Used to specify the largest possible file size that can be uploaded; useful for preventing malicious users from eating up your web server's hard drive space by uploading incredibly large files. (The default value, 0, specifies that no limit on file size should be imposed.)
OverWriteFiles	A Boolean value that specifies whether an existing file on the web server should be overwritten if a file with the same file-name is uploaded. The default value for OverWriteFiles is **True**.
Path	Specifies the default directory for uploading files. If this is not specified, the system-defined Temporary Path is used.
TotalBytes	Reports the total number of bytes written to the web server from the uploaded file. If MaxBytes is set to a value other than 0, TotalBytes will never exceed the value of MaxBytes.
UserFileName	The name and path of the file on the client's machine that was selected for uploading.

Table 8-6. SA-FileUp's Methods Serve One Purpose: to Assist in Uploading a File from the Client to the Server

Method	Description
Delete(*FileName*)	Deletes the file `FileName` from the web server.
Save	Saves the uploaded file to disk in the directory specified by the Path property and with the original file's filename (the value of the UserFileName property).
SaveAs(*FileName*)	Saves an uploaded file to the web server with the filename specified by `FileName`. If no path is specified in the `FileName` parameter, the value of the Path property is used.
SaveAsBlob(*ADOField*)	Saves an uploaded file to the database. We'll look at how to use this method in "Uploading Binary Objects to a Database."
SaveInVirtual(*VirtualLoc*)	Saves the uploaded file to the specified virtual location, `VirtualLoc`.

The code for *SaveUploadedFile.asp*, which can be seen in Example 8-9, is fairly straightforward. We start by performing a little error checking, ensuring that the user selected a file to upload and that his or her browser can support binary uploads. Next, we set the Path property to *C:\Temp* and save the file using the Save method. This will save the file using the same filename as the file on the client's machine. Therefore, if the client uploads the file *C:\SomeDirectory\SomeFile.jpg*, the uploaded file will be saved on the web server at *C:\Temp\SomeFile.jpg*. Since the OverWriteFiles property defaults to **True**, if a file named *SomeFile.jpg* already exists in the *C:\Temp* directory, the existing file will be overwritten. If the file is successfully uploaded, the user will see a confirmation message.

Example 8-9. SaveUploadedFile.asp Writes the Uploaded File to the Web Server's Disk

```
<%@ LANGUAGE="VBSCRIPT" %>
<% Option Explicit %>
<%
  'Create an instance of SA-FileUp
  Dim objUpload
  Set objUpload = Server.CreateObject("SoftArtisans.FileUp")

  If objUpload.IsEmpty then
    'The user did not specify a filename in the text box to upload
    Response.Write "Please specify a file to upload."
    Response.End
  End If


  'Check to make sure the multipart/form-data ENCTYPE is supported
  'by the user's browser
  If objUpload.ContentDisposition <> "form-data" Then
    Response.Write "Your browser does not support binary uploads."
    Response.End
  End If
```

*Example 8-9. SaveUploadedFile.asp Writes the Uploaded File to the Web
Server's Disk (continued)*

```
'If we've reached this point, the file was successfully uploaded.
'Now we just need to save it to the web server!
'Set the path to save the file to, saving it as the same name as the
'name of the file uploaded by the client.
objUpload.Path = "C:\Temp"
objUpload.Save

'To save the file to the root directory in the web site, use:
'objUpload.SaveInVirtual "/challenges"

Response.Write "Your file (" & objUpload.UserFileName & _
               ") has been saved to the web server!"

Set objUpload = Nothing
%>
```

 When saving an uploaded file to the web server, the IUSR_
machinename account must have write permissions to the directory
specified by the Path property. If the IUSR_*machinename* account
does not have the required permissions, an error message will be
displayed explaining the problem.

Uploading Binary Objects to a Database

Databases such as Microsoft Access and Microsoft SQL Server can store a number
of different datatypes. The more commonly used datatypes include simple scalar
datatypes, such as numeric and string variables. These databases can also store
binary objects, or BLOBs (Binary Large OBjects). For example, a table storing
employee information (**Employee**) might contain a column named **Picture** that
would be a BLOB containing a picture of the employee.

Allowing the user to upload a binary to the server and then save that binary object
to the database is fairly simple using SA-FileUp. In fact, it only requires a slight
modification to the ASP page that is responsible for saving the uploaded file to the
web server. The HTML page that provides the form for selecting a file to upload
does not need any changes.

For this example, let's assume we have a table named **Property** that contains
information about various real estate properties. This table contains the following
columns:

PropertyID

    A Primary Key/AutoNumber field that uniquely identifies each row in the
    table.

To Use BLOBs or Not to Use BLOBs?

If a database table needs to have some binary information associated with it, such as an employee's picture, there are two methods that can be used: store the picture in the database using a BLOB datatype, or store the image on the web server and store just the path and filename of the image in the database.

Storing the binary object on disk and a path and filename in the database has one primary advantage: speed. The advantage is especially pronounced if your database and web server reside on different machines. Since this BLOB must be transmitted to the database whenever saving the information, and retrieved from the database whenever it needs to be downloaded or viewed, this can serve as a bottleneck if there are many simultaneous requests for the binary data.

However, by placing binary objects on the web server, you are limiting the scalability of the database. For example, what if a Visual Basic application wanted to query the database and display the images? Tough luck, since the images are off on the web server. Or what if you had two or more database servers spread around the world and you wanted to replicate the database information? You'd be up a creek if you had the binary objects stored on the web server and not in the database.

The decision to store binary data in the database or on the web server, then, is one that depends upon the situation. While storing binary objects on the web server will likely lead to performance increases, it adversely affects the scalability of the database application.

Description

A textual description of the property.

Cost

The cost of the property.

Picture

A BLOB column that stores a picture of the property. (In SQL Server, this would have a datatype of *image*; in Access, this datatype would be *OLE Object*.)

Example 8-10 contains the source code for *UploadFileToDB.htm*, an HTML page that displays an "Add a New Property" form with three form fields: a text box for the **Description**, a text box for the **Cost**, and a file upload text box/Browse button to select the property image to save in the database.

Example 8-10. UploadFileToDB.htm: Adds a New Row to the Property Table

```
<HTML>
<BODY>
  <H1>Add a New Property to the Database</H1>
  <FORM ENCTYPE="multipart/form-data" ACTION="SaveUploadedFileToDB.asp" METHOD="POST">
    Description: <INPUT TYPE=TEXT NAME=Description><BR>
    Cost: $<INPUT TYPE=TEXT NAME=Cost SIZE=8><BR>
    Enter the picture to upload: (<I>GIFs only!</I>)<BR>
    <INPUT TYPE="FILE" NAME="UploadFile">

    <P><INPUT TYPE="SUBMIT" VALUE="Add the Property"
  </FORM>
</BODY>
</HTML>
```

A screenshot of the form created by the HTML code in Example 8-10 can be seen in Figure 8-12. Note that the form indicates that only GIFs should be uploaded to the database. This is done so we have consistent BLOBs in the database. For example, we do not want the user to upload a ZIP file into the `Picture` column of the `Property` table. In *SaveUploadedFileToDB.asp*, the form-processing script that is responsible for adding the new row to the `Property` table, we'll examine how to ensure that the file uploaded by the client was a GIF file.

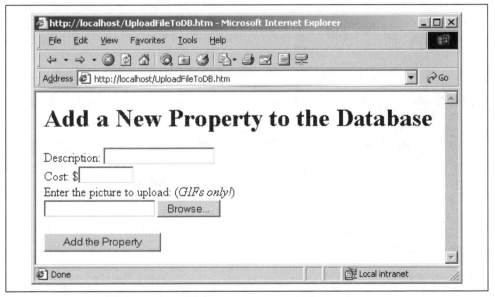

Figure 8-12. Adding a new row to the property table includes entering a description and cost and choosing a GIF file that is a picture of the property

Now that we have created the HTML page that displays the upload form, we need to create the ASP page that grabs the uploaded file and inserts it into the database (along with the Description and Cost information). This ASP page, *SaveUploadedFileToDB.asp*, is fairly similar to the simple upload file we looked at in Example 8-9, *SaveUploadedFile.asp*. However, instead of using the Save method of SA-FileUp, we'll use the SaveAsBlob method to save the image to the database. Example 8-11 contains the source code for *SaveUploadedFileToDB.asp*.

Example 8-11. The SaveAsBlob Method Saves an Uploaded File to a Database

```
<%@ LANGUAGE="VBSCRIPT" %>
<% Option Explicit %>
<%
  'Create an instance of SA-FileUp
  Dim objUpload
  Set objUpload = Server.CreateObject("SoftArtisans.FileUp")

  If objUpload.IsEmpty then
    'The user did not specify a filename in the text box to upload
    Response.Write "Please specify a file to upload."
    Response.End
  End If

  'Check to make sure the multipart/form-data ENCTYPE is supported
  'by the user's browser
  If objUpload.ContentDisposition <> "form-data" Then
    Response.Write "Your browser does not support binary uploads."
    Response.End
  End If

  'Make sure the image is a GIF
  If UCase(Right(objUpload.UserFileName, 4)) <> ".GIF" then
    Response.Write "You must upload a GIF of the property."
    Response.End
  End If

  'Grab a snapshot of the table Property
  Dim objRS
  Set objRS = Server.CreateObject("ADODB.Recordset")
  objRS.Open "Property", "DSN=PropertyDB", adOpenStatic, adLockOptimistic, adCmdTable


  objRS.AddNew                                    'Add a new record

  'Set the values for our three columns based upon the form values
  objRS("Cost") = objUpload.Form("Cost")
  objRS("Description") = objUpload.Form("Description")
  objUpload.SaveAsBlob objRS("Picture")

  objRS.Update                                    'Save the changes
  objRS.Close                                     'Close and clean up...
  Set objRS = Nothing

  Response.Write "Your file (" & objUpload.UserFileName & _
                 ") has been saved to the Web server!"

  Set objUpload = Nothing
%>
```

Reading Textual Form Information Using SA-FileUp

When submitting a form that contains both textual information (such as the Description and Cost fields in *UploadFileToDB.htm*) and binary information (such as the file we are uploading), the textual data can be picked out in the form-processing script using the Form collection of the SA-FileUp object. For example, when setting the **Description** and **Cost** columns of the Recordset object, we read in the user's entries for those two form variables using:

```
objUpload.Form("Cost")
```

and:

```
objUpload.Form("Description")
```

Due to the fact that the SA-FileUp component uses a **Request.BinaryRead** call to obtain the posted form information, you cannot use the Request.Form collection in the form-processing script. (If you attempt to use the Request.Form collection, you'll receive an error: "Cannot use Request.Form collection after calling BinaryRead.") Rather, use the SA-FileUp component's Form collection.

To prevent users from uploading non-GIF files for the property's picture, a quick check is done on the uploaded file's filename. If the last four characters are not equal to *.gif*, the user is shown a message indicating that they can only upload GIF files for the property's picture. A more thorough technique for validating that a given file is indeed a GIF file can be seen at: *http://www.4guysfromrolla.com/webtech/050300-1.shtml.*

Displaying a property's pictures

Displaying the BLOB object in the **Property** table is not exactly straightforward. It would be nice to be able to do:

```
objRS.Open "Property", "DSN=PropertyDB"

'Display the picture
Response.Write objRS("Picture")
```

However, displaying binary objects it is not quite that simple. To display the **Picture** column, we'll use a separate ASP page, one called */images/ShowPropertyPicture.asp*, whose sole purpose is to display the proper GIF from the **Property** table. This page is strikingly similar to the */images/TrafficReport.asp* page we looked at in Example 8-4. As with */images/TrafficReport.asp*, in */images/ShowPropertyPicture.asp*, we will use the Response.ContentType property to let the browser know we are sending it a GIF. We will then use the BinaryWrite method of the Response object to send the binary content of the BLOB column to the browser.

/images/ShowPropertyPicture.asp will show a single property's picture. To specify what property's picture to display, */images/ShowPropertyPicture.asp* should be passed the value of the property's `PropertyID`. Example 8-12 contains the source code for */images/ShowPropertyPicture.asp*.

Example 8-12. /images/ShowPropertyPicture.asp Sends the Binary Content of the Picture Column to the Client, Instructing to the Browser to Interpret the Binary Content as a GIF

```
<% @LANGUAGE="VBSCRIPT" %>
<% Option Explicit %>
<%
  'Get the passed-in property ID
  Dim iPropertyID
  iPropertyID = Request("PropertyID")

  'Retrieve exactly one row from the Property table.
  Dim strSQL
  strSQL = "SELECT Picture FROM Property WHERE PropertyID = " & iPropertyID

  Dim objRS
  Set objRS = Server.CreateObject("ADODB.Recordset")
  objRS.Open strSQL, "DSN=PropertyDB"

  'Only display if we found a row
  If Not objRS.EOF then
    Response.ContentType = "image/gif"     'Tell the browser we are sending it a GIF
    Response.BinaryWrite objRS(0)          'Send the BLOB to the client
  End If

  'Clean Up...
  objRS.Close
  Set objRS = Nothing
%>
```

To view a particular property's image, use an **IMG** tag. For example, the following snippet of code would display a property's picture:

```
<IMG SRC="/images/ShowPropertyPicture.asp?PropertyID=ValidPropertyID">
```

Example 8-13 contains the source to *DisplayProperties.asp*, which will display the Description and Cost information about all of the properties available, along with a picture of the property.

Example 8-13. To Display the Picture for a Particular Property, Use an IMG Tag

```
<%@ LANGUAGE="VBSCRIPT" %>
<% Option Explicit %>
<%
  Dim objRS

  'Open a snapshot of the Property table
  Set objRS = Server.CreateObject("ADODB.Recordset")
  objRS.Open "Property", "DSN=PropertyDB"

  'Loop through each record in the Property table
  Do While Not objRS.EOF
    Response.Write "<TABLE ALIGN=CENTER BORDER=0 WIDTH=""80%"">"
    Response.Write "<TR><TD><B>" & objRS("Description") & "</B></TD><TD>"
    Response.Write FormatCurrency(objRS("Cost"), 0) & "</TD></TR>"
    Response.Write "<TR><TD ALIGN=CENTER COLSPAN=2>"
    Response.Write "<IMG SRC=""ShowImage.asp?PropertyID=" & objRS("PropertyID") & """>"
"
    Response.Write "</TD></TR>"
    Response.Write "</TABLE><P><HR><P>"

    objRS.MoveNext
  Loop

  'Clean up...
  objRS.Close
  Set objRS = Nothing
%>
```

Figure 8-13 contains a screenshot of a browser visiting *DisplayProperties.asp*.

Other SA-FileUp Features

SA-FileUp is a very robust upload component and offers many features not outlined in this chapter. Some of its especially interesting capabilities include:

- Transactional uploads
- Uploading a file with a progress indicator
- The option to upload an entire directory and all of its files and subdirectories from the client

A full list of SA-FileUp's features can be seen at: *http://www.softartisans.com/softartisans/comcom.html*.

Why Reinvent the Wheel?

Throughout this chapter, we've looked at various third-party components that can greatly enhance your IIS/ASP web site. While most of these components come at a cost, it is almost guaranteed to be much lower than the cost in man-hours needed to develop a similar component inhouse.

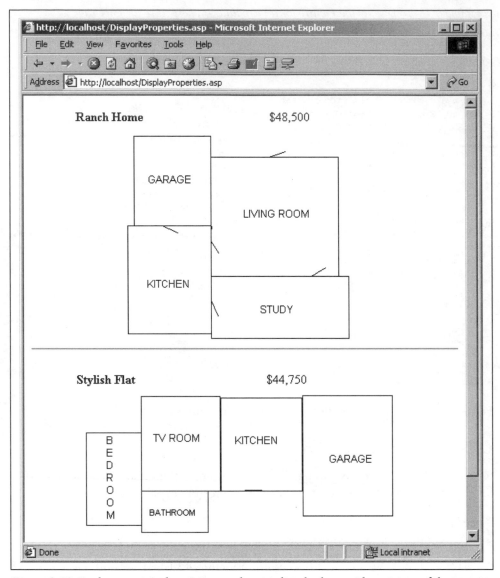

Figure 8-13. Each property's description and cost is listed, along with a picture of the property

Since its Introduction, this book has promoted code reuse repeatedly for several reasons:

- Code reuse decreases the time needed to complete a project.

- Code reuse decreases the time needed to complete future projects.

- Code reuse leads to fewer bugs, since the reused code is more thoroughly tested than newly written code (and it has already been checked time and time again for typos and silly mistakes).

COM components, if they are Microsoft-created, third-party created, or developed in-house, are shining examples of code reuse and are guaranteed to save you time in development and debugging. My advice: if you can find a third-party COM component that can meet your needs, by all means, use it!

The only disadvantage of using third-party or Microsoft COM objects is you don't have access to the source. This, in my opinion, has two disadvantages:

- Sometimes it's nice to be able to see under the hood of the car. With third-party COM components, you are in the dark as to how, exactly, they work. While this black-box implementation has its advantages in encapsulating the implementation complexity, there are still those times when you need to know what makes the component tick. For example, use of the Request object's QueryString and Form collections is not available when using SA-FileUp, since SA-FileUp issues a BinaryRead. Since SA-FileUp is a compiled COM component, we cannot see the code that issues the BinaryRead. While the SA-FileUp help files thoroughly explain why you can't use the QueryString and Form collections on a web page that uses SA-FileUp, it would be nice to be able to dissect the code ourselves, rather than having to rely on the help file.

- It's impossible to reuse COM component code. Perhaps a small portion of a COM object could be used in a future project. With VBScript classes (or COM objects developed in-house), you can take advantage of the existing COM component's source code, creating a new component that reuses the needed section of the source code form the existing component.

Further Reading

With the explosive growth in the popularity of Active Server Pages, an entire component-development industry has arisen. This industry is a testament to ASP's ability to quickly and easily create powerful, dynamic web sites. The links below are to lists of available third-party components and numerous third-party vendors. If you need a specific tool for your web site, say a threaded message board system, check out these lists and vendors to quickly find a complete third-party COM object that fits your needs.

- For a list of available third-party ASP COM components, check out the component list on *ASPAlliance.com*: *http://www.aspalliance.com/components/*.

- If you are looking for an ASP e-commerce component, look no further than iisCart: *http://www.iiscart2000.com*.

- Doug Dean Consulting builds a number of COM objects that can be used in an ASP web site. If you are in the market for a threaded forum, calendar, or web-based memo system, check out: *http://www.dougdean.com.*

- ASPdb is a component designed to aid in publishing database information on the Web. Easily display table information in a number of different formats and styles: *http://www.aspdb.com/.*

- Looking to add a chat system to your site? Why write your own when you can use ASPChat? It's available from *ASPHelp.com* at *http://www.asphelp.com/ASPChat/?*

- Offer your users the option to spellcheck their inputs; check out *http://www.xde.net/spellchecker/.*

- While the FileSystemObject was developed to work exclusively with text files, it can be used to access binary files as well. Check out *http://www.pstruh.cz/help/ScptUtl/library.htm* to learn how to upload files using just ASP code and the FileSystemObject!

Index

<% %> code block delimiters, 22
& bitwise operator, 53
<< bitwise operator, 53
>> bitwise operator, 53
| bitwise operator, 53
~ bitwise operator, 53
∧ (caret), bitwise operator, 53
@ symbol, in ASP directives, 20
@ symbol (PerlScript array), 32
% symbol (PerlScript associative array), 32
$ symbol (PerlScript scalar variable), 25

A

ACTION property (FORM tag), 107, 124
Active Server Pages (see ASP)
ActiveX Data Objects (ADO), 142, 249
  enumerated constants, 143–145
  schemas, 142, 145–149
ActiveX Scripting Engine, 19, 20
Ad Rotator, GetAdvertisement method, 255
Ad Rotator component, 250–267
  Redirection file, 252–253, 257–258
  Schedule file, 252–255
AddEmployee method, source code
      for, 286
AdInfo database table, 257
administration pages
  creating page forms, 185–213

"Delete an Existing Record", 202
"Edit an Existing Record", 208
"Insert a New Record", 194–201, 181
interfaces, 138
maximizing code reuse, 228
reusable, 150
AdminPageAction.asp, 214, 217
AdminPageGenerator class, 186–201
  member variables, 186
  methods, 190
  properties, 186
AdminPageMenu class, 229, 234–241
ADO (see ActiveX Data Objects)
adovbs.inc, 143
AdRotation class, 261
  methods, 263
adSchemaPrimaryKeys schema,
      opening, 162
adSchemaTables, 148
AND operator, 53
applications, design and development
      of, 1–2
ASP (Active Server Pages)
  code block delimiters (<% and %>), 22
  COM, using, 247–290
  downloadable source code, x
  information on web, ix–xi
  pages (see ASP pages)
  Release 3.0, exception handling, 58
  scripting language, choosing, 19, 24–38
  scripts, defining classes, 88

ASP pages
  code reuse, 105
    server-side validation, 116
  design of, 3
  DisplayAdminPage.asp, 242
  for displaying GIFs from a database, 333
  execution on the server of DOS and
    Windows applications, 292
  form creation pages, 106–110
  form processing scripts, 106–110
  form validation, 111–124
  for getting content from other
    servers, 303
  information displayed in, 176
  for processing forms, 108
  for provision of non-HTML output to
    client browsers, 307
ASP upload components, 325
ASPEmail components, 319
  SendEncrypted method, 321
ASPEncrypt component, 315–324
  range of uses, 316
ASPError object, 30, 42, 57–66
  Category property, 62
  error reporting, 69
  instance of, 60
  properties, 58, 62
ASPExec component, 292
  command-line program execution, 293
  properties and methods, 292
  security concerns, 295
ASPHTTP component, 303–309
  installing, 303
  instantiating, 304
  methods, 304
  properties, 303
asymmetric cryptography, 312
authentication, 313–314, 321
  of email from server, 321
AutoNumber columns, 152, 187
  determining, 162

B

banners
  impression tracking with Ad
    Rotator, 259
  statistics, tracking, 257

binary data
  client-to-server upload, 324
  retrieval with ASPHTTP, 305
Binary Large Objects (see BLOBs)
binary objects, displaying, 333
bitwise operators, 53
bitwise shift-left operator, 53
bitwise shift-right operator, 53
BLOBs (Binary Large Objects), uploading to
  a database, 329
browscap.ini, 297, 298
Browser Capabilities component, 297
  vs. BrowserHawk, 297
  collecting information with, 298
BrowserHawk, 297–303
  vs. Browser Capabilities
    component, 297
  instantiating, 300
browsers
  client-side scripting languages,
    support, 296
  determining configuration settings, 302
  properties, 298
  request header information, 298
  standards, 296
business logic, 5
  implementation through ASP pages, 276

C

case-sensitivity, 26
CDATA tag, 286
CDONTS (Collaborative Data Objects for
  NT Server), 99
  for error reporting, 67
certificate authorities, 315, 317
CheckForError subroutine, 50
  for error reporting, 67
class developers, 88
Class statement (VBScript), 89
classes
  AdminPageGenerator, 186–201
  AdminPageMenu, 229, 234–241
  AdRotation, 261
  ColumnInformation, 155
  Columns, 155
  DataTypeFormElementInformation, 176
  for databases, 138–246

for form creation and validation, 125
form field element objects, 125
GenerateForm, 128–135
in VBScript, 15, 88
    Release 5.0, 78
MenuItem, 229–234, 239
ModifyDatabase, 214
using in server-side form
        validation, 121–124
Clear method, 46
click-throughs, 257
client certificates, obtaining, 317
client-side form validation, 111–112
client-side scripting languages, 296
code reuse
    administration pages, 228
    advantages of, 104
    in ASP pages, 105
    databases, 105, 138–246
    exception handling with subroutines, 50
    forms, 124
    for server-side form validation, 116
    with third-party components, 337
collections, use of properties and
        methods, 109
column information, collecting, 155
ColumnInformation class, 155
    testing, 165
Columns class, 155, 157
    member variable, 158
COM (Component Object Model), 248
    inconsistent exceptions and, 47
    using in Active Server Pages, 247–290
COM components
    advantages of, 279
    categories of, 276
    compiled vs. interpreted
        components, 289
    creating with Windows Script
        Components Wizard, 280–290
    for determining browser capabilities of
        users accessing web pages, 297
    disadvantage of, 280
    for encapsulating database and business
        logic, 278
    enhancement with non-portable
        methods, 267, 275

as examples of code reuse, 337
included with IIS, ASP, 250
third-party, 291
compile-time errors, 40, 63
ComputeTotalWithSalesTax function, 5–7
consistent exceptions, 47
constants
    ADO, 143
    vbObjectError, 46
constructors, 88, 89
Content Linker, 250, 267–275
    list file for, 267, 269, 273
control flow with Server.Execute, 16
CreateList, helper function, 203–208
cryptography, 309–324
    asymmetric, 312
    symmetric, 310
custom HTTP error pages, creating, 74

D

databases
    access to backup while primary is
        unavailable, 71
    classes, 138–246
    code reuse for access to, 105
    connecting to with private member
        variables, 187
    data model for, 150
    displaying BLOB datatypes, 333
    enumerations in ADO (ActiveX Data
        Objects), 143
    insertions, deletions, and updates using
        an ASP page, 214
    requirements for administration
        pages, 140
    reusable code, 138–246
    web pages for administrating, 139
DataTypeFormElement property, 180, 184
DataTypeFormElementInformation
        class, 176, 187
    member variables, 180
    testing, 183
datatypes
    JScript, 25
    mapping to form elements, 176
    setting with DataTypeFormElement, 184

declarations, JScript variables, 25
decryption, 309
default scripting language, 21
"Delete an Existing Record", 139
DeleteRecordForm
    methods, 203
    parameters, 203
DeleteRecords method
    ModifyDatabase class, 217, 226
    multiple deletions, 228
DES algorithm, 311
design
    Active Server Pages, 1–18
    scripts, 2
    web pages, 2
destructors, 89
digital certificates, 314
digital signatures, 314
digital signing of email, 321
Dim statement, for defining public
        properties, 91
directory structure for storage of ASP
        modules, 7
displaying information in ASP pages, 176
displaying non-HTML output with
        MIME, 307
displaying tables with foreign key
        constraints, 192
DLL's, for server-side includes, 9
dollar sign ($), 25
DOS applications, execution on the server
        via an ASP page, 292
dynamic evaluation and execution
    security risks, 101
    support in VBScript, 78

E

"Edit an Existing Record" option, 139
"Edit an Existing Record" administration
        page, 208
"Edit an Existing Record" form, 222
email
    acquiring client's certificate for
        encryption, 316
    authenticating with the server certificate,
        security concerns, 322

digital signing, 321
encrypting
    ASPEmail component for, 319
    with client's public key, 319
encryption, 309
    of email, 319
    using S/MIME, 315
ENCTYPE, for binary uploads, 324
end developer, 88
Err object
    methods, 46
    Number property, 46
    properties in VBScript, 45
error detection, 51
error handling
    enabling with VBScript, 44
    (see also exception handling)
error messages, 41
error numbers, hexadecimal formatting, 52
error-detection, 42
errors
    ASPError object, catching with, 30
    compile, 40
    halting, 40
    in programming, 39
    non-halting, 40
    runtime, 40
    syntactical, 40
    (see also exceptions)
event handlers, 89
    Columns class, 158
    ForeignKeys class, 171
    ModifyDatabase class, 215
exception handling, 39–76
    AdRotation class, 264
    for ASP pages using functions and
        subroutines, 48
    enabling and disabling scripting
        language error handling, 71
    error messages, 66
    JScript, 51–57
    support team notification, 67
    (see also error handling)
exceptions, 41
    consistent and inconsistent, 47
    error messages for, 41
    (see also errors)

Execute method, RegExp object, 81, 85
Execute statement, 102
ExecuteDOSApp, 293
ExecuteWinApp, 293
ExecuteWinAppAndWait, 293
external COM object errors, 64

F

file checking, verification of format on
    upload, 333
File extension mapping, 9
file naming
    Content Linker list file, 270
    rotator schedule files, 254
files, uploading from client to server, 324
FileSystemObject
    dynamic includes, 11
    limitations for binary uploads, 325
filetypes, for server-side includes, 8
foreign key columns, management in
    administration pages, 168
foreign key constraints, 153
ForeignKeyExists method, 171
ForeignKeyInformation class, 170
    testing, 174
ForeignKeys class, 171
    testing, 174
Form collection, 108
form creation web page, 106
form elements, 107
    defining datatypes with classes, 176
    standardization, 124
form field NAME value, use of quotes
    in, 118
form interfaces, for database access, 138
form processing script, 106
form reuse, 105
FORM tag, 107
form validation, 111–124
    client-side, 111
    server-side, 113
FormElement class, 125
FormHint method, AdminPageGenerator
    class, 192
forms
    code reuse, 124
    creating, 106

    formatting of entered data, 117
    validation, server-side, 28

G

GenerateForm class, 128–135
GET method, 107
GetAdvertisement method, Ad Rotator, 255
GetColumnInformation method, 158
GetCurrentPrimaryKeys method, 163
GetForeignKeyInformation method, 171
GetLastError method, for retrieval of
    ASPError object instance, 60
GetPrimaryKeys method, 163
GetURL method, ASPHTTP
    component, 304
GIF files, obtaining from other servers, 305
Global property, RegExp object, 79

H

halting errors, 40
helper function, CreateList, 203–208
HIDDEN form fields, passed to
    AdminPageAction.asp, 218
Home Directory tab, Internet Services
    Manager, 21
HTML
    forms, 107
    non-HTML output, displaying, 307
    SCRIPT blocks, 23
HTTP errors
    automated handling, 59
    codes list on Web, 57

I

IgnoreCase property, RegExp object, 79
IIS (Internet Information Server), 24
    creating custom error pages, 74
    default scripting language, 21
    file-extension mapping, 9
    specifying handling of HTTP errors, 59
implementation errors, 39
importing one ASP into another, 8
impressions, banner advertisements, 257
include directive
    cyclical includes and, 8
    file and virtual keywords, 7

include directive (*continued*)
  operation, 9–10
  rules for using, 7
  syntax, 7
include files
  file extensions, 15
  naming conventions, 12
  nesting, 8
  security, 14
  (see also server-side includes)
inconsistent exceptions, 47
inheritance, 88
Initialize event handlers, 89
  AdminPageGenerator class, 188
INPUT tags, 108
"Insert a New Record", 139, 194–201
InsertRecord method, ModifyDatabase
        class, 217–222
instances, 86
instantiation
  ASPHTTP component, 304
  BrowserHawk component, 300
  Content Linker, 270
  Windows Script Components, 288
internal ASP errors, 64
Internet Information Server (see IIS)
iterating through collections, 109

J

JavaScript, 25
JPG files, obtaining from other servers, 305
JScript
  ASP example, 30
  bitwise operators, 53
  case-sensitivity, 26
  creating ASP pages in, 25–31
  datatypes, 25
  error detection, 51
  error handling vs. ASP Error object, 42
  Error object, 52
  exception handling, 51–57
    vs. VBScript, 57
  regular expressions in, 27–29
  script block, use of, 23
  statement termination, 25
  throw statement, 54
  try ... catch blocks, 51
    variables, 25
    variants, 25
    vs. VBScript, 19

K

key length, security concerns, 311
keys (cryptography), 309

L

language directive, 20
LANGUAGE parameter, 22
logical errors, 39
LogonUser method, ASPEncrypt object, 321

M

"Man in the Middle" attacks, 313
match method (JScript String object), 27
member functions, 90
member variables, 90
  AdminPageGenerator class, 186
  Columns class, 158
  DataTypeFormElementInformation
        class, 177, 180
  ForeignKeyInformation class, 170
  ForeignKeys class, 171
MenuItem class, 229–234, 239
METADATA tag, Global.asa, 143
METHOD property (FORM tag), 107
methods, 90
  AdminPageGenerator class, 190
  AdRotation class, 263
  ASPExec component, 292
  ASPHTTP component, 304
  Columns class, 159
  Content Linker list file, 270
  DeleteRecordForm, 203
  ForeignKeys class, 171
  GenerateForm class, 128
  GetLastError, 60
  MenuItem class, 230–234
  RegExp object, 81
  SA-FileUp component, 326
  setting for Windows Script
        Components, 282
  VBScript, 86
  VBScript classes, 90

MIME (Multipurpose Internet Mail Extensions), 307
ModifyDatabase class, 214
    DeleteRecords method, 217, 226
    InsertRecord method, 217–222
    UpdateRecord method, 217, 224
    UpdateSelect method, 222

N

NAME property (FORM tag), 124
NAME property, of FORM tag, 107
NaN (Not a Number), 26
non-halting errors, 40
non-HTML output, displaying, 307
NOT operator, 53
Number property (Err object), 46

O

objColumnDict variable, 158
objConn, 166
objDataTypeDict, 177–180
objDataTypeFormElements member variable, 187
object instances, assigning to properties with Property Set statement, 98
object-oriented programming, 86
objects, 86
objFKDict, 171
objFormDescriptionDict, 177, 180
objFormHints, 187
objFormNameDict, 177, 180
On Error Goto statement, 44
On Error Resume Next statement, 44, 48
Option Explicit statement, 6, 25
OPTION tags, 108
OR operator, 53

P

parameters
    DeleteRecordForm, 203
    for OpenSchema, 147
    PopulateColumns method, 166
Pattern property, RegExp object, 79
PerlScript, creating ASP pages with, 31–37
Personal Web Server (see PWS)
ping, 293–295

placeholders, 179
PopulateColumns method, 159–163
    parameters, 166
PopulateForeignKeys method, 171
POST method, 107
    for binary data uploads, 324
primary keys (database), 152
private key (cryptography), 312
Private keyword, 91
private properties, retrieval with Property Get statement, 92
properties, 86, 90
    AdminPageGenerator class, 186
    AdRotation class, 261
    ASPError object, 58
    ASPExec component, 292
    ASPHTTP component, 303
    Columns class, 158
    ForeignKeys class, 171
    FORM tag, 107
    FormElement class, 125
    JScript Error object, 52
    MenuItem class, 229
    ModifyDatabase class, 215
    SA-FileUp component, 326
    setting for Windows Script Components, 282
    of VBScript Err object, 45
    of VBScript's RegExp object, 79
Property Get statement, 158
    arglist, 94
Property Let statement, 94
Property Set statement, 97
    argument list, 98
public key, 312
Public keyword, 91
PWS (Personal Web Server)
    default scripting langage, 21
    VBScript as default scripting language, 24
Python, creating ASP pages with, 37

Q

QueryString collection, 108
QueryType, 145
QuotedValue, private member function, 163

R

Raise method, 46
Redirect property, 188
redirection file, 251, 256
redirection of users based on browser
        capabilities, 302
referential integrity, 154
RegExp object
    methods, 81, 85
    properties, 79
    syntax, 79–81
regular expressions
    form validation and, 115, 28
    in JScript, 27–29
    in PerlScript, 35
    in VBScript, 78
RegularExpression in FormElement
        class, 127
replace method (JScript String object), 27
Replace method, RegExp object, 81, 85
Request object, ClientCertificate
        property, 317
reusable administration pages, 150
reusable database classes, 138–246
RSA keys, 312
runtime errors, 40

S

SA-FileUp, 325–335
    properties and methods, 326
sales tax, computing (example code), 5
SaveFileTo property of ASPHTTP, 305
SchemaEnums, 145
schemas (ADO), 142
    opening, 145–149
SCRIPT blocks, 22–24
script design, 3
SCRIPT tag (see SCRIPT blocks)
scripting engines, downloads, 51
scripting language, 19–38
    choosing, 24
    default for ASP, 21
    in errors, 62
    JScript, 25–31
    PerlScript, 31–37
    Python, 37

specifying, 20–24
    VBScript, 19–24
scripts, advantages of good design, 2
search method (JScript String object), 27
Secure Socket Layer (SSL), 315
    setup, 317
Secure/Multipurpose Internet Mail
        Extensions (see S/MIME)
security
    ASPExec component, 295
    client-side form validation, 112
    digitally signed email from the
        server, 322
    dynamic evaluation and execution, 101
    server-side form validation, 120
SELECT tags, 108
SendEncrypted method, 321
SendOffSite method, AdRotation class, 263
server certificate, obtaining, 317
Server.Execute method, 5, 12, 16
server-side form validation, 113
server-side includes, 5–15
    CheckForError subroutine, 50
    declarations of variables, 6
    dynamic, 10–12
    filetypes, 8
    for importing adovbs.inc into ASP
        pages, 143
    importing one ASP into another, 8
    (see also include files)
Server.Transfer method, 5, 17
ShowAd function, 260
ShowAd method, AdRotation class, 263
SIZE property, FormElement class, 127
S/MIME Certificate-based encryption, 315
source code
    for AddEmployee method, Windows
        Script Component, 286
    format,Windows Script
        Components, 284
special characters in regular expression
        patterns, VBScript, 79–81
SSI (see server-side includes)
statement termination, JScript, 25
static evaluation and static execution, 99
strAction constant, 214

strColumnName, 170
String object, regular expression matching
    methods, 27
symbol (JScript statement terminator), 25
symmetric cryptography, 310
syntactical errors, 40
sysobjects, 142

T

tags
    CDATA, 286
    Windows Script Components, 284
Terminate event handler, 89
    AdminPageGenerator class, 188
Test method, RegExp object, 81, 85
testing
    ColumnInformation class, 165
    DataTypeFormElementInformation
        class, 183
    ForeignKeyInformation class, 174
    ForeignKeys class, 174
    MenuItem class, 234
TEXTAREA tags, 108
third-party components, disadvantages
    of, 337
three-tiered web sites, 278
throw statement, 54
tilde-delimited strings as placeholders, 179
tree structures, representing web site
    layouts, 268
try ... catch blocks
    nesting, 55–57
    using for error detection in JScript, 51
TYPE property, FormElement class, 127

U

UpdateRecord method, ModifyDatabase
    class, 217, 224
UpdateRecordForm, 211
UpdateRecordList, 210
UpdateSelect method, ModifyDatabase
    class, 214–227
UploadFile.htm, HTML component for
    file-uploading ASP page, 326
uploading binary objects to a database, 329
uploading files from client to server, 324

URLs, specifying non-relative, 252
User-Agent string, 298

V

ValidateForm.asp, 116–124
VALUE property of the INPUT tag,
    FormElement class, 127
values, assigning to private properties
    with Property Let statement, 94
var keyword (JScript), 25
variables
    JScript, 25
    PerlScript, 32–33
variants, 25
vbObjectError, constant, 46
VBScript, 19–24
    Boolean values and, 79
    case-sensitivity vs. JScript, 26
    classes, 15, 88, 90
    enabling error handling, 44
    Err object, 45
    error handling vs. ASP Error object, 42
    exception handling vs. JScript, 57
    vs. JScript, 19
    methods, 90
    object-oriented programming, 85–99
    properties, 90
    RegExp object properties, 79
    Release 5.0, new features, 78
    script block, use of, 23
virtual keyword, 7
Visual Basic, downloadable source code for
    ASP pages, x

W

web browsers (see browsers)
web page design, 2
    accomodation of different browsers, 302
    impact of browser standards on, 296
web pages
    for database administration, 139
    displaying content from other
        servers, 303
    error-handling, 42
    use of forms for, 106
Windows applications, executing on server
    via ASP page, 292

Windows Script Component Wizard, 281
Windows Script Components (WSC), 280–290
    performance vs. compiled
        COM objects, 289
write-only properties, 99

X
XMP tag, 184
XOR operator, 53

Z
ZIP files, obtaining from other servers, 305

About the Author

Scott Mitchell is the cofounder of one of the most popular ASP resource destinations on the Internet, *http://www.4guysfromrolla.com*. Originally started as a college project, the site quickly blossomed into a community of serious web developers. *4Guys* attracts tens of thousands of experienced ASP developers every day; unlike other communities, it offers a warm welcome and advice for those new to Active Server Pages. In addition to *http://www.4guysfromrolla.com*, Scott has extensive experience building real-world web sites using Active Server Pages, including building intranet tools for Microsoft's Office Group.

Colophon

Our look is the result of reader comments, our own experimentation, and feedback from distribution channels. Distinctive covers complement our distinctive approach to technical topics, breathing personality and life into potentially dry subjects.

The animal on the cover of *Designing Active Server Pages* is a night monkey (*Aotus*). The night monkey, also known as the owl monkey, is found in South America, specifically in Northern Argentina, Bolivia, Brazil, Colombia, Costa Rica, Equador, Guyana, Panama, Paraguay, Peru, and Venezuela. It lives in trees and subsists on a diet of fruit, leaves, insects, flowers, and bird eggs. As its name suggests, it is nocturnal and in fact, is the only nocturnal member of the monkey species. It is one of the smaller primates; adults usually weigh about two pounds and are about 11–16 inches long. A night monkey's eyes are larger than any other South American primate's and are a great asset to their nighttime lifestyle.

Night monkeys are monogamous and travel in family packs. The mother cares for a newborn in its first week of life; after that, the father takes over all parental duties except for nursing. The father carries the baby for approximately six months. The baby begins easing more into family play and foraging for food on its own in the second half of its first year. A night monkey reaches maturity between two and three years of age, at which point it leaves its family group and strikes out on its own.

Mary Sheehan was the production editor and proofreader for *Designing Active Server Pages*. Nancy Kotary was the production manager. Ellie Maden was the copyeditor, and Colleen Gorman and Mary Anne Weeks Mayo provided quality control. John Bickelhaupt and Brenda Miller wrote the index.

Edie Freedman designed the cover of this book, using an image from Johnson's Natural History. Emma Colby produced the cover layout with QuarkXPress 4.1 using Adobe's ITC Garamond font.

Alicia Cech and David Futato designed the interior layout based on a series design by Nancy Priest. Mike Sierra implemented the design in FrameMaker 5.5.6. The text and heading fonts are ITC Garamond Light and Garamond Book. The illustrations that appear in the book were produced by Robert Romano using Macromedia FreeHand 8 and Adobe Photoshop 5. This colophon was written by Mary Sheehan.

Whenever possible, our books use a durable and flexible lay-flat binding. If the page count exceeds this binding's limit, perfect binding is used.

 # *More Titles from O'Reilly*

Web Programming

CGI Programming with Perl, 2nd Edition

By Shishir Gundavaram
2nd Edition July 2000
470 pages , ISBN 1-56592-419-3

Completely rewritten, this comprehensive
explanation of CGI for those who want to
provide their own Web servers features Perl 5
techniques and shows how to use two popular
Perl modules, CGI.pm and CGI_lite. It also
covers speed-up techniques, such as FastCGI and mod_perl, and
new material on searching and indexing, security, generating
graphics through ImageMagick, database access through DBI,
Apache configuration, and combining CGI with JavaScript.

Dynamic HTML: The Definitive Reference

By Danny Goodman
1st Edition July 1998
1088 pages, ISBN 1-56592-494-0

Dynamic HTML: The Definitive Reference is an
indispensable compendium for Web content
developers. It contains complete reference
material for all of the HTML tags, CSS style
attributes, browser document objects, and
JavaScript objects supported by the various standards and the latest
versions of Netscape Navigator and Microsoft Internet Explorer.

PHP Pocket Reference

By Rasmus Lerdorf
1st Edition January 2000
120 pages, ISBN 1-56592-769-9

The *PHP Pocket Reference* is a handy
quick reference for PHP, an open-source,
HTML-embedded scripting language that
can be used to develop web applications.
This small book acts both as a perfect
tutorial for learning the basics of PHP
syntax and as a reference to the vast
array of functions provided by PHP.

JavaScript: The Definitive Guide, 3rd Edition

By David Flanagan
3rd Edition June 1998
800 pages, ISBN 1-56592-392-8

This third edition of the definitive reference
to JavaScript covers the latest version of the
language, JavaScript 1.2, as supported by
Netscape Navigator 4 and Internet Explorer
4. JavaScript, which is being standardized
under the name ECMAScript, is a scripting language that can be
embedded directly in HTML to give Web pages programming-
language capabilities.

ASP in a Nutshell, 2nd Edition

By A. Keyton Weissinger
2nd Edition July 2000
492 pages, ISBN 1-56592-843-1

ASP in a Nutshell, 2nd Edition, provides
the high-quality reference documentation
that web application developers really need to
create effective Active Server Pages. It focuses
on how features are used in a real application
and highlights little-known or undocumented
features.

Programming ColdFusion

By Rob Brooks-Bilson
1st Edition November 2000 (est.)
500 pages (est.), ISBN 1-56592-698-6

Programming ColdFusion covers everything
you need to know to create effective web
applications with ColdFusion, a powerful
tool for rapid web site development. The
book starts with the basics and quickly
moves to more advanced topics, providing numerous examples
of common web application tasks, so you can learn by example.
Covers ColdFusion 4.5.

O'REILLY®

TO ORDER: **800-998-9938** • *order@oreilly.com* • *http://www.oreilly.com/*
OUR PRODUCTS ARE AVAILABLE AT A BOOKSTORE OR SOFTWARE STORE NEAR YOU.
FOR INFORMATION: **800-998-9938** • **707-829-0515** • *info@oreilly.com*

Web Programming

Writing Apache Modules with Perl and C

By Lincoln Stein & Doug MacEachern
1st Edition March 1999
746 pages, ISBN 1-56592-567-X

This guide to Web programming teaches
you how to extend the capabilities of the
Apache Web server. It explains the design
of Apache, mod_perl, and the Apache API,
then demonstrates how to use them to
rewrite CGI scripts, filter HTML documents on the server-side,
enhance server log functionality, convert file formats on the fly,
and more.

Webmaster in a Nutshell, 2nd Edition

By Stephen Spainhour & Robert Eckstein
2nd Edition June 1999
540 pages, ISBN 1-56592-325-1

This indispensable book takes all the
essential reference information for the
Web and pulls it together into one volume.
It covers HTML 4.0, CSS, XML, CGI, SSI,
JavaScript 1.2, PHP, HTTP 1.1, and
administration for the Apache server.

DocBook: The Definitive Guide

By Norman Walsh & Leonard Muellner
1st Edition October 1999
652 pages, Includes CD-ROM
ISBN 1-56592-580-7

DocBook is a Document Type Definition
(DTD) for use with XML (the Extensible
Markup Language) and SGML (the Standard
Generalized Markup Language). DocBook
lets authors in technical groups exchange and reuse technical
information. This book contains an introduction to SGML, XML,
and the DocBook DTD, plus the complete reference information
for DocBook.

JavaScript Application Cookbook

By Jerry Bradenbaugh
1st Edition September 1999
478 pages, ISBN 1-56592-577-7

JavaScript Application Cookbook literally
hands the Webmaster a set of ready-to-go,
client-side JavaScript applications with
thorough documentation to help them
understand and extend the applications.
By providing such a set of applications, *JavaScript Application
Cookbook* allows Webmasters to immediately add extra
functionality to their Web sites.

Practical Internet Groupware

By Jon Udell
1st Edition October 1999
524 pages, ISBN 1-56592-537-8

This revolutionary book tells users,
programmers, IS managers, and system
administrators how to build Internet
groupware applications that organize the
casual and chaotic transmission of online
information into useful, disciplined, and documented data.

Java Servlet Programming

By Jason Hunter with William Crawford
1st Edition November 1998
528 pages, ISBN 1-56592-391-X

Java servlets offer a fast, powerful, portable
replacement for CGI scripts. *Java Servlet
Programming* covers everything you need
to know to write effective servlets. Topics
include: serving dynamic Web content,
maintaining state information, session tracking, database
connectivity using JDBC, and applet-servlet communication.

Web Programming

Java in a Nutshell, 3rd Edition

By David Flanagan
3rd Edition November 1999
668 pages, ISBN 1-56592-487-8

The third edition of this bestselling book covers Java 1.2 and 1.3. It contains an advanced introduction to Java and its key APIs and provides quick-reference material on all the classes and interfaces in the following APIs: java.lang, java.io, java.beans, java.math, java.net, java.security, java.text, java.util, and javax.crypto.

VBScript in a Nutshell

By Paul Lomax, Matt Childs, & Ron Petrusha
1st Edition May 2000
512 pages, ISBN 1-56592-720-6

Whether you're using VBScript to create client-side scripts, ASP applications, WSH scripts, or programmable Outlook forms, *VBScript in a Nutshell* is the only book you'll need by your side – a complete and easy-to-use language reference.

Enterprise JavaBeans, 2nd Edition

By Richard Monson-Haefel
2nd Edition March 2000
492 pages, ISBN 1-56592-869-5

Enterprise JavaBeans, 2nd Edition provides a thorough introduction to EJB 1.1 and 1.0 for the enterprise software developer. It shows you how to develop enterprise Beans to model your business objects and processes. The EJB architecture provides a highly flexible system in which components can easily be reused, and which can be changed to suit your needs without upsetting other parts of the system. *Enterprise JavaBeans* teaches you how to take advantage of the flexibility and simplicity that this powerful new architecture provides.

In a Nutshell Quick References

Web Design in a Nutshell

By Jennifer Niederst
1st Edition November 1998
580 pages, ISBN 1-56592-515-7

Web Design in a Nutshell contains the nitty-gritty on everything you need to know to design Web pages. Written by veteran Web designer Jennifer Niederst, this book provides quick access to the wide range of technologies and techniques from which Web designers and authors must draw. Topics include understanding the Web environment, HTML, graphics, multimedia and interactivity, and emerging technologies.

Webmaster in a Nutshell, 2nd Edition

By Stephen Spainhour & Robert Eckstein
2nd Edition June 1999
540 pages, ISBN 1-56592-325-1

This indispensable books takes all the essential reference information for the Web and pulls it together into one volume. It covers HTML 4.0, CSS, XML, CGI, SSI, JavaScript 1.2, PHP, HTTP 1.1, and administration for the Apache server.

Internet in a Nutshell

By Valerie Quercia
1st Edition October 1997
450 pages, ISBN 1-56592-323-5

Internet in a Nutshell is a quick-moving guide that goes beyond the "hype" and right to the heart of the matter: how to get the Internet to work for you. This is a second-generation Internet book for readers who have already taken a spin around the Net and now want to learn the shortcuts.

O'REILLY®

TO ORDER: **800-998-9938** • **order@oreilly.com** • **http://www.oreilly.com/**
OUR PRODUCTS ARE AVAILABLE AT A BOOKSTORE OR SOFTWARE STORE NEAR YOU.
FOR INFORMATION: **800-998-9938** • **707-829-0515** • **info@oreilly.com**

In a Nutshell Quick References

AOL in a Nutshell

By Curt Degenhart & Jen Muehlbauer
1st Edition June 1998
536 pages, ISBN 1-56592-424-X

This definitive reference breaks through the hype and shows advanced AOL users and sophisticated beginners how to get the most out of AOL 4.0's tools and features. You'll learn how to customize AOL to meet your needs, work around annoying idiosyncrasies, avoid unwanted email and Instant Messages, actually understand Parental Controls, and turn off intrusive advertisements. It's an indispensable guide for users who aren't dummies.

Perl in a Nutshell

By Ellen Siever, Stephen Spainhour &
Nathan Patwardhan
1st Edition December 1998
674 pages, ISBN 1-56592-286-7

The perfect companion for working programmers, *Perl in a Nutshell* is a comprehensive reference guide to the world of Perl. It contains everything you need to know for all but the most obscure Perl questions. This wealth of information is packed into an efficient, extraordinarily usable format.

How to stay in touch with O'Reilly

1. Visit Our Award-Winning Web Site

http://www.oreilly.com/

★ "Top 100 Sites on the Web" —*PC Magazine*
★ "Top 5% Web sites" —*Point Communications*
★ "3-Star site" —*The McKinley Group*

Our web site contains a library of comprehensive product information (including book excerpts and tables of contents), downloadable software, background articles, interviews with technology leaders, links to relevant sites, book cover art, and more. File us in your Bookmarks or Hotlist!

2. Join Our Email Mailing Lists

New Product Releases

To receive automatic email with brief descriptions of all new O'Reilly products as they are released, send email to:
listproc@online.oreilly.com
Put the following information in the first line of your message (*not* in the Subject field):
subscribe oreilly-news

O'Reilly Events

If you'd also like us to send information about trade show events, special promotions, and other O'Reilly events, send email to:
listproc@online.oreilly.com
Put the following information in the first line of your message (*not* in the Subject field):
subscribe oreilly-events

3. Get Examples from Our Books via FTP

There are two ways to access an archive of example files from our books:

Regular FTP

- ftp to:
  ftp.oreilly.com
  (login: anonymous
  password: your email address)
- Point your web browser to:
  ftp://ftp.oreilly.com/

FTPMAIL

- Send an email message to:
  ftpmail@online.oreilly.com
  (Write "help" in the message body)

4. Contact Us via Email

order@oreilly.com
To place a book or software order online. Good for North American and international customers.

subscriptions@oreilly.com
To place an order for any of our newsletters or periodicals.

books@oreilly.com
General questions about any of our books.

software@oreilly.com
For general questions and product information about our software. Check out O'Reilly Software Online at **http://software.oreilly.com/** for software and technical support information. Registered O'Reilly software users send your questions to: **website-support@oreilly.com**

cs@oreilly.com
For answers to problems regarding your order or our products.

booktech@oreilly.com
For book content technical questions or corrections.

proposals@oreilly.com
To submit new book or software proposals to our editors and product managers.

international@oreilly.com
For information about our international distributors or translation queries. For a list of our distributors outside of North America check out:
http://www.oreilly.com/www/order/country.html

5. Work with Us

Check out our website for current employment opportunites:
www.jobs@oreilly.com
Click on "Work with Us"

O'Reilly & Associates, Inc.
101 Morris Street, Sebastopol, CA 95472 USA
TEL 707-829-0515 or 800-998-9938
     (6am to 5pm PST)
FAX 707-829-0104

International Distributors

UK, EUROPE, MIDDLE EAST AND AFRICA (EXCEPT FRANCE, GERMANY, AUSTRIA, SWITZERLAND, LUXEMBOURG, LIECHTENSTEIN, AND EASTERN EUROPE)

INQUIRIES
O'Reilly UK Limited
4 Castle Street
Farnham
Surrey, GU9 7HS
United Kingdom
Telephone: 44-1252-711776
Fax: 44-1252-734211
Email: information@oreilly.co.uk

ORDERS
Wiley Distribution Services Ltd.
1 Oldlands Way
Bognor Regis
West Sussex PO22 9SA
United Kingdom
Telephone: 44-1243-779777
Fax: 44-1243-820250
Email: cs-books@wiley.co.uk

FRANCE

INQUIRIES
Éditions O'Reilly
18 rue Séguier
75006 Paris, France
Tel: 33-1-40-51-52-30
Fax: 33-1-40-51-52-31
Email: france@editions-oreilly.fr

ORDERS
GEODIF
61, Bd Saint-Germain
75240 Paris Cedex 05, France
Tel: 33-1-44-41-46-16 (French books)
Tel: 33-1-44-41-11-87 (English books)
Fax: 33-1-44-41-11-44
Email: distribution@eyrolles.com

GERMANY, SWITZERLAND, AUSTRIA, EASTERN EUROPE, LUXEMBOURG, AND LIECHTENSTEIN

INQUIRIES & ORDERS
O'Reilly Verlag
Balthasarstr. 81
D-50670 Köln
Germany
Telephone: 49-221-973160-91
Fax: 49-221-973160-8
Email: anfragen@oreilly.de (inquiries)
Email: order@oreilly.de (orders)

CANADA (FRENCH LANGUAGE BOOKS)

Les Éditions Flammarion ltée
375, Avenue Laurier Ouest
Montréal (Québec) H2V 2K3
Tel: 00-1-514-277-8807
Fax: 00-1-514-278-2085
Email: info@flammarion.qc.ca

HONG KONG

City Discount Subscription Service, Ltd.
Unit D, 3rd Floor, Yan's Tower
27 Wong Chuk Hang Road
Aberdeen, Hong Kong
Tel: 852-2580-3539
Fax: 852-2580-6463
Email: citydis@ppn.com.hk

KOREA

Hanbit Media, Inc.
Chungmu Bldg. 201
Yonnam-dong 568-33
Mapo-gu
Seoul, Korea
Tel: 822-325-0397
Fax: 822-325-9697
Email: hant93@chollian.dacom.co.kr

PHILIPPINES

Global Publishing
G/F Benavides Garden
1186 Benavides Street
Manila, Philippines
Tel: 632-254-8949/637-252-2582
Fax: 632-734-5060/632-252-2733
Email: globalp@pacific.net.ph

TAIWAN

O'Reilly Taiwan
No. 3, Lane 131
Hang-Chow South Road
Section 1, Taipei, Taiwan
Tel: 886-2-23968990
Fax: 886-2-23968916
Email: taiwan@oreilly.com

CHINA

O'Reilly Beijing
Room 2410
160, FuXingMenNeiDaJie
XiCheng District
Beijing, China PR 100031
Tel: 86-10-66412305
Fax: 86-10-86631007
Email: beijing@oreilly.com

INDIA

Computer Bookshop (India) Pvt. Ltd.
190 Dr. D.N. Road, Fort
Bombay 400 001 India
Tel: 91-22-207-0989
Fax: 91-22-262-3551
Email: cbsbom@giasbm01.vsnl.net.in

JAPAN

O'Reilly Japan, Inc.
Yotsuya Y's Building
7 Banch 6, Honshio-cho
Shinjuku-ku
Tokyo 160-0003 Japan
Tel: 81-3-3356-5227
Fax: 81-3-3356-5261
Email: japan@oreilly.com

ALL OTHER ASIAN COUNTRIES

O'Reilly & Associates, Inc.
101 Morris Street
Sebastopol, CA 95472 USA
Tel: 707-829-0515
Fax: 707-829-0104
Email: order@oreilly.com

AUSTRALIA

Woodslane Pty., Ltd.
7/5 Vuko Place
Warriewood NSW 2102
Australia
Tel: 61-2-9970-5111
Fax: 61-2-9970-5002
Email: info@woodslane.com.au

NEW ZEALAND

Woodslane New Zealand, Ltd.
21 Cooks Street (P.O. Box 575)
Waganui, New Zealand
Tel: 64-6-347-6543
Fax: 64-6-345-4840
Email: info@woodslane.com.au

LATIN AMERICA

McGraw-Hill Interamericana
Editores, S.A. de C.V.
Cedro No. 512
Col. Atlampa
06450, Mexico, D.F.
Tel: 52-5-547-6777
Fax: 52-5-547-3336
Email: mcgraw-hill@infosel.net.mx

O'REILLY®

O'REILLY®

O'Reilly & Associates, Inc.
101 Morris Street
Sebastopol, CA 95472-9902
1-800-998-9938

Visit us online at:
www.oreilly.com
order@oreilly.com

O'REILLY WOULD LIKE TO HEAR FROM YOU

Which book did this card come from?

_____

Where did you buy this book?
❏ Bookstore   ❏ Computer Store
❏ Direct from O'Reilly   ❏ Class/seminar
❏ Bundled with hardware/software
❏ Other _____

What operating system do you use?
❏ UNIX   ❏ Macintosh
❏ Windows NT   ❏ PC(Windows/DOS)
❏ Other _____

What is your job description?
❏ System Administrator   ❏ Programmer
❏ Network Administrator   ❏ Educator/Teacher
❏ Web Developer
❏ Other _____

❏ Please send me O'Reilly's catalog, containing
a complete listing of O'Reilly books and
software.

Name _____ Company/Organization _____

Address _____

City _____ State _____ Zip/Postal Code _____ Country _____

Telephone _____ Internet or other email address (specify network) _____

Nineteenth century wood engraving
of a bear from the O'Reilly &
Associates Nutshell Handbook®
Using & Managing UUCP.

BUSINESS REPLY MAIL

FIRST CLASS MAIL   PERMIT NO. 80   SEBASTOPOL, CA

Postage will be paid by addressee

O'Reilly & Associates, Inc.
101 Morris Street
Sebastopol, CA 95472-9902